Medieval & Renaissance Literary Studies

GLUTTONY AND
GRATITUDE

GLUTTONY AND GRATITUDE

MILTON'S PHILOSOPHY OF EATING

EMILY E. STELZER

The Pennsylvania State University Press

University Park, Pennsylvania

Library of Congress Cataloging-in-Publication Data

Names: Stelzer, Emily E., author.
Title: Gluttony and gratitude : Milton's philosophy of eating /
Emily E. Stelzer.
Other titles: Medieval and Renaissance literary studies.
Description: University Park, Pennsylvania : The Pennsylvania State
University Press [2017] | Series: Medieval & renaissance
literary studies | Includes bibliographical references and index.
Summary: "Explores the philosophical significance of gluttony in
Paradise Lost, arguing that a complex understanding of gluttony
and of ideal, grateful, and gracious eating informs the content of
Milton's writing"—Provided by publisher.
Identifiers: LCCN 2017042071 | ISBN 9780271081007 (cloth : alk. paper)
Subjects: LCSH: Milton, John, 1608–1674. Paradise lost. | Gluttony
in literature. | Food in literature.
Classification: LCC PR3562 .S74 2017 | DDC 821/.4—dc23
LC record available at https://lccn.loc.gov/2017042071

The Pennsylvania State University Press is a member of
the Association of University Presses.

We conclude then that temperance would not be a kind of
quietness, nor would the temperate life be quiet, as far as this
argument is concerned at any rate, since the temperate
life is necessarily an admirable thing.
— PLATO, *Charmides*

Eating with the fullest pleasure — pleasure, that is, that does not
depend on ignorance — is perhaps the profoundest enactment of
our connection with the world. In this pleasure we experience and
celebrate our dependence and our gratitude, for we are living from
mystery, from creatures we did not make and powers we cannot
comprehend. When I think of the meaning of food, I always
remember these lines by William Carlos Williams, which seem to
me merely honest:
There is nothing to eat,
    seek it where you will,
        but of the body of the Lord.
The blessed plants
    and the sea, yield it
        to the imagination
intact.
—WENDELL BERRY, *Bringing It to the Table*

CONTENTS

ACKNOWLEDGMENTS

This project would have never materialized without the encouragement, support, wisdom, and expertise of many people. I begin by thanking Michael Bauman, John Alvis, and David Davies, gracious teachers who first introduced me to the serious (and for me, exhilarating) study of John Milton, his thought, and his works. Bauman may not remember his kindness in offering an undergraduate course on Milton at my request the summer after I received my B.A., and then letting me audit that same course, but I will never forget this gift. Davies and Alvis advised me in a dissertation that became my first foray into the cornucopia of Milton's food metaphors. A seedling of this project was published in *Early English Studies*, now the *Early Modern Studies Journal*, and so I thank the editors, especially Amy Tigner, for early advice and permission to reprint. Many thanks are due to the Miltonists and early modernists who have encouraged me in my project at its various stages of development, among them Rebecca Totaro, Nigel Smith, Kristin Pruitt, Dennis Danielson, and Lara Dodds, and to the Milton Society of America, the Murfreesboro Conference on John Milton, the National Humanities Center, and the Lanier Theological Library for cultivating environments of inquiry, gracious conversation, and thoughtful debate. My gratitude extends to my colleagues in the School of Humanities at Houston Baptist University, whose conversations not only have provided the gentle pressure I needed to complete this project but also have enticed me to consider a few of countless interdisciplinary trails, that, if all followed, would make this project interminable. My anonymous readers and the editors at Duquesne University Press deserve no small thanks for their patience and attention to this monograph, which is much improved for their criticism and advice. I am immensely indebted to Susan Wadsworth-Booth and all those who have striven on behalf of the Press in its final year of operation, and to those at Penn State University Press for their support and adoption of the Medieval and Renaissance Literary Studies Series. All above share in the credit for what is good in this book, while the responsibility for its weaknesses is solely mine. Finally, I am deeply grateful to my husband, Stephen, for his love, kindness, patience, good humor, encouragement, and companionship at table.

ABBREVIATIONS

AV   *The Holy Bible: Authorized (King James) Version*. First published 1611. All quotations not otherwise cited are from this version.

CM   *The Works of John Milton*. 18 vols. Edited by Frank Allen Patterson et al. New York: Columbia University Press, 1931–40.

CPEP   *The Complete Poetry and Essential Prose of John Milton*. Edited by William Kerrigan, John P. Rumrich, and Stephen M. Fallon. New York: Random House, 2007.

CPMP   *John Milton: Complete Poems and Major Prose*. Edited by Merritt Y. Hughes. 1957. Reprint, Indianapolis: Hackett, 2003.

A Maske   *A Maske Presented at Ludlow Castle*

OED   *Oxford English Dictionary*

OW   *The Complete Works of John Milton*. 11 vols. Edited by Thomas N. Corns and Gordon Campbell et al. Oxford: Oxford University Press, 2009–.

PL   *Paradise Lost*

PR   *Paradise Regain'd*

SA   *Samson Agonistes*

YP   *Complete Prose Works of John Milton*. 8 vols. Edited by Don M. Wolfe et al. New Haven, CT: Yale University Press, 1953–82.

A NOTE ON THE TEXT

Citations from John Milton's poetic works are from *CPMP*. Unless otherwise noted, citations from Milton's prose are from YP. Citations from Milton's *De doctrina Christiana* are mostly taken from OW. Occasionally, where comparison would prove illuminating, I will refer to John Carey's translation of *De doctrina Christiana* in YP and to Charles Sumner's translation as found in CM. My understanding of Milton's authorship of *De doctrina Christiana* follows the general consensus of the contributors to *Milton and the Manuscript of "De Doctrina Christiana,"* ed. Gordon Campbell et al. (Oxford: Oxford University Press, 2007). Where biblical passages are quoted, I use the Authorized (King James) Version unless otherwise mentioned. When quoting untranslated Anglo-Saxon or Middle English texts, I silently convert thorn (þ) and eth (ð) to *th*, and ligatures (e.g. ash, æ) are separated.

Introduction: "Unsavory Food Perhaps"

In the opening lines to a section of one of the lengthiest and most enduring poems in the English language, a sage and serious poet wrote of man's first disobedience. He retold the story of the human race's first parents and of the eating of forbidden fruit, an act bringing death, woe, and corruption into paradise. It was the close of the fourteenth century. The poet was John Gower, and he was writing about gluttony.

The sixth book of Gower's *Confessio Amantis*, on gluttony, is one of many textual artifacts representative of a historically prominent yet all-but-forgotten tradition regarding the story of Adam and Eve. The tradition deserves note not simply because it has been neglected but because it has had influence, and one of the most sophisticated and imaginative adaptations of this tradition may be found in *Paradise Lost*. Familiar with Gower's *Confessio Amantis*, as with many other late antique, medieval, and early modern works depicting or assuming a gluttonous fall from a state of innocence, John Milton had no dearth of source material at his disposal when he considered the Fall in his own poetry. In using this material, Milton constructed a philosophy of eating that explores not only the expansive boundaries of gluttony but also the outer limits of knowledge and the space governed by charity.

The pages that follow demonstrate how Milton pays tribute to and builds upon the tradition of the gluttonous Fall—a tradition Milton acknowledges directly in his prose and incorporates into his poetry in a significant way, and one affecting the entire created cosmos of *Paradise Lost*. As the angel Raphael leads Adam to discern, what begins as a rule for eating bears upon Raphael's guidelines for the pursuit of knowledge—for example, "be lowly wise"—and for interacting with human

1

companions — for example, "In loving thou dost well, in passion not" (*PL* 8.173, 8.588). A philosophy of eating takes shape as the physical sphere of Milton's cosmopoiesis becomes enfolded in and digested by intellectual and moral spheres, and as gluttony's role in the Fall bears upon the ontological, epistemological, and ethical concerns of the poem. In *Paradise Lost*, eating fundamentally affects being, knowing, and doing. These three categories — the physical, the intellectual, and the moral — are interconnected areas of personal growth for Adam and Eve, making Eden the soil for extraordinary transformation. Thus by turns Milton describes the prelapsarian scale of nature in *Paradise Lost*, first as one of physically metabolic and symbiotic processes, then as one of inquiry, dialectic, and contemplation characterized by self-knowledge and self-restraint, and ultimately as a scale of love. From the tradition of the gluttonous meal, Milton proceeds to test the confines of temperance and the extravagances of charity. In doing so, Milton envisions the Chain of Being as a path toward God involving body, mind, and will, or physical, intellectual, and moral activity. As I will argue, this path is still partly accessible to Adam and Eve after the Fall and becomes a key part of Milton's project in justifying the ways of God.

Attending to the links among the physical, intellectual, and moral spheres of *Paradise Lost*, I have situated this project in the territory of the medieval synthesizers, and in some respects this book is about a "medieval Milton," about how several predominantly late antique and medieval ideas and traditions inform *Paradise Lost*. John Mulryan has encouraged scholars "to study Milton, not as a medieval writer, but as a thinker and as a poet who was profoundly aware of the rich heritage of the medieval tradition, and who was perfectly capable of picking and choosing from its history, philosophy, theology, art, and literature, without necessarily accepting its version of Christianity or civil government."[1] Gluttony once headed the list of deadly sins, and patristic and medieval theologians (e.g., John Cassian, Augustine of Hippo, and Gregory the Great) and medieval poets (e.g., Dante Alighieri, John Gower, and Geoffrey Chaucer) have variously promoted a complex and broad definition of gluttony and the story of a gluttonous Fall. Milton's use of this tradition also pulls from interrelated medieval concepts and poetic features, including triadic structuring, emphasis on the will in moral law, and the cultivation of a relationship between eating and poetics. The roots of these concepts and features were established much earlier and may be found in Jewish and Christian sacred Scriptures and in ancient Greek and Roman philosophy. Their influence persists in and beyond the early modern period. Milton's peculiar treatment of gluttony in *Paradise Lost* depends on Plato, Aristotle, Augustine of Hippo, Evagrius of Pontus, John Cassian, Gregory the Great, Dante, Chaucer, Gower, and Edmund Spenser, and the qualities and consequences of gluttony as once perceived cast new light on the drama of *Paradise Lost*.

Gluttony has a literal, significant role in the Fall in *Paradise Lost*, but the full significance of this narrative is lost if gluttony is not also acknowledged as a symptom and symbol of more abstract corruption. Gluttony would not be so formidable if it had no relation to the mind and the will; it would not be so vivid if it were not for the body. Accordingly, this book both examines the gluttonous and gustatory metaphors of *Paradise Lost* and analyzes the philosophic ideas at stake in an account of a literally gluttonous Fall. I argue that gluttony plays a critical if not obvious role in the Fall in this poem, and that this vice as understood by Milton was more complex, more intellectual, and more consequential than has been expressed before now.

This is not, then, a book on temperance in the narrow and austere sense in which that virtue is sometimes considered. Ever the classicist, Milton thought of temperance in terms of the ancient Greek concept of *sophrosynē*, a virtue that signifies soundness of mind, pleasant restraint, self-awareness, and just moderation, but one that does not represent — at least not for Aristotle in the *Nicomachean Ethics* — the pursuit of an objectively stable ethical mean.[2] Although commonplace expressions of the golden mean often suggest that virtue is a stable target, Milton's concept is more sophisticated and closer to Aristotle's explanation of the virtuous mean as variant and dependent on occasion, situation, and persons involved.[3] For Aristotle, "the desiring part of a temperate person needs to be in harmony with reason, for the aim to which both look is the beautiful, and the temperate person desires what one ought, as one ought, when one ought, which is what reason also prescribes."[4] While Aristotle suggests a somewhat precise but moving target, Milton emphasizes both the need for discernment and the danger of being too "nice" (e.g., *PL* 4.241, 5.433). For both Milton and Aristotle, one cannot pinpoint an exact and static location of virtue from which, at any given moment, any deviation of excess or defect is vicious; in Milton especially, temperance lies in a moderate middle ground that permits fluctuation and is governed by both reason and charity. For example, in *Paradise Lost* sometimes zealous action is laudable as a healthy superflux of courage, which nevertheless is not as extreme as rashness; sometimes restraint or standing is praised, which is certainly not cowardly but does not seem to be at all times a full expression of the active virtue of courage, either. Abdiel is the model angel who demonstrates both active zeal and patient standing at critical moments. His self- and situational awareness make him an exemplary practitioner of *sophrosynē*.

Temperance as *sophrosynē* is philosophical and introspective; it requires self-knowledge that in turn facilitates discursive reasoning. It includes knowing one's dignity as well as one's proper limits. When in book 8 of *Paradise Lost* Adam tells Raphael how he asked God for a human companion, the story that unfolds is a test of self-knowledge that leads to a fit conversational partner. Adam must first articulate his position as intellectually superior to the beasts:

> Of fellowship I speak
> Such as I seek, fit to participate
> All rational delight, wherein the brute
> Cannot be human consort.   (8.389–92)

Adam voices the limitations of seeking companionship among the animals he names. Seeing male and female among the other species, he looks for a sexual partner but also one that, as "human consort," would share with him in "rational delight." He is aware of his peculiar dignity. Subsequently, Adam demonstrates his knowledge that it is not good for him to be alone, that he is not, like God, his own best society (427–28). As Adam explains to God,

> Thou in thyself art perfet, and in thee
> Is no deficience found; not so is Man,
> But in degree, the cause of his desire
> By conversation with his like to help,
> Or solace his defects.   (415–19)

Adam's gift of "sudden apprehension," with what knowledge he has accumulated from a few short hours of life, leads him to conclude that he has both a dignity beyond that given to the other animals and a subordinate position in relation to his Creator, whom he calls "Supreme of things" (8.354, 414). Neither beast nor god, Adam meets Aristotle's time-honored description of man as a political and social animal.[5] Following Milton's description of a healthy marriage in the *Doctrine and Discipline of Divorce*, Adam's request for a companion is clearly and repeatedly tied to the human need for conversation and communion (*PL* 8.396, 408, 418, 429, 431, 432; YP 2:246, 251). God approves of Adam's expression of self-knowledge, an important component of the broad virtue of temperance: "Thus far to try thee, Adam, I was pleas'd, / And find thee *knowing* not of Beasts alone, / Which thou hast rightly nam'd, but *of thyself*" (*PL* 8.437–39; emphasis added). Here is the famed directive *gnōthi seauton*, "Know thyself," which was inscribed into the ancient temple at Delphi, and which crystalizes much of Greco-Roman philosophy. Milton presents self-knowledge as a key characteristic of temperance, one important in readying the self to engage graciously with others. Passing this test of *sophrosynē*, aware of his nobility as well as his needs, Adam is prepared for the surgery that leads to his heart's desire — the creation of Eve.

Milton's concept of temperance, therefore, involves more than the body, and it includes more than the intellect; it ultimately depends on charity. As *Paradise Lost* concludes, the archangel Michael exhorts Adam to "Love, / By name to come call'd Charity, the soul / Of all the rest" of the virtues (*PL* 12.583–85). Milton's understanding of charity stems from Augustine's *caritas*, the Latin church father's preferred term for selfless, divinely ordered love, which he places in opposition to selfish *cupiditas*.[6] More than an eleemosynary donation to a worthy cause, "charity" for Milton is the word for the costliest of undeserved gifts. God's most momentous request in *Paradise Lost* is a call for charity, the only way to preserve the human race:

> Say Heav'nly Powers, where shall we find such love,
> Which of ye will be mortal to redeem
> Man's mortal crime, and just th' unjust to save,
> Dwells in all Heaven charity so dear? (3.213–16)

In context, the dearness of this charity refers to the extravagant expense of the sacrifice as well as the quality of the sentiment motivating such a sacrifice, but it could also bear a third connotation, one signifying glory, honor, and worthiness.[7] For an early modern example, Shakespeare's *Troilus and Cressida* puns on this word when Hector prepares for his final battle despite Andromache's pleas and Cassandra's warnings. The warrior dismisses the women's call to disarm: "Mine honor keeps the weather of my fate; / Life every man holds dear, but the dear man / Holds honor far more precious-dear than life."[8] The "dear man" here pursues the honor and glory of great enterprise, which in turn is "dear" with respect to the value and affection he places in noble action. A similarly polysemous reading of the above-quoted passage of *Paradise Lost* would underscore the glorious extravagance of charity (in contradistinction to the virtue of temperance, which observes limits even if those limits are flexible, allowing for occasions of excess). In book 3, the Son of God answers this call to extravagant charity, a foil to Satan's apparently heroic volunteerism among the powers of hell in book 2. In Augustinian terms, the difference between the two heroic enterprises is the vast chasm separating *caritas* and *cupiditas*. As I will demonstrate, both Augustine and Milton insist that charity has a broad compass, involving how one should love God and others as well as oneself, without neglecting the peculiar importance of the more narrowly delimited virtues of the self, prudence and temperance. Temperance becomes the tipping point between two opposed sorts of boundlessness, one selfish, one sacrificial. And although gluttony and charity are both involved in extravagance, the lips of charity kiss more than the jaws of gluttony can devour.

Charity, then, is an antidote to gluttony that is nevertheless unopposed to fit extravagance. A necessary part of any examination of Milton's views on temperance, charity supports the important idea of heavenly superfluity and excess. It is the nature of love to be extravagant without being ostentatious. Charity may be said to serve as xylem and phloem in the great Tree of Life, described by Raphael as a representation of all creation's movement in relation to God, "from whom / All things proceed, and up to him return, / If not deprav'd from good" (*PL* 5.469–71). Raphael suggests that humans may be sublimated to higher orders of being, just as "flow'rs and thir fruit / Man's nourishment, [are] by gradual scale sublim'd" (5.482–83). Later, Raphael makes clear that this scale of sublimation is powered by love:

> Love refines
> The thoughts, and heart enlarges, hath his seat
> In Reason, and is judicious, is the scale
> By which to heav'nly Love thou may'st ascend.   (8.589–92)

Love or charity enables translocation, a sign of vitality, producing not only the perfume of praise, represented by the flower, but also the fruit, "Man's nourishment." Gratitude (movement upward) and grace (movement downward) are impossible to measure in this system, and these offshoots of charity are signs of fit excess, which in *Paradise Lost* is rooted in temperance.

As presented in *Paradise Lost*, the Great Chain of Being and the great Tree of Life support the cultivation of charity and a *sophrosynē*-derived self-awareness that checks arrogance even as it allows for radical growth. Temperate self-knowledge, gratitude, grace, and charity save Milton's adaptation of the hierarchical Chain of Being from becoming an ideological power ladder. Rooted in Diotima's description of love in Plato's *Symposium*, the depiction of the cosmos from ground to God as a ladder, line, or living tree was a cherished medieval trope, one not only found in the writings of Neoplatonic Christian mystics but also in the image in William Langland's *Piers Plowman* of the Tree of Charity, called so for its fruit: a tree commonly named Patience, planted in humanity by God, rooted in mercy, and cultivated by free will.[9] This too is a vision of a paradise within, of charity-producing faith supported by a state of virtuous self-composure that may also fall under the term *sophrosynē*.

Radical charity makes Milton's cosmopoiesis more than a defense of temperance; gluttony makes this project more than a book on food metaphors. Both charity and gluttony are involved in excess and extremes, but they represent two very opposed sorts of boundlessness. It makes a world of difference whether one approaches the throne of God beseeching or besieging, and it makes a world of difference whether socio-cosmic border crossing is due to greed and gluttony or to gratitude and grace. When in book 3 the Son of God responds to God's plan to offer grace to Adam and Eve, the narrator describes the Son not only as "most glorious" among the heavenly spirits but also as one showing "Love without end, and without measure Grace" (*PL* 3.139, 142). When the Son then offers his life to redeem the human race, God exalts the Son for his sacrificial charity, "because in thee / Love hath abounded more than Glory abounds" (3.311–12). Such abundance contrasts markedly with the boundless and shadowy figure of Death, emblem of gluttony. Surveying the spoils of paradise after the Fall, Death, "Sin-born Monster," tells his mother he is consumed with the self-centered, never-ending quest "To stuff this Maw, this vast unhide-bound Corpse" (10.596, 601). Inward-turning temperance depends on outward-turning charity to oppose gluttony in a satisfactory way. In *Paradise Lost*, charity enjoys its traditional prominence among the virtues, while it becomes apparent that certain shapes of abstinence can be much more dangerous than certain types of over-indulgence. Where there is energetic temperance, gratitude, and grace, there is also room for grateful vicissitude, guiltless errantry, and beneficent excess and extravagance.

Accordingly, both prelapsarian Eden and heaven contain a remarkable capacity for change, variety, and excess—a capacity that serves as an alternative to gluttony by enabling the proper sort of extravagance on which charity depends. Even the existence of the Tree of Knowledge of Good and Evil points to the variety and excess of paradise—a tree fulfilling a necessary role as a pledge of obedience and a sign of moral choice but superfluous as a food source: "Fruit be here to excess," Eve tells the serpent (*PL* 9.648). The mobility, mutability, and diversity of creation can be incorporated in a psalm of divine goodness and power, as evident in Adam and Eve's morning hymn.[10] In that hymn, the elements that "mix / And nourish all things" are invoked to "let [their] ceaseless change / Vary to our great Maker still new praise" (*PL* 5.182–84). The "Mists and Exhalations"—also part of the metabolic Great Chain of Eating—are exhorted to rise gratefully in honor of God and to descend graciously to "wet the thirsty Earth" (185–90); even the falling motions of creation still advance God's praise (191). And paradisal motion is wed to paradisal excess. The narrator explains that at midday in pre-Fall Eden the sun disperses "more warmth than *Adam* needs," gently recommending that he relax with Eve in their cool bower (5.302); the trees of paradise are so bounteous and varied that God instructs Adam to "Eat freely" and "fear here no dearth," to accept paradise "To Till and keep, and of the Fruit to eat" (8.320, 322). Adam is at once guest, steward, and lord, invited to enjoy Eden's abundance and instructed to care for the garden so that its produce and its beauty may be shared with others, whether celestial guest, human offspring, or friendly beast. When Raphael visits Eden, Adam humbly receives his angel guest, offering with largess the bounties of paradise, skillfully and lovingly prepared by Eve, yet he wonders whether earth's provisions could satisfy heavenly tastes, or if what he has to offer is "unsavory food perhaps" (5.401). For his part, Raphael reassures Adam of the real need, real digestion, and real pleasure that accompany their shared meal. Together, "with meats and drinks they had suffic't, / Not burd'n'd Nature" (5.451–52). In a pure, bounteous, and active *locus amoenus*, Adam and Eve may eat without gluttony and serve without envy.

The vicissitude, diversity, and superfluity that characterize heaven and the earthly paradise indicate that the presence of evil (viz., Satan in the garden) or even the potential for evil (represented by the Tree of Knowledge of Good and Evil) is not a prerequisite for the expression of free will. The motions and excesses of Eden establish the conditions necessary for the exercise of free will and practical judgment, and

Adam and Eve are continually pleased to make decisions beyond the basic choice of obedience or disobedience, decisions that demonstrate their good taste. That is, in a cosmopoiesis where environments often reflect the moral condition of their inhabitants, the changes in paradisal spaces not only imitate the energy and variety within prelapsarian living, but they also encourage change in human activity, permitting intervals of restraint and anticipation as well as seasonable indulgence.

Variety and excess within Milton's paradise invite a relaxed, expansive view of prelapsarian eating. The first observed meal in paradise follows a no-less-delightful period of activity:

> after no more toil
> Of thir sweet Gard'ning labor than suffic'd
> To recommend cool *Zephyr*, and made ease
> More easy, wholesome thirst and appetite
> More grateful, to thir Supper Fruits they fell. (*PL* 4.327–31)

A little labor helps Adam and Eve appreciate the gentle breeze, and periods of work make the periods of rest and repast more pleasurable, and "ease / More easy." In this first description of eating in Eden, Adam and Eve's supper requires little preparation: they recline and pluck fruit from hanging boughs, using the rinds to scoop water from a nearby stream (4.332–36). "To thir Supper Fruits they fell" — the verb promotes a sense of nostalgia through the sharp contrast of this scene with the portrait of fallen eating in book 9, but it also highlights the spontaneity and simplicity of this prelapsarian meal in contrast to a more elaborate but no less delightful alternative.

The meal shared with Raphael in book 5 showcases Eve's great artistry:

> She turns, on hospitable thoughts intent
> What choice to choose for delicacy best,
> What order, so contriv'd as not to mix
> Tastes, not well join'd, inelegant, but bring
> Taste after taste upheld with kindliest change. (*PL* 5.332–36)

The meal Eve prepares demonstrates her elegance, expertise, thoughtfulness, hospitality, and artistry. "Taste after taste" marks the alimentary correlative to the "Grateful vicissitude" charging Milton's heavenly and paradisal spaces (6.8); variety enabling "kindliest change," the delightful progression from one good thing to another, enables choice and the exercise of reason and free will in prelapsarian contexts. There is no one way to eat in Eden, but, whether expertly prepared or casually enjoyed, the meal is marked by grace, graciousness, and gratitude. During both prelapsarian meals, the discourse naturally turns to expressions of gratitude for God's bounty. In the scene of the pastoral supper fruits, Adam remarks, "needs must the Power / That made us, and for us this ample World / Be infinitely good" (4.412–414); a satisfying meal invites him to comment on the goodness of the giver. When Raphael joins the couple in book 5, the dinner begins at Adam's invitation, his words showing not only his graciousness as a host but also his gratitude in recognizing the meal's ultimate source:

> Heav'nly stranger, please to taste
> These bounties which our Nourisher, from whom
> All perfet good unmeasur'd out, descends,
> To us for food and for delight hath caus'd
> The Earth to yield. (5.397–401)

The produce of paradise, Adam observes, is intended to delight as well as to nourish. Raphael assures Adam that the meal, prepared by Eve and originating in God's bounty, is "No ingrateful food" for angelic palates (5.407; cf. 5.430–38, 469–70). Nevertheless, as the poet prepares to narrate the Fall in book 9, he reflects on the loss of this idyllic commensality and communion,

> where God or Angel Guest
> With Man, as with his Friend, familiar us'd
> To sit indulgent, and with him partake
> Rural repast. (9.1–4)

In this nostalgic description of prelapsarian eating, the familiarity of the commensals and the rural simplicity of the customary meal described here do not detract from its indulgence. Before dramatizing the myth of the gluttonous Fall, Milton pauses to grant the reader one last glimpse into a golden world where the divine and the human, and the eaters and the eaten, exist in grateful harmony—a world without prey or predation, rapacity or scarcity, ingratitude or begrudged service, calorie counting or binging. It is, nonetheless, a world of options, of relaxed and kindliest change. Book 9 of *Paradise Lost* shows how easily the expansive code of hospitality of a bygone epoch can be abused. Paris abused it in the story of the Trojan War. Penelope's suitors abused it in *The Odyssey*. Dido was certain Aeneas had abused the code by leaving Carthage. This abuse also occurs in the Fall in *Paradise Lost*, where it can be summed up in one word: Gluttony.

As explored in *Paradise Lost*, body, mind, and soul are interrelated parts of the human experience, and so gluttony has become the starting point for an inquiry into a physiology of eating, a philosophical temperance, and a social and moral view of charity in Milton's poem. The full argument of this book proceeds in similar fashion, from gluttony to temperance to charity, culminating in some observations about poetry, the poetic process, and Milton's philosophy of eating in *Paradise Lost*.

Chapter 1 introduces the theological and literary tradition of a gluttonous Fall and provides an overview of some influential patristic, medieval, and early modern ideas and texts examining or imagining gluttony. The case for Milton's adaption of this tradition begins with an examination of Tertullian's arguments for fasting, which Milton points to in his Commonplace Book entry on gluttony. The chapter considers the development of lists of vices where gluttony frequently was given first place, whether from belief in its role in the Fall or from its perceived position as a "gateway sin" leading to graver faults. I examine the broad definitions and extensive ramifications of gluttony as presented in late antique and medieval theological texts, and the myth of the gluttonous Fall and its conventional relationship to the wilderness temptations of Jesus are given particular attention, as this elucidates Milton's pairing of *Paradise Lost* and *Paradise Regain'd*. The chapter then considers how these theological texts influenced medieval and early modern poetry, with emphasis on works by Dante, Gower, Chaucer, and Spenser. Representative examples of how gluttony has been listed, categorized, and imagined in patristic, medieval, and early modern texts lay a foundation for examining Milton's own use of gluttony in *Paradise Lost*.

Building from this historical and intertextual foundation, chapter 2 considers Milton's use of gluttony's role in the story of the seduction and fall of Adam and Eve. Milton's debt to the gluttonous Fall tradition is further supported in part by *De doctrina Christiana*. In book 9 of *Paradise Lost*, Milton's account of the Fall employs the medieval notion of pretentious eating as a form of gluttony, with gluttony as ill-advised choosiness leading to gluttony as ravenous consumption. Chapter 2 also begins to look into Milton's presentation of gluttonous and temperate knowledge: the forbidden tree is joined to the knowledge of good and evil and Raphael draws an analogy between knowledge and food from the need for temperance and the problem of surfeit. A philosophy of eating starts to unfold as gluttony expands to affect the mental space of the eater.

Chapter 3 turns to examine Milton's presentation of gluttony among the infernal powers, and of the "foul descent" of Satan and his rebel angels, who are "gross by sinning grown" (*PL* 6.661, 9.163). After Adam and Eve's fall, Milton more clearly depicts the repulsiveness of gluttony in the demon's serpentine metamorphosis in book 10. The corporealizing effects of fallenness indicate not a dualistic universe separating body and spirit or mind, and not simply a single sliding scale from grossly corporeal to purely incorporeal but also a general hierarchical principle animated by the dynamism of creatures endowed with free will. Milton's association of the infernal powers with vulgar punning, scatological metaphor, and gluttonous consumption indicates the ignominious consequences of willful deviation from the scale of nature in the poem. Although several scholars make the case for erotic or reproductive rather than digestive metaphor in these passages, I focus on the equally conventional and relevant association of Death with gluttony.

The transformation of Satan and his followers becomes a *de casibus* tale of warning both for Adam and for Milton's readers, but chapter 4 explores the positive potential for change in human nature within Milton's poetic universe. Adam and Eve have the potential to ascend the scale of nature to God; this chapter examines the possibilities for their divinely ordered metamorphoses into higher forms of being, with emphasis on the relationship in the poem between angels and humans. Of the similarities and differences between unfallen angels and humans, those manifest through bodily consumption remain especially significant to this inquiry, since Raphael proposes that obedient eating might raise Adam and Eve to godhood. Through an analysis of Raphael's hypothesis, I examine Milton's use of humoral physiology and the sources for his perception of perfect digestion and excretion. Milton transforms the myth of the perfectly assimilable meal, whether ambrosia or manna, into a representation of prelapsarian eating and excretion as worshipful aspiration. Eating becomes an occasion for virtuous exercise, cultivation of social bonds, and liberating worship. Raphael's opinion of humans' potential to elevate their nature is examined in relation to Galen's *On the Natural Faculties*, Pico della Mirandola's *Oration on the Dignity of Man*, Augustine's *City of God*, and the halakhic midrash *Sifré to Numbers*.

With ideal eating established as no less than the path to a satisfying life and to God, chapter 5 then expands the philosophical implications of good taste to consider a more comprehensive structuring of Milton's poetics and his poetic cosmos. It also considers whether earlier articulations of the power of temperate, obedient eating retain any relevance in Milton's postlapsarian spaces. Throughout *Paradise Lost*, Milton introduces three different methods of ascent to God: the scales of nature, contemplation, and love. In the beginning of book 9, Adam defends the goodness of the three corresponding foods of the body, the mind, and love. Milton employs the triadic outline of philosophy in Augustine's *City of God* to organize the argument of his poem, and he consistently defends the role of bodily regulation and self-governance as a foundation for perfecting the intellect and the will. Unlike some instances of Augustinian Neoplatonism, Milton's most speculative philosophy never leaves the material world behind. Michael's advocacy of the "paradise within" at the conclusion of the poem endorses a Stoic concept — one to which Augustine does not entirely assent — by suggesting that prelapsarian conditions of human nature, the intellect, and the will are partly recoverable through physics, logic, and ethics, or bodily, intellectual, and moral discipline (*PL* 12.587). Bodily temperance then becomes a foundation that supports prudence in philosophical endeavors and charity in interacting with others. In championing *sophrosynē* and the "paradise within," Milton nods to Athens; in seeking complete physical and spiritual glorification through the doctrine of the resurrection of the body, Milton looks to the New Jerusalem. For Milton, both the mental and the heavenly paradise require a synergy of human effort and divine grace, and of bodily and intellectual discipline freely motivated by gratitude.

Chapter 6 asserts that Milton's scheme of consumption has implications for the poet as well as his characters. As early as "Elegia sexta," Milton continued a tradition of associating sober poetics with abstemious eating. Urania is, among other things, a muse of temperance, and the invocation in book 7 of *Paradise Lost* intimates the significance of temperance in diet as well as in the pursuit of knowledge and acclaim, not only for the well-being of the characters within the poem but also for the inspiration sought by the bard himself. Milton's espousal of reason and "slow-endeavoring art" radically dissents from the convention of the ecstatic poet, and even suggests one may presume to solicit a heavenly muse through careful regulation of body and mind. Without denying prevenient grace or poetic inspiration, Milton's persona is a better Bellerophon because he, knowing his human limitations, will curb his poetic presumption. By espousing temperance not only in preparing the poet for imaginative flight but also in guiding the poet's descent, Milton reinforces the relevance of poetry and elegant speech to earthly concerns. This final chapter revisits the medieval concept that gluttony could include any sin of the mouth, including sins of speech, and that gluttony could be atoned for with words of eloquence and praise. *Paradise Lost* itself, then, can be viewed as a work of art seeking in part to repair the ruins caused by a gluttonous Fall.

1

Patristic, Medieval, and Early Modern Views of Gluttony

Whan Adam of thilke Appel bot,
His swete morscel was to hot,
Which dedly made the mankinde.
And in the bokes as I finde,
This vice, which so out of rule
Hath sette ous alle, is cleped Gule.

—John Gower, *Confessio Amantis*

The first sin ever committed by humankind, the sin of the Fall, was gluttony, or so we may read in several late antique patristic writings, and in some of the most influential medieval and early modern theological and literary texts. John Milton had access to many of these texts, and when in the seventeenth century he composed his rendition of the Genesis narrative of Adam and Eve, he incorporated and adapted the tradition of a gluttonous Fall into *Paradise Lost*. This tradition depended on a definition of gluttony that encompassed far more than overeating, and ecclesiastic epistles, homilies, and biblical commentaries offered Milton broad definitions of gluttony, with various arguments regarding its relationship to other vices, and with long and varying lists of its peculiar ramifications. In early and medieval Christian writings on the vices, even casual references to gluttony often bifurcated the vice into quantitative and qualitative branches, or gluttony of the belly and of the palate. Gluttony also appeared as the first of three moral faults, which together represented all physical, intellectual, and social sin, or as the sin that opened its gullet to comprise all sins. From sacred texts and theological commentaries, the expansive portrait of this vice and its association with the Fall soon appeared in poetry and other imaginative literature, including that of Dante Alighieri, John Gower, Geoffrey Chaucer, and Edmund Spenser. This chapter will highlight key examples of late antique, medieval, and early modern attitudes and opinions about gluttony, all contributing to shape a tradition Milton used in his own portrait of a gluttonous Fall in *Paradise Lost.*

TERTULLIAN: FASTING AND THE FALL

One of the earliest Christian authors to examine gluttony was Quintus Septimius Florens Tertullianus, better known as Tertullian (ca. 150–223). His late work *De jejuniis* (On Fasting) identifies gluttony as the sin of the Fall, reproving Adam for having "yielded more readily to his belly than to God, heeded the meat rather than the mandate, and sold salvation for his gullet"; consequently, Tertullian advises fasting as a corrective for the Fall.[1] Tertullian wrote this treatise after he converted to Montanism, a sect known primarily for ecstatic prophesying but also for ascetic behaviors, including periods of fasting and xerophagy, promotion of celibacy and disapproval of remarriage, and strict standards for modesty in dress and behavior. *De jejuniis*, then, sits comfortably with Tertullian's other Montanist writings, especially *De monogamia* and *De pudicitia* (On Modesty). With the enthusiasm of a Montanist, Tertullian promoted rigorous fasting in *De jejuniis*, going so far as to argue that abstaining from food could atone for the Fall and save the soul:

> I hold, therefore, that from the very beginning the murderous gullet was to be punished with the torments and penalties of hunger. Even if God had enjoined no preceptive fasts, still, by pointing out the source whence Adam was slain, He who had demonstrated the offense had left to my intelligence the remedies for the offense. Unbidden, I would, in such ways and at such times as I might have been able, have

habitually accounted food as poison, and taken the antidote, hunger; through which to purge the primordial cause of death — a cause transmitted to me also, concurrently with my very generation; certain that God willed that whereof He nilled the contrary, and confident enough that the care of continence will be pleasing to Him by whom I should have understood that the crime of incontinence had been condemned. Further: since He Himself both commands fasting, and calls *"a soul wholly shattered"* — properly, of course, by straits of diet — *"a sacrifice,"* who will any longer doubt that of all dietary macerations the rationale has been this, that by a renewed interdiction of food and observation of precept the primordial sin might now be expiated, in order that man may make God satisfaction through the self-same causative material through which he had offended, that is, through interdiction of food; and thus, in emulous wise, hunger might rekindle, just as satiety had extinguished, salvation, contemning for the sake of one unlawful more lawful [gratifications]?[2]

Fasting thus became a way to punish the flesh for its sinful appetites and "murderous gullet"; the explicit reference to gluttony in the Fall was interpreted as an implicit recommendation to fast in the present day. Tertullian recognized all "dietary macerations" and "interdiction of food" simply and grandly as attempts to expiate the "primordial sin," and posited that, through asceticism, eschewing even lawful gratification of the appetite, "man may make God satisfaction." Such emphasis on human merit is far from the later and more prevailing Anselmian satisfaction theory of atonement, for which the Crucifixion of Jesus Christ is central; nevertheless, the moralistic idea of naysaying one's way into paradise is not unique to Tertullian.[3] Tertullian's rhetorical position in the above passage produces an expectation of agreement — "who will any longer doubt?" — yet, while controlling one's diet as a means to sacrificial worship is a common enough idea among Christian writings in late antiquity, both his admonitions and the effects he anticipates are extreme. He even goes so far as to opine, "An over-fed Christian will be more necessary to bears and lions, perchance, than to God."[4] His declared habit of treating food as poison and hunger as antidote is physically and spiritually anorexic, yet he has the highest expectations for this regimen. Tertullian continues, "For if the eternal God will not hunger, as He testifies through Isaiah, this will be the time for man to be made equal with God, when he lives without food."[5] In fasting Tertullian finds a path to pursue godhood.

Tertullian's influence on John Milton is apparent through Milton's direct references to the early father of the Latin church in many of his writings. *Of Reformation, Of Prelatical Episcopacy, Colasterion, The Doctrine and Discipline of Divorce, Tetrachordon, The Tenure of Kings and Magistrates,* and *A Defense of the People of England* all cite Tertullian (YP 1:552, 644, 645; 2:236, 644, 736; 3:202; 4:392–93, 414). Most of these works are relatively early in Milton's corpus, and it is unsurprising that the young Milton, who praised and defended virginity (including his own), and who prescribed fasting for those aspiring to write serious poetry, could find much common ground with these stringent attitudes toward the body and its pleasures, and that later in life when defending his opinions he would occasionally call upon the authority of the polemicist and moralist from Carthage.[6] Milton's Commonplace Book, composed during his years of private study at Horton (1636–38), mentions Tertullian on four occasions (YP 1:362, 367, 433, 489–90); the first of these, under the subheading "*Gula*" (gluttony), records his familiarity with the tradition of the gluttonous Fall and with the passage from Tertullian's *De jejuniis* quoted above: "*Tertullianus* eleganter vocat homicidam gulam, et suppliciis inediae puniendam ait, etiamsi deus nulla jejunia praecepisset, quia in eam primus parens lapsus est" (Tertullian tastefully calls gluttony a murderer, and says it must be punished by the torment of not eating, even if God had not commanded any fasting, because in this [vice] our first parent fell).[7] The gloss concludes with a page number (703) identifying Milton's source as Nicholas Rigault's edition of Tertullian's *Opera* (Basel, 1634). Thomas Roebuck has noticed that this passage on gluttony may be easily discovered by looking through Rigault's index, and he questions how thorough Milton's engagement with Tertullian had been in compiling his Commonplace Book. Roebuck argues that there is "no necessary connection between Tertullian and writing about gluttony: this is…a historically decontextualized *sententia*"; Milton's "historical engagement [with Tertullian] is slight and context-free."[8] Nevertheless, however Milton comes upon the passage, and despite the lack of attention to historical context, what concerns me is the simple fact that the young Milton does choose to preserve this particular passage from Tertullian on the gluttonous Fall and the corrective of fasting. Why he does so is another question, perhaps unanswerable, but we do have evidence that Milton was attracted to and approved of Tertullian's sentiment.

The young Milton's praise for Tertullian's expression, suggesting assent, is contained in the Latin adverb *eleganter*. Derived from *elego* (I pick out, I select), *eleganter* carries connotations of proper selectivity and supports the Miltonic definition of reason as choice (*PL* 3.108; YP 2:527). The adverbial form may also be translated "tastefully," through double entendre, pitting Tertullian's eloquence against the gluttony he condemns (YP 1:367).[9] The pun supports a significant idea found in many Christian writings on gluttony and repeated within Milton's work: tasteful words counter inelegant eating. Variations of the food pun on "elegant" in *Paradise Lost* strengthen the case for its intentionality in the Commonplace Book and elsewhere; for example, in book 5 unfallen Eve, skilled in "What choice to choose for delicacy best," prepares a tasteful, "not…inelegant" meal fit for an angel (*PL* 5.333–35). The correlation of the tasty and the tasteful in *eleganter*, or of food and knowledge, is further supported by Milton's frequent punning on "sapience," which in the Latin unites flavor and understanding. The extent to which Adam's intellectual vision has been darkened by the Fall is then doubly evident when he dubs Eve "elegant, of Sapience no small part" for her choice to eat of the forbidden fruit (*PL* 9.1018). In his praise for Tertullian's elegant words approving fasting to counter the sin of the Fall, the young Milton intimates that not only restraint in diet but also beautiful and fitting words of praise or truth may appropriately oppose the sins of the mouth, including sins of eating.[10] As will be evident over the course of this book's argument, I observe a tension between such an extreme position on abstinence as Tertullian's and the ethical stance of the mature Milton. Nevertheless, this early Commonplace Book jotting remains significant to my argument for two reasons: first, it establishes Milton's awareness of and interest in the tradition of the gluttonous Fall; and second, it suggests that Milton noted a connection between speech and diet, and between reason and food. The consequence of this second observation is that, in indicating the power of elegant speech to reprove gluttony, even as a youth Milton adjusts Tertullian's message of asceticism, his exhortation to respond to the Fall by rejecting food, into a more positive message of action through writing.

FROM CASSIAN TO GREGORY:
GLUTTONY LISTED, DIVIDED, AND MULTIPLIED

Since Tertullian, other Christian authors and ascetics have considered and categorized sin and morality with increasing complexity. The list of vices that came to be known as the Seven Deadly Sins began in the Nitrian and Scetis deserts of Egypt with the highly influential fourth and fifth century monastic writings of Evagrius of Pontus (345–399 AD) and Saint John Cassian (c. 360–435). For the ascetic desert monks, gluttony led the vices. In his *Praktikos*, Evagrius placed gluttony (the Greek word *gastrimargia*) at the beginning of his list of eight tempting *logismoi* (thoughts); the other seven were *porneia* (sexual immorality, prostitution), *philarguria* (love of money, avarice), *lupē* (pain, grief, distress, dejection), *orgē* (anger), *akēdia* (sloth, lack of concern for others), *kenodoxia* (vainglory), and *huperēphania* (pride).[11] The desert fathers also first anatomized gluttony; its parts, its relation to other vices, and its consequences were variously enumerated and considered. In the beginning of the fifth century, Cassian brought Evagrius of Pontus's teachings, including his list of capital sins, to Western Christianity. His *Conferences* record the words of desert monks from the Scetis Valley in Egypt, and in the fifth conference, Abbot Serapion repeats the eight *logismoi* of Evagrius, placing melancholy just before sloth, but otherwise keeping the list the same, with gluttony (the Latin *gula*) first.[12] The ordering most familiar today was initiated in the sixth century by Pope Gregory I, who added *invidia* (envy), subsumed vainglory into pride, and used the term *tristia* (melancholy) to comprise both sloth and dejection from Evagrius's and Cassian's lists. Gregory listed pride first and placed gluttony in the penultimate position, just before lust, and his ordering — *superbia, invidia, ira, tristia, avaritia, gula, luxuria* — became the basis for the prevailing list of capital sins.[13] This reordering in effect reprioritized the vices and helped to obscure, but not eradicate, the tradition of the gluttonous Fall.[14]

Cassian provides reasons for placing gluttony first among the vices. It was the first of three sins in Adam's fall: "For it was gluttony through which he took the fruit of the forbidden tree, vainglory through which it was said 'Your eyes shall be opened,' and pride through which it was said 'Ye shall be as gods, knowing good and evil.'"[15] Cassian describes the first six principal faults from Evagrius's list as causally linked, the excess of one leading to the next. Gluttony opens the door to lust, avarice, anger, melancholy, and sloth. (The last two faults, vainglory and pride, are peculiar in that a monk's successful striving against the first six faults could make him more susceptible to the temptation to exult in the self; nevertheless, Cassian also lists pride among the vices escorted into the soul by gluttony.[16]) Cassian notes an especially close link between lust and gluttony, in part because he thinks it peculiar that their consummation requires the body.[17] In general, gluttony came first because it made the soul less able to resist other sins. To combat these sins, Cassian argues, one must first extirpate the root of gluttony:

> [The first six principal faults] have a sort of connexion with each other, and are, so to speak, linked together in a chain, so that any excess of the one forms a starting point for the next. For from superfluity of gluttony fornication is sure to spring, and from fornication covetousness, from covetousness anger, from anger, dejection, and from dejection, accidie. And so we must fight against them in the same way, and with the same methods: and having overcome one, we ought always to enter the lists against the next. For a tall and spreading tree of a noxious kind will the more easily be made to wither if the roots on which it depends have first been laid bare or cut.... Wherefore in order to overcome accidie, you must first get the better of dejection: in order to get rid of dejection, anger must first be expelled: in order to quell anger, covetousness must

be trampled under foot: in order to root out covetousness, fornication
must be checked: and in order to destroy fornication, you must chastise
the sin of gluttony.[18]

All fruits, roots, and ramifications of this tree of vice were the out-
growth of gluttony. A response to the temptation of gluttony thus ushers a person into a path of either vice or virtue, marking a terrifically
consequential fork in the road of ethical living.

In addition to drawing the lines of causation between gluttony
and the other capital sins, Cassian also separates gluttony into different branches. In the second and fifth conferences, Cassian bifurcates
gluttony into the sin of the belly and the sin of the palate, implicating fastidious taste buds as well as the voracious appetite.[19] One mark
of gluttony among the monks, for example, was asking one's host for
a condiment, sauce, or relish to add to one's fare: such a request was
not only a breach of hospitality and a potential exposure of the host's
poverty, but it was also a sign of the monk's moral weakness: "For one
who is upset by taking an unsavoury morsel once and in a way, and
who cannot even for a short time overcome the delicacy of his appetite
will never succeed in curbing the secret and more important desires
of the body."[20] Cassian's division of gluttony into sins of the belly and
of the palate became part of the traditional understanding of the vice
and alternatively has been configured by William Ian Miller into masculine (quantitative) and feminine (qualitative) versions of gluttony:
"One style is gendered vulgar masculine, the other vulgar feminine;
one low-class, the other pretentiously claiming for itself the superiority
of expertise and highness, but often taking the style of an unintended
parody of highness."[21] Quantitative and qualitative gluttony, the sins of
the gourmand and the gourmet, were also configured as drunkenness
and delicacy, respectively, for gluttony encompassed excessive drinking as well as excessive eating, and this excess was not merely quantitative.[22] Gluttony included both indiscriminate and fastidious eating, and
marked both spiritual and corporal weakness.

Cassian's bifurcation of gluttony almost immediately leads to more
complex categorizations. In the *Conferences*, Cassian also divides

gluttony into three branches: "(1) that which drives a monk to eat before the proper and stated times; (2) that which cares about filling the belly and gorging it with all kinds of food; and (3) that which is on the lookout for dainties and delicacies."[23] In addition to the sins of the belly and the palate, the requirement of honoring "the proper and stated times" for virtuous eating emphasizes the need for patience.[24] Cassian also condemns certain instances of delay in taking food. He shares the story of the "gluttony of brother Benjamin," who prolonged his fast an extra day, reserving his allotment of two biscuits that he might combine them with the next day's portion, gaining thereby a greater sense of satiety upon breaking his fast.[25] In this case, one's attitude in taking food is just as important as timing. The triad of eating too soon, too much, or too fastidiously expanded with others' consideration. In the sixth century, Gregory the Great enumerated five basic categories of gluttony in *Moralia in Job*: eating *praepropere* (too soon or hastily), *laute* (too expensively or luxuriously), *nimis* (too much), *ardenter* (too avidly or greedily), and *studiose* (too daintily or elaborately).[26] Of Gregory's five branches, *gula studiose*, or dainty gluttony, not only permits the idea of qualitative excess but also, as a studied, artistic version of the vice, is arguably the most willful and intellectual branch of gluttony. The gluttonous gourmand may eat without thinking; the gluttonous gourmet, however misguided, eats intentionally. Gregory's fivefold division of gluttony persisted in medieval thought, regularly appearing in influential texts of the high medieval period, including a hagiographical text widely used in medieval homilies, the *Dialogus miraculorum* of the German Cistercian monk Caesarius of Heisterbach (ca. 1180–ca. 1240), the Spanish Dominican friar Raymond of Peñafort's *Summa de poenitentia et matrimonio* (c. 1224–26), Thomas Aquinas's *Summa theologica* (c. 1265–74), and the Anglo-Latin manuscripts of the *Gesta Romanorum* (c. fourteenth century).[27] Gluttony had loosened its belt, expanded its compass.

As a capital sin, gluttony grew in consequence by fathering a brood of lesser sins. Cassian identifies "surfeiting and drunkenness" as peculiar offshoots of the vice.[28] Gregory the Great identifies five daughters of gluttony: *immunditia* (moral filth, wantonness), *scurrilitas* (coarse humor), *inepta laetitia* (unfit or foolish joy), *multiloquium* (excessive talking), and *hebetatio sensus circa intelligentium* (weakening of the understanding); the list is affirmed by Caesarius of Heisterbach, Raymond of Peñafort, Thomas Aquinas, and the *Gesta Romanorum*.[29] Furthermore, the consequence of gluttony could be catastrophic. The vice was thought to have caused the Flood as well as the Fall.[30] Milton seems to concur, at least in part, for he describes the world before the Flood as "luxury and riot, feast and dance," progressing "from Cups to civil broils" (*PL* 11.715, 718). Gluttony destroyed cities; early and medieval Christian writings attribute the destruction of Sodom to gluttony, citing Ezekiel 16:49: "But this was the iniquity of Sodom, that she waxed wanton in pride and in fullness of bread, and in abundance of luxury."[31] There was even a tradition that gluttony caused the Babylonian destruction of Jerusalem, since King Nebuchadnezzar's commander Nebuzaradan was mistakenly identified in the Septuagint as *archimageiros*, "chief cook or butcher" (2 Kings 25:8, 11).[32] Although blaming such catastrophes on gluttony seems quaint and darkly comic, to the desert monk or ascetic such appetitive indulgence was bound to have repercussions. Ostensibly diminutive and forgivable, gluttony was an undomesticated pet sin that usually left disaster in its wake.

One further reason Cassian and other late antique and early medieval moralists placed gluttony first in their lists of vices was its ease of commission. As a seemingly innocuous but potentially destructive action, gluttonous eating became a foundational vice providing a critical, explicable link in the transition from innocence to sin. At one point Cassian even proposes that gluttony in itself would be no sin if it did not lead to worse vices, "because the love of good things, i.e., gluttony, would not be in itself harmful, were it not that it opened the door to other passions."[33] Gluttony's involvement with "good things" makes this vice particularly easy to commit and difficult to quell; for Cassian, the need for food makes gluttony the only vice for which one may never hope to eradicate daily temptation.[34] In this we see a key difference between Tertullian's and Cassian's writings against gluttony: The former's extreme asceticism treats eating itself as a moral failure, while Cassian more temperately warns against excessive fasting, for "excessive abstinence is still more injurious to us than careless satiety: for from this latter the intervention of a healthy compunction will raise us to the right measure of strictness, and not from the former."[35] Cassian recognizes that extreme asceticism hinders true virtue and is harder to correct than overeating, while gluttony's generative properties, its pervasive threat, its seemingly innocuous beginnings, its perversion of a basic human need, and the indistinct boundaries between virtuous and vicious eating make the vice an understandable gateway sin, supporting the tradition of the gluttonous Fall.

AUGUSTINE: GLUTTONY IN THE GARDEN, TEMPERANCE IN THE DESERT

If gluttony was humanity's first offense, it had to be conquered by anyone who would check the impact of the Fall. A tradition consequently arose in which Adam's fall in the garden in Genesis 3 was set against Jesus's withstanding of temptation in the desert in Matthew 4 and Luke 4. Significantly, the test of obedience on both occasions began with the temptation to gluttony. In this tradition, the Fall represented all human sin, divided into three broadly defined categories: gluttony, avarice, and pride. Alternatively, these three categories were named in accordance with the threefold division of sin in 1 John 2:16: lust of the flesh, lust of the eyes, and the pride of life. Lust of the flesh, or sensual sin, included sexual sins, of course, but started with gluttony. In practice and in consequence, gluttony is the least concealable example of fleshly indulgence, a most visible representation of the sins of the body. Lust of the eyes was traditionally considered an intellectual sin and was often narrowed to *curiositas*, the avaricious desire for excessive, unnecessary knowledge. The pride of life was the sin of excessive self-love. Adam's gluttonous eating, avaricious curiosity, and selfish pride represented all sin in the single act of the Fall. In the role of Second Adam, Jesus countered this failure by resisting three corresponding temptations in the wilderness — temptations involving the nourishment of bread (lust of the flesh), the wonders of the world (lust of the eyes), and the status of godhood (pride of life). Elements of this reading are found in the writings of many late antique and medieval theologians, including Cassian, Jerome, Caesarius of Heisterbach, Ambrose, Aquinas, and Pseudo-Chrysostom.[36]

More than these, however, Augustine of Hippo delighted in the neat correspondence drawn between Adam in the garden and Christ in the desert, and he promoted the taxonomy of sin according to 1 John 2:16 several times in his writings. For example, in his second homily on the first epistle of John, Augustine asserts, "These three there are, and you can find nothing whereby human cupidity can be tempted, but either by the lust of the flesh, or the lust of the eyes, or the pride of life. By these three was the Lord tempted of the devil."[37] Augustine analyzes these three divisions of sin further in book 10 of *The Confessions*, devoting sections 31–33 to considering the lust of the flesh, sections 34–35 to the lust of the eyes, and sections 36–41 to the pride of life, or vainglory. Section 31 examines gluttony more particularly, where, contra Tertullian, who "habitually accounted food as poison," Augustine approves of "the medicine of nourishment."[38] The effect of sin is cumulative; gluttony leads to other lusts of the flesh — those involving senses other than taste — and then lust of the flesh leads to lust of the eyes, defined as "a certain vain and curious longing, cloaked under the name of knowledge and learning, not of having pleasure in the flesh, but of making experiments through the flesh."[39] Pride of life follows as a sin that often results from exultation in one's physical or intellectual gifts. Augustine elaborates on the connection between these three categories and the temptation in the desert in his exposition on Psalm 8:

> Now these three kinds of vice, namely, the pleasure of the flesh, and pride, and curiosity, include all sins. And they appear to me to be enumerated by the Apostle John, when he says, "*Love not the world; for all that is in the world is the lust of the flesh, and the lust of the eyes, and the pride of life*" [1 John 2:15–16]. For through the eyes especially prevails curiosity. To what the rest indeed belong is clear. And that temptation of the Lord Man was threefold: by food, that is, by the lust of the flesh, where it is suggested, "*command these stones that they be made bread*" [Matt. 4:3]: by vain boasting, where, when stationed on a mountain,

all the kingdoms of this earth are shown Him, and promised if He would worship [Matt. 4:8–9]: by curiosity, where, from the pinnacle of the temple, He is advised to cast Himself down, for the sake of trying whether He would be borne up by Angels [Matt. 4:6].[40]

The citations in this edition are from Matthew, but Augustine describes the temptations following the order in Luke. Augustine associates "vain boasting" with the pride of life and with the mountaintop, and he associates the *curiositas* of the lust of the eyes with the temple pinnacle. Augustine connects the first temptation — to turn stones into bread — to the lust of the flesh, and together all three temptations represent all possible sin.

The division of sin in 1 John 2:16 and its relevance to the fall of Adam and the temptation of Christ well accords with the structure of *Paradise Regain'd*, which retells the temptation of the Son of God in the desert rather than the Passion of Christ (a subject Milton tended to avoid addressing directly since leaving unfinished his 1630 poem on the same). The Son symbolically redeems what was lost in the Fall — and in triumphing over three temptations he conquers all. At the beginning of *Paradise Regain'd*, the bard explains he will "now sing / Recover'd Paradise to all mankind, / By one man's firm obedience fully tried / Through all temptation," resulting in "*Eden* rais'd in the waste Wilderness" (PR 1.2–5, 7), and at the end of the poem the angels praise the Son for succeeding where Adam failed: "Now thou hast aveng'd / Supplanted *Adam*, and by vanquishing / Temptation, hast regain'd lost Paradise" (4.606–08).[41]

As Frank Kermode and Roy Flannagan have both demonstrated, the Son in *Paradise Regain'd* resists the three temptations as follows: (1) gluttony or lust of the flesh in the banquet scene and in the temptation to turn stones to bread, (2) the lust of the eyes (*curiositas*) in the mountaintop temptation, which includes all the learning of Athens, and (3) the pride of life (*superbia*) on the pinnacle of the temple.[42] Milton reverses the sins Augustine associated with the mountaintop and temple pinnacle, while the Augustinian tradition of glossing the temptation of Christ using 1 John 2:16 helps explain some of Milton's more peculiar additions to the Luke 4 narrative. For example, the temptation to eat forbidden fruit was paired with the temptation to turn stones into bread, and under this scheme gluttony — a synecdoche for lust of the flesh — retained significance as a foundational vice. Milton elaborates on the Gospel narratives' modest temptation for lust of the flesh by adding the banquet scene with its delicacies. This, too, the Son rejects: "Thy pompous Delicacies I contemn" (PR 2.390).

Cassian argued that since Christ withstood the temptation to gluttony, he was unsusceptible to the temptation to erotic lust, for lust has gluttony as its root and arises from its superfluity; Augustine also saw lust as the product of gluttony.[43] This likely influences Milton's fashioning of Belial's proposal (after the Son withstands the temptation to turn stones to bread) to tempt the Son with women, which is quickly overturned by Satan (PR 2.153–81).

The parallels between 1 John 2:16 and the temptations in the desert also explain why Milton includes the temptation of Athenian learning on the mountaintop scene, which corresponds with *lust of the eyes* or *curiositas*. Once we understand that the lust of the eyes is an intellectual sin, and accept Augustine's explanation that "through the eyes especially prevails curiosity," it makes perfect sense that Milton would have Satan discuss philosophy with the Son of God while pointing to the wonders of the world.

Significantly, hunger and the temptation to gluttony persist as recurring concerns throughout the entire series of temptations. The intellectual gluttony characterizing the mountaintop temptation is not abstracted from more physical urges but, rather, builds from them. The Son rejects the wealth of nations that Satan offers, "though thou should'st add to tell / Thir sumptuous gluttonies, and gorgeous feasts / On *Citron* tables or *Atlantic* stone" (4.113–15). The Son still thirsts and hungers, and gluttony still lurks on the mountaintop after the Son has withstood the temptations to turn stones to bread and to select delicacies from a lavish banquet. Satan compounds the temptations upon first rejection rather than abolishing them. Upon the Son's successful renunciation of the third and final temptation, angelic ministers serve him "a table of Celestial Food" and repair "What hunger, if aught hunger had impair'd, / Or thirst" (4.588, 592–93). Though the Son rejects gluttony as a lust of the flesh, ultimately he eats and is nourished.

Milton followed the church fathers in counterbalancing the Fall with the temptation of Christ, but not all agreed on the significance of this comparison. For rigid moralists like Tertullian, Jesus's success marked him as an exemplar of the religious ascetic. Tertullian proposed asceticism as a path to salvation, and while Cassian and Augustine also felt the ascetic call to what Cassian approvingly named the "desert of virtue," they despaired of ever living up to its demands.[44] Augustine, like Cassian, identified gluttony as a particularly difficult temptation to resist, more so than its partner sin, lust, because the need for food made the vice a daily temptation. Augustine writes of learning to control his sexual passions, yet the indelible temptation to gluttony leads him to lament, "But is there anyone, O Lord, who is never enticed a little beyond the strict limit of need?"[45] His distress is complicated by the ascetic idea that the line between temperance and gluttony is crossed as soon as one enjoys bodily pleasure beyond that which is required for survival, the "strict limit of need." This strictness was also found earlier in Cassian, where the two biscuits per diem located gluttony in the feeling of repletion.

The tradition of opposing gluttony with asceticism, however, only tells part of the story. More important, Augustine also saw gluttony as being opposed to the ultimate rule of charity. And so in *The Confessions* Augustine affirms in his characteristically prayerful style, "It is not continency alone that You have enjoined upon us, that is, from what things to hold back our love, but righteousness also, that is, upon what to bestow it, and hast wished us to love not You only, but also our neighbor."[46] Consider again Augustine's second homily on the first epistle of John, in which one may find Augustine's exposition of the three categories of sin Milton uses in *Paradise Regain'd*, and which is effectively a treatise on charity. The first epistle of John, after all, is devoted to the doctrine of Christian love, and in the homily quoted above, Augustine lays out his trademark sermon distinguishing cupiditas, a selfish love drawn to things of the earth, and caritas, a selfless love drawn to the things of God. The peroration of this homily is saliently Augustinian: "Holding these things fast, you shall not have the concupiscence of the world: by not having concupiscence of the world, neither shall the lust of the flesh, nor the lust of the eyes, nor the pride of life, subjugate you: and you shall make place for Charity when she comes, that you may love God."[47] Augustine's persistent call to charity is a reminder of the basis of Judeo-Christian ethics — love of God and love of neighbor. Gluttony, or lust of the flesh, was the first step away from this abstract of the Ten Commandments. Even theologians who reject the tradition of the gluttonous Fall still note the seriousness of gluttony in undermining the law of love.[48]

Consequently, Augustine's view of Christian dietary regulations emphasizes liberty and attitude. In book 10 of *The Confessions*, Augustine prayerfully appeals to Scripture to counter legalistic asceticism and to draw attention to the importance of gratitude when eating:

> You have taught me, good Father, that *"unto the pure all things are pure"* [Titus 1:15]; but *"it is evil for that man who eats with offense"* [Rom. 14:20]; *"and that every creature of Yours is good, and nothing to be refused, if it be received with thanksgiving"* [1 Tim. 4:4]; and that *"meat commends us not to God"* [1 Cor. 8:8]; and that no man should *"judge us in meat or in drink"* [Col. 2:16]; and that he that eats, let him not despise him that eats not; and let not him that eats not judge him that eats [Rom. 13:23]. These things have I learned, thanks and praise be unto You, O my God and Master, who dost knock at my ears and enlighten my heart; deliver me out of all temptation. It is not the uncleanness of meat that I fear, but the uncleanness of lusting.[49]

Recognizing gluttony's complexity and its psychological variations, Augustine exhorts his readers to respond to others' eating behaviors with charity — not to accuse others of the vice too quickly, without gracious consideration of context. Regarding dainty gluttony, Augustine emphasizes that the nature of the dainty dish is not so important as the attitude directed toward that delicacy. The quality of the meal is less significant than the gratitude of the eater.

Augustine also advises ascetic readers not to view the path to temperance as a challenge to subsist on the basest of meals. He cautions against the snobbery of the ascetic as well as the gourmand:

> We must, therefore, consider carefully what is suitable to times and places and persons, and not rashly charge men with sins. For it is possible that a wise man may use the daintiest food without any sin of epicurism or gluttony, while a fool will crave for the vilest food with a most disgusting eagerness of appetite. And any sane man would prefer eating fish after the manner of our Lord, to eating lentils after the manner of Esau, or barley after the manner of oxen. For there are several beasts that feed on commoner kinds of food, but it does not follow that they are more temperate than we are. For in all matters of this kind it is not the nature of the things we use, but our reason for using them, and our manner of seeking them, that make what we do either praiseworthy or blameable.[50]

Augustine argues that alimentary delicacies are not in themselves the mark of gluttony, but they must be consumed wisely. At the same time, one may turn the palate as well as the belly into one's god, showing an undignified prioritization of sensual gratification over reason and temperance. While Augustine easily condemns Esau's sale of his birthright for a pot of lentils as gluttonous, occluding a definition of temperance that is confined to the simplest of meals, he warns the reader that it is not so easy to discern the motives of the eaters with more elegant tastes.

Essentially, these motives, reasons, and mental attitudes toward eating determine whether gluttony is committed. Augustine may appear to disregard qualitative gluttony, for the attitude of the eater takes precedence over the nature of the eaten, but this Augustinian emphasis on the will also insists that identifying gluttony requires more than measuring quantities eaten. Because one may eat too daintily, expensively, hastily, or avidly, gluttony may appear in times of drought and famine as well as in times of paradisal plenty.

Granted, the Augustinian opposition of gluttony to charity, and not just to asceticism or temperance, is not a focal point of all Milton's works. In *A Maske*, the young Milton has his moralizing Lady counter

Comus's intemperance by proclaiming the goodness of faith, hope, and…chastity (213–15). Nor is charity the obvious virtue opposite gluttony in *Paradise Regain'd*. Richard Douglas Jordan argues in *The Quiet Hero* that Milton's Son of God is a recurring model for the temperate hero, and his case is strongest in this poem. Nevertheless, in *Paradise Lost* charity regains its traditional position of prominence among the virtues, and when one considers Milton's works as a whole, it is clear that unqualified asceticism is antithetical to Milton's own understanding of Christian liberty. Given Milton's high view of love, companionship, and human worth and potential, as well as his positive portrait of Edenic excess in *Paradise Lost*, I presume Milton would agree with Shakespeare's King Lear that transcending bare physical necessity is a marker of human dignity: "O reason not the need! Our basest beggars are in the poorest things superfluous. Allow not nature more than nature needs, man's life's as cheap as beast's."[51] As one with Milton's love of books and appetite for learning would readily conclude, being fully human demands more than what is required for bodily survival.

DANTE: GLUTTONY AND THE SWEET NEW STYLE

We may now turn to consider representations of gluttony in medieval imaginative literature, how these representations perpetuated the ideas of gluttony found in late antique theological writings, and how they became poetic precedents for Milton's own imaginative treatment of gluttony. Even if gluttony still retained the primary meaning of consuming to excess, medieval poetic references to this capital sin often mentioned Adam and Eve and reflected the broad definition of gluttony in patristic and ecclesial writings, including gluttony as a qualitative and psychological error, and even associating the sin with other nonalimentary sins of the mouth, reinforcing the connection between eating and speech. We see these motifs in Dante, Gower, and Chaucer, for example.

Dante Alighieri's *Divine Comedy* provides a transition from the early Christian writings on the vices to their portrayal in medieval imaginative literature. Quantitative gluttony (the sin of the belly, not the palate) is the branch most obviously punished in canto 6 of Dante's *Inferno*, where Ciacco ("The Hog"), supine and pelted with filthy rain, suffers fit *contrapasso* for a life of slovenly self-indulgence. Cerberus guards the gluttons, but Virgil distracts him by throwing a fistful of mud for him to gobble, parodying the passage in the *Aeneid* where the Sibyl of Cumae feeds Cerberus a drugged honey cake. A triple-mouthed monster distracted by the crudest of food, Dante's version of this classical hellhound is itself a portrait of the indiscriminate glutton.

More complicated is the treatment of the penitent gluttons in Dante's *Purgatorio*, where those who "gorg'd themselves" and "had drunk too avidly" are purified.[52] Both words and hunger atone for gluttonous consumption on earth, as the souls sing the hymn "Domine labia mea" ("*O Lord, open thou my lips*, and my mouth shall shew forth thy praise," from Psalm 51:15). It is on this terrace that Dante encounters the poet Bonagiunta da Lucca, who credits Dante with creating the *dolce stil novo*, the sweet new style of Italian poetry characterized by intense introspection, incorporation of philosophical and theological ideas, the praise of female beauty and the idealization and spiritualization of that beauty, and, above all, the theme of love.

Dante has Bonagiunta identify a poet's response to divine, inspiring love as the factor distinguishing the sweet new style from Bonagiunta's own work. "I am one who, when Love breathes / in me, takes note," Dante the pilgrim says, and Bonagiunta assents: "I clearly see how your pens follow closely / behind him who dictates, and certainly / that did not happen with our pens"; there is "no other difference between / the two styles."[53] In this context, the response to divine love becomes the link between Dante's sweet new style of poetry and the atonement for gluttony. Richard Abrams argues that Dante adroitly reserved discussion of his *dolce stil novo* for the sixth terrace because the activity of poetry (of Dante and Bonagiunta) counteracts the "stay-at-home" vice of gluttony.[54] A habit of selfishly cramming food into the mouth is combatted and atoned for by giving of the self through elocution, eloquence, and praise.

Gluttony becomes an especially significant vice among the poets Dante encounters, since poetic output is arrested by undue deference to bodily appetite. The inordinate eating by the glutton-poets leads to constipated words, to a selfish and impatient ingestion that obstructs any response to divine love, any expression of graciousness and gratitude. Maggie Kilgour has masterfully made this connection in light of Augustine's *Confessions*, which, as she explains, describes human development as a natural progression from feeding to speech to writing.[55] Kilgour elaborates:

> Literal food represents for Dante, as it did for Augustine, all sources of immediate gratification that are chosen instead of the deferred satisfaction promised by God.... If there are poets among the gluttons, one might expect they cared more for stuffing their mouths with food than opening them with words. In Purgatory, the gluttons are taught not to reject bodily impulses but rather to restrain them, "quanto è giusto" (24.154), both to hunger after what is just, and to hunger as much as is just.... The opposite of the greedy, self-centered mouth that simply takes food in is the mouth that also opens to let words out and, specifically, to praise others. So further on, in part of the paradisal counterpart to these cantos, Peter and James will appear to Dante as doves, "laudando il cibo che là sù li prande" ("praising the food which feeds them thereabove," *Paradiso* 25.24): God is food that is both eaten and praised, that goes in but causes words to come out as well.[56]

In this sense, to return to the terrace of the glutton-poets, the hymn "Domine labia mea" purges forbidden fruit. The penitent gluttons are tantalized, curiously enough, with fruit from a scion of the Tree of Knowledge of Good and Evil, and then warned away from it by voices advocating temperance (24.116–17). The placement of this tree on the terrace of Gluttony bears theological and poetic significance for Dante. In her classic work on Dante and Milton, Irene Samuel suggests that Milton acknowledges Dante's association of gluttony with dubious trees when she compares the tree in *Purgatorio* 24 with "the sham trees" appearing in hell in book 10 of *Paradise Lost*.[57] And while Adam in *Paradiso* distinguishes his primary transgression of disobedience from the mere tasting of the tree, the gluttons in purgatory reinforce the connection between food and the Fall, and the role of poetry and hymns in counteracting this failure.[58]

Dante's gluttons in *Purgatorio* exemplify a curious medieval tradition that associated gluttony with other sins of the mouth, including lying, swearing, blasphemy, complaining, boasting, and perjury.[59] We are reminded that loquacity is listed among the five "daughters of gluttony" categorized by Gregory and others, and yet, although gluttony may incite loose speech, speech as an indicator of potential rationality may also be the means through which gluttony finds expression. Under this wide definition, even a poet as poet may be susceptible to charges of gluttony. Gluttony defined broadly as any sin of the mouth thereby retains its viciousness even for those who, like Milton, would iterate Jesus's words against dietary legalism: "Not that which goeth into the mouth defileth a man; but that which cometh out of the mouth, this defileth a man" (Matt. 15:11; cf. Mark 7:15 and YP 2:513–14). Gluttony in speech became a verbal expression of deep-seated moral corruption, for "of the abundance of the heart [the] mouth speaketh" (Luke 6:45). Dante's gluttons remind us that there are multiple ways to understand (or commit) gluttony, but also that spoken words can become the appropriate penance for bad eating.

MILTON AND GOWER ON MAN'S FIRST DISOBEDIENCE

The idea of the gluttonous Fall continues in fourteenth century Middle English literature. In Gower's *Confessio Amantis*, the confessor Genius tells Amans (the lover) that "the grete Senne original" was committed "Whan Adam of thilke Appel bot," and that "This vice, which so out of rule / Hath sette ous alle, is cleped Gule."[60] Milton's familiarity with *Confessio Amantis* is demonstrated by citation in his Commonplace Book and by quotation in *Apology against a Pamphlet* (YP 1:497, 946–47; cf. YP 4:641).[61]

In his adaptation of the gluttonous Fall tradition, Milton was particularly influenced by the sixth book of Gower's *Confessio Amantis*, on gluttony. When the confessor Genius glosses the vice of gluttony in that book, he says that the branches of the vice are many, but he must limit himself to describing two: "Dronkeschipe" and "Delicacie."[62] Before receiving absolution, Amans must understand the ways in which he falls guilty of these two branches of the vice. Genius begins by describing the man enslaved to the first branch, drunkenness, as one who loses his self-awareness and his sanity:

> All hise wittes he foryet
>
> ....
>
> That he ne wot so moche as this,
> What manner thing himselven is,
> Or he be man, or he be beste.
> That holde I riht a sori feste,
> Whan he that reson understod
> So soudeinliche is woxe wod.[63]

Of this indictment Amans might be secure if his confessor had not continued to explain that even the wisest men fall prey to this vice when falling in love. Erotic love, like drunkenness, makes a man forget his reason, and Amans admits he is guilty of gluttony because he is *lovedrunke*.[64] When removed from his lady, Amans explains, he would "suffre such a Passion" that would elicit the pity of all.[65] The condition is not relieved in his lady's presence:

> For whanne I mai upon hir stare,
> Hire wommanhede, hire gentilesse,
> Myn herte is full of such gladnesse,
> That overpasseth so mi wit
> That I wot nevere where it sit,
> Bot am so drunken of that sihte.[66]

That sight, which Amans thinks to be "of Paradis the moste joie," engenders in the heart of the lover "a gret desir, / The which is hotere than the fyr."[67] There is an ambivalence in Amans's encounters with his beloved: a paradise of joy mingled with the hellfire of desire. Such is drunkenness, the first species of gluttony to which Genius leads Amans to confess.

If this first of Gower's two branches of gluttony involves forgetting one's intellect, the second involves the misuse of the intellect. "Delicacie" is a sin of those who already possess the good and yet presumptuously desire something different.[68] As Genius explains, in eating, the guilty seek outlandish cuisines; in love, they seek pleasure outside their marriages; the desired exotic delicacies promise to improve one's nature, but they ultimately prove to be unhealthy.[69] Feeding on such scraps of love as the sight of his lady and the sound of her voice — all he does, he complains, is "hiere and se" — Amans raises some question as to whether he, who has in no other sense tasted of his beloved, could be guilty of the sin of delicacy. Genius reminds him that delicacy is a sin of the mind:

> It been delices wonder smale,
> Whereof thou takst thi loves fode.
> Bot, Sone, if that thou understode
> What is to ben delicious,
> Thou woldest noght be curious
> Upon the lust of thin astat
> To ben to sore delicat,
> Whereof that thou reson exceed.[70]

The lover's food is limited to sound and sight — wondrously small fare for his appetite, and yet a marvelous indulgence. Could Milton have been thinking of the words of Genius when his Adam identifies "looks and smiles" as the food of love, food extracted from reason and talk (*PL* 9.237–40)? Postlapsarian smiles, Genius intimates, can fuel a dangerous curiosity and illicit desires as well as love, and can be acted upon in a way that exceeds reason.

In choosing to describe only two species of gluttony, Amans's confessor selects one traditionally quantitative, material, and "masculine" variety (drunkenness), and one traditionally qualitative, intellectual, and "feminine" variety (delicacy). In further explaining how these two species of gluttony might apply to a character like Amans, who is only interested in the food of love, Genius elaborates his definitions of gluttony in a way that may be compared to Milton's and others' ideas of the Fall: Adam's uxoriousness is a type of love-drunkenness, and Eve's presumption for forbidden knowledge is a type of psychological delicacy. As such, book 6 of the *Confessio Amantis* appears to be yet another source from which Milton might have extracted the bifurcation of gluttony.

But there are indications that Milton may have been using Gower more directly. At the beginning of book 6, before Gower's Middle English, there is an epigraph in medieval Latin:

> Est gula que nostrum maculavit prima parentem
> Ex vetito pomo, quo dolet omnis homo.
> Hec agit vt corpus anime contraria spirat,
> Quo caro fit crassa, spiritus atque macer.
> Intus et exterius si que virtutis habentur,
> Potibus ebrietas conviciata ruit.
> Mersa sopore, labris, que Bachus inebriat hospes,
> Indignata Venus oscula raro permit.

> [It is Gluttony that first tainted our parents, by the primeval apple for which every human being mourns. This sin makes the body yearn for things contrary to the soul, by which the flesh is made stout and the spirit thin. If anything virtuous belongs to a man, within or without, loathsome drunkenness destroys it with tippling. Indignant Venus rarely imprints kisses languid with sleep on lips that Bacchus the tavern host has made drunken.][71]

Andrew Galloway's translation masks something more apparent in the Latin. *Vetito*, which Galloway translates as "primeval," in this context should mean "forbidden"; *pomo* can mean "apple" but also more generically means "fruit" — together, the phrase *vetito pomo* is a medieval Latin idiom that translates to "forbidden fruit."[72] *Dolet*, from *doleo*, is where we get *dolor*, or "woe," translated as "mourns" above. *Nostrum . . . parentem* is masculine or feminine accusative singular; while translated as "our parents," above, the number of the phrase positions the direct object in this context to refer to the collective man, or to Adam. The placement of *prima* next to *parentum* in Gower reminds us that "our first parents" is a Miltonic idiom (cf. *PL* 1.29, 3.65, 4.6, 12.638), but syntactically Gower's *prima* could be a medieval Latin adverbial, an elision of the adverbial phrase *in prima hora*, or an adjective modifying *gula* (both are nominative singular feminine).[73] *Maculavit* (tainted) may appear to be a mild consequence of a correspondingly mild sin, but this was the word commonly used in medieval Latin to describe the stain that sin, especially original sin, left on the human soul, a deadly stain, indelible without the effects of grace and penance.[74]

Now compare this to Milton's opening lines of *Paradise Lost*. The individual words appear, and even if the syntax has changed the meanings are similar. *Prima* appears as "First Disobedience." Forbidden fruit is there, as well as the singular eater. The word *omnis* modifies *homo* in Gower ("every human being"); in Milton the "all" goes with "our woe." The "our" in Milton we find, of course, in Gower's *nostrum*. The words may be rearranged and the modifiers may be paired differently, but the important adjectives, adverbs, and nouns are all there. What is missing in Gower's Latin epigraph is the *mortal* taste — the reference to death, but this is not only implicit in the theological term *macula*, but also found in line 7 of the Middle English: "Which dedly made the mankinde." Take, furthermore, the Latin lines "Hec agit vt corpus anime contraria spirat, / Quo caro fit crassa, spiritus atque macer." Although in Milton's thought body and soul were intricately combined, a notable consequence of the Fall is the positioning of appetite and reason at variance (*PL* 9.1126–31, 12.83–90). Finally, the Latin *crassa*, translated "made thick," is to my mind properly translated as "made gross" in the sense we find in *Paradise Lost* (5.416, 6.661).[75] It is important for Milton that the rebel angels are "now gross by sinning grown."

If these correspondences are not coincidences, they indicate that Milton is not only aware of the tradition of a gluttonous Fall; he's also consciously playing with the connection in the very opening lines of *Paradise Lost*. "Of Man's First Disobedience," then, is in the position of Gower's "*Est gula*" — that is, it is gluttony. If Milton intended this correspondence, at the very least a reader familiar with both *Confessio Amantis* and *Paradise Lost* would note the change of *gula* to the more general "disobedience" and contemplate the alteration. If Milton wanted to intimate by the change that gluttony is *not* particularly associated with the Fall, why draw attention to Gower's book on gluttony in the first place? The similarities between Gower's consideration of gluttony and the proem to *Paradise Lost* may be the most curious evidence so far that the vice is not to be ignored.

CHAUCER AND THE GLUTTONOUS FALL

For a final example of the tradition of the gluttonous Fall in influential medieval poetry, we turn to Chaucer. *The Canterbury Tales* repeatedly mentions gluttony, frequently with reference to Adam and Eve. The Pardoner exclaims against the vice; the Parson anatomizes it, and their conclusion is the same: gluttony first corrupted the world. When the Pardoner warms up for his sermon against avarice, he first turns to gluttony:

> O glotonye, ful of cursednesse!
> O cause first of our confusioun!
> O original of oure dampnacioun,
> Til Crist hadde boght us with his blood agayn!
> Lo, how deere, shortly for to sayn,
> Aboght was thilke cursed vileynye!
> Corrupt was al this world for glotonye.[76]

The Pardoner, whose text "is and ever was, *Radix malorum est cupiditas*," juxtaposes gluttony and avarice. The close relationship between the vices is supported by the lexical facts that *gula* could be translated as greed as well as gluttony and that the Latin *cupiditas* could mean any excessive desire, not just the love of money. Given Augustine's opposition of *caritas* and *cupiditas*, Aquinas's description of gluttony as "inordinate concupiscence" (*inordinatam concupiscentiam*, from the same linguistic root as *cupiditas*), and the common theological reference to gluttony as *gula concupiscientia*, the opposition between gluttony and charity grows increasingly clear.[77] The Pardoner also confirms the association of gluttony with lust, mentioning "the fyr of lecherye, / That is annexed unto glotonye."[78] Chaucer's Physician concurs: "For win and youthe dooth Venus encresse, / As men in fir wol casten oille or gresse."[79] In the "Summoner's Tale," a mendicant friar tries to establish credibility before asking for a hefty donation, claiming his temperance at table and his sexual abstinence earn him divine approval and visionary powers:

> And therefore may ye se that oure preyeres —
> I speak of us, we mendynantz, we freres —
> Been to the hye God more acceptable
> Than youres, with youre feestes at the table.
> Fro Paradys first, if I shal nat lye,
> Was man chaced for his glotonye;
> And chaast was man in paradys, certeyn.[80]

The Friar delights in his own pun: Adam was "chaast" in his behavior until he committed gluttony and was consequently "chaced" from the garden. The passage and the succeeding narrative are filled with irony and bad logic: Paradise is a place of abstinence; all friars are abstinent; friars have God's special blessing (but they need more than that to survive); you should therefore trust this particular friar and give (only) him your money.

If one refuses to accept the hypocritical Pardoner's word on this subject, or the words a vindictive Summoner places in a manipulative friar's mouth, one may turn to the words of a nobler, more authoritative (if less interesting) pilgrim, the Parson. In his sermon on penitence and the Seven Deadly Sins, the Parson explains, "Glotonye is... unmesurable appetit and desordeynee coveitise to eten or to drynke. / This synne corrumped al this world, as is wel shewed in the synne of Adam and of Eve."[81] In agreement with Aquinas, the Parson also notes that gluttony is especially dangerous because it leads to other sins: "He that is usaunt to this synne of glotonye, he ne may no synne withstonde. He moot been in servage of alle vices, for it is the develes hoord ther he hideth hym and resteth."[82] Following Gregory the Great, the Parson defines gluttony broadly, including aspects of dainty eating in a list of variations of his vice: "The seconde is whan a man get hym to delicaat mete or drynke.... The fourthe is curiositee, with greet entente to maken and apparaillen his mete." The Parson's application of *curiosi-tee*, a customarily intellectual sin, to Gregory's *studiose*, the most artful branch of gluttony, furthers the analogy between knowledge and food. The Parson's *Remedium* for gluttony, insofar as it lies within human willpower, is "abstinence...attemperaunce...shame...suffisance...mesure...sobrenesse...sparynge."[83] Although (or perhaps because) Milton's familiarity with Chaucer is overt, not much scholarship has been devoted to examining it, except to note that Milton's copy of Chaucer's works was certainly John Specht's 1602 edition.[84] Milton's use of Chaucer in his Commonplace Book annotations (YP 1:402, 406, 416, 472–73), his reference to the "Squire's Tale" in *Il Penseroso* (lines 109–15), and his regard for "our learned Chaucer" in *Animadversions* (YP 1:667) attest to his early familiarity with the *Romaunt of the Rose*, the *Parlement of Foules*, the *Book of the Duchess*, and, of course, *The Canterbury Tales*, where no fewer than three pilgrims repeat the story of a gluttonous Fall.

THE ELIZABETHAN HOMILY ON GLUTTONY

In the early modern period, the connections between gluttony and the Fall become less frequent and less overt, but a couple of texts deserve consideration here. The official Anglican homily "Agaynst Gluttony and Drunkennesse" uses the story of a gluttonous Fall to warn against excess:

> If our first parents Adam and Eve had not obeyed their greedy appe-tite in eating the forbidden fruit, neither had they lost the fruition of GODS benefites which they then enjoyed in paradise, neither had they brought so many mischiefs both to themselves, and to all their pos-teritie (Genesis 3.6). But when they passed the bonds that GOD had appointed them, as vnworthy of GODS benefits, they are expelled and driuen out of paradise, they may no longer eate the fruites of that gar-den, which by excesse they had so much abused.[85]

In this homily, as in earlier medieval writings, Adam and Eve become primary characters in a string of *de casibus* tales, in which Noah, Lot,

Amnon, Holophernes, the cities of Sodom and Gomorrah, and Alexander the Great each follow Adam and Eve's example in becoming "a slave by excesse" in the form of gluttony.[86] The homily strictly warns its Elizabethan audience against both "daintie and ouerlarge fare," reminding them that Saint Paul "numbreth gluttonie and drunkennesse among those horrible crimes, with the which (as he saith) no man shall inherite the kingdome of heauen."[87] Threatening would-be gluttons with such dangers as "sodaine death by banqueting," the homily asserts that digestion is a divine blessing: "For except God blesse our meates, and give them strength to feede us [and] strength to nature to digest, so that we may take profit by them, either shall we filthily vomite them up againe, or els shal they lie stinking in our bodies, as in a loathsome sink or chanell, and so diversely infect the whole body."[88] The homily also indicates less drastic but no less important consequences of gluttony; the vice prevents one from honoring God and serving others. A mind "made sluggish by cramming in meate, and powring in drinke... cannot lift up it selfe to the glory and prayse of God"; gluttony-induced sluggishness makes the body "unable and unfit to serve either God or man."[89] Gluttony again opposes a sound mind and a charitable soul; it disregards the ancient law to love God and one's fellow humans.

SPENSER: THE MIND OF THE GLUTTON AND THE TEMPERATE KNIGHT

For a final example, Milton may have most carefully pondered the tradition of imagining a gluttonous Fall while reading Spenser. Systematic, allegorical, and concerned with chivalric morality, *The Faerie Queene* is as comfortably medieval as it is Elizabethan. The poem follows medieval chivalric works in which a knight must combat the Seven Deadly Sins. For example, gluttony threatens knighthood in one of the most important and successful works on the medieval chivalric code, Ramón Llull's Catalan *Llibre qui es de l'ordre de cavalleria* (1274–76), which Gilbert Hay (c. 1403–?) loosely translated into the Scots *Buke of Knychthede* at least ten years before William Caxton's independent translation (1484). Llull's original manuscript and Caxton's English printed translation both list the traditional Seven Deadly Sins with gluttony first.[90] Hay's edition, peculiar for its many variations and additions, substitutes this list for an extended passage on gluttony, explaining how the sin is the consummation of all Seven Deadly Sins:

> Off the quhilk sevin synnis, glutany is ane of the werst; forthy, that quhen a glutoun has chargit him our mekle with metis and drinkis than bringis it in suerenesse [sloth], that he mon slepe or rest; and in his rest than desyris he luxure; and quhen he seis that all his charge may nocht be uphaldyn bot grete gudis and richesse, than cummys covatise, that settis nocht by how that gude be wonnyn bot he have it. Of the quhilk conquest cummys ire, and invye, and redy murther and slauchter, quhilkis cummys seldyn, bot that pryde be in thair falouschip. And thus throu glutony is gaderit and assemblyt all the foule company of the vii dedely synnis.[91]

Note that gluttony is presented as "ane of the werst" sins for the same reason that some theologians thought that it was one of the lesser sins within its tribe: gluttony started it all. Hay describes the progression from one vice to the next as if it were inevitable that gluttony would expand to comprise all deadly sins. It is clear from Hay's *Buke of Knychthede* that, with the company that gluttony keeps, being a good knight begins at the table.

Such books of chivalry as the *Llibre de cavalleria* and the *Buke of Knychthede* provide strong precedents for Guyon's noble bouts against gluttony in Spenser's *Faerie Queene*, even though Spenser's book on temperance is second to the book on holiness. In book 1 of *The Faerie Queene*, Redcrosse visits the House of Pride, whence Lucifera progresses with Gluttony and his expected companions. Riding on an ass, Idleness leads the procession, which would not advance at all without Sathan whipping him into action. By the side of Idleness, Gluttony rides "on a filthie swyne," gorging himself, vomiting, drunk and drinking, sweating, wreathed in ivy like Bacchus or Silenus, hardly able to hold himself up, bloated, swollen-eyed, and suffering from dropsy, an allegorical figure "whose mind in meat and drinke was drowned."[92] Although in the description of this procession Idleness precedes Gluttony, their order is reversed when afterward Gluttony serves up a feast that occasions Idleness to call the rest of the sins to join.[93]

Gluttony's first appearance bears no sign of Eden, but there may be allegorical allusions to a gluttonous Fall in book 2 of Spenser's *Faerie Queene*, when Guyon's temperance is tested in the Cave of Mammon with a tree of golden apples. Although the tree in Eden is not mentioned here, one cannot help but pick up echoes of that same tree reverberating in Spenser's Garden of Proserpina, the call to temperance, and Guyon's temptation to eat forbidden fruit.[94] The fruit of Milton's Edenic arbors was like those of Spenser's forbidden tree and those of the fabled Garden of the Hesperides: golden (*PL* 4.146–49, 216–20, 246–49, 9.575–78).

Reason is opposed to intemperance in *The Faerie Queene*. Spenser's allegorical figure of gluttony is the picture of intellectual torpor, and from Spenser Milton directly considered the role reason played in combating gluttony. Perhaps the most interesting information on Milton's opinion on the relationship between reason and temperance is found in *Areopagitica* in a passage honoring but misreading Spenser. In this passage, Milton retells how "our sage and serious poet *Spenser*, whom I dare be known to think a better teacher than *Scotus* or *Aquinas*, describing true temperance under the person of *Guion*, brings him in with his palmer through the cave of Mammon, and the bowr of earthly blisse that he might see and know, and yet abstain" (YP 2:516). What has intrigued critics most about this passage is that Milton was wrong. In the *Faerie Queene*, the Palmer, the voice of reason, assists Guyon through the Bower of Bliss but leaves him to his own devices in the Cave of Mammon. The significance of Spenser's depiction, according to Ernest Sirluck, is that Guyon exhibits continence (the restraint of powerful desires through the force of reason) when he sojourns in the Bower of Bliss with the Palmer, but temperance (understood in Spenser by Sirluck as the Aristotelian state of having become virtuous through habit and without the need of active reason) when he faces the temptations in the Cave of Mammon alone. The significance of Milton's misreading, according to Sirluck, is that, in contrast to the Aristotelian model, the efficacy of habit is less important for Milton, while virtuous striving according to one's reason is always necessary in the exercise of temperance. While I (in considering Aristotle as well as Milton) use the word "temperance" to signify a rational, active virtue, and although "temperance" is, of course, the word Milton uses, under the terminology Sirluck uses in reading Aristotle, Milton does not emphasize temperance as much as continence. Temperance, as habituated virtue, once attained, makes right action easier, such that reason can relax its vigil. And since continence requires the exercise of reason but no habituation, it is presumably easier to attain yet harder to maintain.[95]

The particular significance of Milton's reading of this Spenserian episode to *Paradise Lost* lies in Dryden's comment in the preface to his *Fables* that "Milton has acknowledg'd to me that Spenser was his original."[96] As Edwin Greenlaw argues, this comment was most likely made in connection with *Paradise Lost*, for Dryden conversed with Milton about his epic poem and sought permission to "tag his verses" as the foundation for his *State of Innocence*.[97] The applicability of Milton's misunderstanding of Spenser to his understanding of his own epic is apparent because for Milton, as Sirluck argues, "the peculiar glory of virtue resides in the conquest, not the placidity, of appetite."[98] One must fight gluttony with reason, not habit.

Sirluck's comment is insightful and well accords with the writings of desert ascetics like Evagrius of Pontus and Cassian, who knew the persistent desire for food meant that one must maintain constant vigilance against gluttony, but I must emphasize that Milton would consider this "conquest of appetite" to be its taming, not its destruction, for appetite, when controlled, is a natural source of pleasure. The importance of appetite and desire is bound up in Milton's insistence on the interdependency of free will, love, reason, and temperance in the garden of Eden: "We our selves esteem not of that obedience, or love, or gift, which is of force: God therefore left [Adam] free, set before him a provoking object, ever almost in his eyes; herein consisted his merit, herein the right of his reward, the praise of his abstinence. Wherefore did he creat passions within us, pleasures round about us, but that these rightly temper'd are the very ingredients of vertu?" (YP 2:527).

Just as Milton thought the continual presence of the Palmer was necessary for Guyon, reason must continually guide Adam and Eve in their quest for temperance, but never by quarantining delight. Although the quest becomes easier as one becomes more virtuous, reason is never left behind.

I do not think it too hasty to conclude that the Fall of humankind and the viciousness of gluttony were fertile topics for the medieval imagination. Drawn from scriptural exegesis and concerns about fasting and ethical living in early Christian patristic letters, homilies, polemical writings, systematic theologies, and penitential manuals, medieval texts promoted the tradition of the gluttonous Fall. Though less pronounced, the tradition persists into early modernity, contributing to a wealth of precedents for a seventeenth century poet interested in our first disobedience. Familiar with the fathers of the Christian church and, of course, with such poets as Dante, Gower, Chaucer, and Spenser, Milton was indeed exposed to a long tradition depicting the first sin as gluttony.

2

An Anatomy of Gluttony in *Paradise Lost*

Atque ait, Heu quanto satius fuit illa coloni
(Parva licet) grato dona tulisse animo!
Possem ego avaritiam frenare, gulamque voracem:
Nunc periere mihi et fetus et ipsa parens.

—John Milton, "Apologus de rustico et hero"

In Aesop's Fable of the Peasant and the Lord, a peasant gives the best produce of his fruit tree to his landlord every year. Eager for more of it, the landlord seizes the tree and transplants it into his own garden, but the move to new soil causes the tree to wither and become barren. Milton fashioned this fable into a Latin poem following a model in Baptista Mantuanus's *Sylvarum*. The lord's didactic lament appears in the final lines of Milton's poem, which serve as the epigraph above. If only the lord had received the peasant's gift with gratitude and contentment; gluttony caused him to lose both the fruit and its parent tree. The poem bears the marks of a schoolboy's exercise, but its publication in the 1673 *Poems* suggests that it retained significance for the mature poet.[1] What also comes across in the apologue is a prime example of Milton's tendency to pit a grateful spirit ("grato...animo") against greed and voracious gluttony ("avaritiam...gulamque voracem"). But did Milton, like others before him, think gluttony played a significant role in the Fall?

I have already discussed in chapter 1 Milton's awareness of the tradition of the gluttonous Fall as documented in his Commonplace Book; Milton's other ongoing project, *De doctrina Christiana* (composed while

51

he was also writing *Paradise Lost*), also refers to a gluttonous Fall. Here, as in the Fable of the Peasant and the Lord, Milton again connects gluttony and ingratitude. In the chapter "On the Fall of the First Parents and on Sin," Milton catalogs the sins compounded in this first disobedience, calling Adam ungrateful (*ingratus*) and gluttonous (*gulosus*):

> Sub hoc enim quid non perpetravit homo, credulitate in Satanam, incredulitate in Deum iuxta damnandus, infidelis, *ingratus*, inobsequens, *gulosus*, uxorius hic, mariti illa inobservantior, uterque suae prolis, totius generis humani, parricida, fur, et alieni raptor, sacrilegus, fallax, divinitatis insidiosus, et indignus affectator, superbus, arrogans. (OW 8:412; my emphasis)

> [For under this head what sin did man not perpetrate — to be damned equally for his trustfulness toward Satan and for his trustlessness towards God; faithless, ungrateful, disobedient, gluttonous; he uxorious, she all too heedless of her husband; each of them a killer of their own progeny (the whole human race), a thief, and a preyer on what was not theirs; sacrilegious, deceitful, a crafty and unworthy pretender to divinity, haughty and arrogant?] (Hale and Cullington translation, OW 8:413)

In this congeries, Milton is careful to remember ingratitude and gluttony amid a hoard of more impressive sins, including sacrilege, pride, and the murder of all humanity. (We recall that Gluttony itself is called a murderer in Milton's paraphrase of Tertullian in the Commonplace Book.) In the John Hale and J. Donald Cullington translation above, as in Charles Sumner's translation in the Columbia *Works of John Milton*, gluttony applies to both Adam and Eve (CM 15:180–83). John Carey's translation in the Yale *Complete Prose Works* renders *gulosus* peculiar to Adam, with the masculine singular *hic* the subject of everything from *infidelis* to *uxorius*, but the logical and grammatical parallelism of the passage favors the translators of the Columbia and Oxford editions: Adam is too deferential, Eve is too inconsiderate (YP 6:383). And while Carey prefers to translate *gulosus* more broadly as "greedy," Sumner and Hale and Cullington use the most precise definition of the word: "gluttonous." Important as these distinctions are, in all three translations Adam and Eve together represent humankind (*homo*, not *vir*), and their shared sin affects the entire human race (*totius generis humani*): In Adam's fall we are gluttons all.

Milton underscores all humanity's participation in the Fall, whether or not it is relished, in the passage introducing the above catalog of sins: "Omnium commune, quod aniecta prorsus obedientia, fructuque vetitae arboris degustado, primi parentes atque in iis omnes eorum posteri commiserunt" (The common sin of all is that which the first parents, and in them all their descendants, committed when they cast obedience completely aside and took a taste of the forbidden tree's fruit) (OW 8:412–13). The Latin reveals how even this description of the Fall as simple disobedience is laden with connotations that focus on eating. All share in the banquet of sin — "Omnium commune" — and the disobedience of this great communion is marked by the palate. Full participation does not require a voracious appetite, for *degustado* means "to taste, lick, sip, sample, or touch slightly upon."[2] Bad banqueting includes more than stuffing the belly; in accordance with the doctrine of original sin, through Adam, we all "took a taste" — and a taste is all it takes to be guilty of gluttony.

At the encouragement of one of Milton's earliest prose writings and one of his latest, let us turn to consider how the tradition of the gluttonous Fall influences book 9 of *Paradise Lost*. Of course, proof of Milton's awareness of the tradition in his prose writings should not alone convince us that he makes use of it in his poem; moreover, no matter how many images and metaphors of eating or gluttony appear in the poem, this preponderance in itself does not prove that Milton assigns gluttony a critical role in the Fall. It does, however, create an environment that encourages the curious reader to inquire into the significance behind such images and metaphors, and to be alert to discover how a broadly medieval perspective on gluttony works its way into *Paradise Lost*.

PARADISE LOST AND THE GLUTTONOUS FALL

Adam and Eve's partaking of forbidden fruit marks the perversion not only of eating but also of rational discourse and social intercourse. This theme is introduced in book 9 with repeated references to physiological consumption, references that would be entirely gratuitous if Milton meant to emphasize the arbitrariness of the prohibition rather than the peculiar role of eating in the Fall. From the opening lines of book 9, the Fall is contrasted with the "Rural repast" and its "Venial discourse unblam'd" as depicted in books 5 through 8 (*PL* 9.4–5).[3] "On the part of Heav'n," the response to the Fall is one of "distaste" (9.8–9). As the bard contrasts the "higher Argument" of the poem with the spuriously heroic theme of martial exploits, he also indicates that feasts in themselves are inadequate subjects for the truly heroic poem approving patience and martyrdom — further preparing the reader for a tale of bad eating (9.31–32, 37–38, 42).

As the narrative resumes, the references to food and to consumption prevail. Significantly, once Eve suggests separation from Adam, she articulates an altered perspective on eating. "Let us divide our labors," she suggests, lest dalliance or discourse bring their day's work to little, "and th' hour of Supper comes unearn'd" (*PL* 9.214, 225). She sees their noontime meal as a respite from labor that must be earned, not as a response of thanksgiving for God's bounty. Her focus shifts from divine providence to her own efforts, preparing the way for eating as an ironic expression of autonomy. Alimentary metaphors predominate as Adam urges Eve to remain at his side. While praising her desire for fruitful labor, Adam seeks to temper any extravagance in this desire by reminding Eve of the importance of rest and receiving the various foods available for their refreshment:

> Yet not so strictly hath our Lord impos'd
> Labor, as to debar us when we need
> Refreshment, whether food, or talk between,
> Food of the mind, or this sweet intercourse
> Of looks and smiles, for smiles from Reason flow,
> To brute deni'd, and are of Love the food,
> Love not the lowest end of human life.
> For not to irksome toil, but to delight
> He made us, and delight to Reason join'd. (9.235–43)

Adam explains that he and Eve were created to enjoy the refreshments of paradise, including physical nourishment (literal food), discourse (the "food of the mind"), and "looks and smiles" ("of Love the food"). These three "foods" gratify the whole human — body, intellect, and will — and are interrelated, with "delight to Reason join'd." Adam claims that when he and Eve properly indulge in such pleasures, they are acting in accordance with God's will and with their purpose in creation. "To delight / He made us," Adam affirms — that is, we are more than wage earners, and our relationship with God is not merely contractual — and love is "not the lowest end of human life" — not a bad example of litotes from the poet who calls love the soul of all virtues (*PL* 12.583–85).

Despite Adam's rhetorical efforts, Eve departs, but the food metaphors remain as the bard compares Eve to a series of goddesses associated with eating. As Eve leaves Adam she is likened to Pomona, goddess of fruit trees, and to virginal Ceres, goddess of grain (*PL* 9.393–96).[4] The metaphors presage the transition from a frugivorous golden age to an agricultural society and to the curse of needing to toil for bread. Soon afterward, as Satan observes Eve alone, Milton compares her charms to those of Circe, the enchantress who, like Eve well-versed in the virtues of plants, lures Odysseus's men with food and then turns them into the swine their natures signify (*PL* 9.522; cf. *A Maske*, 50–53, 64–77).[5] In Renaissance emblem books, Circe is frequently a representative of gluttony and the consort of Bacchus, the figure for drunkenness. As a figure of intemperance, Circe is opposed to reason, symbolized by moly, the divinely proffered herb that renders ineffectual Circe's charms — in this, moly is like the haemony of Milton's *A Maske* (638).[6] The Renaissance interpretation of the rational powers of moly builds on Circe's understanding of Odysseus's invulnerability to her powers: "There is a mind in you no magic will work on."[7] As the metaphors shift — Pomona, Ceres, Circe, all food goddesses with their respective pastoral, georgic, and domestic/civic connotations — one may wonder if the temptation Eve will face and the comestible she will offer Adam is best thought of as forbidden fruit, bread from cursed toil, or *pharmakon* (ambiguously medicine and poison).

When Satan tempts Eve as a speaking, intelligent serpent, he tells her his extraordinary rational and elocutionary powers came from eating of the forbidden tree. "Hunger and thirst," he acknowledges, are "Powerful persuaders" (and who would disagree?), but Satan's tactics also include the belittling of physical appetite (*PL* 9.586–87). Before his transformation, Satan in the serpent says, he was a beast "of abject thoughts and low, / As was [his] food, nor aught but food discern'd, / Or sex, and apprehended nothing high" (9.572–74). Satan speaks deprecatingly of the bodily desires for food and sex as a subtle means to tempt Eve to eat something. It is as if he were saying to her, "Eating isn't important. There are so many other, more philosophic things that should demand the attention of such a noble creature as you are. What you eat does not signify anything. Mere animals care for food and sex."[8] And ironically, after the Fall her desires for food and sex are exacerbated and inordinate, while her capacity for reason (which sets her above the beasts) is checked (8.390–92, 9.1127–30). Because Eve neglects the divine mandate and follows her appetite rather than right reason — though she says that "Reason is [her] Law" — she becomes like the lawless, virtueless man of Aristotle's *Politics:* "full of lust and gluttony" (*PL* 9.654).[9]

The temptation is not one of merely physical appetite; Eve eventually believes the apple offers not only bodily nourishment, but also the food of the mind and the food of love. Contemplating the trespass, she calls the fruit "This intellectual food" (*PL* 9.768). She eats to "feed at once both Body and Mind," and then ponders keeping the forbidden fruit to herself "to add what wants / In Female Sex, the more to draw [Adam's] Love" (9.779, 821–22). The bounties and fecundity of paradise, the quality of her prelapsarian mind (endued with sudden apprehension, developed by dialogue and permissible experiment, and fortified by divine message), and the love she shares with a faultless partner no longer satisfy. In choosing forbidden fruit she compromises the delights available to her: the food of the body, of the mind, and of love. She discards moly and reaches for Circe's cup, but in doing so she becomes not Circe but the anti-Lady of Milton's masque. Eve's sin, attended by a wealth of food metaphors, involves her physical appetite as well as her intellect and will. Her mindset and actions are partly comparable to those of the belly-serving, navel-gazing glutton, but are they gluttonous?

Consider all the indications of gluttony within the description of the Fall. Eve's appetite is awakened as she approaches the tree, and desiring its alleged intellectual and apotheosizing benefits, she eats of its fruit. The seduction of Eve is sensual, involving her eyes, ears, nose, appetite, hands, and finally, her palate (*PL* 9.735–42). At the climax of this catalogue, Eve is "Inclinable now grown to touch or taste" — the very actions of which she says the prohibition consists (9.742; cf. 9.651). In addition to following the Genesis account, the emphasis on taste and touch corresponds nicely with Aristotle's understanding of temperance's particular involvement in the bodily pleasures of touch and taste.[10] After that first crucial bite, "Greedily she ingorg'd without restraint / And knew not eating Death" (9.791–92). Eve feels "Satiate at length" — and "satiate," as Kristin Poole points out, has both positive connotations of satisfaction and negative connotations of glut.[11] Eve is intoxicated by her sin, "hight'n'd as with Wine," but the satiety soon vanishes (9.793); in less than ten lines, she begins planning her next meal, meals beyond that, and a ritual of abject adoration of her food source:

> henceforth my early care
> Not without Song, each Morning, and due praise
> Shall tend thee, and the fertile burden ease
> Of thy full branches offer'd free to all;
> Till dieted by thee I grow mature
> In knowledge, as the Gods who all things know.   (9.799–804)

A single experiment becomes a plan for repeat offense, which contrasts with the fitly timed but unpremeditated "prompt eloquence" of Adam and Eve's unanimous morning and evening prayers (4.736, 5.149). She plans to become a slave to her diet and thinks this is the path to godhood. Michael Lieb sees Eve's self-love in her plans for the tree, as "powers of God are here transferred to the self projected in the Tree and worshipped in that form."[12] Her meal breeds discontent and the desire for more of the fruit and its effects. She begins to recognize that her transformation is not as complete as expected, while death might be imminent. Desperately resolved that Adam will participate in her "bliss or woe," Eve takes not one apple but an entire "bough of fairest fruit" to offer Adam (9.831, 851). Eve has neglected her spouse, for in feeding herself she has failed to make their noontide prandial rendezvous. Adam awaits her return, weaving for her a wreath of flowers worthy of a harvest queen, but, his heart filled with misgivings, he intuits Eve's "falt'ring measure" and hastens to find her beside the Tree of Knowledge (9.846). He sees on his beloved's face some signs of the glutton: "excuse," "Apology," and a "Count'nance blithe" yet feverish, for "in her Cheek distemper flushing glow'd" (9.853–55, 886–87). Flowers fall. Astonished that his wife boldly presumed to eat the fruit "sacred to abstinence" (924), Adam must pause before the idea of sin sinks in. Nevertheless, once resolved, Adam does not eat sparingly, for as Eve offers him the fruit "With liberal hand," "he scrupl'd not to eat / Against his better knowledge" (9.997–98). Earth trembles, an event that Peter McCluskey has interpreted as Nature's sympathetic flatulence at the Fall, her entrails reacting to Adam's bad meal.[13]

It is also possible that in composing this passage Milton had in mind the words of Proverbs 30:21–22: "For three things the earth is moved: yea, for four it cannot sustain itself"; the second of these earth-shakers is "a fool when he is filled with meat" (Geneva Bible). Milton cites parts of this proverb three times in *De doctrina Christiana* (OW 8:389, 1097, 1205), and if he refers to it here, the trembling would indicate not only the gluttonous consumption of the human pair, but also the entrance of folly (the intellectual analogue to bodily gluttony) rather than heightened wisdom at this act of disobedience. Adam "took no thought / Eating his fill, nor *Eve* to iterate / Her former trespass fear'd" (*PL* 9.1004–06). Eve's second helping of sin goes beyond the satiety she experienced earlier, complicating an already criminal act (9.792). Poole argues that Eve's gluttony far surpasses that of her husband's: "Eve's sin is not simply that she ate; it is also that she over-ate. (Compare to Adam, who merely 'Eat[s] his fill' [9.1005].)"[14] Nevertheless, gluttony is not limited to quantitative indicators, and as Donald Davis notes, Adam joins Eve in the psychology of gluttony, for he "remarks that the fruit is so tasty that he wishes the Lord had forbidden ten trees rather than only one — an unwittingly ravenous appetite for death that Death himself would have applauded."[15] As gluttons experiencing "mortal taste," Adam and Eve are allied to the infernal character most representative of gluttony, "devoted to death," "to Death devote" (*PL* 1.2, argument to book 3, 9.901).

The natural effects of eating well do not attend this meal. The resulting state of intoxication contrasts with the "inoffensive must" of the crushed grape served earlier (*PL* 5.345). Eating in a way that impairs their reason, leading to their own destruction, both consume gluttonously. Inebriation is not their sin, but it is a symptom of it, one of Gregory's daughters of gluttony. Following the conventional consequences of this vice, gluttony leads to drunkenness, which then leads to newfound lust, "Carnal desire inflaming" (9.1013). Although Eve praises the "exceeding Love" that draws Adam to follow her lead, the narrator takes care to disillusion the reader: "in Lust they burn" (9.961, 1015). *Cupiditas* supplants *caritas*. Post-fall sex leads to an oppressive weariness. The "pure digestion" and "temperate vapors bland" which customarily "bred" Adam's "Aery light" sleep are replaced by "the force of that fallacious Fruit," first intoxicating Adam and Eve with "exhilarating vapor bland," and concluding in an "Oppress[ive]," "grosser sleep / Bred of unkindly fumes" (5.1–5, 9.1045–50). Even Adam and Eve's most involuntary, primal operations — sweat and sleep — have been drastically changed by the excessive and unseasonable gratification of appetite. From this one act, all subsequent meals are tainted: Adam will grieve, "All that I eat or drink, or shall beget, / Is propagated curse" (10.728–29). Failing to grasp the significance of the Fall's effects on the most basic of sustaining bodily processes, Richard Bentley subjected these lines to one of his infamous emendations, changing the "Typographical Fault" of "eat or drink" to "act or think."[16] He missed the meaningful *contrapasso*: the alimentary and digestive effects of the

Fall are correlative to the act. In accordance with the broad medieval perspective on gluttony, Adam and Eve's sin is presented as gluttonous in commission and in consequence.

Consider how the Gregorian divisions of gluttony might unfold in *Paradise Lost*. Eve sees in the apple a shortcut for Raphael's plan of sublimation over "tract of time," and she contemplates achieving *too soon* the benefits of eating, an indicator of the hurried consumption (eating *praepropere*) that Gregory, Aquinas, and others list among the branches of gluttony (*PL* 5.498). Not without significance did Eve previously prepare meals "due at her hour" (5.303). In book 9, Eve tries to sidestep the routine of alternating labor and rest, now interpreted as a system of chores and wages. Despite lengthy preliminaries, the act itself is sudden and dreadful: Eve's "rash hand in evil hour" plucks and eats (9.780). Although the Fall occurs at the time of "Noontide repast," Eve does not wait until returning to the bower to eat, and her failure to meet her engagement with Adam further indicates unseasonable, over-hasty consumption (9.403). In her desire for divinely forbidden food, her dismissal of the cost, and her improperly zealous speeches before and after eating, Eve eats both *laute* (too expensively or luxuriously) and *studiose* (too daintily or elaborately). The intended move from spontaneous praise of the Creator to ritual adoration of the tree also marks a transition from acting *eleganter* to acting *studiose*: "Henceforth my early care…each Morning…Shall tend thee," Eve promises the tree (9.799–801). "Intent now wholly on her taste," Eve eats too avidly (*ardenter*), as if the apple intensified what Adam earlier described as permissible, leisurely refreshment (9.786). Finally, her greed leads her to eat too much (*nimis*), far beyond the point of satiety. In different ways, Eve eventually demonstrates all the traditional expressions of gluttony.

Gregory the Great's classification of gluttony includes not only eating with the gourmand's rapacity, but also eating with the gourmet's snobbish, overdiscriminating palate, that is, eating a certain type of food in a certain way.[17] This duality is a helpful gloss on the complexity of gluttony as presented in *Paradise Lost*. Eve first commits gluttony of the discriminating type, and then of the undiscriminating. In an "unintended parody of highness" (to return to William Ian Miller's description of feminine, qualitative gluttony) Eve first chooses to act beyond her human limits — that is, beyond the dictates of right reason and against the divinely revealed prohibition. At first, her sin is not that she wants too much food or excessive knowledge; it is that she wants *forbidden* fruit and attendant *forbidden* knowledge, "sciental sap, deriv'd / From Nectar, drink of Gods" (9.837–38). At her fall, her pride is not in her place in the created hierarchy; it is in her assumption that she, too, must be "as the Gods" (9.804). Ironies attend Eve's qualitative gluttony, for the forbidden fruit has no certain, inherently peculiar worth; it is special simply because it is forbidden, and it offers new knowledge of good and evil only as a consequence of disobedience. Moreover, insofar as the temptation to be as "the Gods" means to become like the *angels*, such aspiration, through licit means, has already received the approval of the angel Raphael. In accordance with Cassian's understanding of the vice, Eve's gluttony may initially be involved with good things — desire to refresh her body, to be like the angels, to perfect her moral knowledge, and to increase the love she shares with Adam — but she locates the means to these desires in the wrong tree and eats with the wrong disposition. Eve presumptuously decides she deserves an immediate promotion. Her sin begins with a nicety — with dainty, qualitative gluttony.

Only after Eve fails to choose well — a qualitative sin — does she eat excessively, fully succumbing to her bodily desires. Adam reenacts this pattern, as the choice to ignore his rational misgivings and to disobey the mandate leads to his intemperate consumption. The choice to eat forbidden fruit is qualitative, and the choice to continue eating leads to compounded, quantitative sins. Gluttony as a sin of vicious selectivity soon degenerates into its visually repulsive counterpart, marking the disillusioning transition from snob to slob. The qualitative and the quantitative, palate and belly, thereby converge in the communal first sin of Adam and Eve. From this act, a horde of sins and disorders soon follow: intoxicated Lust first, and then "high Passions, Anger, Hate, / Mistrust, Suspicion, Discord" and the like (9.1123–4). As a result of Adam's and Eve's gluttony, their tripartite souls are lodged in "distemper'd breast[s]," for

> Understanding rul'd not, and the Will
> Heard not her lore, both in subjection now
> To sensual Appetite, who from beneath
> Usurping over sovran Reason claim'd
> Superior sway.   (9.1127–31)

Thus gluttony as ill-advised fastidiousness leads to gluttony as ravenous consumption, which leads to a host of other sins and to the subjection of reason to appetite. Eve's dainty gluttony — the supposition that prohibited fruit ought to be for her own enjoyment — results in the gluttonous tyranny of the appetitive part of the soul. Both Adam and Eve end up "Bewailing thir excess" (11.111). The Son tells Adam he must now labor for his meals: "Curs'd is the ground for thy sake, thou in sorrow / Shalt eat thereof all the days of thy Life," and "In the sweat of thy Face shalt thou eat Bread" (10.201–02, 205). As Michael Schoenfeldt remarks, "Where in Paradise eating was simply an appropriate response to God's generous plenitude... after the Fall it becomes both a reward and a punishment."[18] The assumptions about eating that Eve voiced as she separated from Adam have been ironically fulfilled. Now, the hour of supper must be earned.

At the same time, there is evidence that the Fall in *Paradise Lost* follows the threefold division of sin in 1 John 2:16: the lust of the flesh, lust of the eyes, and the pride of life, where lust of the flesh initiates the series with the more specific sin of gluttony. In chapter 1 I examined how these categories of sin and the consequent parallels drawn between the Fall of Adam and the temptation of Christ affect the structure of *Paradise Regain'd*. One may consider whether Milton's use of this triadic structuring also appears in *Paradise Lost*. It is possible, of course, that Milton used this traditional application of 1 John 2:16 in the later poem without doing so in the earlier, but the opposite possibility deserves our inquiry as well. After all, Milton quotes 1 John 2:16

in the chapter of *De doctrina Christiana* devoted to the providence and blamelessness of God, a topic certainly salient to the great argument in *Paradise Lost* (OW 8:327). And in fact, there is a triadic structure to the Fall in *Paradise Lost*, with gluttony in the initial position. Eve experiences the lust of the flesh, the lust of the eyes, and the pride of life. Her aspirations are not only appetitive, but also intellectual and, ultimately, selfish. Satan's temptations mirror these three aspects of sin, as he first speaks of physical appetite, then of philosophy, then of godhood (*PL* 576–97, 598–605, 679–97, 708–30). Eve's response likewise follows this pattern, as her appetite is aroused first; then she considers the virtues of the Tree of Knowledge of Good and Evil, and finally she questions God's motives in denying her its fruit (735–79). After she plucks and eats, the bard once more recapitulates this three-fold sin of qualitative gluttony as Eve grows "Intent now wholly on her taste.../...through expectation high / Of knowledge, nor was God-head from her thought" (9.786, 89–90). Eve chooses to gratify her physical appetite by means of the wrong fruit, and thereby com-mits the sin of lust of the flesh. She seeks to stimulate her intellect by means of the wrong tree and thereby commits the sin of lust of the eyes. She wants to satisfy her will and her desire for love in the wrong way, by asserting her autonomy, gratifying inordinate desires, and despis-ing God, and thereby demonstrates pride of life. Lust of the flesh, lust of the eyes, and pride of life: The Fall perverts the three "foods" Adam discusses in book 9: bodily refreshment, food of the mind, and the food of love.

While portraying the first sin, Milton can at once draw from the tra-dition of applying the three sins of 1 John 2:16 to the Fall, the Gregorian explication of the fivefold nature of gluttony, and the simplified divi-sion of these types into quantitative and qualitative versions. Despite objections that gluttony is only one of many contributors to the Fall, or only one of many consequences of it, within this Augustinian and Gregorian structure it is apparent that gluttony has a principal place in Milton's rendition of the Fall.

WHY NOT GLUTTONY?

One might reasonably resist this reading of the prominent presence of gluttony in the Fall in *Paradise Lost*, but I do not think the expectation of a more metaphysical "great argument" is a good enough reason to do so. Milton can soar above the Aonian mount and into the empyrean, but he also digs his pen into the earth. He defends the poetic and polemical use of the vulgar image (YP 1:895).[19] He cares about the physical, sensual world enough that the *Oxford English Dictionary* proposes Milton coined the word "sensuous" so that his descriptions of the natural world and his good opinion of the senses would be free from the connotations of immorality associated with the word "sensual" in seventeenth century England.[20] Of the 20 instances of the word "flesh" in the poem, 15 are positive, associated with the intimacy of Adam and Eve's relationship, with the doctrine of the incarnation, or with the regeneration of the repentant heart. Disregard for the vice of gluttony could intimate a dualistic disregard for the physical world itself, for the material substances that can become either the stuff of the Fall or part of the very ingredients of virtue.

In fact, there are two dualistic interpretive paths that might reject my reading and its serious consideration of gluttony. The first is part of Satan's rhetoric of temptation and of gloating; it is the message that decisions about eating are inconsequential and it is the expression of contempt for those who take commands about apples seriously, for those who could be tempted with an apple, and for those (including God) who could be offended by such a meal. Satan tells his demons that such a transgression and offense is "worth [their] laughter" (*PL* 10.488; cf. *Paradise Regain'd* 2.348–49). His rhetoric is linked to what Stephen Fallon has identified as "infernal Cartesianism," the alluring idea that the mind is its own place to the extent that it may contemn the external world, hell, apples, and all (*PL* 1.254).[21] The satanic mindset assumes that one can think or imagine oneself into heaven or godhood without the external forces of faithful action and supernal grace, and without responsibly and honestly acknowledging one's environment.

The second interpretive path veering away from consideration of gluttony avoids analyzing the physical act to emphasize the *will* of Adam and Eve in the Fall. Perhaps "Man's First Disobedience" is most simply and most accurately identified as just that — disobedience. It does not matter that there is fruit — only that there is something forbidden. God just as easily could have provided Adam and Eve a pledge of obedience by drawing a line in the sand and saying "None shall pass." In this reading, the apple is an accessory; where the real sin originates is in the will, as an unnatural evil intention or inordinate desire, even if the Fall subsequently consists in a physical act of disobedience. This reading has the theological weight of Augustine on its side: "Thus, the evil act, — that is, the transgression of eating the forbidden fruit — was done only by human beings who were already evil: such an evil fruit could have come only from a corrupted tree. Moreover, the corruption of that tree came about contrary to nature, because it certainly could not have happened without a defect in the will, and such a defect is against nature."[22] In Augustine's metaphor, the "fruit" is the action of the Fall; the "tree" is the mind of the eater. While the will is of primary concern, there remains an organic relationship between mind and body, between will and action.

Such a focus on the mind and its desires need not remove gluttony from a position of primacy, for the vice is wide enough to encompass such mental activity. As we have seen, gluttony can be a state of mind, an attitude about eating: one may commit qualitative gluttony with the mere expectation of eating something qualitatively superior, regardless of the true quality of the meal. Diners can be snooty about peanut butter and jelly or about caviar; they can exult in an expensive oil without the taste buds perceiving that it has gone rancid. Presumably, one can also commit the sin of gluttony by pretentiously choosing *not* to eat.

This focus on the will has a correlative and more troublesome argument — that the Fall consisted in *mere* disobedience. In this reading, it is irrelevant that the sin includes eating, and the apple itself has no intrinsic powers to convey knowledge: The "force of that fallacious Fruit" consists only in the fact that God has forbidden it (*PL* 9.1046). This reading deserves consideration, especially since it corresponds to Milton's description of the Fall in *De doctrina Christiana*, which argues that the forbidden tree "was called [the tree] of the knowledge of good and evil from the outcome [*ab eventu*], for ever since its tasting not merely do we know evil, but we do not even know good except through evil" (OW 8:361).[23] The tree's name depends on what *results* from eating it, not from what it *is*. Milton explains that the prohibition had to be arbitrary to test man's voluntary deference to divine mandate — "so that there might be some scope for him to attest his obedience" — rather than test his powers of reason (OW 8:359). This idea is connected to *Paradise Lost* in C. S. Lewis's *Preface*, where Lewis affects surprise that "great modern scholars have missed what is so dazzlingly simple," that the apple is an apple, not an allegory, and that "The Fall is simply and solely disobedience — doing what you have been told not to do: and it results from Pride."[24] Lewis's logic is too breezy here, yet I accept the reading that *Paradise Lost*'s forbidden fruit had no intrinsic power to convey knowledge. It is uncertain that the fruit, once eaten, had any immediate extraordinary effect on the senses beyond the placebic and temporary euphoria of disobedience, such effects felt "whether true / Or fancied so" (*PL* 9.788–89). Eve expects knowledge and divinization, but we are only on solid ground when it comes to the eating itself: "Greedily she ingorg'd without restraint" (9.791).

The "force of that fallacious Fruit" is real and noticeable in its digestive consequences: bad eating causes bad sleep and bad vapors, physical signs of a physical, mental, and spiritual Fall. Digestive outcomes pale in comparison to the more spiritual consequences, but "all our woe" surely includes suffering in the physical realm along with its correspondent and interconnected spiritual grief. One may very well suppose that the arguments made by Augustine, Lewis, and Milton himself (in the prose treatise) for focusing on the *will* (preceding the first bite) or the *event* (*ab eventu*, the outcome) rather than the apple itself could also be made against emphasizing the matter of eating. Nevertheless, the action of the poem cannot be disconnected from the stuff and flesh of the world Milton creates.

Whatever we make of the prose treatise, to read the poetic Fall as *mere* willful disobedience would account neither for Milton's alimentary metaphors nor for his interest in the material world. If focusing on the psychology of sin is taken so far as to devalue the physical world and movement within it, we have once again the infernal Cartesian mindset. Gluttony may be committed in the mind, but even thoughts are, in their most basic form, linked to the sensible realm. One might argue that in focusing on gluttony I follow Lewis in erroneously proposing a too-simple narrative of the Fall, but my intention is different: to uncover the complexity of gluttony, with its earthiness, psychic qualities, potential for metaphor, and so on, both in the medieval mindset and in Milton's application of the same in *Paradise Lost*.

Other objections remain. Perhaps gluttony is only one of the sins compounded in the Fall, following Milton's explication in *De doctrina Christiana* (presented at the beginning of this chapter), where *gula* might seem inconspicuous amid 15 other vices involved in the Fall (OW 8:412–13). Or perhaps, following Aquinas, Milton presents gluttony as merely a consequence of the Fall, not the act of the Fall itself. Maybe pride comes before the Fall, and the Fall before gluttony. After all, Eve first partook, and then she partook ravenously. Perhaps the death our first disobedience brings into the world is not, as chapter 3 will argue, an allegory of gluttony, but most simply and accurately an allegory for itself—Death. Yet again, perhaps the mortal taste of forbidden fruit brings into the world of Milton's poem not only a gluttonous Death, but also a deadly gluttony. While the passage from *De doctrina Christiana* serves to emphasize the comprehensiveness of the Fall, relegating gluttony to a position of one among many sins fails to account for its rhetorical prominence in Milton's poetic narrative. For the same reason, one cannot dismiss gluttony in the poem simply by relegating it to a place of consequence, for such a maneuver fails to explain why the poem includes so many signifiers that more readily point to gluttony over any other proposed consequence of the Fall.

Perhaps one might object that Milton, like Aquinas, draws attention to the tradition of a gluttonous Fall in order to displace it. If there is one contender for gluttony's position as primal sin, it is pride. Pride's claim may have the advantage of the authority of Aquinas and Gregory, but gluttony has more explanatory power in *Paradise Lost*. The building block of gluttony may create complex, vice-ridden towers, and its manifold nature can explain the foundations of sins of many other names. Pride may be expressed as gluttonous self-esteem, but gluttony encompasses more than the gates of pride can admit, since gluttony may entice the slovenly, servile, or destitute as well as the pretentious. As Milton describes the Fall, pride alone cannot account for Eve's lack of abstinence or Adam's uxoriousness, but gluttony, understood as quantitative or qualitative intemperance, and grounded in the failure to know oneself — one's proper limits as well as one's proper dignity — can do so. Furthermore, by way of analogy, gluttony may explain the intellectual as well as physical failures of the Fall. Thomas Aquinas himself names gluttony-induced dullness of sense and lust-induced blindness of mind as the vices opposed to knowledge and understanding.[25] When listed first among the vices, gluttony — often a visible example in action and in consequence of exceeding the virtuous mean — presents itself as a grotesque gloss on all the others.

As presented in *Paradise Lost*, gluttony holds a reasonable claim to the title of primary sin in the Fall of humanity. In his preponderance of alimental metaphors, allusions, and other rhetorical devices, Milton is not merely following the Genesis account. Even if the specific nature of the prohibition in Scripture is arbitrary, Milton makes eating a point of emphasis in his poem. The reader may demand further explanation for this poetic decision. If we grant the evidence for gluttony in the Fall, how does this affect our reading? Traditional interpretation or not, can one really expect Milton to reduce the "cause of all our woe" to "the great myth of the evil meal," as William Kerrigan puts it?[26] We are led to ask, what might this evil meal *mean*? And once eaten, what are its effects?

THE AFTERMATH OF GLUTTONY AND THE CALL TO TEMPERANCE

In confirmation of the involvement of gluttony in the Fall, Milton weaves the theme of temperance into the end of his poem. The final books of *Paradise Lost* are especially important because they take place in, and seek to explain, a postlapsarian world. Although C. S. Lewis has famously stated that books 11 and 12 constitute a prosaic, "untrans-muted lump of futurity," it is here that one may receive the poem's final word on the ethics of consumption, and where it is clear that prelapsarian depictions of temperance are not merely reminiscences of a lost ideal but also a reinforcement of a standard of self-regulation and fruition worth striving to attain, however imperfectly.[27] Mindful of this, Michael calls Adam to temperance repeatedly. Preparing him for visions of the future, the angel advises Adam to

> temper joy with fear
> And pious sorrow, equally inur'd
> By moderation either state to bear,
> Prosperous or adverse: so shalt thou lead
> Safest thy life.   (*PL* 11.361–65)

Later, Michael reminds Adam that moderation ought to govern Adam's opinion of his condition; "Nor love thy Life, nor hate," he commands (11.553). At the conclusion of his visit, Michael's final string of exhortations includes the call to temperance (12.583).

Before Adam can begin to understand this call and envision its allure, he must receive medical treatment from an angel. One debilitating effect of the Fall on the human condition is the impairment of sight, along with the weakening of the cognitive and philosophical powers suggested by this sense. Consequently the extraordinary vision and narrative of books 11 and 12 require special preparation:

> *Michael* from *Adam's* eyes the Film remov'd
> Which that false Fruit that promis'd clearer sight
> Had bred; then purg'd with Euphrasie and Rue
> The visual Nerve, for he had much to see;
> And from the Well of Life three drops instill'd.   (11.412–16)

Michael counters human limitations and the effects of the Fall with nature's gifts in the medicinal herbs euphrasy and rue, herbs known in Milton's day for their power to restore failing eyesight. As euphrasy and rue were herbs any London apothecary might sell, it is probable that Milton tested their effects on his own failing eyesight, for early biographers record his "tampering with physic" in the hope of staving off blindness.[28] While Milton's medical experiments were ultimately ineffective, he makes Adam's treatment far more powerful, if only because it is mingled with spiritual elements, drops from the well of life, and administered by an angel who begins by removing the distorting film of fallenness from Adam's eyes. The divine elements become important active ingredients in Adam's physic, but so are the earthly herbs, and these herbs support Michael's message of temperance. Milton's choice of euphrasy and rue was based on wordplay, as Alistair Fowler has noted: "The name 'euphrasy' is from Gk. Euphrasia, cheerfulness, while the bitter rue puns on rue = sorrow, pity, or repentance (a pun so common that no fewer than five instances are given in OED s.v. *Rue* sb.2 1 b). In other words the herbs are correlates of the 'joy' and 'pious sorrow' that Michael told Adam to temper, at ll. 361 f. Note, however, that the tempering is connected with the operation of the *well of life*: true Christian patience depends on grace and repentance."[29] This reading of euphrasy and rue as cheerfulness and sorrow is suited to Michael's exhortations toward moderation, to God's own tempered response to the Fall, and to the paradoxical and complex state of Adam and Eve at the end of *Paradise Lost*.

But there may be yet another sense in which euphrasy and rue are significant here. If euphrasy and rue point to the tempering of cheerfulness and sorrow essential to the human response to the Fall, they may also indicate another tempering in the poem's expression of a dynamic synergy between divine grace and human effort. Rue was commonly known as the herb of grace, and, as David O. Davies has explained, euphrasy has a homophonic resonance in *eu* + *phradzein*, which could mean "good phrasing" or "eloquence," perhaps even "poetry."[30] In this reading, euphrasy and rue are emblems of the best that human beings can offer God — eloquent words of praise, or a life well lived, which is (as Milton asserts in his *Apology for Smectymnuus*) "a true Poem, that is, a composition, and patterne of the best and honourablest things" — and the best that God gives humans: favor and blessing preceding one's virtuous deeds and extending far beyond one's deserving (YP 1:890). Such a reading proposes that Milton envisioned *Paradise*

Lost (and indeed, his very life) as both a deeply reverent hymn to divine grace and an exultantly vigorous example of human poetic action. For Milton, a temperate response to the Fall includes both cheerfulness and sorrow, and relies upon both divine and human agency.

Intemperance in its specific sense of gluttonous eating also appears in the final books of the poem. The dominant cause of death, Adam learns, will be "Intemperance...In Meats and Drinks" (*PL* 11.472–73). Michael shows Adam a vision of a lazar house where many of the diseases there pertain to the digestive system: "Intestine Stone and Ulcer, Colic pangs...Marasmus...Dropsies" (11.479–88). Bodily sickness, Adam learns, is the fruit of "th' inabstinence of *Eve*" and of his own poor choice (11.476). And when Adam asks if all humans are destined to die through violence or excruciating pain, Michael tells him that a regimen of proper eating and drinking will soften the effects of sin on the body. Michael then exhorts Adam,

> Well observe
> The rule of not too much, by temperance taught,
> In what thou eat'st and drink'st, seeking from thence
> Due nourishment, not gluttonous delight,
> Till many years over thy head return:
> So may'st thou live, till like ripe Fruit thou drop
> Into thy Mother's lap, or be with ease
> Gather'd, not harshly pluckt, for death mature. (11.530–37)[31]

This preventative diet can only partially undo the deleterious effects of fallen human nature. Even with rigorous attention to "due nourishment," Michael warns, old age will eventually give way to melancholy caused by the now natural imbalance of the humors (11.544). After the Fall temperance is still as necessary as ever, though the consequences of intemperance are invasive, and the cure — "the rule of not too much" — is incomplete.

Nature as well as human nature suffers from the Fall. When God decrees Adam and Eve's expulsion from paradise, he personifies the garden of Eden as a nauseated dyspeptic who can no longer contain the tainted Adam and Eve:

> Those pure immortal Elements that know
> No gross, no unharmonious mixture foul,
> Eject him tainted now, and purge him off
> As a distemper, gross to air as gross,
> And mortal food, as may dispose him best
> For dissolution wrought by Sin, that first
> Distemper'd all things, and of incorrupt
> Corrupted.   (11.50–57)

In depicting the land as a queasy stomach, Milton follows a metaphor within Hebrew sacred Scripture.[32] In Leviticus 20:22, Yahweh warns the Israelites, "Ye shall therefore keep all my statutes, and all my judgments, and do them: that the land, whither I bring you to dwell therein, spue you not out" (AV).[33] Eden, acting like a healthy body encountering a toxic substance, "eject[s]" the human pair, "purg[ing them] off / As a distemper" (a catch-all word for illness in the seventeenth century). Perhaps because these words are put into the mouth of God, or perhaps because the eventual redemption of Adam and Eve is in the background (foretold as early as the fourth line of the poem), the diction here is rather gentle for the action it describes. Nevertheless, the polyptoton and other figures of repetition here ("gross...gross... gross"; "distemper...Distemper'd"; "incorrupt / Corrupted") intensify the images of revulsion. Eden's natural rejection of sin attests to its continued health; resisting the deleterious "change on Sea and Land," Eden in its integrity is no longer a fit region, soil, or clime for tainted Adam and Eve. The garden remains intact only as a *hortus conclusus*, and there is a wistful propriety in its destruction at the Flood (10.693, 11.829–35). The moral Michael draws from this — "God attributes to place / No sanctity, if none be thither brought / By Men who there frequent, or therein dwell" — advises Adam in turn to examine his interior landscape and to cultivate a "paradise within," while the personified garden demonstrates its own figurative sanctity — a state of being set apart, of good refusing to compromise with evil (11.836–38). Although the bodily and moral integrity Eden represents may be irreproducible in a fallen world, it imitates what Milton deems the appropriately holy response of heaven: distance and distaste.

When Milton describes Nature's response to human intemperance, he imagines pure regions vomiting out the impure inhabitants, and places so corrupt that, as if in vicious sympathy, the environment imitates the vomiting gluttons within. While God describes Eden purging itself, its "pure immortal Elements" ejecting Adam and Eve, ancient Egypt is the symbolic land of bondage that best illustrates intemperance for Milton: her pharaoh a tyrant, her people luxurious, and her river "disgorging at seven mouths" (*PL* 12.158). The Nile's delta imitates the four rivers of hell, which "disgorge / Into the burning Lake thir baleful streams"; in sharp contrast, the four rivers of Eden, though "wand'ring," "Ran Nectar, visiting each plant, and fed / Flow'rs worthy of Paradise," and which "perpetual draw thir humid train" (*PL* 2.575–76; 4.234, 240–41; 7.306). Infernal rivers vomit, paradisal rivers nourish. As in books 1 and 2, the final books of *Paradise Lost* refer to Busiris's Egypt and to the exodus of the Israelite slaves to oppose gluttony to liberty, providing a narrative frame reinforcing the dual concepts that intemperance enslaves the self and nauseates Nature. Milton's description of the postlapsarian Nile in book 12 is an ironic but pointed reminder that hellish environs can make their way to earth, pervert natural fecundity, and threaten liberty.

In associating ancient Egypt with gluttony and tyranny, Milton does nothing new. John Cassian, for example, made ancient Egypt a symbolic land of gluttony, although the fault might more properly be attributed to the grumbling, hungry Israelites who, unmindful of liberty, resented leaving a land of abundance (Exod. 16:3). While Milton's temperate locales are "delicious" spots, far from arid, the "fleshpots of Egypt" conventionally represent the abundance of general wickedness, and gluttony in particular, which tempts the ascetic from virtuous restraint (cf. *PL* 4.132, 4.729, 7.537, 9.439, 10.746). In his fifth conference, Cassian associates a deadly sin with each of the seven nations God promises to destroy for Israel in Deuteronomy 7:1–2. But Cassian counts eight principal vices, and so as a counterpart to gluttony he adds Egypt, a land to be forsaken but not destroyed. The distinction, he explains, signifies that the force of appetite can never be completely eradicated, and eating should be moderated but not rejected. As chapter 1 has noted, Cassian also argues that fasting itself ought to be moderated, lest extreme hunger and excessive abstinence cause a monk to "return again to the land of Egypt, i.e., to our former greed and carnal lust," to the depravity that Cassian summarizes as gluttony.[34] Aquinas acknowledges this conventional reading of Egypt with its "fleshpots" as a metaphor for gluttony, citing Psalm 135:10: "[Give thanks] to him that smote Egypt in their firstborn, for his mercy endureth forever."[35] The scriptural text has nothing to say about gluttony, but Aquinas cites an anonymous gloss of the verse, one that regards Egypt and her "firstborn" as gluttony and the other sins issuing from this parent sin. Curiously, Aquinas objects to the gloss's conclusions about gluttony but takes no issue with the metaphor used to draw those conclusions. Milton also assumes the connection between Egypt and gluttony is commonly accepted enough that it needs little explanation.

Milton consistently thought of temperance as a salient characteristic of citizens of a free society. In the *Second Defense*, Milton argues that "to be free is precisely the same thing as to be pious, wise, just, and temperate, careful of one's property, aloof from another's, and thus finally to be magnanimous and brave" (YP 4:684). And when Milton proposes a modified republican system of choosing a leader through a series of refined elections in *The Readie and Easie Way to Establish a Free Commonwealth*, he advises, "To make the people fittest to chuse… teach the people faith not without vertue, temperance, modesty, sobrietie, parsimonie, justice" (YP 7:443). Conversely, gluttony enslaves. In *The History of Britain* and in his the Commonplace Book, Milton holds gluttony responsible for the Norman Conquest, the dissipation and lassitude of the English nobles in war, and the fall of Harthacnut, the last Danish king of England (YP 1:367, 5:402; cf. 5:370–73). Gordon Campbell and Thomas N. Corns demonstrate how the conclusion to the *History* ends with a dark assessment of the contemporary moral environment of England: "His closing depiction is of an age of gluttony" but also "an age...characterized by the perseverance of a godly remnant."[36] In Milton's "Letter to a[n Unknown] Friend," dated October 20, 1659, Milton comments upon "the sad & serious discourse which we fell into last night concerning these dangerous ruptures of the common wealth, scarce yet in her infancy, which cannot be without some inward flaw in her bowells" (YP 7:324). Gluttony provided a metaphor for the disease of the body politic, as well as a literal threat to domestic, political, and religious liberty.

Milton also made gluttony a metaphor for immoderate pursuit of glory. In a letter to Richard Jones, son of Lady Ranelagh, Milton exhorts his young advisee, "Learn now, from early youth, to consider and recognize great examples, not on the basis of force and strength, but of justice and moderation [*temperantia*]" (YP 7:493). A life of moderation may at times seem unfruitful and inglorious, but in the closing books of *Paradise Lost* Milton advocates temperance even at the expense of the epic battle tradition. In book 9, the heroic legends of Achilles, of "the *Greek*" famously "Perplex'd" by the god of the sea (Odysseus), and of "*Cytherea's* Son" (Aeneas) are opposed to "the better fortitude / Of Patience and Heroic Martyrdom," which is presumably a guiding theme for Milton's own "Subject for Heroic Song" (*PL* 9.13–33). Milton elaborates upon this opposition in book 11 by adhering to the conventional depiction of warfare as gluttonous.[37] Even though the battles Adam envisions occur much earlier in history than those of the Greek epics, the association of the two historical periods is patent. Michael relates,

> For in those days Might only shall be admir'd
> And Valor and Heroic Virtue call'd;
> To overcome in Battle, and subdue
> Nations, and bring home spoils with infinite
> Man-slaughter, shall be held the highest pitch
> Of human Glory, and for Glory done
> Of triumph, to be styl'd great Conquerors,
> Patrons of Mankind, Gods, and Sons of Gods,

Destroyers rightlier call'd and Plagues of men.
Thus Fame shall be achiev'd, renown on Earth,
And what most merits fame in silence hid.   (11.689–99)

Michael thus condemns the intemperance of human warfare, while
Milton presents his poem as superior to the classical martial epics
of antiquity. Excoriating the edacious and "infinite Man-slaughter"
of war, the veteran angel strips these future conquerors of their false
glory, preferring to call them "Destroyers" and "Plagues." Following the
depiction of the War in Heaven, war on earth is destructive, violent,
and yes, gluttonous: Adam weeps at the vision of the "brazen Throat of
War" (11.674, 713). The epic battle heroes are further associated with
gluttony when, in times of peace, after having "done much waste," they
then revert to "sloth, / Surfeit, and lust," the traditional offspring of
gluttony (11.791–95). Gluttony in its most basic, visible form — eating too much — never leaves the poem even when it is attended by more
honored or more sophisticated sins: the intemperate pursuit of glory in
battle, for example, or the luxuriant sloth of peacetime.

Even the rewards of industry can prove a challenge to temperance.
Michael foretells that bountiful harvests in times of antediluvian peace
will induce gluttony in fallen humans,

for th' Earth shall bear
More than anough, that temperance may be tri'd:
So all shall turn degenerate, all deprav'd,
Justice and Temperance, Truth and Faith forgot.   (11.804–07)

Earth's prolific bounty is no new occasion for temperance, but fallen
reason exacerbates the temptation to misuse that abundance, and the
new threat of scarcity instigates hoarding and gorging in times of plenty.
Scarcity also binds gluttony to injustice, following a common medieval
and early modern assumption that for every rich glutton there must be
a starving beggar, in accordance with the parable of Dives and Lazarus
in the Gospel of Luke.[38] In a world where honor and feasting cannot
be accessible to all, the would-be heroes are unjust gluttons in war and

in peace, by negative example reinforcing Michael's instructions to seek "Due nourishment, not gluttonous delight" (11.533).

In championing temperance Milton undercuts the classical epic while advocating classical moral philosophy, especially the Aristotelian concept of *sophrosynē*, the Greek word for self-control, self-knowledge, soundness of mind, and calmness of spirit. As Richard Douglas Jordan argues in *The Quiet Hero*, "*sophrosynē* was a Greek virtue that found little positive expression in the characterization of Greek [literary] heroes" — that is, it was rarely idealized in Greek epic, comedy, tragedy, or romance.[39] Instead of glorifying a dubious character trait — the wrath of Achilles, for instance — Milton deglamorizes violence, whether done to a fellow human or an angel, to God's laws, or to the environments of heaven and earth. Milton is no pacifist, and he understands war as necessary in a fallen world where some yet strive for justice and liberty, but in the *Second Defense* he affirms that the "warfare of peace" — striving to master the self and the temptations of avarice, ambition, and luxury — is "far more noble than the gory victories of war": "For, my fellow countrymen, your own character is a mighty factor in the acquisition or retention of liberty. Unless your liberty is such as can neither be won nor lost by arms, but is of that kind alone which, sprung from piety, justice, temperance, in short, true virtue, has put down the deepest and most far-reaching roots in your souls, there will not be lacking one who will shortly wrench from you, even without weapons, that liberty which you boast of having sought by force of arms" (YP 4:680–81).

Similarly in *Paradise Lost*, despite his feats of prowess in the War in Heaven, the Son's heroism depends upon his temperance, obedience, and love (*PL* 12.403). Exhibiting "the better fortitude / Of Patience and Heroic Martyrdom," Milton's Son of God is a recurring model for the temperate hero, most conspicuously in *Paradise Regain'd* for abjuring the temptations of bread and banquet, as Jordan explicates in detail, but also in *Paradise Lost*, for more general expressions of temperance (*PL* 9.31–32; cf. *PR* 2.378, 2.408, 3.92, 4.110–42). The Son is temperate in moderating righteous wrath with kindness; in his plans to judge the human pair, he tells the Father, "I shall temper so / Justice with Mercy" (*PL* 10.77–78). Repentant Adam remembers God's "mild / And gracious temper" (the various senses of the verb and noun are not unrelated) and anticipates divine mercy once he seeks forgiveness (10.1046–47).

However, like Adam, who acts upon prevenient grace, the "quiet hero" in *Paradise Lost* goes beyond Jordan's definition of one "who achieves important successes... by not acting, by merely waiting, or by undertaking (at the end of a period of restrained or thwarted action) a climactic action that has a symbolic relationship to the outcome rather than being a major cause of it."[40] *Paradise Lost* does reinforce the idea in Milton's Sonnet 19 that "They also serve who only stand and wait": God approves Abdiel for having "fought / The better fight," for "this was all [his] care / To stand approv'd in sight of God." The Son tells the faithful angels to "Stand still" while he singlehandedly routs the demonic hordes, and Raphael exhorts Adam to "stand" in obedience (*PL* 5.522; 6.29–30, 35–36, 801; 8.640–41). But throughout Milton's oeuvre, standing requires not inactivity and denial but balance, faith, and readiness for action — even as these conditions rely on grace. Laura L. Knoppers beautifully points out that the Son's stance in the final temptation of *Paradise Regain'd* is ambiguously positioned within the divine grace/human effort dynamic that charges much of Milton's poetry and thought: "The word 'pinnacle' (πτερυγιον; a turret or battlement, a pointed roof or peak; Vulgate *pinnaculum* and *pinna*) in Matt. 4:5 and Luke 4:9 is variously interpreted and hence does not resolve the issue of whether or not the Son can stand by human powers alone."[41] In book 3 of *Paradise Lost*, God insists that he created man "Sufficient to have stood, though free to fall," but that, once fallen, "Man shall not quite be lost, but sav'd who will, / Yet not of will in him, but grace in me.../ Upheld by me, yet once more he shall stand" (3.99, 173–74, 178). The balance required for standing depends not upon motionless, mindless obedience, but upon the dynamism between faith-inspiring grace and the active, rational condition of temperance. This is the ultimate message of the final books of *Paradise Lost*, reinforced by negative example through metaphors of gluttony: temperance must be wed to grace, and virtuous human striving to divine motion, if humanity is to live well in a postlapsarian world.

GLUTTONOUS AND TEMPERATE KNOWLEDGE

Milton thought temperance involved and affected the mind as well as the body. Recall that Evagrius of Pontus, whose list of vices becomes the basis for the Seven Deadly Sins, names gluttony (*gastrimargia*) and its associates as tempting *thoughts* (*logismoi*) rather than actions. Among these tempting thoughts, gluttony is peculiarly related to the mind. Considering conventional opinions on consumption, digestion, and excrement with an eye for philosophic analogs, one might ask if there are boundaries to knowing, if such boundaries are qualitative or quantitative, and if one stands in danger of unwisely pursuing knowledge too soon, too avidly, too expensively, and too nicely, as well as pursuing too much of it, following Gregory's fivefold definition of gluttony. To what extent does "lust of the eyes" betoken intellectual gluttony? Could the acquisition of knowledge or the pursuit of wisdom lead to unhealthy excess? In *Paradise Lost*, Raphael announces his "Commission from above / ... to answer [Adam's] desire / Of knowledge within bounds"; beyond these bounds, he instructs, "abstain / To ask" (*PL* 7.118–21). But how is one to know where the boundaries of permitted or beneficial knowledge lie, or the questions one should abstain from asking?

The interrelation between the health of body and mind was a commonplace from antiquity, and there is a correlative relationship between gluttony and intellectual torpor. We have observed how temperate eating and knowing meet in the Greek *sophrosynē*, which signifies soundness of mind as well as sobriety and moderation in diet, and how they meet again in the Latin *eleganter* (tastefully, well-chosen, from *elego*, to choose) and in *sapientia* (good taste, intelligence, from *sapor*, taste, flavor). The physician of Plato's *Symposium* argues that a sound body leads to proper desires of the soul, while Aristotle states that "the unrestrained person [with respect to bodily pleasures] is one who stands aside from his reasoning."[42] Cicero describes gluttony as a sickness of the mind, and Juvenal, in his tenth satire, praises a *mens sana in corpore sano*.[43] A sound body supports a sound mind, while sickness, neglect, or misuse of the body enervates the intellect and the spirit. As Timothy Reiss elucidates in his work on personhood and passibility in early modernity, Galen, Seneca, Cicero, and Plutarch each drew analogies between body and soul, and between medicine and philosophy.[44] Using ancient authority and early modern commonplaces, Stephen Pender explains that physicians were to be skilled philosophers, for *medicine begins where philosophy ends*.[45] Rhetoric became involved in this interrelationship as well; Pender discusses widespread ancient, medieval, and early modern belief in the physical healing power of well-spoken words, a belief based not only on awareness that "Knowledge of the embodied self is found at the intersection of medicine, philosophy, and rhetoric," but also on the truism, supported by Hippocrates, Galen, Cicero, and Burton, that wise words carry psychosomatic benefits.[46]

Conversely, gluttony enervates the mind. The inscription to Pieter Bruegel the Elder's 1557 painting *Gula* translates to "Shun drunkenness and gluttony, because excess makes man forget God and himself," while his 1560 *Temperantia* painting opposes temperance and ignorance: "We must look to it that, in the devotion to sensual pleasures, we do not become wasteful and luxuriant, but also that we do not, because of miserly greed, live in filth and ignorance."[47] Similarly, Shakespeare's misanthropic Timon of Athens links gluttony, ingratitude, and mindlessness, irate that "ungrateful man, with liquorish draughts / and morsels unctuous, greases his pure mind, / That from it all consideration slips."[48] Even *gula studiose*, dainty gluttony, was thought to be mentally debilitating. In the opening scene to *Love's Labour's Lost*, for example, drawing an analogy between eating and sexual gratification, Longeville observes that "fat paunches have lean pates, and dainty bits / Make rich the ribs, but bankrupt quite the wits."[49] And in *Paradise Lost*, gluttonous actions lead to intellectual complications: eyes opened to evil, minds darkened (*PL* 9.1053–54).

As the Tree of Knowledge of Good and Evil joins forbidden fruit to forbidden knowledge, Milton's angels insist that the consumption of information, like food, needs temperance. Raphael unfolds an analogy between knowledge and food both to satisfy and to check Adam's curiosity. The explanation for curbing the intellectual appetite is physiological:

> But Knowledge is as food, and needs no less
> Her Temperance over Appetite, to know
> In measure what the mind may well contain,
> Oppresses else with Surfeit, and soon turns
> Wisdom to Folly, as Nourishment to Wind.   (7.126–30)

The knowledge-food analogy introduces the concept of gluttonous, even flatulent knowing.[50] Adam is asked to know his intellectual as well as physical limits, to realize "In measure what the mind may well contain," for excessive and indiscriminate consumption turns wisdom to folly.

Though Milton never overtly anatomizes gluttony in his writings, in *De doctrina Christiana* he does list the branches of its counterpart in the "Knowledge is as food" analogy: folly. Instead of directly inquiring into "what the mind may well contain" and then categorizing all else as folly, we may proceed by a *via negativa*, first reviewing Milton's definition of folly, and from there determining his opinion on the proper sphere of knowledge. Milton anatomizes folly into four branches: folly includes, first, "disregard [or ignorance] of God's will"; second, "a false persuasion of wisdom"; third, "Prying into hidden things, as when our first parents went prying into the forbidden knowledge of good and evil"; and fourth, "human wisdom," or the inferior brand of knowledge "that is often [really] punishment for contempt of true, divine wisdom" (OW 8:927–31).

Opposed to these examples of folly is prudence, "the virtue by which we foresee when and where each thing ought to be done" (OW 8:931). Glossing Hebrews 5:14 under the heading of prudence, Milton explains that "solid food is the mark of adults: of those, that is, who because of habit have senses trained for the discrimination of good and evil"; directly following this he calls prudence "a seasoning of every virtue, as salt once was of every sacrifice" (OW 8:933). Prudence is thus both sustenance and seasoning to ethical living. If prudence, as Milton argues, requires the distinction of good from evil, then one may presume that, in a certain sense, knowledge of good and evil is not forbidden but, indeed, is necessary to prevent folly. If Milton's definitions in the ethical section of *De doctrina Christiana* apply to *Paradise Lost*, then the Tree of Knowledge of Good and Evil must signify something apart from the ability to distinguish good from evil: what is forbidden is an empirical knowledge that requires participation in evil.

Temperance is to gluttony as prudence is to folly, but the virtues and vices are so interwoven that avoiding gluttony requires prudence, and avoiding folly requires temperance. Folly, like gluttony, can be divided into quantitative and qualitative branches: one may seek to consume too much too soon, and one may devote oneself to the wrong sort of knowledge at the wrong time, in contradistinction to the fitting "what . . . and when . . . and where" of Milton's definition of prudence. Both quantitative and qualitative folly exceed permitted "knowledge within bounds," although, like the line between nourishment and gluttony, the boundaries of knowledge may be indistinct and variable (*PL* 7.120). As with the application of humoral theory to early modern medicine, knowledge of the self is needed to clarify these intellectual boundaries. Quantitative folly (or intellectual gluttony of the quantitative variety) is best illustrated by the knowledge-food analogy: one can oppress the self with surfeit of knowledge just as one can become bloated with overeating. But the knowledge-food analogy also presupposes the existence of qualitative folly (or intellectual gluttony of the qualitative sort); prudent intellectual exercise requires knowing "*what* the mind may well contain," and not just how much of it (my emphasis). Thus, Raphael warns Adam against seeking "Things not reveal'd," for "Anough is left besides to search and know" (*PL* 7.122, 125). *Paradise Lost* repeatedly addresses two types of qualitative folly: the empirical knowledge of evil gained by committing sin, and a type of vague speculation more difficult to define. While the first sort was positively forbidden, the second was advised against by an angel guest, but then partly exercised, under supervision. This leads to one of the dramatic cruxes of *Paradise Lost*: the troublesome possibility that, through conversation, Raphael incites Adam to intellectual gluttony.

Even before eating forbidden fruit, Adam may be led by Raphael into "Seeking for knowledge of things which are hidden from mankind," the species of folly Milton particularly associates with Adam and Eve in his anatomy of folly in *De doctrina Christiana*. In book 5 of *Paradise Lost*, Eve's dream brings to her imagination the possibility of disobedience, and Raphael's visit introduces Adam to this possibility through rational discourse. Some of God's creatures have already fallen, Adam learns, and he is free to follow suit. When Adam asks about the War in Heaven, Raphael, "After short pause," as if questioning the wisdom of such a revelation, agrees to tell a tale "perhaps / Not lawful to reveal" (5.562, 569–70). His story is beyond the limits of what reason may discover: "I have reveal'd / What might have else to human Race been hid" (6.895–96). While in *De doctrina Christiana* Milton's high view of divine revelation in sacred Scripture is evident from its first page, Raphael's uncertainty about the bounds of permissible knowledge may cloak Milton's own anxiety about creating a new "revelation" in his narrative of the War in Heaven. "Into the Heav'n of Heav'ns" the bard has presumed, not entirely certain if he can express what he imagines there without blame (*PL* 7.13, 3.3).

The dangers or futility of transgressive and presumptive knowing are patent in *Paradise Lost* because for Milton this is a real challenge confronting anyone who faithfully exercises his or her mind. Rather than closing off all inquiry, Milton endorses the pursuit of knowledge by providing his readers with a template for approaching the unknown. So it is with Raphael. Raphael instructs Adam in cosmic speculation even before he warns Adam against it, but, "measuring things in Heav'n by things on Earth," he provides a reason for his revelation: "that thou mayst beware / By what is past" (6.893–85). When Adam, having heard "Things above Earthly thought, which yet concern'd / [his] knowing" (7.82–83), desires of Raphael a follow-up narrative of the Creation, he prudently adds,

> if unforbid thou mayst unfold
> What wee, not to explore the secrets ask

> Of his Eternal Empire, but the more
>
> To magnify his works, the more we know.   (7.94–97)

Raphael assents: "This also thy request with caution askt / Obtain" (7.111–12). While these passages signal that Raphael ushers Adam through some extraordinary and dangerous territory, they also indicate the proper disposition toward such inquiry — tentative, humble, reverent steps.

Cautious inquiry is then supported by the ethical usefulness of knowledge remote from the normal bounds of human reason. As Adam's astronomical fancies lead him to wonder whether the universe is heliocentric or geocentric, Raphael interrupts: "Solicit not thy thoughts with matters hid.... Heav'n is for thee too high / To know what passes there; be lowly wise" (*PL* 8.167, 172–73). An eager pupil, once checked, Adam earnestly agrees that

> not to know at large of things remote
>
> From use, obscure and subtle, but to know
>
> That which before us lies in daily life,
>
> Is the prime Wisdom; what is more, is fume,
>
> Or emptiness, or fond impertinence,
>
> And renders us in things that most concern
>
> Unpractic'd, unprepar'd, and still to seek.
>
> Therefore from this high pitch let us descend
>
> A lower flight, and speak of things at hand
>
> Useful.   (8.191–200)

It is the usefulness of "That which before us lies" in daily life that legitimizes knowledge.

When speculation is not useful, Raphael cuts it short, as when Adam ponders the layout of the universe. Confirmed heliocentrism or geocentrism might distemper Adam's self-opinion: From one perspective he is a small being on the periphery of an immeasurable expanse; from another, he is the dignified darling of heaven, the centerpiece of the cosmos, with planets and their motions solicitous to his needs.[51] To choose one or the other model might upset the balance of Adam's wonder and his confidence — and Milton's ideal of *sophrosynē* needs both. Raphael is not against confidence: "Oft-times nothing profits more / Than self-esteem," he assures Adam (*PL* 8.571–72). Neither is he against wonder; in fact, wonder is the appropriate response to God's works — "For wonderful indeed are all his works," Uriel says (3.702) — and as Raphael explains to Adam, "what [knowledge of God's works] thou canst attain…may serve / To glorify the Maker" (7.115–16). Instead, Raphael opposes the futile attempt to reason one's way to the ineffable, and cautions against the presumption of inquiring into "Things not reveal'd, which th' invisible King, / Only Omniscient, hath supprest in Night, / To none communicable in Earth or Heaven" (7.122–24). What Raphael himself reveals is safely short of this threshold simply because his message is both revealed and communicable (at least through the comparison of great things to small), while it more strictly meets the criteria of knowledge worth pursuit and expression because Raphael has a "Commission from above," because his revelation is useful to his audience, and because that audience receives the messenger and message without presumptuousness (7.118). Once again, following Augustine, it is the attitude and will of the eater or learner that determines whether bodily or intellectual consumption transgresses into gluttony.

The Raphael discourse suggests that, when explored with an attitude of dignified humility, the territory of useful, permitted inquiry is broad and more than enough to satisfy an acute, contemplative mind. Given the discourse of books 5–8, useful knowledge includes that which strengthens human relationships and (as this is a daily practical concern for Adam and Eve) that which strengthens relationships between humans and God. Purposeful, reverent inquiry even permits speculation in due measure. In agreeing with Raphael's admonishment against intemperate knowledge, Adam does not forgo all "things remote" but only speaks against knowing of them "at large" (*PL* 8.191). The twenty-first century reader might feel safely immured against trespassing into intellectual gluttony; the grounds of inquiry are too broad and too deep to know of them "at large." A Miltonic exuberance for scholarship underlies the call to intellectual temperance. As Adam interprets Raphael's words, the problem with investing too much time in "things remote" is not that the subject matter is objectively futile, but that, if useless — that is, if great, inaccessible things are not comparable to the small — speculation directs one's attention from "things at hand," making one "unpractic'd, unprepar'd" for living wisely on earth, for "the prime Wisdom" (8.194, 197, 199). Adam is exhorted not to dream of other worlds in Milton's potential multiverse — not because they are insignificant but because these dreams, at least for the present, would not be put to any good use. The criterion of usefulness, then, is associated with the command to love God and one's fellow humans, and to do something good with the knowledge one has gained, rather than harboring or hoarding it within. This is the law of excretion in Milton's cosmos: the consumer must choose food wisely, process it, and with that produce something beneficial not only to the self, but to others. As poor digestion can bloat the belly, knowledge untransmuted into something that may benefit others will collect into a congested head of bad vapors or hot air. Knowledge puffeth up, but charity edifieth (1 Cor. 8:1).

Though the pursuit of knowledge, like food, should be moderated according to the useful, this criterion allows for more intellectual freedom than would a slavishly indiscriminate quest of knowledge for the mere sake of having knowledge. Permitted knowledge is at least as various and as spectacular as the permitted trees of paradise; both contain branches and fruits "yet unknown" (*PL* 9.619). At the same time, the fact that almost any scrap of knowledge could be defended as useful permits the breadth of intellectual freedom that we expect from the writer of *Areopagitica*, who acknowledges "the benefit which may be had of books promiscuously read" — reading and hearing "all manner of reason" being the safest means of "scout[ing] into the regions of sin and falsity" (YP 2:517). Even "bad books" may be put to good use. Milton explains that individual pieces of information cannot be separated into objectively decadent and warranted indulgences: "a wise man like a good refiner can gather gold out of the drossiest volume, and . . . a fool will be a fool with the best book"; of the more questionable works, "to all men such books are not temptations, nor vanities; but usefull drugs and materialls wherewith to temper and compose effective and strong med'cins, which mans life cannot want" (YP 2:521). Adapting the portrait of Socrates as physician of the soul, Milton also describes Jesus as "a wise Physician, administering one excesse against another to reduce us to a perfect mean" (YP 2:282–83). The success of both metaphysicians depends on their knowledge of the condition of the individual soul. As with the medical wisdom in, for example, *Bald's Leechbook*, treatment must be administered with careful attention to the peculiar condition of the patient: "Apply the leechdoms according as thou seest the state of the body. For a mickle difference is there, in the bodies of a man, a woman, and a child; and in the main or constitution of a daily wright or labourer, and of the idle, of the old and of the young, of him who is accustomed to endurances, and him who is unaccustomed to such things."[52] As a doctor must adjust his "leechdoms," or prescriptions for medical conditions, to the patient, so a regimen for the healthy mind will vary from person to person.

This is a persistent idea in early modern literature. For example, when Carolyn Merchant examines early modern organic utopias, she especially attends to Tommaso Campanella's *City of the Sun* (1602). Alternation of food supplies, variety in meals, and attention to the requirements of bodies differing in age, activity, and humoral constitution are each essential to Campanella's imagined society. As Merchant explains, "Diversity in diet was considered especially essential to the maintenance of a healthy body," with the amount eaten varied to accommodate the needs of each person.[53] A philosopher-king and the harmonious guidance of Power, Wisdom, and Love ensured a natural and social organic unity.[54] As if to confront the related evils of gluttony and injustice, Campanella gives the ideally ordered society a diet based on careful economical stewardship, variety based on supply, and respect for natural seasons and for animal breeding cycles. While *City of the Sun* emphasizes that dieting must be individualized and in harmony with self-knowledge, Campanella elsewhere argues that all humans were designed and commanded by God to learn:

As Aristotle has said, "All men by nature desire to know," and as Moses said in Genesis 1, "God put man in paradise to cultivate and take care of it." But this was not manual labor or the caring for animals.... Rather man's work was to know things, and to observe the heavens and the natural world out of curiosity, so that he would as a result investigate everything to meet his obligation to venerate God, which cannot be done without first having knowledge, for "the invisible things of God are known through what He has made," as the Apostle said [Rom. 1:20].

Even if it be granted that all the sciences were infused into Adam, still he lacked experiential knowledge. Further, this command to learn was given to him, not as an individual person but as head of the human race, and hence it has also been given to us, his descendants.[55]

For Campanella, theology and science, Scripture and the Book of Nature, were compatible and mutually supportive. The obligation to venerate God was adequate justification for seemingly infinite inquiry and experience, even if it excluded the experiential knowledge of disobeying God's commands. Presumably, an attitude of worship kept healthy curiosity from being sinful *curiositas*, and virtuous pursuit of self-knowledge from degenerating into selfish pride. Campanella's utopia is filled with a wealth of food, and his paradise is stocked with a wealth of material to learn, but both eating and learning were to be responsibly, purposefully accomplished.

For the sake of comparison, consider *The Blazing World* of Margaret Cavendish, which presents a more complicated treatment of mental space, focusing on the power of the imagination. This visionary work (described by Cavendish as successively "romancical, ... philosophical, and ... fantastical") features an extraterrestrial paradise (Adam once lived there) governed by a newly arrived Empress who is a "determined utopian" in her penchant for reform.[56] As Lara Dodds elucidates, "Cavendish's primary innovation in the utopian tradition can be found in the Empress's creation of multiple imaginary worlds," or the "theoretically infinite proliferation of the good place as a psychological state."[57] When the Duchess, soulmate of the Empress, expresses an "extream Ambition" to conquer and appropriate a "gross material world" of her own, spirits of the Blazing World curb that wish by assuring her that, anytime she or the Empress desires, they may create carefree, delightful, effortlessly renewable worlds within the self through the power of Fancy. While such mental exertions are "truly satisfying" to the Empress and Duchess, Dodds considers these imaginary worlds with caution and nuance: "At once immensely attractive and a sad confirmation of the limitations on women's public agency, the imaginary worlds created by the Duchess and the Empress are a sublime representation of the paradoxes of utopia."[58] They are also ambiguously beneficial to the imaginer. As Dodds explains, these worlds may be comparable to Milton's image of the "paradise within," "a similar form of consolation, a means of cultivating self-knowledge and growth in potentially hostile circumstances," or they may be "that image's mirrored, satanic opposite: the mind as 'its own place,' . . . a form of rigid self-absorption that reveals a psyche cut off from authentic forms of meaning." In *Paradise Lost*, Dodds notes, "the subject's orientation toward God provides the grounds for answering this question," while *The Blazing World* has "no such arbiter," suggesting that a utopia limited to the imagination is "both absolutely necessary and severely limited."[59] Cavendish's literary imagination thus provides a beautifully elusive survey of the paradoxically infinite and restrictive powers of the imagination.

Of course, the immeasurable and yet restricted allure of the mind and of learning is a temptation the Son faces on the mountaintop in *Paradise Regain'd*: "So let extend thy mind o'er all the world, / In knowledge, all things in it comprehend," Satan proposes (*PR* 4.223–24). Such knowledge, Satan promises the Son, would make him "a King complete / Within [him]self," and, in contradistinction to the expectations for the exercise of the imagination in *The Blazing World*, the acquisition of learning would also prepare the Son for a material, earthly kingdom (4.283–84). The Son refutes Satan and, without revealing the boundaries of what he knows or does not know, he successively dismisses Socrates, Plato, the Skeptics, Aristotle, Epicurus, and the Stoics, asking, "what can they teach, and not mislead; / Ignorant of themselves, of God much more" (4.309–10)? Alluding to Ecclesiastes 12:12, the Son reiterates the importance of self-knowledge to the would-be philosopher:

> However, many books
> Wise men have said are wearisome; who reads
> Incessantly, and to his reading brings not
> A spirit and judgment equal or superior
> (And what he brings, what needs he elsewhere seek)
> Uncertain and unsettl'd still remains,
> Deep verst in books and shallow in himself,
> Crude or intoxicate, collecting toys,
> And trifles for choice matters, worth a sponge;
> As Children gathering pebbles on the shore.   (*PR* 4.321–30)

The Son concludes that the finest of hymns, of eloquence, and of rules of civil government are plainest, easiest, and best found in the Hebrew Scriptures.

According to the Pauline expression of Christian liberty, all things may be permissible but not all are beneficial, and the need for prudence resides in this qualification.[60] In accordance with prudence, certain dispositions toward knowledge are infelicitous, and certain dispositions toward consumption are proscribed by right reason and the law of nature. Yet there is much freedom in this. From *Areopagitica* to *De doctrina Christiana*, Milton, following Paul, vividly describes intellectual and Christian liberty with respect to dietary laws (see, e.g., OW 8:717–23). He finds all manner of knowledge permissible if used wisely, but he never challenges the necessity of temperance:

> When God did enlarge the universal diet of man's body, saving ever the rules of temperance, he then also, *as before*, left arbitrary the dieting and repasting of our minds; as wherein every mature man might have to exercise his own leading capacity. How great a virtue is temperance, how much of moment through the whole life of man! Yet God commits the managing of so great a trust, without particular law or prescription, wholly to the demeanor of every grown man.... Solomon informs us that much reading is a weariness to the flesh; but neither he nor other inspired author tells us that such or such reading is unlawful; yet certainly had God thought good to limit us herein, it had been much more

expedient to have told us what was unlawful than what was wearisome. (YP 2:513–14; emphasis added)

This passage draws a distinction between the prelapsarian bounds of eating and of knowing. In Genesis, Yahweh does not officially approve of humans eating animal flesh until the Noahic covenant, although after the Fall he accepts the burning of animal sacrifices.[61] But while Milton writes of God "enlarg[ing] the universal diet of man's body," he notes that God, "as before, left arbitrary the dieting and repasting of our minds." While temperance remains necessary in feeding both body and mind, the liberal boundaries of knowledge in paradise before the Fall correspond to the generous limits to knowing that Milton defends in his prose. One might even infer from this passage that the analogy between food and knowledge is even more applicable after the Fall (and after the Noahic covenant) than before it.

Moreover, in Milton's prelapsarian paradise, knowledge immediately off-limits to human reason might have become accessible once humans would have become more like the angels, their knowledge becoming more intuitive. Before the Fall, through eating the permitted fruits of paradise, Adam and Eve would grow to be as the angels and participate in angel food, and through the "contemplation of created things" they would grow in the wisdom that would prepare them for further intellectual acquisition (PL 5.511). This calls for patience, or prudence and temperance with respect to time. To rashly pluck forbidden physical or intellectual fruit in an evil hour is not to achieve godhood, but to demonstrate impatient dissatisfaction with the divinely ordered plan for ascent, and to fall prey at best to curiositas, the pursuit of useless knowledge, or at worst, to superbia, the prideful presumption of having attained knowledge one is not able (at least not yet) to understand or use. Conversely, to refuse to cultivate the mind may be to commit the sin of the unfaithful servant who buries his talent (Matt. 25:14–30; Luke 19:11–27), or to languish in the spiritually infantile condition of demanding doctrinal milk, without progressing to solid food (Heb. 5:12; cf. 1 Cor. 3:2).

Self-knowledge, then, is both a fitting subject of study and a pre-ventative against prematurely exceeding one's limits or not properly esteeming one's intellectual abilities. It is necessary for knowing "what the mind may well contain." As Aristotle explains in his anecdote of Milo the wrestler in book 2 of the *Nicomachean Ethics*, the amount of food necessary for one person's temperate diet might be the mark of gluttony in another.[62] In a similar way, fit subjects of study, approaches to knowing, and depths of inquiry will vary from person to person, and will healthily expand with the self-regulated exercise of the pro-ductive mind. The acquisition of temperance is not a formulaic matter of counting calories or calculating an intelligence quotient, but it does require maintaining a disposition that recognizes one's worth as well as one's weaknesses. Milton demonstrates that we must know our true position in the divine order of the cosmos — thinking of ourselves as neither lower nor higher than we ought — in order to maintain temper-ate self-knowledge.

The introduction to this book has already examined how Adam demonstrates his understanding of both upper and lower boundaries when God tests Adam's self-knowledge as a precursor to the creation of Eve. In seeking a fit partner, Adam first gives a speech declaring his difference from the beasts and then admits his difference from God (*PL* 8.379–97, 412–33). In accordance with Aristotle's *Politics*, Milton has Adam express his awareness that humanity lies between these two alternatives and that he is therefore in need of companionship, of "con-versation with his like" (8.418). God speaks approvingly (though still testing him) of Adam's "nice and subtle" desire (8.399) and ultimately affirms Adam's assessment of his own nature and of his need for a fit companion: "Thus far to try thee, *Adam*, I was pleas'd / And find thee knowing... / ... of thyself" (8.437–39).

At the Fall, however, Adam demonstrates a willful self-ignorance, for the Son tells Adam that his submission to Eve's governance in this one fatal instance would not have happened "hadst thou known thy-self aright" (10.156). To "know thyself" requires knowing one's proper authority, limits, and needs. In this way the exhortation to know thy-self aright and the "rule of not too much" that Michael endorses are interdependent. Philosophers and scholars have recognized them as interdependent since antiquity. Both injunctions were inscribed over the entrance to the temple of Apollo at Delphi — *mēden agan*, or "nothing too much," joined with the temple's most famous inscription, *gnōthi seauton*, "Know thyself."[63] Together, these axioms command an attention to practical, philosophical introspection, but warn against excess. Apollo's temple and oracle at Delphi were dedicated to prophetic knowledge, and the temperance advocated in *Paradise Lost* is likewise applicable to intellectual aspirations, including those that require divine assistance. The Delphic inscriptions are in accord with the messages of Raphael, the Son, and Michael.

Returning to the closing books of *Paradise Lost*, we realize that Michael's final exhortation is one of thoughtful activity. After hearing Michael's prophetic narrative, Adam replies,

> Greatly instructed I shall hence depart,
> Greatly in peace of thought, and have my fill
> Of knowledge, what this Vessel can contain;
> Beyond which was my folly to aspire.
> Henceforth I learn, that to obey is best,
> And love with fear the only God, to walk
> As in his presence, ever to observe
> His providence, and on him sole depend,
> Merciful over all his works, with good
> Still overcoming evil, and by small
> Accomplishing great things, by things deem'd weak
> Subverting worldly strong, and worldly wise
> By simply meek; that suffering for Truth's sake
> Is fortitude to highest victory,
> And to the faithful Death the Gate of Life;
> Taught this by his example whom I now
> Acknowledge my Redeemer ever blest.   (*PL* 12.557–73)

Michael immediately approves: "This having learnt, thou hast attain'd the sum / Of wisdom; hope no higher" (12.575–76). Yet, as if to aggravate the reader's curiosity, there is some ambiguity regarding what

"This," the "sum / Of wisdom," is: The Christian message of the Gospel, taught by the "Redeemer"? *Sola scriptura?* The entire spectrum of human history, as has just been revealed to Adam? The goodness and reliability of Eternal Providence within that spectrum? The ultimate victory of those who suffer "for Truth's sake"? All of the above? Any effort to delineate hard and fast boundaries to knowing is interrupted by angelic exhortations to faith and action:

> add
> Deeds to thy knowledge answerable, add Faith,
> Add Virtue, Patience, Temperance, add Love,
> By name to come call'd Charity, the soul
> Of all the rest: then wilt thou not be loath
> To leave this Paradise, but shalt possess
> A paradise within thee, happier far.[64]   (12.581–87)

Schoenfeldt argues that this "paradise within" is "not a geographical place but rather a series of social and dietary practices that cultivate the inner spaces of the postlapsarian subject."[65] I believe this is taking the food metaphor too far; it is, in fact, destroying the simile between knowledge and food by limiting it to a too physiological, literal interpretation. For Milton, not all reality can be accounted for by physiology, though physiological terms may adequately illustrate philosophical concepts. Milton's world is created *de Deo*, "one first matter all," descending from God and ultimately "up to Him return[ing]," but it is also a world of "Orders and Degrees" (*PL* 5.470, 472, 792). The analogy between food and knowledge depends on difference as well as sameness. Another remark from Schoenfeldt better preserves the integrity of the food/intellect simile: "Digestion is then not simply a function of some lower bodily stratum, to borrow a phrase from Bakhtin, but a central process of psychological and physiological self-fashioning"[66] — and philosophical, moral, and spiritual self-fashioning, one might add, if these are not already subsumed under "psychological." If Milton's interior paradise is in part the peace that comes from the physiological tempering of humors and passions, it is also the cultivation of the virtuous soul that opposes vice in the "warfare of peace." The seven qualities Michael calls for at the conclusion of his visit may fitly oppose the Seven Deadly Sins: for avarice, or lust of the eyes, there is knowledge answerable; for sloth, there are deeds; for inward-turning pride, there is outward-turning faith; for envy, which looks outside the self to begrudge and to crave, there is virtue, which looks into the self in order to cultivate the integrity of one's own moral garden; for wrath, there is patience; for gluttony, there is temperance, and for lust, there is love. Michael's words illustrate the hope that Adam through moral striving may partly recover a felicitous internal balance no longer possible outside the self due to the changed nature of a world fallen askew.[67]

Milton's knowledge/food analogy suggests that due diligence in maintaining the body is beneficial in itself, but it also significantly instructs us in something else, even as that something else, upon further inspection, is not so very different. Knowledge is as food, as in Raphael's story, heaven is as earth; but "food alike [to human food] those pure / Intelligential substances require," and what if "Each to other [are alike] more than on Earth is thought" (PL 5.407–08, 576)? Knowledge and food are two distinct goods within Milton's unified and hierarchical view of creation, but one illumines the other. By way of analogy, perverse eating may also uncover the dangers of folly and false philosophy.

One final observation to make here is that the role of gluttony in the Fall does not denigrate the body, nor does it exclude the role of the mind. Despite the seemingly omnivorous threat of gluttony, Milton assuredly maintains the dignity of the body. After all, as Raphael explains, "Whatever was created, needs / To be sustain'd and fed" (PL 5.414–15). The mind also seeks nourishment, wisely selected and wisely savored. The distinction of the good from the bad, and the nutritive from the indigestible, as well as the pursuit for the temperate balance that avoids the varied extremes of gluttony, is a task that requires reason and promises delight. Both the fastidious and the vulgar representations of gluttony show us the unpalatable alternatives to this rational endeavor.

3

Scatology and Devilish Glut in *Paradise Lost*

> Alle the sowlys he cast owt,
> That wer yscateryd rond abowt,
> He swalowyd hom ageyn ychon
> With smok of pycche and of brymston.
>
> — *Vision of Tundale*, 1393–96

After bard and muse usher the reader into the narrative of *Paradise Lost*, the first character to speak is Satan, and his first utterance is aposiopetic, syntactically and grammatically incomplete. As baleful eyes adjust to the lurid darkness of hell and rest on Beelzebub, Satan checks his first thought: "If thou beest he; But O how fall'n! how chang'd" (1.84). While Satan could simply be confirming the identity of his companion here, it is no stretch to supply for the missing main clause a thought so horrid to Satan that it must be kept to himself: if *you* look like that, then what happened to *me?* Aposiopesis can serve as a rhetorical signpost for great passion, modest reserve, or mental revision, and this broken, discomposed speech may reveal to the reader more of Satan than Satan yet understands of himself, for here he is preoccupied with physical rather than psychological changes, with deteriorated appearance rather than his presumably "fixt mind" (1.97). Though both pride and stupor initially keep Satan from articulating his own degradation, he soon admits he is "chang'd in outward luster" (97).

Still, he glories in the residuum of his brilliance. As the bard describes the great antagonist of heaven,

> his form had not yet lost
> All her Original brightness, nor appear'd
> Less than Arch-Angel ruin'd, and th' excess
> Of Glory obscur'd.   (PL 1.591–94)

The bard subsequently affirms Satan's diminishment and yet ennobles him through epic simile: Satan's glory is that of the sun arising through the mist, "Shorn of his Beams" (594–96) — or he is the moon in "dim Eclipse," shedding a "disastrous twilight" as an omen of change (596–99). Similarly, his army is a forest "of stately growth," but lightning scorched, "scath'd" with "singed top" (612–15). He surveys his followers, a formidable yet diminished crew, "Thir Glory wither'd" also (1.612). Significantly, he does not scorn his former brilliance: from "Eternal Splendors flung," Satan still has a taste for beauty (1.610). His first positive remark is about the "happy Realms of Light," a sign that Satan is not immediately fluent in his new language, in "Evil be thou my Good," especially when goodness and evil are respectively associated with beauty and ugliness (1.85, 4.109). He has a tendency to call ugliness ugly until he sees a personal advantage in seeing and calling it otherwise. Thus, at the gates of hell in book 2, he bluntly tells Sin and Death he has never seen "Sight more detestable than him and thee," before shifting to acknowledge them as "Dear Daughter" and "fair Son," "the dear pledge / Of dalliance" (2.745, 817–19).

Conversely, when Satan sees Eve alone in the garden in book 9, her beauty will temporarily disarm him, leaving him "Stupidly good" (9.465). Naturally repulsed by ugliness and susceptible to beauty, Satan's encounter with beauty in association with goodness soon excites his envy, his hate, and his plans for mischief:

> the more he sees
> Of pleasure not for him ordain'd: then soon
> Fierce hate he recollects, and all his thoughts
> Of mischief, gratulating, thus excites.   (9.469–72)

Cut off from pleasure, rejecting goodness, and diminished in beauty, Satan clings to what remains of his physical splendor. Thus, in book 4 the words of the cherub Zephon, "Severe in youthful beauty" (4.845), sorely aggravate him:

> Think not, revolted Spirit, thy shape the same,
> Or undiminisht brightness, to be known
> As when thou stood'st in Heav'n upright and pure;
> That Glory then, when thou no more wast good,
> Departed from thee, and thou resembl'st now
> Thy sin and place of doom obscure and foul.   (4.835–40)

Satan is disarmed here as well:

> abasht the Devil stood,
> And felt how awful goodness is, and saw
> Virtue in her shape how lovely, saw, and pin'd
> His loss; but chiefly to find here observ'd
> His lustre visibly impair'd.   (4.846–50)

His obsession with luster and with sensual, physical, and visible attributes is cursedly matched with a diminishment of the same in his own appearance. Yet he accepts this foul descent, for "what will not Ambition and Revenge / Descend to?" (9.168–69). Satan's loss of splendor is one example of the ways the fallen angels become "gross by sinning grown" (6.661); Milton dooms his fallen angels to wallow in a morass of gluttonous imagery, crude corporeality, vulgar puns, and scatological metaphors.

CORPUS DIABOLI: DEMONIC BODIES ENGROSSED

Satan's plans to overthrow God fail to materialize, but his disappointment is not without physical consequences. When Satan first makes his appearance on the lake of fire, he looks more like a Cartesian *res extensa* than an intelligential *res cogitans*. The narrator's attention, like Satan's, is drawn to the physical before the psychological. "Confounded though immortal," Satan is transfixed by adamantine chains and the will of heaven, "stretcht out huge in length" (*PL* 1.53, 209). His body,

> Prone on the Flood, extended long and large,
> Lay floating many a rood, in bulk as huge
> As whom the Fables name of monstrous size,
> *Titanian*, or *Earth–born*
>
> ....
>
> or that Sea-beast
> *Leviathan.*   (1.195–201)

Satan's bulk is reinforced by the famous simile of the Leviathan, mistaken for an island by an unsuspecting navigator (1.203–07). The simile, an early modern topos, alerts the reader to the lurking danger of attraction to this figure at the same time that it establishes Satan's massive proportions. As a unit of measure (about six to eight yards according to the *OED*), *rood* emphasizes the materiality of Satan. More subtly, Milton's choice of this word to describe the extended, fixed body of Satan simultaneously represents this fallen angel as an enormous, horizontal, upside-down crucifix. With the addition of Promethean chains, Satan appears a potential victim and a martyr. If Milton leads his readers to imagine Satan's position as cruciform, he draws attention to his antagonist's body while clearly warning his Protestant readers. In this vein Paul J. Voss argues that *rood* as crucifix in this first epic simile at once reminds the reader of "Christ's execution," becomes "the symbol of Christ executing his victory over Satan," and presents through "anti-Catholic, anti-Laudian sentiment" a "critique of idolatry" in line with Milton's iconoclastic beliefs.[1] From a generic seventeenth century Puritan perspective, the opening portrait of Satan would be reminiscent of the icon-turned-idol, of Roman Catholic overattention to the material wounds of the crucified body of Christ rather than the spiritualized Resurrection body. Even unconsciously, Satan proves a religious decoy, visually impressive in the reader's imagination but, in actuality, only a tremendously deceptive alternative to the one, already accomplished, and unrepeatable sacrifice.[2] As if fixed to a cross, his posture invites our anatomizing scrutiny; in this he is also like *Vitruvian Man*. He is a specimen not of Adam or of angel, but of an imposing, physical, tangible evil; however, like Leviathan, his very monstrosity helps him hide his true identity.

Perhaps there is no better symbol of Satan's new corporeal limitations than his adamantine chains, heavy, bulky, and restrictive. Yet these chains also release the possibility of assigning Satan a Promethean role, not only as defiant thief but also as giver of divine fire, of new and forbidden knowledge.[3] The narrative allusively positions Satan as Titan light-bearer, if only to admonish and unsettle the quick-judging reader. And so it is with Satan's chains, which restrict him and yet seem ineffectual without the will of heaven to bind (1.209–13). With no explanation other than the permission of heaven, with no description or narrative drama, Satan's doffing of his chains is suggestively incidental and effortless. Hard as it is to exclude or restrain "Spiritual substance with corporeal bar," and easy as it is for spirits "not ti'd or manacl'd with joint or limb" to "execute their aery purposes," we are on unstable ground when pondering the materiality of the fallen spirits (4.584–85; 1.426, 430).

Satan's subsequent motion is both a parody of a scriptural narrative and a result of his materiality. He displaces the liquid of the lake of fire as he rises:

> Forthwith upright he rears from off the Pool
> His mighty Stature; on each hand the flames
> Driv'n backward slope thir pointing spires, and roll'd
> In billows, leave i' th' midst a horrid Vale. (PL 1.221–24)

As Satan parts a red sea, he prefigures what he parodies, assuming the role of a deliverer. His Mosaic (or Aaronic) role continues when, within a few lines, his voice signaling his followers is compared to "the potent Rod / Of *Amram's* Son" that, when raised, not only splits the Red Sea (that liminal space between deliverance and the land of gluttony and servitude) but also calls up "a pitchy cloud / Of *Locusts*" (1.338–41). His ability to summon demonic locusts is more directly a power of plaguing than of deliverance, and once again his initial appearance as a savior gives way to a darker and yet less powerful identity.

Just as the reader recalls that Satan's prone posture is due to the fact that he is confounded, in recalling the story of the crossing of the Red Sea, "whose waves o'erthrew / *Busiris* and his *Memphian* Chivalry," the reader shifts associations; this figure of a charismatic liberator, whose voice assembles legions, transforms into a tyrannical pharaoh whose struggle to stand creates parting waves of fire (1.306–07). The bard informs us that, having been "Left…at large to his own dark designs," Satan "heav'd his head" from the lake only to "Heap on himself damnation" (1.211–15). Satan's parting of the lake of fire reveals not a passageway to safety but a "horrid Vale," a synecdoche of the "hollow Deep / Of Hell," whose closure promises nothing but "floating Carcasses" or soulless materiality (1.224, 314–15, 310). And while Satan's parodic movement exhibits his massiveness, the tumult he causes intimates his own displacement. His extraordinary heaviness is not characteristic of his previous existence in heaven. He feels "unusual weight" as he flies from the lake of fire to "the burning Marl," caused not only by the oppressive atmosphere of his new environment but also by his new susceptibility to it (1.227, 296). Later, his movement through chaos is laborious: "on he fares / Treading the crude consistence," "O'er bog or steep, through strait, rough, dense, or rare" (2.940–41, 2.948). Weight becomes an accident of fallenness. G. K. Chesterton once quipped that angels can fly because they take themselves lightly. Satan, burdened by his heroic self-perception, moves with heavy pace, and heavier doom (cf. 3.159, 6.551).

INFERNAL ERUCTATIONS, ERUPTIONS, AND OTHER EMISSIONS

After rising from the lake of fire and flying through heavy air with unusual weight, Satan alights on the burning marl. With Virgilian metaphor Milton compares the terrain of hell to Mount Aetna, the anthropomorphized volcano notorious for its grumbling and churning of the bowels. In the *Aeneid*, "Aetna thunders with horrifying ruin while hurling forth black clouds and balls of flame that lick the stars, vomiting from its depths, with a roar, its entrails of boulders and liquefied stone."[4] Milton follows Virgil in personifying the mountain. But while

Virgil is content with metaphors of the mouth (*lambit*/lick, *eructans*/ vomiting, *tonat*/roar — the entrails regurgitated), Milton descends to a lower humor in his version:

> As when the force
> Of subterranean wind transports a hill
> Torn from *Pelorus*, or the shatter'd side
> Of thund'ring *Aetna*, whose combustible
> And fuell'd entrails thence conceiving Fire
> Sublim'd with Mineral fury, aid the Winds
> And leave a singed bottom all involv'd
> With stench and smoke: Such resting found the sole
> Of unblest feet.   (*PL* 1.230–38)

Deep within the body of a mountain, pressurized wind and combustible entrails culminate in an explosion, a singed bottom, and a stench. This is in part Milton's more eloquent, grown-up version of the schoolboy flatulence jokes and taunts of "Aetna breath" in Prolusion 6; in part it looks further back to a medieval convention uniting the diabolic with the scatological.[5] It is this tradition that sets the stage for the characterization of Satan and his companions as vulgar and gluttonous.

Medieval and Renaissance renderings of hell frequently depict Satan eating and excreting the damned. Perhaps the Last Judgment mosaic (1240–1300, attributed to Coppo di Marcovaldo) on the vault of the baptistery of San Giovanni in Florence, Giotto's *Last Judgment* fresco (1304–05) in the Scrovegni Chapel, and Dante's *Divine Comedy* (1308–20) provide the most recognizable, vivid depictions of Satan masticating sinners. Of these, Giotto's fresco most clearly includes Satan's defecation of those he consumes. In his study of the sources, influences, and artistic analogs for the infernal vision of Chaucer's prologue to the "Summoner's Tale," John F. Plummer catalogs and describes an extensive but by no means exhaustive group of fourteenth through sixteenth century paintings and woodcuts featuring Satan or his devils eating and excreting condemned souls. Plummer's list includes works by Giotto, Tadello di Bartello, Francesco Traini, Giovanni Dall'Orto, Giovanni da Modena, Hieronymus Bosch, and Lucas Cranach the Elder.[6] There are other famous examples: Luca Signorelli's fresco of *The Damned Cast into Hell* (1499–1504) in the San Brizio chapel of the Orvieto Cathedral contains devils biting human flesh; the theme persists in the lower part of Michelangelo's *Last Judgment* (1536–41) in the Sistine Chapel. Giorgio Vasari and Federico Zuccari's *Last Judgment* frescoes (1568–79) in the cupola of the Duomo of Santa Maria del Fiore in Florence feature a ravenous, many-mouthed Satan with human legs dangling from each set of devilish jaws. Fra Angelico's *Last Judgment* (c. 1425–31) in the Museo di San Marco depicts Satan chewing the damned, and while the composition of the picture does not admit a view of his nether parts, what is visible provides yet another example of a gluttonously vulgar prince of hell. Luther Link finds the earliest example of the "ingesting Satan" motif in the dragon heads that gobble the damned while adorning Satan's throne in the Last Judgment mosaic (late twelfth century) on the west wall of the Cathedral of Santa Maria Assunta in Torcello; he indicates the Last Judgment Tympanum over the west portal of Sainte-Foy at Conques (ca. 1130) as an early example of demons devouring the damned.[7]

The threat of devouring devils in medieval and Renaissance renderings of the Last Judgment was usually visually compounded by the topos of the jawed and toothy mouth of hell. So the Last Judgment Tympanum at Conques features demons feeding the damned to a beastly hell-mouth, and in the Florence Duomo's *Last Judgment* multiple hell-mouths bordering the lower edge of the dome complement the multiple mouths of Satan. Other notable depictions of the mouth of hell in fine art include an illumination in the Winchester Psalter (c. 1150), the stained glass window in the Bourges Cathedral depicting the Last Judgment (c. 1215), and the painting of St. Michael weighing the souls and the Doom painting in the South Leigh, St. James the Great Church in Oxfordshire (fifteenth century). All these works of art portray hell as a grotesque region of fierce and insatiable consumption. In medieval drama, the hell-mouth was a spectacular feature of mystery and morality plays, though early modern drama largely abandoned this theatrical convention. Milton, however, pays homage to the topos of the gluttonous hell-mouth.[8] When Satan first exits hell's gates, the aperture is described as a furnace mouth, emitting fire and smoke (*PL* 2.888); to prepare the way for his return, Sin and Death plough and shove chaotic materials indiscriminately toward the mouth of hell, which hell receives with remarkable ease (10.288).

Depictions of hell in medieval literature also commonly featured obscene, flatulent devils, or a devil vomiting or excreting the damned. V. A. Kolve and others have examined how obscene diabolical portraits in the medieval cycle plays influenced Chaucer's works; the prologue to the "Summoner's Tale" and the satirical conclusion of *The Romaunt of the Rose* ribaldly threaten evildoers with a doom of confinement in "the develes ers."[9] Dante's Malebranche in *Inferno* 21 also exemplify the medieval commonplace of the flatulent devil; their leader, Malacoda, signals to the other devils by making "a trumpet of his ass."[10]

One of the most popular and widely translated examples of medieval literature featuring obscene devils eating and excreting the damned is the Vision of Tundale/Tnugdalus/Tondal, the story of a wealthy but virtue-impoverished Irish knight whose gluttonous banqueting at a debtor's expense brings him to a violent fit and into a dream-vision of hell. The Middle English *Vision of Tundale* (fourteenth century, from twelfth century Latin sources) depicts the lurid horrors of eternal consumption and evacuation. Passus 8 describes a beast who perpetually consumes and casts out the damned:

> That best was bothe fell and gredy
> And swollod tho sowlys that wer redy,
> And when the sowlys wer theryn,
> Ther wer thei peynod for her syn.
> In strong fyr ther brand thei ay,
> Too thei wer ner wastud away,
> And than ycast fro that peyn
> Tyll thei wer covert agayn.[11]

This particular punishment was so compelling that a variation of it appeared in Tundale's later vision of Satan chewing and casting out the damned, in the passage serving as the epigraph to this chapter. The Getty *Visions du Chevalier Tondal* (c. 1475) is especially notable for its series of miniature paintings by Simon Marmion, featuring punishment of murderers bobbing in a glowing red bowl of blood soup, the beast Acheron devouring the avaricious (the first punishment Tondal must participate in), the House of Phristinus (Preston in the Middle English translation) gaping to receive gluttons and fornicators, a stork-billed dragon eating and excreting unchaste monks and nuns, and a prickly Lucifer, mouth agape, lying supine across the portal of hell.

A similarly grotesque vision of hell may be found in the third book of Mechthild de Magdeburg's Middle Low German *Flowing Light of the Godhead* (c. 1250–80). This hell has three basic divisions, where self-identifying Christians, Jews, and heathens are respectively punished, with the lowest region, the worst pains, and the closest proximity to Lucifer reserved for the Christians, from whom a greater degree of goodness is expected. There a succession of punishments reveal a pre-Dantean understanding of *contrapasso*, many such punishments involving digestive and excretory processes: "[Lucifer] gnaws at the moneylender incessantly"; "All the sodomites pass down through his throat and live in his belly; when he draws breath they are pulled into his belly, but when he coughs they are pushed out again"; "the avaricious man Lucifer devours, because he always wanted to have more. After he has swallowed him he excretes him from under his tail"; "Those who here applied themselves so vigorously to drinking and eating in excess must stand everlastingly hungry before Lucifer and eat burning stones and drink sulphur and pitch. There all sweetness is exchanged for sourness."[12] It is worth recalling here that in the writings of several early church fathers, the sin of Sodom was considered to be gluttony primarily, rather than any particular sexual act, although gluttony was frequently thought to incite lust. Avarice was often linked to gluttony as well, hence the moneylenders and the avaricious are eaten, too. Keeping these associations in mind may help explain the *contrapasso* of the particularly alimentary punishments listed above. In Mechthild de Magdeburg's vision of hell, judgment is consummated with a gulp: "After the Day of Judgment Lucifer...shall on occasion inflate himself to such an extent and his jaws open so wide that he shall swallow in one intake of breath Christians, Jews and heathens. Then they shall reap their full reward in his belly and have their special feast."[13]

As John N. King demonstrates, the convention of the grotesquely humorous devil persisted into the early modern era: "Although the scurrility of polemical moments in *Paradise Lost* troubled Addison, Johnson, and other readers, *Gargantua and Pantagruel, The Faerie Queene*, and *The Locusts* afford rich precedents for bodily disorderliness and grotesque sexual misconduct associated with Satan's encounter with Sin and Death, the Paradise of Fools, War in Heaven, and other episodes."[14] To King's list one might add Thomas Lupton's *All for Money* (1578), in which Sinne, who has planned to abandon Satan but begrudgingly agrees with Satan's children Pride and Gluttonie to stay, peevishly calls their father "Snottienose Sathanas."[15] The rift between Satan and Sinne is soon mended, but the snub reveals that even Satan's closest companion can find material for insult in bodily effluvia.

In *Paradise Lost* infernal emissions are at first most forcefully projected onto the hellish environment using bodily metaphor, but it is clear from the beginning of the narrative that the rebel angels also experience new corporeal limitations. We have noted how the terrain of hell suffers a "singed bottom all involv'd / With stench and smoke," and how the "four infernal Rivers... disgorge / Into the burning Lake thir baleful streams" (2.575–76); even as the opening books present Milton's grandest and most formidable portrait of Satan, the deflating ridicule of satire presides in descriptions of the landscape of hell. Satan quickly learns that to be fallen is to be changed, and for the worse. The bard introduces the other fallen angels "intrans't / Thick as Autumnal Leaves," "bestrown" on the lake of fire "under amazement of thir hideous change"; by the time Satan's underlings recover from their fall enough to survey their doomed habitation in hell, they have become a distinctly "imbodied force" against which all future armies of earth could only be compared to pygmy troops (1.301–02, 311, 313, 574–76). Like "the hollow Deep / Of Hell" that encloses them, the rebel angels are at once massive and vacuous (1.314–15).

Subsequently, the corporealization of the demons is qualified: directly after the Mount Aetna metaphor appears the famous passage on the incorporeality of the demons who, "in what shape they choose, / Dilated or condenst, bright or obscure, / Can execute thir aery purposes" (*PL* 1.428–30). Certainly the demons have not lost all of their heavenly attributes. The apparent disjunction between the "unusual weight" experienced by Satan in hell and the "aery purposes" that the demons execute unencumbered can be explained in part by a change in narrative style between these two passages. At the latter point, Milton is more firmly positioned within the world of classical epic. By then he has invoked his muse a second time and has begun listing the ranks of the demons in imitation of the Homeric catalog of the ships in *Iliad* 2 or Virgil's listing of Italian captains in *Aeneid* 7. At that moment, Satan's lofty diction overpowers any satirical and authorial commentary. Yet even in the loftiest moments of the poem, fallen ethereal powers exhibit the more adverse characteristics of materiality, whether dilated or condensed. The more martial-spirited demons travel in "Squadrons and gross Bands" (2.570); like the shape their army forms in the War in Heaven, the demons themselves are intrinsically hollow but superficially "gross and huge" (6.552).

The demons' retained incorporeal attributes qualify their descent into gross materiality while simultaneously preparing the reader for the pun-filled conclusion to book 1, where the minor demons "reduced their shapes immense and were at large" as abject dwarves, and the leaders, who "in close recess and secret conclave sat," occasion yet another of those anti-Catholic jibes Milton found irresistible (*PL* 1.795). Despite the force of Satan's rhetoric and heroic stature, Milton's narrator then describes hell as grossly putrid and its demons as puny and papist in book 1. In an extensive analysis of such passages, John N. King examines how the satirical narrative voice demotes Milton's high church and royalist contemporaries by literarily demonizing them. For example, as King explains, in comparing the demons Satan summons from the lake of fire to a plague of locusts (1.341), Milton makes use of a recognizable early modern Protestant symbol for rapacious Catholic clergymen.[16] King's argument follows and draws support from Patrick Hume's annotations for *Paradise Lost* (1695), proving that the poem has lent itself to historicizing readings for hundreds of years. Yet it is simultaneously probable in these passages that Milton reminds his reader of the nefariousness of his demonic characters by associating them with the ecclesiastical and political trappings he opposes. In *Paradise Lost*, Milton inveighs against his spiritual villains at least as much as he does against the historical, human opponents to whom they may correspond, and unsympathetic descriptions of the denizens of hell often appear without obvious contemporary satirical targets. Milton wanted his readers to be wary of demons, not just of cardinals and councilmen.

Milton's depiction of Satan illustrates a physical law operating within the cosmos of his poem: turning away from God means descending — not simply deviating from — the scale of Nature. In other words, Satan cannot escape his creatureliness by rejecting his creator. The demon-enervating parodies and satirical puns of book 1 may be less rhetorically potent than the impressive heroic portrait of Satan, but these intimations of deflated sails to come set a precedent for their description in the (chronologically earlier) War in Heaven in books 5 and 6. As Raphael describes the machinations of Satan and his minions in the War in Heaven, Satan becomes more physically limited even as he challenges his creation. He thinks the Son has "ingross't / All Power," hoarding heavenly honor and commanding bended neck and knee (*PL* 5.775–76, 787–88). While implying that he objects to the concretization of abstract power, he is in fact resentful that this power is not instead engrossed in himself. For Satan, who tells Abdiel, "Our puissance is our own," power is the mark of a brutish tyrant in God, but the seal of divinity in himself (5.864). He refuses to afford the Son any bodily gesture of obsequy because of his envy, but he attributes this refusal to his dignity, his ethereal nature (5.662, 863).[17] Satan then awkwardly presents his ignorance of the particulars of his creation as evidence of autogenesis, but this declaration of independence ironically lowers him in the scale of nature. He has been created with free will, and his use of this, even when in rebellion against his creator, does not remove him from the ranks of the created; Satan's choices ironically demote and restrict him, limiting his freedom and resulting in weighty corporealizing effects.

"INTESTINE WAR" AND "MATERIALS DARK AND CRUDE"

The demon most engrossed in materiality is Mammon, the "least erected Spirit," whose "looks and thoughts" are "downward bent," even in heaven (PL 1.679–81). Mammon seeks something more substantial and self-satisfying than the beatific vision, more measurable and aggregate than airy offerings rendered to God, and more foundational to the building of his own reputation as infernal architect. He therefore turns from God to gold, and from the heights of heaven to the bowels of hell. Resentful of God's expectation of worship, Mammon ends up as a cog in the machine of an infernal regime; he labors to accumulate the stuff of Pandaemonium and of Satan's throne.

Mammon's digging is neither his own idea nor is it at his leisure: he digs at Satan's command and follows Satan's precedent. Nor is Satan's idea truly original or creative; it is a perversion and interruption of the natural growth process from root to flower that Raphael describes in book 5 (479–82). Looking for new war tactics after the first day of battle in heaven, Satan draws his angels' attention to the "Plant, Fruit, Flow'r Ambrosial, Gems and Gold" of heaven, and then asks,

> Whose Eye so superficially surveys
> These things, as not to mind from whence they grow
> Deep under ground, materials dark and crude
> Of spirituous and fiery spume, till toucht
> With Heav'n's ray and temper'd they shoot forth
> So beauteous, op'ning to the ambient light[?]   (PL 6.475–81)

Satan is a perceptive natural philosopher here, and his inquiry into the causes of natural phenomena proves to be a powerful weapon. From natural beauty above the surface of the earth he ponders hidden "materials dark and crude," through which Milton yokes the rebel powers with the potentially good but God-removed, chaotic, and formless material antecedents of the cosmos. Nonetheless, in several ways Satan's application of his scientific observations is unnatural. The natural growth process involves response to the light of "Heav'n's ray," yet Satan organizes bowel-digging under the cover of heaven's night. Natural growth

requires time and tempering, but Satan's project is violent and prema-
ture. In heaven, natural growth requires no strenuous angelic effort,
but Satan's perversion requires the labors of excavation. While natural
growth is illustrated by the beauteous opening of a flower at the touch
of light, Satan instead seeks the "fiery spume" of gunpowder:

> in a moment up they turn'd
> Wide the Celestial soil, and saw beneath
> Th' originals of Nature in thir crude
> Conception; Sulphurous and Nitrous Foam
> They found, they mingl'd, and with subtle Art
> Concocted and adusted they reduc'd
> To blackest grain, and into store convey'd:
> Part hidd'n veins digg'd up (nor hath this Earth
> Entrails unlike) of Mineral and Stone,
> Whereof to found thir Engines and thir Balls
> Of missive ruin; part incentive reed
> Provide, pernicious with one touch to fire.   (6.509–20)

The digging up of the elements "in thir crude / Conception" is more an
act of abortion than of delivery. Satan's expectations are fulfilled, however, as he has advised that these buried materials "in thir dark Nativity
the Deep / Shall yield us, pregnant with infernal flame" (6.482–83).
The concocting, adjusting, and reducing performed after this rifling
of heaven's bowels imitates digestion and alchemy, but the process is
destructive rather than preservative. It produces not a flower nor its
essence but a quintessence of dust, volatile "blackest grain." In opposition to the natural process of heavenly growth, the flower of Satan's
uprooting is a destructive, even if spectacular, explosion. The purpose
is "pernicious," "missive ruin." Satanic discovery is thus demonstrably
earthy, violent, and ostensibly creative but unnatural and ultimately
destructive.

Raphael, it must be remembered, is narrating the story of the War
in Heaven, and he pauses here to confirm the evil of satanic excavation
with a foreboding prophecy of the destructive use of firearms among
men. He warns Adam,

> yet haply of thy Race
> In future days, if Malice should abound,
> Some one intent on mischief or inspir'd
> With dev'lish machination might devise
> Like instrument to plague the Sons of men
> For sin, on war and mutual slaughter bent.   (6.501–06)

Here, Milton does not excoriate the evils of mining or metallurgy, but condemns the violent aftermath of such excavation. At other times, following Spenser in book 2 of *The Faerie Queene*, and a long tradition of condemning perverse digging as an assault on Mother Earth, he describes the violence of the act of excavation itself, especially when performed in avarice:

> By [Mammon] first
> Men also, and by his suggestion taught,
> Ransack'd the Center, and with impious hands
> Rifl'd the bowels of thir mother Earth
> For Treasures better hid.[18]   (*PL* 1.684–88)

The bard warns against the enslaving powers of excessive devotion to material wealth that mining and Mammon represent. Earth is "ransacked" and "rifl'd" rather than "temper'd" and "toucht / With Heav'n's ray," the violence betraying satanic preoccupation with power rather than love.

Raphael's narrative of the rebel angels' actions in the War in Heaven is rife with puns and metaphors of scatology and indigestion. References to civil strife within heaven as "Intestine War" and to chaotic "intestine broils" emphasize that the body of heaven is upset, and scatological puns color descriptions of satanic warfare (2.1001, 6.259). In Walter Savage Landor's *Imaginary Conversations*, the character based on Robert Southey remarks of *Paradise Lost*, "It appears, then, on record that the first overt crime of the refractory angels was *punning*: they fell rapidly after that."[19] It may appear odd that Milton, a lover of wordplay, would particularly associate punning with the infernal powers, but the doubletalk here stylistically reinforces the rebel angels' crude duplicity. Satan introduces his secret weapons with "ambiguous words" in imitation of a peace talk: "We discharge / Freely our part.... Briefly touch / What we propound, and loud that all may hear" (*PL* 6.564–68). Words of truce mask aggressive meanings as Satan's troops prepare their artillery, and the exclamations create a jarring dissonance between the rhetoric of confidence and that of ambivalence. The unfolding of the vanguard exposes the hollow of both the demonic phalanx and the proposed truce. When at the cannons' blast Michael's angels fall, Satan in mock astonishment describes his enemies' reaction to his "open front" as a strange dance: the master equivocator affects inability to interpret the action of retreat or the confusion of being under fire. Urging reloading, he advises his demons to "compel [the faithful angels] to a quick result," or a *jumping again* at a second firing of the cannons (6.619). Belial contributes "in like gamesome mood," a sign of his confidence in satanic powers of destruction: "Leader, the terms we sent were terms of weight, / Of hard contents, and full of force urg'd home" (6.620–22). Excessive punning — the lowest form of wit according to neoclassical hierarchy — suggests the affective and intellectual as well as the physical degradation of the rebel angels.[20]

Yet the fallen angels are not the only punsters; Raphael and Milton's bard also have their fun at the demons' expense. Punning of the narrators here is partly attributable to colored narrative and indirect discourse befitting a poetic description of Satan's rebellion, but Milton hardly avoids wordplay at loftier artistic occasions, beginning with the very first line of the poem. (The polysemy in "fruit" has been well noted, but Milton might be punning with the very first phrase, for "Of Man" is a loose definition of both the English word "woman" and its Hebrew cognate *ishshah* in Genesis 2:23.)[21] Nevertheless, Milton here exceeds his wonted wordplay, and his punning takes a distinct turn to the bodily as he recounts the maneuvering of the demonic troops. Their war strategies are represented with bodily metaphors of emission — sexual and natal, and digestive and excretory. Michael Lieb explicates the "markedly sexual overtones" in Satan's battle plans and in the narrative description of the rebel angels' artillery: Satan will "violate the 'pregnancy' of the Deep"; "the engines are 'long,' 'round,' 'thick,' and 'dilated' or swollen instruments that 'send forth' their contents furiously"; the rebel phalanx approaches "gross" and "huge."[22] John N. King also notes the "sexualized cannonry": "The meticulous application of phallic 'reeds' to a 'narrow vent' (i.e., a small touch-hole) with 'nicest touch' refers literally to the firing of cannon with flaming reeds, but bawdy quibbles add a layer of sexual raillery."[23] King reminds us that "vent" according to seventeenth century usage could denote "anus, vulva or the touch-hole of a firearm, in addition to the standard senses of a slit or aperture."[24] Kent Lehnhof also argues for a pun here, asserting that "Milton maps Satan's weaponry onto the lower bodily stratum," but his interest is in the digestive metaphor in these same instances of wordplay, the scatological innuendos that both Lieb and King admit but do not always emphasize.[25]

Following Lehnhof, I see digestive metaphor predominating in the War in Heaven. Mammon's devilish engines are intestinelike, "hollowed bodies" with "mouths" gaping with "hideous orifice" (*PL* 6.574, 576–77). They operate as dysfunctional digestive systems:

> Immediate in a flame
> But soon obscur'd with smoke, all Heav'n appear'd
> From those deep-throated Engines belcht, whose roar
> Embowell'd with outrageous noise the Air,
> And all her entrails tore, disgorging foul
> Thir devilish glut.   (6.584–89)

W. B. C. Watkins notes the effectual cacophony of this passage, as "the noise of the new satanic artillery, as actively destructive as the explosion, eviscerates the air."[26] Milton's normally mellifluous blank verse here is punctuated by harsh gutturals, dentals, and long vowel sounds. The sound of the lines spurts and explodes. Watkins's description of the atmospheric evisceration reflects upon Milton's description of the tearing of the figurative entrails of the air, reminding us that not only do Mammon's cannons disgorge their contents upon the air, "embowell[ing]" it, but they also simultaneously *dis*embowel the air in the explosion. Here is a return to the volcanic rumbling, roaring, belching, and spewing of Virgil's description of Mount Aetna. The image is chaotic and unsettling: the devilish engines and the rarefied ether are both personified, the former eructating its own insides while violating the insides of the latter. The grotesquerie is compounded because the cannons, an invention of devilish art, emit insides not originally their own but untimely ripped from the womb of heaven, and better left undiscovered. Rammed with "blackest grain," the cannons violate and vomit upon the figurative insides of heaven's atmosphere (6.515). The "grossness," then, of satanic weaponry is not simply its bodily activity but also its rupture of all delineations of form without consent.[27] The ammunition in the War in Heaven is not in itself nefarious; it is the elemental stuff of heaven, and for a moment, at the explosion "all Heav'n appear[s]." Nevertheless, the devilish engines are presented as nauseated bodies, unable to digest and incorporate heavenly matter, while metaphors of glutting, belching, and disemboweling leave no question that the demons have become not merely expendable but repeatedly and violently noxious to heaven's figurative body. Nevertheless, as the demons become more materially gross, they also become more contemptible, their actions noisy and troublesome but ultimately ineffectual. Like Mount Aetna, their efforts sputter, ending in stench and smoke.

The rebel angels, however, cannot expel the evil from themselves, for Milton insists that evil ultimately redounds upon its initiator. Satan's engines backfire — or at least they have a "kick" that provides no insignificant discomfort to their operators. This mechanical defect in Satan's cannons correlates to the bard's repeated descriptions of the psychological effects of Satan's rebellion: "his dire attempt" to pervert humankind "boils in his tumultuous breast, / And like a devilish Engine back recoils / Upon himself" (4.15–18). Even when not directly suffering under the red right arm of God, Satan's actions betray psychic disturbance and self-destructive impulses. He carries "horror and doubt...and...Hell within him" (4.18–20). He "heap[s] on himself damnation," dedicated to "desperate revenge, that shall redound / Upon his own rebellious head" (1.215, 3.85–86). More generally, in the War in Heaven "the evil soon / Driv'n back redounded as a flood on those / From whom it sprung" (7.56–58). Thinking of their freedom as tyrannically restricted rather than their minds and bodies as clogged and diseased, the rebel angels are bound up in their sin and, like Mammon the materialist, resent "Forc't Halleluiahs" (2.243). Consequently, "what redounds" in them collects, hardens, and putrefies.

As the war proceeds, the disadvantages of bodily confinement become apparent even among the unfallen angels, but the rebel angels alone experience "sense of pain," resulting from their new degree of corporealization (6.394). Such is not the case with Michael's troops:

> Far otherwise th' inviolable Saints
> In Cubic Phalanx firm advanc'd entire,
> Invulnerable, impenetrably arm'd,
> Such high advantages thir innocence
> Gave them above thir foes, not to have sinn'd,
> Not to have disobey'd; in fight they stood
> Unwearied, unobnoxious to be pain'd
> By wound, though from thir place by violence mov'd.   (6.398–405)

Here, the innocence of the unfallen angels is their armor. On the second day, however, either Michael's angels have exchanged their abstract but impenetrable arms for a more concrete but less effective defense, or innocence is no longer the analog to their armor. The cry of vigilant Zophiel gives new emphasis to their resistance: "Arm, Warriors, Arm for fight...let each / His Adamantine coat gird well" (6.537, 541–42). Michael's troops wear adamantine armor that, correlative to the materials of the earth, simulates the effects of corporealization. When faced with Mammon's engines, the heavenly warriors are only encumbered by their armor: "Unarm'd they might / Have easily as Spirits evaded swift / By quick contraction or remove" (6.595–97). Thus clad and weighed down, the angels learn quickly to discard their armor, and instead pluck up mountains, "arms / Against such hellish mischief fit to oppose" (6.635–36). At this retaliation, Satan's troops learn the encumbrance of their own armor, and they feel an added pain clearly due to substantial change:

Thir armor help'd thir harm, crush't in and bruis'd
Into thir substance pent, which wrought them pain
Implacable, and many a dolorous groan,
Long struggling underneath, ere they could wind
Out of such prison, though Spirits of purest light,
Purest at first, now gross by sinning grown.   (6.656–61)

Milton's vision of spirits imprisoned in body armor draws a sharp distinction between the shades of materiality on opposite sides of the spectrum of created beings. The difference between armor and spirit is also compounded by the difference between fallen and unfallen spirits. The rebel angels are "now gross by sinning grown," inferior and impaired. Thus "pain[ed]" and "pent," they are increasingly subject to the discomforts and limitations of corporealization (6.661).

While rebel angels lose the advantages of full permeability and become subject to bodily pain, and while the violent spewing of devilish engines tears through the entrails of the ether, a more comprehensive set of metaphorical entrails are set in motion. Heaven, like a healthy body, cleanses herself of impurities, and a new scatological form of excretion appears — if only metaphorically. In accordance with the Elizabethan homily on gluttony, the whole digestive process requires divine supervision. On the third day of the war, routed by the Son of God, the demonic hordes are

pursu'd
With terrors and with furies to the bounds
And Crystal wall of Heav'n, which op'ning wide,
Roll'd inward, and a spacious Gap disclos'd
Into the wasteful Deep; the monstrous sight
Struck them with horror backward, but far worse
Urg'd them behind; headlong themselves they threw
Down from the verge of Heav'n, Eternal wrath
Burn'd after them to the bottomless pit.
Hell heard th' unsufferable noise . . .

. . . .

Disburd'n'd Heav'n rejoic'd, and soon repair'd
Her mural breach, returning whence it roll'd.   (6.858–67, 878–79)

In referring to "Disburd'n'd Heav'n," Milton obliquely puns on the Latinate synonym *exonerate* (from L. *onus*, burden), which in early modern England could refer to the relieving of the bowels.[28] Heaven purges itself, and the "wasteful Deep" receives Satan and his followers. Drawing attention to the "unsufferable noise" attending the event (*PL* 6.867), Kent Lehnhof describes this expulsion as a "flatulential episode in which [God] disburdens heaven by expelling Satan and his offending forces from out of heaven's breach/breech." The final push is still purgative in this reading: "Too filthy for the Father's kingdom, the rebellious angels are cast out and consigned to an excremental existence in hell."[29] For Lehnhof, the entire rebellion in heaven is "a gastronomic event, namely the onset of unwholesome intestinal gas." This reading is paradigmatic for Lehnhof: when Satan "mines the digestive tract of heaven," he is actively seeking "intestinal gas"; in book 4, acting as poisonous toads were supposed to act, Satan vexes Eve not only with disturbing dreams, but also with "flatulential vapors"; in book 9, when taking possession of the body of the serpent, Satan plays on the beast "as an arse trumpet"; and when the demons greet Satan in hell with involuntary hissing in book 10, they are filled with pestilential vapors, and cannot hide the "inadequacy of their anal parody of divine power."[30] The emphasis on intestinal gas and flatulence then effectively betrays demonic impotence and bluster.

I read the scatological metaphors of the War in Heaven as more defecatory than flatulential in emphasis.[31] Satan mines crude, dark materials that are digested into blackest grain, and the "huge...rout / Incumber[ing]" chaos is better described as solid rather than merely gaseous waste matter (*PL* 6.873–74). This distinction is worth mentioning because it reinforces the description of the demons as compacted matter, gross by sinning grown. Of course, demonic "engrossment" and flatulence are not mutually exclusive; the demons grow more corporeal and windier at once. The disburdening of heaven is a new model for defecatory excretion, the first of its kind in the chronology of the poem. Although, as I will demonstrate in chapter 4, excess and its moderation are part of natural heavenly and paradisal cycles, and perfect bodies routinely excrete superfluities, defecation is unnecessary until Satan's rebellion; while Milton's perfect worlds allow for the excretion of superfluities, the metaphor of defecation does not appear until the expulsion of the rebel angels. To compare great things to small, heaven's imitation of the postlapsarian body in its expulsion of the rebel angels is a larger-scale production of the eventual expulsion of Adam and Eve from the garden for their own sin. The metaphor of celestial defecation in the former scene corresponds to the metaphor of Edenic vomiting in the latter — both signs that the body is working as it should in emitting what is noxious to it.

As an alternative to this understanding of the disburdening of heaven, Michael Lieb, primarily finding reproductive imagery where I find digestive metaphor, sees in this passage a metaphorical birth. Lieb compares the disburdening of heaven to the cultivation of fertile Eden, what Eve describes for the serpent as the human project of "disburden[ing] Nature of her Birth" (*PL* 9.624). As Lieb explains, Milton often fuses images of generation and consumption, which is particularly noticeable in Milton's repeated use of the image of being swallowed in a womb.[32] Belial fears being "swallow'd up and lost / In the wide womb of uncreated night"; the enclosing spaces of Hell, Chaos, and Limbo are wombs that yawn, devour, and enshroud in darkness (2.149–50; 2.434–41, 911, 10.476–77). Even while maintaining his argument for the dominance of reproductive imagery, Lieb notes the tendency of diabolical environments and peripheral spaces like Chaos to engulf rather than emit: "from the Satanic point of view, 'womb' is a place which negates generation. It manifests itself in images of swallowing rather than in images of giving forth, in images of entering into wide openings rather than in images of exiting from openings."[33] In this context, Denise Gigante reminds us that in the seventeenth century "womb" could refer to the abdomen, stomach, or bowels as well as the uterus.[34] Nevertheless, Lieb's view of the expulsion is especially parturitive: "There seems to be little question as to whether at least a metaphorical birth is occurring in the fall of Satan and his crew. What should concern us, rather, is what kind of 'birth' is being portrayed and what it means."[35] The philosophical and theological consequences of reading the expulsion as a birth can be dualistic if not entirely Manichean, since evil apparently has a positive identity. To accept the dominant metaphor of the expulsion as natal would also suggest that heaven's womb protected, developed, and produced evil, only to abandon her progeny from the moment of birth. Alternatively, to envision the expulsion as defecation, and demons as waste, is metaphorically more compatible with the Augustinian notion of evil as privative, a notion that Milton shared.[36] An expulsion of fecal matter suggests something noxious and unhealthy to retain has been introduced to and naturally rejected by the hale body of heaven. The digestive image does not explain whence this new evil comes, but it does suggest that the cause need not lie within the body of heaven. This waste cannot be considered a scion of the mind of God. Heaven is never called a womb; its "mural breach" operates more like a sphincter expelling waste than a protective, enclosed uterus that will in time bring forth a viable Other. More often than not, instances of possible sexual or procreative metaphor may be alternately read as digestive metaphor. In the case of the demonic expulsion, the context is more purgative than natal.

The expulsion of the demons from heaven is revisited in the initial moments of the divine act of Creation. The Spirit of God separates the vital from the indigestible; it "downward purg'd / The black tartareous cold Infernal dregs / Adverse to life" (PL 7.237–39). Such "divine defecation" (to use Lehnhof's wording) into the "cosmic latrine" (to use Gigante's phrasing) replicates the physical separation of the assimilable and inassimilable parts of Creation that first occurred at the rebel angels' fall.[37] Using Jacques Derrida's language of economics, Gigante argues that a restricted economy of circulation entailing no loss — one like that of her understanding of Milton's prelapsarian cosmos — must be "founded upon an originary loss or expulsion, which once made can never be reclaimed"; the infernal dregs must be rejected to allow for a tasteful creation.[38] Gigante's argument builds from the work of John Rogers, who explains how Milton employs the Paracelsan concept of tartar as the "inassimilable elements purged from the system in the process of digestion" to present the Creation in an "explicitly digestive vocabulary." Envisioning the tartareous dregs as the residue of an external agent introduced to the body through consumption has its metaphysical implications: "A truly monist universe, permeated entirely with divinity, cannot logically accommodate a pocket of inertness that has escaped divinization.... The tartareous dregs of creation introduce into the otherwise monistic world of the poem a residual trace of dualism."[39] Since, according to Rogers, monism is an essential part of Milton's theodicy, "in three simple lines, Milton, it can be safely said, has sabotaged his attempt to justify the ways of God to men."[40]

Yet if we read the purging of infernal dregs not as exclusively Paracelsan, but as at least partly Galenic (an idea the next chapter will explore in greater detail), the removal of the willfully inassimilable dregs is another exoneration of heaven. "Tartareous," after all, could refer to more than one thing: relating to the useless dregs of grapes fermenting into wine, or to the Greek realm of punishment for the unjust dead (*PL* 2.858, 6.54), or to a native inhabitant of central Asia (*PL* 10.431); Marlowe's *Tamburlaine the Great, Part 2,* sets a precedent in employing all of these senses, and recently Eric Song has applied this polysemous use of "tartar" to Milton, too.[41] If Milton's reference to tartar is more than Paracelsan, and if we consider the expulsion in Galenic terms, this expulsion demonstrates the healthy body of heaven excreting superfluous matter that intentionally avoids being digested to nourish or fortify the body, and which, left alone, would be toxic to the body. The angels' freely willed resistance to participation in God's creative plan supports Milton's theodicy. Originally created good and possessing the freedom to choose to turn from goodness, the fallen angels, "self-deprav'd," do not become something new as much as they become defective (3.130). The Augustinian notion of evil as privative is thereby wed to the Galenic digestive theory, where originally good but undigested humoral superfluities, unuseful, turn noxious and must be expelled lest they collect and intoxicate the body.[42] This reading helps distinguish angelic excretions of praise from the divine defecation that serves as a response to (not a cause of) sin. The metaphor of foul expulsion is neither necessary nor natural until foulness has been introduced. God then is not a God who creates waste; the tartareous dregs are the residuum of rebellious angels who choose not to participate in the nutritive system of God's plan; their refusal makes them cosmic refuse. The fact that they get their way by being capable of turning from God does not demand a dualistic reading, nor does it occlude an Augustinian ontology where all that truly exists is good, while evil is rendered merely a defection from good.

A difficulty lies in the direct influence this expulsion has on the human condition. Gigante argues, "Satan is expelled in the constitutive moment of Miltonic creation."[43] Although the expulsion and the Creation appear to be not exactly simultaneous, since a divine speech, an angelic hymn, and the Son's procession separate the narration of the two events, the bard reminds us that "Immediate are the Acts of God, more swift / Than time or motion, but to human ears / Cannot without process of speech be told" (*PL* 7.176–78). Regardless of a possible delay between the expulsion and Creation, there is a dramatic connection between the two events. As John Rumrich explains, "Roughly speaking, Adam and Eve are war babies, part of a creative celebration of victory conveying the resilience and versatility of God in the face of evil and loss. The meaning of our existence is, thus, inextricably linked to the origin of evil and distance."[44] Though God assures his faithful angels that "Heav'n yet populous retains / Number sufficient to possess her Realms," of the "Self-lost" angels, he states, "I can repair / that detriment…and in a moment will create / Another World" (*PL* 7.146–47, 152–54). Earth is consequently fashioned under the divine principle of generating "Good out of evil," and man is designed as a replacement, "instead / Of Spirits malign a better Race to bring / Into their vacant room" (7.188–90).

Nevertheless, the prophecy of Creation was in the angels' consciousness before the expulsion of the rebel angels, rendering it possible that the creation of earth did not depend on the War in Heaven (2.348–49). Moreover, steps are taken to ensure that the goodness of Creation is not tainted by the circumstances leading to its fashioning; for example, Raphael explains his commission to check the steadfastness of hell's gates, preventing the mixture of "Destruction with

Creation," and of evil with goodness (8.236). "Hell's location," Milton argues in *De doctrina Christiana*, "seems to be outside this world," for "the apostasy of the devil took place before the fall of man," and the earth could not have been created cursed (OW 8:893). The argument to book 1 of *Paradise Lost* agrees, pointing to the goodness of Creation: hell is *"not in the Centre"* of earth, "for Heaven and Earth may be suppos'd as yet not made, certainly not yet accurst." Gigante argues that the positioning of Satan's expulsion before the creation of earth and of the earthly heavens supports a dualistic reading where an alternative to God and godliness exists from the beginning of the poem: "the dregs of Miltonic creation...are always already lost."[45] Nevertheless, this reading does not comprehensively account for the narratives of the conception of Sin and of the War in Heaven, stories that do take into consideration a time when Lucifer, however temporarily, enjoyed his status among the faithful angels. I see no definite reason why we cannot apply to Milton's cosmology a passage from Macrobius that Gigante quotes, only to reject: "from the Supreme God even to the bottommost dregs of the universe there is one tie, binding at every link and never broken."[46] The Macrobius passage, as Gigante notes, is representative of traditional *ex Deo* Creation theory, where the dregs still remain part of creation; one thinks of Milton's defense of creation *ex Deo* in *De doctrina Christiana* (OW 8:290), and in *Paradise Lost*, of Milton's hell — still part of the divine plan — "which God by curse / Created evil, for evil only good," or of Abdiel and Satan's conversation about their creation, where Abdiel tells Satan that he remains under God's authority and can choose through obedience or rebellion whether to be governed by a golden scepter or an iron rod (*PL* 2.622–23, 5.886–87). These significant passages serve Milton's theodicy by intimating that evil did not spring from God, nor is it a separate-but-equal alternative to God's plan. Infernal dregs are not a necessary by-product of Creation, but the residue of freely chosen sin; whether they like it or not, the fallen angels still share a part in God's creation, not having won for themselves true autonomy. They have not made themselves anew; they have only nurtured disease associated with the gluttonous body.

"DEVILISH GLUT"

What must appear dramatically enticing in book 9 in Eden, then, becomes repulsive when reconsidered and revised in book 10 in hell. There, the demons transform into serpents and gorge themselves on the new-sprung grove of trees "laden with fair Fruit, like that / Which grew in Paradise, the bait of *Eve*" (*PL* 10.550–51). The description that follows is one of Milton's best representations of the unpalatable quality of gluttony:

> [The demons-turned-serpents] could not abstain,
> But on they roll'd in heaps, and up the Trees
> Climbing, sat thicker than the snaky locks
> That curl'd *Megaera*: greedily they pluck'd
> The Fruitage fair to sight, like that which grew
> Near that bituminous Lake where Sodom flam'd;
> This more delusive, not the touch, but taste
> Deceiv'd; they fondly thinking to allay
> Thir appetite with gust, instead of Fruit
> Chew'd bitter Ashes, which th' offended taste
> With spattering noise rejected: oft they assay'd
> Hunger and thirst constraining, drugg'd as oft,
> With hatefullest disrelish writh'd thir jaws
> With soot and cinders fill'd.   (10.557–70)

Phonetically, the reader experiences the harsh, unpalatable strains of "thirst constraining," "hatefullest disrelish," and "writh'd thir jaws"; in regard to the narrative, the devils' dish of bitter ashes compares with the apples of Sodom Augustine mentions in the *City of God*, the fruit of a region once compared with paradise: "The land of Sodom was certainly not always as it is now. Once, it presented an appearance like that of other lands, and it flourished with a fruitfulness equally great — if not greater, for in the Divine Scripture it is compared to the Paradise of God. But after it was touched by heaven, it became a wondrous, blackened horror.... Also, its apples, under the false appearance of ripeness, contain ashes within. Behold, then: something which was once of one kind, and is now of another."[47] This passage is from book 21 of *The City of God*, dedicated to examining the fate of Satan and the damned. Chapter 5, "That there are many things which reason cannot account for, and which are nonetheless true," introduces the apples of Sodom as evidence that the inexplicable is not impossible, and that such wondrous phenomena may be "permanent features of places which now exist." Chapter 8, containing the long passage quoted above, is designed to prove "that it is not contrary to nature that, in an object whose properties are known to us, there should be found an alteration in those properties known to be natural to it." That is, changes in an object's natural properties are in themselves natural. Transformation — the potential to rise as well as to fall — is part of creation's design.

Thus Augustine compares both young Sodom to the paradise of God and the deceptive and ashen apples of corrupted Sodom to forbidden fruit; Milton follows suit in representing the Fall in the infernal setting of book 10 of *Paradise Lost*. The section on temperance in Milton's *De doctrina Christiana* reinforces these comparisons when, in a list of scriptural passages on gluttony, Milton quotes Ezekiel 16:49: "Behold, this was the iniquity of your [i.e., Jerusalem's] sister Sodom: excess, a satiety of food" (OW 8:1077). Recalling that John Chrysostom, Thomas Aquinas, Caesarius of Heisterbach, and the Elizabethan homilies also indicted ancient Sodom with gluttony, it is apparent that Milton participates in a tradition of a gluttonous Fall by describing the demon snakes "greedily...pluck[ing]...Fruitage" that crumbles into ashes. The infernal reenactment of Adam and Eve's disobedience emphasizes the "hatefullest disrelish" of their actions. Although sin may surprise us in book 9, here it is stripped of its illusive grandeur, its crudity revealed.

Satan himself becomes the first symbol of gluttony to infect Eden. When he enters the garden in book 4, he is as "a prowling wolf / Whom hunger drives to seek new haunt for prey" (4.183–84). Certainly hunger is no sin, but the predation he plans is markedly nefarious. From the boundaries of Eden,

> Up he flew, and on the Tree of Life,
> The middle Tree and highest there that grew,
> Sat like a Cormorant; yet not true Life
> Thereby regain'd, but sat devising Death.   (4.194–97)

The strangeness of Milton's choice to have Satan resemble a seabird in the middle of the garden is alleviated through symbol, by the cormorant's notoriety as an especially voracious bird of prey. Chaucer's *Parliament of Fowls* includes the "hote cormeraunt of glotonye," and from the sixteenth century the cormorant was used figuratively to describe an insatiably greedy person. Shakespeare refers to "cormorant devouring Time," "the insatiate cormorant," and "the cormorant belly."[48] Satan's ravenous appetite is drawn not to the "Ambrosial Fruit / Of vegetable Gold" hanging about him, but to insidious predation (4.219–20). His inability to choose the good before him also marks him guilty of the qualitative errors of the glutton. While perched "like a Cormorant," Satan first sees Adam and Eve, and first observes a temperate communal meal in earthly paradise. Fittingly, in this guise Satan "devis[es] Death," another signal of his involvement with gluttony.

While an infernal pit of snakes exhibits gluttony, and Satan assumes the shape of an emblem of gluttony, Death stands for Gluttony itself. The double allegory of Death as Gluttony appears throughout *Paradise Lost*, and Death's association with excess and selfishness begins *in utero*. Sin carries the "growing burden" of Death to term, her womb "excessive grown" and panged by "Prodigious motion" (*PL* 2.767, 779, 780). When encountering Satan at the gates of hell, Death expands himself tenfold (705). The very form of the "grim Feature" of Death suggests gluttony (10.279), for his indistinct shape, his "vast unhidebound Corpse," replicates the boundlessness of his gluttony, while as a goblin-like hellhound he recalls the three-headed (and three-mouthed) Cerberus, as his snaky mother does Scylla (2.648–61, 688, 724; 10.601, 616, 630). The progeny Death begets on Sin are, like their father, internally and externally unrestrained. Incessantly howling and gnawing, this brood with "wide *Cerberean* mouths" returns "when they list, into the womb / That bred them": "My Bowels, thir repast," Sin frets (2.655, 798–800). Just as Milton's Satan fathers both Sin and then, through incest, Death, Lust is traditionally Gluttony's "sexy sibling sin of the flesh," as William Ian Miller describes her.[49] As sensual sins in a sensual portrayal of the Fall dominated by metaphors of eros and of eating, Lust and Gluttony serve as appropriate analogs for Sin and Death.

In depicting Sin and Death thus, Milton does nothing extraordinary. As Donald Davis notes, citing the work of Robert Fox, Scylla and Cerberus "were associated, respectively, with lust and gluttony in a long, steady tradition."[50] Versions of Scylla's origins present a girl turned into a monster for sexual crimes, but Scylla is also associated more generally with the dangers of excess with respect to physical pleasure. The *Aeneid* describes Scylla as having a "belly of wolves" (*utero...luporum* [*Aeneid* 3.428]); her counterpart, Charybdis, is an insatiate whirlpool (*implacata...gurgite* [*Aeneid* 4.420, 421]). Renaissance mythography records the moralizing interpretation of a hero sailing between these monsters as the one who practices the Aristotelian idea of virtue attained by moderation. Thus we read in Natale Conti's *Mythologiae*: "For what else do our lives consist of, but a continual sailing between various afflictions and immoral pleasures? Indeed, only the person who has lived a pious and holy life, and who scorns the vices that flank either side of his ship, will be able to get to his homeland unharmed. That homeland refers of course to the assembly of blessed souls presided over by God in the afterlife."[51] Temperance, then, becomes a path to paradise in Conti's mythology.

Cerberus joins Scylla and Charybdis as a symbol of inordinate desire. Like Scylla, he was sometimes portrayed with serpents for hair, with his bark and bite reminiscent of Scylla's wolvish waist. Conti's preferred etymology for Cerberus follows Isidore of Seville in associating the hellhound with the grave: "In fact the name Cerberus really means 'tomb,' for κρεας means 'flesh' and βορῶ, 'I devour.'"[52] The etymology itself explains the long-standing connection between Death and Gluttony. "For those who want to relate the story to behavioral patterns and improving the human condition," Conti continues, "Cerberus represents greed and the desire for wealth that arises only from evil thoughts." Lust, Gluttony, Greed — There is good reason for Dante grouping these three together in Dante's *Inferno.* They are the sins of incontinence, the sins of inordinate desires placed in physical or material pleasures, the suburban (or superurban?) sins loitering outside the gates of the City of Dis, where violence, malice, and fraud are punished with greater severity. Lust, Gluttony, and Greed are not only firmly included among the Seven Deadly Sins, they each have been used as an umbrella term for the entire group. Lust may be described as a gluttonous sexual desire, for example, and gluttony as a lust for food. They work well together, and it should not surprise us to see that the taxonomy of these Cerberean, unhidebound sins is indistinct.

At the end of his account of the *Letter to Egbert,* Bede identifies the original sin (both the sin of the fallen angels and the sin of Adam and Eve in paradise) as a three-headed covetousness represented by Cerberus, itself representative of all possible sin to be found in this world:

> The angels were thereby [through covetousness] cast down from heaven, the first created beings expelled from a paradise of endless enjoyment. And if you must know, this is that three-headed dog of Hell, called Cerberus in the fables, from whose ravening teeth the Apostle John would save us, when he says, "Beloved, love not the world nor those things that be therein: if any man love the world, the love of the Father is not in him. For every thing which is in the world, is the desire of the flesh, and the desire of the eyes, and the pride of life, which is not of the Father, but is of the world." Thus much briefly have I said against the poison of covetousness. But if I were to treat in like manner of drunkenness, feasting, luxury, and other contagions of the same kind, my letter would be indefinitely lengthened. May the grace of the Chief Shepherd ever keep you safe for the wholesome feeding of his flock, Prelate, most beloved in our Lord: Amen![53]

Here we once again see that unholy trinity: the lust of the flesh, the lust of the eyes, and the pride of life. Gluttony, Lust, and Pride. Cerberus, Scylla, and Satan. Death, Sin, and the Devil. Milton's Death is indeed a devourer of flesh, and the snaky sorceress is associated with the eyes: confronting Satan at the gates of hell, she inquires, "do I seem / Now in thine eye so foul?" In heaven, she reminds Satan, her attractive graces once pleased him, "full oft / thyself in me thy perfect image viewing" (*PL* 2.747–48, 763–64). As for Satan, "his Pride / Had cast him out from Heav'n" (1.36–37). As pride goeth before the Fall, Satan is also associated with catastrophe. The opening action of *Paradise Lost* is, after all, Satan's fall, and this allows Satan, Sin, and Death to be alternatively read as analogs to catastrophe, lasciviousness, and gluttony — a triad mentioned by Augustine in a passage on the beauties of parallelism in rhetoric.[54] Either way, we have in Sin, Death, and Satan an unholy trinity working together to compound rejection of God and its consequences, and all three bear the marks of Cerberean inordinate desire.

Death, however, retains a special affiliation with Gluttony. "Half starv'd" at the gates of hell, Death would have devoured Sin had he not known that his own death was to be involved in the death of his sister / mother (2.805–07, 10.595). At hearing from Satan that the whole earth is to be his to consume, and that he will "be fed and fill'd / Immeasurably," Death responds with a complacent, "ghastly smile" (2.843–46). After the Fall, Death follows Sin to destroy the earth. Compared to not one bird, but "a flock / Of ravenous Fowl," he exults, "such a scent I draw / Of carnage, prey innumerable, and taste / The savor of Death from all things there that live" (10.273–74, 267–69). Death pines with "eternal Famine," but this is not for lack of food; his prey — the entire created world — "though plenteous, all too little seems / To stuff this Maw" (10.597, 600–01). Without radical divine intervention, what Michael calls "Death's rapacious claim" on sinful humanity may be postponed, but not escaped (11.258). Moreover, though much is made of Adam and Eve's ignorance of the nature of Death before the Fall, afterward Eve recognizes Death's gluttony and so suggests counteracting it with abstinence: "Childless thou art, Childless remain: So Death / Shall be deceiv'd his glut, and with us two / Be forc'd to satisfy his Rav'nous Maw" (10.989–91). By giving the formidable shape of Death a "Rav'nous Maw," Milton depicts not only the rapacity of death but also what he believes to be the morbidity of gluttony. Of course, the suggestion of sexual abstinence or suicide from the "Mother of human Race" is ill advised: even if these methods appear the simplest and fastest ways to thwart Death, they abandon life (4.475). Though the allegorical figure of Sin is associated with lust, the nonbeing that looms with complete sexual abstention is no less a threat.[55] Adam repudiates Eve's suggestion, creating space for a Miltonic view of temperance as a rational virtue flanked by the vice of making the gratification of desire one's god, and the vice of seeking to utterly stifle all desire. Adam and Eve need another plan to counterattack Death.

The foretelling of the eventual destruction of gluttonous Death is a popular Renaissance topos, and Milton's rendition offers one of the best examples of *contrapasso* in early modern English poetry. The promise of such eschatological retribution aptly suits both Milton's construction of Death and the fulfillment of his poetic enterprise. Milton's endeavor to "justify the ways of God to men" is essentially an encounter with theodicy — that is, of making sense of sin and death in a world governed by an omnipotent, omniscient, and benevolent God. As it is for Dante's damned, and as it is for Milton's Satan, the punishments of Sin and Death are in part themselves. Sin as Lust is allegorically portrayed as incestuous and self-destructive — her offspring tearing at her entrails and feeding on her bowels — and Death as Gluttony remains in the agony of perpetual famine.[56] As early as book 3, the Son foretells how Death's present punishment will reach completion at the eschaton: "Death his death's wound shall then receive" (3.252). The Son then describes to God the Father the particularly appropriate means by which ravenous Death shall be vanquished: "by thee rais'd I ruin all my Foes / Death last, and with his Carcass glut the Grave" (3.258–59). After the Fall, God the Father confirms this fate for Sin and Death:

> I call'd and drew them thither,
> My Hell-hounds, to lick up the draff and filth
> Which man's polluting Sin with taint hath shed
> On what was pure, till cramm'd and gorg'd, nigh burst
> With suckt and glutted offal, at one sling

Of thy victorious Arm, well-pleasing Son,
Both *Sin*, and *Death*, and yawning *Grave* at last
Through *Chaos* hurl'd, obstruct the mouth of Hell
For ever, and seal up his ravenous Jaws.   (10.629–37)

In the same redemptive act, not only shall Death die but also the grave shall be glutted with the figure of Gluttony, along with that of Lust, their rapacious appetites forcibly quelled. This promised end counters the horrific image of Sin, with Death at her side, opening the gates of hell, which "like a Furnace mouth / Cast forth redounding smoke and ruddy flame," granting Satan passage into chaos in quest for paradise (2.888–89). Before Satan wins Death over with promises of a world of carnage to feast upon, he antagonizes and taunts the grisly terror: "Taste thy folly" (2.686); ironically, this is just what will happen to Death for his alliance with the author of all ill.

"WORST EXTREMES": HELLISH EXCESS AND EXTREMISM

Hell is a place fit for Death. Its furnace-mouth sucks and spews, it is "fed / With ever-burning Sulfur unconsum'd," its gates "open wide, belching outrageous flame / Far into *Chaos*" (1.68–69, 10.232–33). It is a place of extremes, of insatiate gluttony, of death and of

shades of death,
A Universe of death, which God by curse
Created evil, for evil only good;
Where all life dies, death lives, and Nature breeds,
Perverse, all monstrous, all prodigious things.   (2.621–625)

As the demons explore hell in book 2, they learn their new home suffers a violent jostling of extremes. The adventurers find "No rest," for theirs is a land "where peace / And rest can never dwell," a place of "torture without end" (2.618, 1.65–67). Instead of comfortable meadows of mottled sun and shade, or the undulation of land and water features in the "temperate Clime" of paradise, the demons find a "burning Lake," rivers with "waves of torrent fire," and a "frozen Continent" where "cold performs th' effect of fire" (12.636; 2.576, 581, 587, 595).

Instead of harmonious interchange and "Grateful vicissitude" (6.8), the denizens of hell suffer from both oxymoronic and extreme conditions. The oxymoronic parts — from the "darkness visible" to the "burning Lake" — reflect the collapsed logic, confused rhetoric, and cognitive dissonance behind such statements as Satan's "Evil be thou my Good" or Beelzebub's claim that the War in Heaven "endanger'd Heav'n's perpetual King" (4.110, 1.131). As if in natural sympathy with Satan's inner turbulence, and as fit correlative to the contradictions and mental gymnastics of infernal thinking, hell itself models a new, irregular, and unpleasant experience of extremism, contradiction, and infelicitous change. The fallen angels are doomed to

> feel by turns the bitter change
> Of fierce extremes, extremes by change more fierce,
> From Beds of raging Fire to starve in Ice
> Thir soft Ethereal warmth, and there to pine
> Immovable, infixt, and frozen round,
> Periods of time, thence hurried back to fire.   (2.598–603)

There are heavenly excesses in *Paradise Lost*, but "worst extremes" are reserved for Satan and his followers (1.276). These extremes may be thought of as an excess of excess, a grotesque exaggeration of the undulations of heavenly and paradisal experience.

As a mark of his extremism, Satan does not participate in the routines of temperate angels. He does not eat. He does not sleep. He does not worship. He does not dedicate time to any action that detracts from his monomaniacal mission of revenge. Not content with his heavenly palace, he begins his rebellion by ascending his throne

> as a Mount
> Rais'd on a Mount
> ....
> which not long after, he
> Affecting all equality with God,
> In imitation of that Mount whereon
> *Messiah* was declar'd in sight of Heav'n,
> The Mountain of the Congregation call'd.   (5.757–66)

As a "Mount…on a Mount," Satan recalls the myth of the insurrection of the giants Otus and Ephialtes who, by stacking Mount Ossa on Mount Pelion, hoped to overthrow the gods of Mount Olympus. This mountain-piling simile exemplifies Satan's extremism, while he masks his egoistic tyranny by renaming the place of his throne the "Mountain of the Congregation" — one of many instances of a devilish difference between public message and private agenda. As Satan seeks to imitate the Mount of God, so Mammon thinks he can renovate hell in imitation of heaven (2.269–73), but in both cases the result is a gross caricature diametrically opposed to the spirit of the original.

In an ironic *contrapasso*, the extreme fluctuations in hellish environs are fit punishment for those inflexibly opposed to a perceived rigidity in God's creative order. As Joseph Summers argues, Satan "seems to imagine an order which is static except for his own aspiration," and so, in defiance of the splendid energies he confronts within heaven and paradise, he contemns all law, overleaps natural boundaries, and scoffs at those that protect them (*PL* 4.180–81).[57] When Gabriel accosts him for his trespass — "Why hast thou, *Satan*, broke the bounds prescrib'd?" — Satan scorns Gabriel, calling him a "Proud limitary Cherub" (4.878, 971). Satan aspires far beyond his natural limits and soon develops a self-determined, inflexible resolve that ironically harries him with constant motion — "And in the lowest deep a lower deep / Still threat'ning to devour [him] opens wide" — and commotion — "his face, / Thrice chang'd with pale, ire, envy and despair" (4.76–77, 114–15). Among such extreme conditions, Satan himself is "only Supreme / In misery," the heavy consequence of his futile aspiration (4.91–92).

Milton thus marks devilish extremism with psychological inflexibility and mental inertia matched with physical restlessness exacerbated by newly experienced pain. At the conception of Sin, Satan becomes the first to feel mental pain, and at the sword of Michael, Satan first feels bodily pain (2.752, 6.327). In Milton's infernal world, those confirmed in their defection from God do not, like fallen humans, stagger between pleasure and pain, but rather experience the fluctuation of alternating evils, or at least alternating sensations of pain. At best they can suspend their pains through the charms of harmony or eloquence, but this is a temporary deviation from their regular torments (2.547–56). When demons sing of their own heroic deeds, the narrator informs us, "Thir Song was partial" — partisan and one-sided, but also with various parts resolved into harmony: the music "charms the Sense" and leaves the audience spellbound (2.552, 556). But the song is also partial because it is an incomplete and temporary respite from punishment, deceptively dulling the conscience along with the senses, perhaps, but no permanent solution to this newcomer, pain. Likewise, "false Philosophie" charms less musical demons with "Fallacious hope" and "stubborn patience" against the pain or anguish that would come with self-awareness, but this too lasts only "for a while" (2.565–69).

Satan's abjuration of repentance, confirmed by the reflection that "ease would recant / Vows made in pain, as violent and void," is also a resignation to pain and restlessness (4.96–97). Later, when Satan is caught spying in the garden, he scoffs when Gabriel asks him why he escaped hell: "Lives there who loves his pain?" (4.888). But a retort that plays on Satan's pride soon elicits a new and contradictory approach: "Not that I less endure, or shrink from pain, / Insulting Angel" (4.925–26). Less interested in telling the truth than in winning an argument, Satan is caught in his own lies even as he calls upon his experiences with pain as evidence for his superiority.

But it is also a mark of fallenness that Satan's subordinate demon, Nisroch, seeks nothing but repose. After the first day of battle in heaven, "Sore toil'd, his riv'n Arms to havoc hewn," he laments the advantage of their enemy:

> hard
> For Gods, and too unequal work we find
> Against unequal arms to fight in pain,
> Against unpain'd, impassive; from which evil
> Ruin must needs ensue; For what avails
> Valor or strength, though matchless, quell'd with pain
> Which all subdues, and makes remiss the hands
> Of Mightiest. Sense of pleasure we may well

> Spare out of life perhaps, and not repine,
> But live content, which is the calmest life:
> But pain is perfet misery, the worst
> Of evils, and excessive, overturns
> All patience.   (6.449, 452–64)

Nisroch's opinion of his newly experienced pain as "the worst / Of evils" goes too far in uniting physical sensation with morality. His motivations appear base and nonrational, as if the demon were slavishly bound to comfort, if not to pleasure.[58] His remark that one might well prefer "the calmest life" against one punctuated by pleasurable sensations also suggests a fallen preference for stasis, itself an extremist position. Nisroch is well on his way to being tantalized by the powers of Lethe, "whereof who drinks / Forthwith his former state and being forgets, / Forgets both joy and grief, pleasure and pain" (2.584–86). To desire the mental erasure granted by Lethe is in some respect to forgo active pursuit of *aletheia* — the truth, that which is unforgettable — and to ignore a higher, truer realm of being in order to mask the pain of descent. For this reason Milton keeps among the tantalizations of hell the classical River of Oblivion that Dante reserves for his earthly paradise (*PL* 2.583). For Milton, to desire insensibility is to reject a fundamental aspect of being, even to lose part of one's identity. Nisroch's opinion of the impassivity of angels is inaccurate — he too quickly forgets that even though the unfallen angels do not feel pain since their bodies have not grown gross with sin, they are yet fully capable of experiencing both desire and pleasure in eating, in embracing, and in the experience of "change delectable" (5.629, 8.626). Lethe would have no seductive powers for a perfect being in a perfect environment. Though heaven is filled with pleasant variation and modulating activity, the demons mistakenly and illogically scorn the faithful angels for their limited experience, while they, exasperated by the interchange of extremes, desire a rest that they are doomed not to find.

Demonic restlessness and desire for rest are manifest in variant perversions of ideal repose and activity, and show that gluttony, rather than active temperance, leads to idleness and rigidity. At the Stygian council, Moloch iterates Nisroch's perspective; he abhors the "pain of unextinguishable fire" and seeks rather to "reduce / To nothing this essential, happier far / Than miserable to have eternal being" (2.96–98). Where Nisroch seeks numbness, Moloch desires an expense of spirit concluding in nothingness. Subsequently, Belial's response to Moloch first allies painlessness and annihilation with reference to chaos:

> That must be our cure,
> To be no more; sad cure; for who would lose,
> Though full of pain, this intellectual being,
> Those thoughts that wander through Eternity,
> To perish rather, swallow'd up and lost
> In the wide womb of uncreated night,
> Devoid of sense and motion?   (2.145–51)

Belial argues for the good of a life even such as their own, one characterized by "sense and motion," and he thereby contends with Nisroch and Moloch's desire for numbness, oblivion, or loss of being. But Belial's proposal is itself a variation of the desire for stasis, described by the narrator as "ignoble ease, and peaceful sloth, / Not peace" (2.227–28). Most significantly, Belial's antipathy for "the wide womb of uncreated night," which Satan later describes as the threat of "utter loss of being," turns our consideration to one more realm of excess and extremes: that of chaos (2.440).

Like hell, chaos is a place of "fierce extremes" antithetical to the tempered variety of the created cosmos, yet not without its purpose in the divine plan (7.272). There, the four contraries, "hot, cold, moist, and dry," are "Champions fierce" that in their unordered formlessness embroil the deep (2.898). Negation and affirmation are mixed confusedly, causing some critics to defend the neutrality of chaos, and some to state even more earnestly its nefariousness.[59] For this argument it is important to distinguish between Chaos the quasi-ruler and chaos, his realm. The anarch is inherently allied with Satan the destroyer rather than God the creator, but as heaven has use for twilight, so God brings good out of "his dark materials," stuff that belongs to him properly, to Chaos only as a subsidiary (2.916). The extremes of life and death are confused in chaos, "the Womb of nature and perhaps her Grave" (2.911). The potential for life is stated positively, and that of death, tentatively, which seems to privilege the potential for good within chaotic, unformed matter. Yet Chaos as allegorical figure prevents the actualization of this potential. He and his consort Night, whose "Sable-vested" darkness exceeds that of her heavenly counterpart, "hold / Eternal Anarchy," keeping their realm — if the place they occupy may be called that — antithetical to created heaven and earth (2.962, 2.895–96). Theirs is a place of fearful disarray,

> a dark
> Illimitable Ocean without bound,
> Without dimension, where length, breadth, and highth,
> And time and place are lost.   (2.891–94)

Within this space, the ferocity of the warring rudiments of being and the lurking threat of nonbeing or destruction indicate the danger of the place.[60]

Similarly, at the gates of hell Sin recounts how she was "excessive grown" with Death, morbidly uniting the two extremes of life and death in her pregnancy (2.779). By conflating the grave and the womb in the realm of Chaos and in Sin's body, evil alteration is manifested not only by movement from one evil, pain, or fierce extreme to another but also by the juxtaposition of the good with the bad so that good becomes tainted and bad becomes more appealing, or, as this juxtaposition presents itself in paradise, so that the experience of evil becomes more painful in pleasurable environs.

Thus, in earthly paradise, Satan suffers from the extreme contrast between good and evil. The good of the creation that he views (especially the "sweet interchange" brought on by its natural variety) irritates the evil within him:

> The more I see
> Pleasures about me, so much more I feel
> Torment within me, as from the hateful siege
> Of contraries.   (9.115, 119–22)

Satan, the most extreme creature in evil, cannot avoid the sharp pain of contact with extraordinary good. As a result he finds ease "only in destroying" — in mixing the two other opposites of creation and destruction (9.129, 477).

Here arises a further and crucial distinction between the infernal and heavenly use of good and evil in *Paradise Lost*. Although it is God's tendency to bring forth good out of evil, he always preserves the distinctions between moral opposites (7.188). We have already observed how the angelic rebellion becomes the occasion for God to restock his worshipers by creating earth, but not before sending Raphael to guard the gates of hell to prevent enemy escape, "Lest hee incenst at such eruption bold / Destruction with Creation might have mixt" (8.235–36).[61] Following Jewish tradition, creation is an act first of separation, and then of joining "like things to like," yet the result is harmonious: "Earth self-balanc't on her Centre hung" (7.240, 242).[62] In constructing a temperate universe, God also takes precautions to alienate Chaos, "lest fierce extremes / Contiguous might distemper the whole frame" (7.272–73).

Contrariwise, Satan nefariously mixes evil into good, falsehood into truth, death into life. Satan's mixing confuses and is never creative. His "Evil, be thou my Good" is merely an illogical change of nomenclature. If God were to say this line — and he very well could — such an expression would affect an actual change from disorder and destruction to purposeful, orderly creation. Milton's God reforms and redeems; he is the master of change for the better. Satan can mix good and evil in order to make evil all the more enticing, but he cannot relieve the pain of subjection to the fierce extremes raging within him, and of an evil mind confronting a good world. He operates under the impression that paradise must fall with him if he is to find any lingering modicum of relief.

It is worth noting that the satanic attempt at a static mixture of good and evil, a sin-produced "unharmonious mixture foul," is only temporary, for Milton's narrator assuredly states that "evil...[is] impossible to mix / With Blessedness" indefinitely; the War in Heaven could have no other outcome than evil redounding on evil, ending in the expulsion of the demons and the exoneration of Heaven (11.51, 7.56–59). Such redundancy, though out of the demons' control, is yet another mark of hellish extremism and stasis. In their pain, each demon has lost the angelic perspective — in some cases, the memory — of pleasurable excess, variety, and change. Nisroch's rejection of God's system of positive change manifests itself most in his expressed desire for repose or insensibility; Moloch's, in the desire for annihilation; Belial's, in sophisticated sloth; Chaos, in senseless embroiling, and Satan's, in his indomitable will to pervert good. Each devil has lost the good of the senses, of vigorous, constructive work, and of life itself.

One might rightly wonder why such extreme conditions in hell, such references to vomiting, defecation, and flatulence, and such images of gluttony are embedded in the nobler passages of the epic poem. Vulgar metaphors appear to work against the "answerable style" Milton seeks to obtain from his "Celestial Patroness"; they seem too base to match the height of his "great Argument" (9.20–21, 1.24). Yet these seemingly incongruous passages are intimations of a broader purpose. Dante set a precedent for selectively employing a coarse narrative style when describing infernal regions, and Milton follows suit.[63] Despite the silver tongue of Milton's Satan, the fallen angels have grown "gross by sinning," and correspondingly "gross" passages contribute to Milton's examination of the "foul descent" undergone by those who turn from God (*PL* 9.163). Milton's images and metaphors of flatulence, vomiting, and excretion are even more rhetorically effective, I believe, than the visual degradation of Satan from angel to leviathan, to cormorant, to lion, to tiger, to anuran "peeping Tom," upon which C. S. Lewis bases much of his argument against those who champion Satan's heroism.[64] The poem's satiric metaphors of the lower body and its earthy and scatological associations mark the degradation of the infernal powers. For its purpose, the crude language is entirely suitable. As Milton himself explains in defending potty-mouth polemic in his *Apology for Smectymnuus*, "Christ himselfe speaking of unsavory traditions, scruples not to name the Dunghill and the Jakes" (YP 1:895).[65] The introduction of scatological metaphor in the expulsion of the rebel angels suggests a new type of superfluity, of good-humors-turned-toxic, of that which must be expelled to ensure the economy of heaven and of paradise. Finally, the infernal eating, digesting, and excretion in *Paradise Lost* serves as a negative image of ideal eating, and a starting point for inquiry into the boundaries of prelapsarian bodily and intellectual potential.

4

Perfect Consumption, the Food of the Gods, and the Great Chain of Eating

...the church's banquet...
God's breath in man returning to his birth...
Exalted manna...
The land of spices; something understood.

— George Herbert, *Prayer (I)*

Half of *Paradise Lost* (books 5–8 and 11–12, or 44 percent of the poem's 10,565 lines) is devoted to two Edenic angelophanies, thereby relying on physical and verbal correspondence between humans and heavenly messengers. Raphael and Michael help Adam understand his position and his potential in the cosmos and in history, and each visitation leads Adam to adjust his understanding of his relationship with God and his angels. The angel Raphael, sociable and affable, and selected by God for the prelapsarian discourse, informs Adam that heaven's angels think no less of him than as a fellow servant of God, one who enjoys honor and God's "Equal Love" (*PL* 8.228). Adam is a deferential host, but Raphael graciously insists on their similarity as they share a meal, human fare being "No ingrateful food" to the angel (5.407). Of the similarities and differences between faithful angels and unfallen humans, those demonstrable through bodily consumption are especially significant, since Raphael proposes that eating might raise Adam and Eve to godhood, at which point typical angel fare would pose "no inconvenient diet" to the human couple (5.495). As presented in Milton's cosmopoiesis and in Raphael's account of prelapsarian physiology and natural philosophy, ideal eating, perfect digestion, and celestial viands have key parts to play in Edenic life, where worship and aspiration are complementary. This chapter explores the potential for Adam and Eve's divinely ordered metamorphosis within Milton's poetic universe; doing so leads to examining Milton's use of humoral physiology and the sources for his presentation of perfect digestion and excretion. Galen's *On the Natural Faculties*, Pico della Mirandola's *Oration on the Dignity of Man*, Augustine's *City of God*, and the halakhic midrash *Sifré to Numbers* all contribute to the development of a philosophy of eating in *Paradise Lost*. As this philosophy of eating unfolds, we begin to see how prelapsarian acceptance of the perfectly assimilable meal, whether ambrosia or manna, becomes an occasion for virtuous exercise, cultivation of social bonds, and liberating worship.

HUMAN AND ANGELIC CORPOREALITY

Because both gluttony and temperance deal specifically with attitudes toward bodily pleasures, Milton's peculiar interest in bodies in *Paradise Lost* deserves closer consideration here. Much of the information about bodies in Milton's cosmos comes from Raphael, who identifies himself and the other angels as "incorporeal," "purest Spirits," and "pure / Intelligential substances" (5.406, 407–08, 413). The narrator identifies the fallen angels also as "incorporeal Spirits," but this is not to say that angels, faithful or fallen, lack bodies in all respects (1.789). Uriel, the first unfallen angel *Paradise Lost* describes in detail, has a back, a head, shoulders, hair, a "radiant visage," and a good ear, even though his primary responsibility is to serve as the more symbolic eye of God (3.624–53). Taken from Ezekiel 1, even the "four Cherubic shapes" drawing the Chariot of Paternal Deity are said to have bodies and to be "Distinct alike" (6.753, 847). In some sense even the sun, moon, and stars have or are bodies—a fact Milton repeatedly emphasizes (e.g., 7.353; 8.28, 87; 10.1072). Insofar as Milton is nodding to classical thought here, the term "celestial bodies" is more than metaphor, for the planets were considered to have separate intelligences, and to house light, similar to the body housing the soul.[1] It is this division of body and animating intelligence that allows Milton to explain the different days for the creation of light and for the "Sun's Orb, made porous to receive / And drink the liquid Light, firm to retain / Her gather'd beams, great Palace now of Light" (7.361–63). This concept of a vitalized, intelligent, and embodied creation allows the apostrophe to the stars in Adam and Eve's morning prayer, including the invocation of the Sun to "Acknowledge him thy Greater," to be more than metaphoric anthropomorphism (5.172). While such passages complicate any argument regarding monistic and dualistic vocabulary in Milton's works, from a cursory perspective it is apparent that Milton is interested in the body in its various cosmic configurations, whether angelic, planetary, human, animal, botanical, or telluric, even as these bodies differ greatly from form to form.[2]

The need to account for sameness and difference in Western philosophy is manifest as early as the pre-Socratic Parmenides's *On Nature*, which separated the Way of Truth (reality, unity) from the Way of Opinion (that-which-is-not, built on appearances, presuming variety). *On Nature* (bk. 8) also asserts that there can be no creating from nothing, which makes Parmenides one of the earliest writers on cosmic unity, variety, being, and becoming, topics that were of great interest to Milton in his own thoughts on Creation in *Paradise Lost* and *De doctrina Christiana*. Parmenides's Way of Truth opposed Heraclitus's emphasis on change and strife. Hélène Tuzet describes this opposition as the Parmenidean pathos of Unity and the Heraclitean pathos of Becoming, Variety, and Liberation; the two theories were juxtaposed, Arthur Koestler proposed, in the Aristotelian model of the universe, which "solved the basic dilemma by handing over the sub-lunary region to the Materialists, and letting it be governed by Heraclitus's motto 'all is change'; whereas the rest of the universe, eternal and immutable, stood in the sign of the Parmenidean 'nothing ever changes.'"[3] Koestler acknowledges the oversimplification of his account, which is nonetheless instructive. In time, he explains, this "two-storey universe — all basement and loft—was superseded by an elaborately graded, multi-storeyed structure" surviving for "nearly a millennium and a half."[4] The Great Chain of Being, in this view, has been from its beginning an attempt to envision cosmic sameness and difference, permanence and dynamism, unity and variety.

In Aristotelian terms, if all created things arise from the same original matter, if they share a material as well as an efficient cause, correspondence between created things is greater than what might be supposed under the doctrine of Creation *ex nihilo*. In *De doctrina Christiana* Milton peremptorily rejects this prevailing understanding of Creation: "Most moderns contend that everything emerged out of nothing (out of which nothing, I reckon their own opinion originates!)" (OW 8:287). After explaining that neither the Hebrew word for creating, nor the Greek, nor the Latin, implies creation out of nothing, Milton expounds his doctrine of Creation *ex materia* and *ex Deo*, the doctrine that all things were made out of original matter, itself originating in God (OW 8:286, 290). The passage presents God as the material as well as the efficient, formal, and final cause of all creation (OW 8:290–93). This idea of primordial substance being derived from God is important to Milton's understanding of the beauty and variety of creation, and the sovereignty and providence of God:

> What else is it but a sign of [God's] supreme power and supreme boun-
> teousness that such heterogeneous, multiform, and inexhaustible virtue
> should exist in God and that, substantial as it is (for that virtue cannot
> be accidental which admits both of certain degrees, and as it were of
> giving out and withdrawing according to his will), [that] he does not,
> I say, enclose this heterogeneous and substantial virtue within himself
> but sends it out, propagates it, and extends it as far as and in whatever
> way he himself wills. For indeed that original matter is not to be thought
> of as an evil or worthless thing, but as a good thing, a seed bank of every
> subsequent good. It was a substance, and derivable from no other source
> than from the fountain-head of all substance; at first unarranged and
> disorganized, but afterward God arranged it and made it beautiful.
> (OW 8:293)

Here is the original Latin for the last two sentences translated above: "Neque enim materia illa res mala est, aut vilis existimanda, sed bona, omnisque boni postmodum producendi seminarium; Substantia erat, nec aliunde quam ex fonte omnis substantiae derivanda, indigesta modo et incomposita, quam Deus postea digessit et ornavit" (OW 8:292).[5]

There are two observations to make about the Latin. John K. Hale and J. Donald Cullington translate "materia illa" (that matter) as "original matter," as Charles R. Sumner did before them, and the use of this Aristotelian technical term is warranted by the earlier appearance of "materia...prima" in the beginning of this section of the treatise (OW 8:286). Second, Milton's use of the Latin *indigesta* and *digessit* (which Carey translates as "confused" and "ordered," Sumner as "confused" and "digested," Hale and Cullington as "unarranged" and "arranged") suggests the poet's intentional evocation of physiological connotations in describing the Creation.[6] Digestion in an unfallen world is an act of beauty, of art, of *cosmos*.

More generally, the passage above, which is frequently used to identify Milton as a monist materialist, is used by the author himself in a context that highlights the multifarious splendor of Creation — a stupendously "heterogeneous, multiform, and inexhaustible virtue" that characterizes both God and his creative acts, and a potency for individuation that may be undermined when the word "monism" is too quickly applied to this passage. Indeed, the very word "monism" has its various forms and applications so that, as David Bentley Hart informs us and Phillip Donnelly reminds us, we are in the ironic position of needing to ask, "What kind of monism?"[7] For Donnelly, Hart "aptly points out that none of the available monist precedents (whether Stoic or Neoplatonic) really fits with Milton's account" — a position Stephen Fallon has also taken in *Milton among the Philosophers*, praising Milton for his unique contribution to early modern thought even as he traces some of Milton's philosophical influences — but, as Donnelly argues, a nuanced examination of various applications of the term *materia prima* must also differentiate between the terms "matter" and "body."

In his classic text on Milton's cosmogony, Walter Clyde Curry names Avencebrol as the thinker who, combining elements of Aristotelian and

Neoplatonic thought, conceived of "a plurality of forms and matters rooted in a *materia universalis*...which constitutes the ultimate source of the Miltonic postulation of 'one first matter all.'"[8] While the Jewish philosopher's theory of the world as "the product of a constantly deteriorating emanation" lacks the energy and optimism of Milton's own cosmogony, Curry proposed Avencebrol's influence on Milton through Duns Scotus, who follows Avencebrol in naming three different varieties of *materia prima*. Curry specifies that Milton's idea of first matter "corresponds precisely in all respects with Duns Scotus's *materia primo prima*"; he further mentions that Duns Scotus, like Milton's Raphael, describes the cosmos as a tree (*mundus est arbor quaedam pulcherrima*); Duns Scotus's tree has roots of original matter, foliage of changeable accidents, branches of corruptible creatures (*creata corruptibilia*), flowers of rational souls, and fruits of angelic nature.[9] A note proposes that this tree metaphor is a closer parallel to Milton's than is Robert Fludd's, which Denis Saurat had proposed as Milton's model.[10]

Curry describes Duns Scotus's tree as a hierarchy of intellectual powers that Raphael's tree seems to follow, yet there are noteworthy differences. First, Duns Scotus's tree has a divided root, corporal and spiritual, which lacks the Miltonic fusion of body and spirit; and second, as Curry admits, "alien to Duns and Avencebrol" is Milton's new doctrine "of a dynamic force or power which is able to overleap the bounds proportioned to its kind."[11] Locating any of Milton's ideas in a single primary source is almost certain folly, for he was no less independently minded than he was well read. Curry's enlistment of Origen, Avencebrol, and Duns Scotus's versions of first matter and Stephen Fallon's examination of Anne Conway, Ralph Cudworth, Pierre Gassendi, and others in his analysis of Milton's philosophy wisely remind us not to interpret Milton's view of matter by blind application of pure Aristotelian technical terms, or of the technical terms of any one particular thinker, for that matter. Whether using the terms "material monism," "animist materialism," some version of "hylozoism," whether calling the "dark materials" of Milton's Creation *materia prima, materia primo prima, materia universalis*, or even *ylem*, we must take care not to assume that Miltonic thought may be described by these terms in precisely the way his predecessors and contemporaries used them.[12] Indeed, he may have thought of these terms in more than one way at once.

We return to the passage from *De doctrina* above, beginning with Milton's reference to that matter (*materia illa,* translated "original matter"), which originally was *indigessa,* but which afterward God *digessit.* Neither God's singularity nor the description of the origin of all as first matter coming from God is under question here, but his power and bounties are emitted, extended, and diversely manifest. Milton insists that all existence, all being, all positive good materially originates in God and is further adorned and enhanced by God's shaping, ordering, and *digesting* it. A chasm separates this prolific, giving, multifarious divine action from the monomaniacal, inward-turning egoism of Milton's Satan.

Milton's materialism extends to the concept of the human soul, as Milton (again perfunctorily) states, "Surely almost everyone agrees that all form — to which category the human soul also belongs — is produced from the power of matter" (OW 8:307). He bases his conclusion on the principle "that man is an animate being [animal], inherently and properly one and individual, not twofold or separable — or, as is commonly declared, combined or composed from two mutually and generically different and distinct natures, namely soul and body — but that the whole man is soul, and the soul is man; namely a body or substance which is individual, animated, sensitive, and rational" (OW 8:303).[13] The interdependence between soul and body, along with the connection between God-matter and Creation, implies a constitutional similarity between human and angel, and in fact among all created beings. This connection surfaces in *Paradise Lost* in Raphael's discourse:

> O *Adam,* one Almighty is, from whom
> All things proceed, and up to him return,
> If not deprav'd from good, created all
> Such to perfection, one first matter all,
> Indu'd with various forms, various degrees
> Of substance, and, in things that live, of life;

> But more refin'd, more spiritous, and pure,
> As nearer to him plac't or nearer tending
> Each in thir several active Spheres assign'd,
> Till body up to spirit work, in bounds
> Proportion'd to each kind. (5.469–79)

In this view of Creation, boundaries are still relevant, even though movement beyond them is expected: all creation proceeds from and returns to God, matter "Indu'd with various forms, various degrees / Of substance." The natural mobility of Milton's cosmos is staggering: not only are creatures given room to move within "thir several active Spheres," but even these roomy limits are transcended when "body up to spirit work[s]." There are "bounds / Proportion'd to each kind," that is, limits to what any particular kind of created being can actively do, conforming to the nature of that being, but even these natural boundaries may be transgressed or surpassed, as happens when the flowers and fruit of the Great Tree are "by gradual scale sublim'd" (5.483). Raphael's assertion that everything derives from "one first matter" explains how he may truly eat and incorporate earthly produce. Milton insists that Raphael actually eats the food Adam offers:

> So down they sat,
> And to thir viands fell, nor seemingly
> The Angel, nor in mist, the common gloss
> Of Theologians, but with keen dispatch
> Of real hunger, and concoctive heat
> To transubstantiate. (5.433–38)

Raphael experiences real hunger and truly eats food that is actually metabolized and assimilated into his substance. This process is meant to be both wondrous and natural; the theologically loaded word "transubstantiate" suggests that Edenic and angelic eating exemplify Milton's alternative to the Roman Catholic sacrament of the Eucharist.[14] Raphael's "one first matter" speech continues with an analogy of the cosmos that is also a synecdochic example of the way sublimation works within it:

> So from the root
> Springs lighter the green stalk, from thence the leaves
> More aery, last the bright consummate flow'r
> Spirits odorous breathes: flow'rs and thir fruit,
> Man's nourishment, by gradual scale sublim'd,
> To vital spirits aspire, to animal,
> To intellectual, give both life and sense,
> Fancy and understanding, whence the Soul
> Reason receives, and reason is her being,
> Discursive, or Intuitive; discourse
> Is oftest yours, the latter most is ours,
> Differing but in degree, of kind the same. (*PL* 5.479–490)

Milton's view of matter allows a credible interaction between human and angel within his poetry, as well as a credible potential for human transformation to a more glorified version of the self, one sharing in angelic qualities to a greater degree. These passages from *De doctrina Christiana* and *Paradise Lost* provide the rudiments for the monism-driven criticism of the past century.[15]

Rather than refute or articulate any consensus on Milton's monism, this chapter seeks to provide an alternative perspective, for differences as well as similarities in Milton's cosmos must be acknowledged. We recall that the divine act of Creation involves both the joining of "like things to like," and the preliminary separation of useful, vital matter from tartareous dregs (*PL* 7.240). In poetics, metaphor ceases to exist not only if there is no similarity between compared objects but also if the two become so completely conflated into an individual unity that no distinctions can be made, and every analogy is a false one if it treats the items compared as identical. Similarly, the concept of materialist monism loses its import when one ceases to wonder how a certain part of the corporeal world may be said to be incorporeal. Men becoming angels is no longer remarkable if we tacitly assume that angels are men and no more, or that men are angels and no more. Transubstantiation loses its glory when the focus is only on the shared substance or original matter of all creation. Precisely because many critics of *Paradise Lost* have successfully argued that yes, there are different forms in creation, but it is important to remember that in Milton's world they share the same substance, are all composed of God-matter, I find it worthwhile to iterate that yes, Milton presents the created world as all "God-kind," but it is important to remember that he also presents formal differences. Because Adam acknowledges these differences to the point of obeisance — "As to a superior Nature, bowing low" (5.360) — Raphael finds it worthwhile to propose that things in heaven and earth are "each to other like more than on Earth is thought" (576). As the introduction to this book observes, Adam needs repeated reassurances of the adequacy of his hospitality toward his heavenly guest: "unsavory food perhaps...Food not of Angels, yet accepted so...yet what compare?" (5.401, 465, 467). Adapting his message to suit the disposition of his audience, Raphael begins to relate the War in Heaven by emphasizing resemblances, "lik'ning spiritual to corporal forms" (573).[16] Today, when "on Earth is thought" much about the similarities and less about the distinctions between manifestations of matter in Milton's prelapsarian cosmos, we may need to adjust our interpretation of Raphael's message in order to enjoy again the wonder of the transformation he proposes for Adam — a transformation that is essential to Milton's philosophy of eating.

I acknowledge that the search for terra firma in Raphael's conversation is highly problematic. The angel's words may be doubted since they come from a being distanced from human experience, and since his account of heavenly activity must be accommodated to a human audience through metaphor. In this valley of shadows of interpretive ambiguity, there are pits of indeterminacy and aporia on all sides. This chapter, however, considers Raphael's message on his own terms. Following Milton's approach to the theory of accommodation in *De doctrina Christiana*, my initial approach is to acknowledge that human understanding of the divine is necessarily limited, but that Raphael can best communicate with Adam if Adam accepts his message and his stories as literally true, even as Raphael warns Adam that his message depends on analogies (cf. OW 8:27–33). As the reader of fiction is called upon to suspend disbelief and enter the world of the poem on its own terms, Raphael expects Adam to accept that his message is presented in a way best suited to his own understanding. For the purposes of this chapter's inquiry, Raphael's description of heavenly beings and their activity, and Milton's description of angels like Raphael, will be evaluated as if literally true within the world of the poem. This approach extends to the evaluation of Raphael's hypothesis that humans could become like the angels, a change that is only meaningful if humans and angels are essentially different. Of the changes to the human form that would attend its metamorphosis to the angelic, three will receive particular attention in this space: the angels have a flexibility of form, a more glorious proper form, and the diffusion of senses and bodily aspects.

Earth may be the shadow of heaven, and earthly beings may even rise to celestial heights, but the shape-shifting of ethereal forms distinguishes angels, even fallen ones, from humankind:

> For Spirits when they please
> Can either Sex assume, or both; so soft
> And uncompounded is thir Essence pure,
> Not ti'd or manacl'd with joint or limb,
> Nor founded on the brittle strength of bones,
> Like cumbrous flesh; but in what shape they choose
> Dilated or condens't, bright or obscure,
> Can execute their aery purposes. (PL 1.423–30)

Since angels are unconstrained by a definite bodily shape, and since, traditionally considered, constraint or delineation of one's being is a primary attribute of the body with respect to the soul, angels are, at least in this sense, incorporeal. Lewis explains Milton's angelic beings using Thomistic terms: "A *body* is in a place in such a way as to be bounded by it, i.e. it occupies a place *circumscriptive*. An angel is in a place not *circumscriptive*, for it is not bounded by it, but *definitive*, because it is in that one place and *not* in any other."[17] Chapter 3 observes how the fallen angels have the residual advantage of having once been closer to God; their nature contrasts with the human form, which is "ti'd" and "manacl'd" by "brittle...bones" and "cumbrous flesh." Thus the narrator relates the shrinking of "incorporeal Spirits" filling the great hall of Pandaemonium — incorporeal not because they are immaterial but because they are of ether, rarefied matter, an "empyreal substance" (*PL* 1.789, 1.117). Walter Clyde Curry explains the ether of which Milton's angels are composed: "Here it is necessary to understand that Milton is not following that tradition which conceives of ether as a fifth essence which differs in kind from all the four elements. He holds rather to the historical theory that ether is a matter sublimated from the four elements, or merely a purer form of air and fire."[18] This understanding of ether accounts for Milton's apparently interchangeable use of the words "ethereal" and "empyreal," and is compatible with Uriel's account of the creation of the elements in *Paradise Lost* 3.714–19. In *De doctrina Christiana*, Milton divides all being into the visible and the invisible world, the latter of which belongs to the angels, yet all forms, visible or invisible, derive from original matter (OW 8:291–97). The stuff of angels may be "Dilated or condensed," but, rarefied and flexible as it may be, it is still "stuff."

Despite their shape-shifting powers, Milton's angels have a proper form that further distinguishes them from humans even as it invites human companionship. This, however, depends on angelic (gracious) condescension. Generally anthropoid with wings, the angel form allows conversation with humans to turn on common or analogous experiences — eating, for example, or an embrace (5.633, 8.626). When God commissions Raphael, "sociable Spirit," "affable Arch-angel," to meet Adam "as friend with friend," Raphael visits in "his proper shape," with the six wings of a seraph (5.221, 5.229, 5.276, 7.41). Yet even in his human perfection, Adam first addresses the angel with a politeness and formality that recognizes their difference: "Native of Heav'n, for other place / None can than Heav'n such glorious shape contain" (5.361–62). Adam, of course, is engaging in the rhetoric of the gracious host, but it is true within the poem that angels are distinct from humans not only in that they are unrestricted by shape, but also in that their "proper shape" is far more "glorious" than those of humans. That one form or shape of an angel is more identifiably his own than any other shape he may choose to assume is evident not only from the bard's narration of Raphael's appearance but also from the effect of Ithuriel's spear, which returns the form of a toadlike Satan "to its own likeness" (4.813). Even the rebel angels are described as "Godlike shapes and forms / Excelling human" (1.358–59).[19]

Milton especially emphasizes this formal superiority after the Fall. Now "Insufferably bright" to the human senses, Michael visits Adam "not in his shape Celestial, but as Man / Clad to meet Man," yet, rather than "as friend with friend," Michael arrives as a warrior-king to meet a subordinate (9.1084, 11.239–40). Michael's condescension to human form thus far does not show similarity between man and angel but rather suggests the added difference of human sin that widens the natural gap between them. As divine glory becomes oppressive to Adam's sin-darkened eyes, it is no longer meet that "God or Angel Guest / With Man, as with his Friend, familiar . . . / . . . sit indulgent, and with him partake / Rural repast" (9.1–4). Formal differences between human being and angel are then accentuated after the Fall, partly by this new need for greater angelic condescension, and partly by the manner in which Michael fulfills his commission: as an aloof and authoritative messenger, conveying majesty without terror (11.111, 232–37). Even if we attribute the tonal difference between the pre- and postlapsarian angelophanies as greatly due to the disparate "personalities" of Raphael and Michael, God carefully selects his messenger on both occasions — the sociable six-winged seraph before the Fall, the majestic military commander obscuring his angelic form afterward. Surely the visible change in God's delegates unsettles Adam, for it is another sign of heaven's distance and distaste for sin. Even before Michael speaks a word, Adam has observed enough to question whether Raphael's hypothesis of sublimation was yet viable. To become as the angels, he would have to acquire a flexibility of form, but his default form must also be glorified.

A third key distinction between human and angel is that each sense is diffused throughout the angelic body. It appears that angels have the advantage for which Milton's Samson pines:

> why was the sight
> To such a tender ball as th' eye confin'd?
> So obvious and so easy to be quench't,
> And not as feeling through all parts diffus'd,
> That she might look at will through every pore?   (*SA* 93–97)

While the human body comprises distinct organs, angelic "Spirits…
live throughout / Vital in every part"; "All Heart they live, all Head,
all Eye, all Ear, / All Intellect, all Sense" (*PL* 6.344–45, 350–51). The
division of labor among the organs of the human body and the lack of
that division within the angelic body is significant even if the poem's
dramatic content does not always support this information. An angel
may be, for example, "all Eye," but Uriel, whose particular duty is to act
as God's eyes, cannot see Satan when his back is turned (3.624, 650).

The fact that the angels, those "pure / Intelligential substances,"
are, among other things, "all sense," implies the union of body and
spirit (5.407–08). Yet the angels are not said to be "all entrails" or "all
viscera," as if this were too ignoble to be said of a spiritual creature.
Although Raphael politely enjoys human food, digesting it seems to
be not a typical activity but an act of extraordinary condescension.
The omission of digestive organs in Milton's angelic blazon is initially
unimpressive, but it becomes noteworthy when, by contrast, this passage describes "frail man" as having "Entrails, Heart or Head, Liver or
Reins [kidneys]," each of which performs a specific function, and none
of which can perform the tasks of another (6.345–46). Milton then
appears to include in his anatomy of angels the analogues to the human
nervous and circulatory systems (William Harvey published his work
On the Motion of the Heart and Blood in 1628), but not to the digestive
or excretory systems. As Raphael demonstrates, Milton's angels literally digest food; however, like angelic lovemaking, the angelic digestive
process is completed without specific organs of the lower body. Since
"if Spirits embrace, / Total they mix," one may surmise that angelic
eating, a second means of incorporating another, likewise involves
one's entire being (8.626–27). In the world of *Paradise Lost*, there are
similarities between eros and eating, and between Adam and angel,

but even in the midst of presenting his case for the similarity and connection between humans and angels, Milton acknowledges their differences. The angels eat, drink, speak, embrace, and, when necessary,
engage in war, but their modes of participating in these activities differ
from human modes. That angels participate in lovemaking betokens
their similarity to humans; that they do so without the constraints of
flesh betrays their essential difference. That an angel can partake of an
earthly meal "with keen dispatch of real hunger" further demonstrates
their sameness, but the distinction between human and angel is held
in place when we consider the limits to this reciprocity. Angels have
no abdominal viscera, and Adam has no organs designed to digest a
heavenly meal — at least not yet.

TRANSFORMATIVE EATING

All this may seem insignificant, but the differences between humans
and angels become especially meaningful once Raphael hypothesizes
that humans have the potential to be transformed — presumably to a
form more flexible, more glorious, and less dependent on organs with
specialized functions. Milton's task is to make this hypothetical transformation both credible and incredible, at once acceptable to the imagination and marvelous, natural and yet supernatural. And to do this
he attends to correspondences and differences among created beings
using Aristotelian language, and he borrows from Galenic theories of
digestion to introduce to quotidian rhythms the wondrous possibility
of metamorphosis.

More specifically than the principle that all derives from "one first
matter," the principle that higher beings contain all the faculties of
lower beings provides credence to angelic condescension and human
aspiration. Milton partly follows Aristotle's *De anima*, which posits that the human (rational) soul contains the powers of the lower
nutritive soul of plants and the sensitive soul of animals.[20] Milton's *De
doctrina Christiana* coincides with this ancient idea: "Spirit, being the
more excellent substance, virtually (as they say) and eminently contains
within itself what is undoubtedly the inferior substance — just as the

spiritual and rational faculty contains the corporeal one, that is, the sentient and vegetative faculty" (OW 8:295). So in *Paradise Lost* the faculties of inferior natures are nestled within higher ones, a concept that lends further credence to all analogies between human and angel, and legitimizes their shared pleasure in material food. As Raphael assures Adam,

> What [God] gives
> ...to man in part
> Spiritual, may of purest Spirits be found
> No ingrateful food: and food alike those pure
> Intelligential substances require
> As doth your Rational.   (5.404–09)

Again, Raphael is a gratifying and grateful guest, reassuring Adam by acknowledging both his need to eat and his pleasure in their shared meal. The similarity of angelic to human eating is tempered by the fact that, in Raphael's analogy, angels, those "pure / Intelligential substances," correspond not to the entire human being, but to the rational part of humans in particular; however, as Raphael explains, the angels and the rational part of humans both depend on and include the "grosser" aspects of being:

> and both contain
> Within them every lower faculty
> Of sense, whereby they hear, see, smell, touch, taste,
> Tasting concoct, digest, assimilate,
> And corporeal to incorporeal turn.   (5.409–13)

Milton accounts for correspondences between humans and angels both because the rational part of humanity is similar to the intelligential angels, and because both angels and humans "contain / Within them every lower faculty / of sense." As members of a higher order of being, angels have the abilities of humans as well as those powers more distinctively angelic. This nestling hierarchy of properties works within the orders of the angels as well, and has been used convincingly to explain Milton's seemingly arbitrary use of angelic titles. Raphael and Uriel are each named both seraph and archangel, for example; according to Dionysian angelology, a seraph may be called by the name of any lower degree of angel, a cherub may be called anything but a seraph, and so on.[21] Yet exclusive properties are not indefinitely so. Raphael describes how plants, through a series of nutritive sublimations, "to vital spirits aspire, to animal, / To intellectual," in which each higher stage enfolds the faculties of the lower stages (5.484–85).

Among the orders of creation, the higher, "purer" creatures have a greater debt to the "grosser" creatures below them, and so ascent enjoins gratitude, not gloating. As Burton writes in *The Anatomy of Melancholy*, referring to Aristotle's *De anima*, "the inferior [divisions of the soul] may be alone, but the superior cannot subsist without the other; so *sensible* includes *vegetal*, *rational* both; which are contained in it (saith Aristotle) as a triangle in a quadrangle."[22] While gratitude is at its simplest a looking upward in thanksgiving to a superior being, it also includes respect and appreciation for the lower creatures and aspects of being on which one's existence depends. The airiest fragrance of the most delicate flower depends on its rootedness.

The material nourishment humans depend upon and Raphael enjoys, however, requires a conversion before it may be assimilated into the body. Like Adam, Raphael eats "with keen dispatch / Of real hunger, and concoctive heat / To transubstantiate," yet the transubstantiating effects of digestion complicate the comparison (*PL* 5.436–38). Angels convert food into their own substance; humans convert the same food into *their own* substance; it does not follow that angelic and human substances are the same. It is not simply that you are what you eat; what you eat also becomes changed into *you*.[23]

By emphasizing the metabolic properties of digestion, Milton is in one respect preferring the Galenic to the Paracelsan understanding of digestion: Paracelsus argued that the nutrients forming our bones, blood, bodily tissue, and so on, were present in the food we consume, and that digestion was ultimately separation; the older Galenic model emphasizes the transformative conversion of bread into blood. For Galen, digestion requires *alteration* (*alloiōsis*), a technical term for qualitative change, directly derived from Aristotle's work "On Complete

Alteration of Substance," and originating in Hippocrates. Examples of Galenic alteration include *genesis*, in which "something comes into existence which did not exist previously," and *assimilation*, in which "inflowing material becomes assimilated to that which has already come into existence," as when food is converted to bodily tissue.[24] Regarding digestion, Galen argues, "nobody will suppose that bread represents a kind of meeting-place for bone, flesh, nerve, and all other parts, and that each of these subsequently becomes separated in the body and goes to join its own kind; before any separation takes place, the whole of the bread obviously becomes blood.... And clearly this disproves the view of those who consider the elements unchangeable."[25] With similar impatience Galen dismisses his detractors in the opening pages to *On the Natural Faculties*, insisting on substantial, not merely accidental, alteration: "The Sophists, however, while allowing that bread in turning into blood becomes changed as regards sight, taste, and touch, will not agree that this change occurs in reality.... Others (such as Anaxagoras) will have it that the qualities do exist in it, but that they are unchangeable and immutable from eternity to eternity, and that these apparent alterations are brought about by separation and combination. Now, if I were to go out of my way to confute these people, my subsidiary task would be greater than my main one."[26]

Galen's hasty dismissal ironically reminds us that there were indeed alternative theories available during his lifetime, some resurrected in the early modern period. Paracelsus's concept of generation and digestion as separation was a prominent sixteenth century alternative to the Galenic understanding of alteration, and since there has been notable scholarship on Milton's Paracelsan influences, the opposition between these philosophical digestive models warrants consideration. The sixteenth century Swiss physician and theologian Thomas Erastus exemplifies the energy with which some early modern thinkers opposed Paracelsan theories of digestion and generation. Walter Pagel summarizes Erastus's censure of Paracelsus with reference to the Anaxagorean ideas Galen dismisses: "Generation to Paracelsus is merely the separation of objects preformed in an Anaxagorean 'Chaos.' Hence in his world there is room neither for corruption nor for the transformation of things. Thus according to Paracelsus, the bread which we eat is not converted into blood, but already contains it. If that were so, however, where is the art which succeeds in making blood from bread? Paracelsus in his pestilential heresy places unlimited faith in this art which is but an ape of nature and unlike the latter is nothing divine."[27] In other words, Erastus insisted that digestion must be transformative and divine — both creative and supernatural.

Paradise Lost draws from both Galen and Paracelsus. John Rumrich mentions that "from the time of Paracelsus..., the phenomenon of digestion justified the work of the alchemists."[28] In a note, he attributes William Empson with "first hear[ing] the echoes of Paracelsan alchemy in Milton's use of digestion to convey the substantial unity of matter and spirit."[29] Michael Lieb asserts that alchemy is "intimately related to the creational dimension of the poem," pointing to "a well-established alchemical tradition associating Christ and the Philosopher's Stone," and quoting Evelyn Underhill to explain that if "alchemy in its truest sense is a spiritualizing art involving a movement from the physical to the spiritual, an 'ascension to that perfect state' which is God, then in *Paradise Lost* natural alchemy is everywhere."[30] It is important to note that Lieb adds, "at his disposal Milton also had the degenerate tradition, alchemy as a charlatan's art used to dupe others for the purpose of material aggrandizement. If Chaucer dramatized such an idea in his Canon and Jonson in his Subtle, Milton made that idea an integral part of his Satan." Lieb then associates the "debased approach to alchemy" with "equating materiality with spirituality and the consequent failure to achieve the spiritual by means of the material."[31] As previously mentioned, John Rogers argues that when Milton follows Paracelsus in describing the necessary purging of tartareous dregs at the onset of Creation — that is, describing creation as separation — he problematizes the monist elements of the poem.[32] I would qualify these notable examinations of Milton's use of alchemy and of Paracelsus by adding that often the sources for Milton's physiology predate Paracelsus, that Paracelsus retained many Galenic ideas even while trying to distinguish his works from those of Galen, and that Paracelsus was not willing to allow for transubstantiative eating, a critical component to the Raphael discourse.

Both Galen and Milton's Raphael extend this transubstantiation to the eater as well as the eaten. According to Galen, alteration affects both food and body, and, though a natural faculty, it demonstrates purposeful artistry through digestion and bodily formation: "this faculty we state to be artistic — nay, the best and highest art [*technēn*] — doing everything for some purpose, so that there is nothing ineffective or superfluous, or capable of being better disposed."[33] Following Aristotelian teleology, Galenic digestion is ingeniously artistic — not only resourceful and sustainable but creative and renovating. The rudiments of a larger transformation are also in Galen: "Just as everything we eat or drink becomes altered in quality, so of course also does the altering factor itself become altered.... Since, therefore, not only is the nourishment altered by the creature nourished, but the latter itself also undergoes some slight alteration, this slight alteration must necessarily become considerable in the course of time, and thus properties resulting from prolonged habit must come to be on a par with natural properties."[34]

Likewise, Raphael famously hypothesizes that this transubstantiative eating over an extended period improves not only the food, but also the eater:

> time may come when men
> With Angels may participate, and find
> No inconvenient Diet, nor too light Fare.
> And from these corporal nutriments perhaps
> Your bodies may at last turn all to spirit,
> Improv'd by tract of time, and wing'd ascend
> Ethereal, as wee, or may at choice
> Here or in Heav'nly Paradises dwell;
> If ye be found obedient, and retain
> Unalterably firm his love entire,
> Whose progeny you are. Meanwhile enjoy

>   Your fill what happiness this happy state
>   Can comprehend, incapable of more.   (*PL* 5.493–505)

The rarefaction over time of the soul who eats well is a more expansive, external manifestation of the transformation that Raphael both describes and exemplifies: the conversion of "corporeal [food] to incorporeal [substance]" through digestion (5.413). There is a critical but surmountable difference between humans and ethereal beings. Raphael speculates that the metamorphosis of human to angel (or rather to a human with angelic properties) would be enacted by the very natural activity of eating, through "corporal nutriments" and the digestive "tract of time," yet in a way this activity is beyond one's nature — it involves alteration, not just in converting food to one's own substance, but also in transforming oneself by means of eating that very food, converting "bod[y] . . . to spirit" and thereby becoming more capable of consuming what was earlier an "inconvenient Diet" and "too light Fare." The suggested means for this evolving includes eating and remaining obedient and steadfast in God's love over time. And, in Eden, obedience and love are one and the same, demonstrated both through actively chosen abstention from forbidden fruit and through its converse — gratefully eating anything else from the vegetable bounties of paradise.

Fundamentally transformative and yet mundanely natural, unfallen eating provides the perfect metonym for the ambiguous corporeality of intelligential spirits, and for the substantial yet gradual metamorphosis of the human form. Both before and after the Fall, from the perspective of Adam looking upward in humility, the differences between him and his angel visitors are vast. From the perspective of Raphael before the Fall, however, there is always an opportunity for the gracious condescension of angels, and the dangling prospect of a means of ascent for humankind. Correspondences between heaven and earth enable angels to find among human fare "no ingrateful food," and offer humans the opportunity in time to find in the food of angels "no inconvenient Diet."

Beyond Galenic alteration, there are several precedents from which Milton could have developed Raphael's ideas about the potential for metamorphosis from human to angelic, from body to "all . . . spirit," from earth to heaven, and indeed from that which proceeds from God to that which returns to him. The angel's hypothesis holds similarities with the Stoic philosophy of creation returning to its origins, and with the classical idea of apotheosis, or the divinization of emperor, hero, or ancestor.

This latter idea has had its detractors, both humorous and reformatory. In Seneca's fanciful *Apocolocyntosis divii Claudii*, the dying Claudius becomes a gourd, not a god. Suetonius provides another reproof of apotheosis in the skeptical lament of the dying emperor Vespasian: "Woe is me. Methinks I'm turning into a god." Dying with all the dignity that the symptoms of diarrhea would permit, Vespasian's last words registered the incongruence between Rome's tradition of divinizing its dead rulers and the crudity of his own passing: "An emperor ought to die standing."[35] When Virgil considers the decorum of divinization in the *Aeneid*, he has the good Arcadian king Evander explain that the way up is not to scorn stooping. "Austere Evander" welcomes Aeneas into his home with a reminder that heroism requires humility:

> In victory Hercules
> Bent for this lintel, and these royal rooms
> Were grand enough for him. Friend, have the courage
> To care little for wealth, and shape yourself,
> You too, to merit godhood. Do not come
> Disdainfully into our needy home.[36]

Virgil reminds those who would be morally endangered by too eagerly embracing the cult of the emperor that such an advantageous transformation depends on both humility and merit.

The connection between humility and growing godlike continues in patristic theology with the doctrine of *theosis*, variously entertained by many early Christian theologians, and variously defined as the complete sanctification, glorification, or even divinization of the faithful. In most configurations of the doctrine, there is an expressed need for both divine grace and human merit in this process. The expounding of the doctrine of *theosis* often included explication of Psalm 82:6 ("I have said, 'Ye are gods'"); Milton cites this verse three times in *De doctrina*

Christiana, and considered with John 10:34 (where Jesus quotes the psalm) this verse becomes a passage of particular interest to Milton in his chapters on the Son of God and on the covenant of grace and the law of God (OW 8:137, 165, 171, 677). To the words of the Psalmist and of John the Evangelist Milton adds "those of Paul — 1 Cor. 8:5–6: *even if there be such as are called Gods...yet for us there is one God, that Father from whom* [are] *all things,*" and "those of Peter — 2 Pet. 1:4: *so that through these things you might be made sharers or partakers of the divine nature*" (OW 8:137; cf. 8:71). Milton emphasizes the paradox that God remains holy and separate from his creation even as humans are granted participation in the divine nature. While patristic exhortations to seek godhood intimate free will and human effort, the simple possibility of *theosis* was usually attributed to grace and the incarnation. The idea that God became human so that humans could become God (or gods, or sons of God) is found in the works of Irenaeus, Clement of Alexandria, Athanasius of Alexandria, Gregory of Nyssa, and others.[37] In his *Exposition on the Book of Psalms,* Augustine considers the doctrine of divinization in his commentary on scriptural references to "gods" and "sons of gods": "See in the same Psalm [82] those to whom he says, '*I have said, You are gods, and children of the Highest all; but you shall die like men, and fall like one of the princes.*' It is evident then, that He has called men gods, that are deified of His Grace, not born of His Substance." Citing John 1:12, Augustine then observes, "If we have been made sons of God, we have also been made gods: but this is the effect of Grace adopting, not of nature generating."[38] Characteristically for patristic advocates of the doctrine of *theosis,* Augustine emphasizes the need for divine grace to effect this radical transformation. In book 8 of *The City of God,* Augustine more mildly speculates that we might become like the angels in spirit if we imitate them in good will.[39] In both of these instances, Augustine's speculations on transcending one's human limits are for a postlapsarian audience, constituting a serious theological doctrine for the fallen that shares ideas with some of the more radical moments in Raphael's hypothesis for human metamorphosis.

The idea of humans growing into some measure of divinity is influentially expressed in Boethius's *Consolation of Philosophy.* Arguing from the idea that God is the source of all things and is happiness itself, Lady Philosophy presents a version of the doctrine of *theosis* to the prisoner: "Since men become happy by achieving happiness, and happiness is itself divinity, clearly they become happy by attaining divinity. Now just as men become just by acquiring justice, and wise by acquiring wisdom, so by the same argument they become gods once they have acquired divinity. Hence every happy person is God; God is by nature one only, but nothing prevents the greatest possible number from sharing in that divinity."[40] The connection between *theosis* and felicity resounds in *Paradise Lost* in the implied parallel between Raphael's hypothesis of human transformative ascent and Michael's endorsement of the "paradise within." For Boethius, these targets are essentially the same, and both the ascent toward God and the interior state of happiness depend on what humans do with their free will. This happy divinity is itself the result of freely choosing to live virtuously. Thus, Lady Philosophy explains, using an Augustinian expression of evil as privative, humans may ascend or descend the Chain of Being, changing their nature through their good or bad behavior:

> Since goodness alone can raise a person above the rank of human, it must follow that wickedness deservedly imposes subhuman status on those whom it has dislodged from the human condition. What follows from this is that you cannot regard as a man one who is disfigured by vices. A man who in seizing the possessions of others is consumed by greed is comparable to a wolf. The aggressive and restless man who devotes his tongue to disputes can be considered a dog. The underhand plotter who rejoices in stealthy theft can be likened to young foxes.... In this sense he who abandons goodness and ceases to be a man cannot rise to the status of a god, and so is transformed into an animal.[41]

The verses that follow exemplify the Christian classicists' habit of moralizing Homer. Boethius reenvisions the doctrine of *theosis* and degeneration, of ethically propelled movement along the Chain of Being, with reference to one of the oldest myths of Western literature, the story of Odysseus and Circe. With mindful temperance and divine moly, Odysseus withstands Circe's charms and saves his shipmates from permanent transformation into beasts. With virtue and grace, so might the Christian attain new heights and support his fellow human being.

Giovanni Pico della Mirandola gives a similar description of Adam's created potential in his *Oration on the Dignity of Man* (1486). Joseph Wittreich argues for Milton's familiarity with and use of this influential manifesto for Renaissance humanism, shaping his argument from *Areopagitica*.[42] There are similarities to be found in *Paradise Lost* as well. In Pico della Mirandola's *Oration*, God tells newly formed Adam of his especially malleable form:

> The nature of all other creatures is defined and restricted within laws which We have laid down; you, by contrast, impeded by no such restrictions, may, by your own free will, to whose custody We have assigned you, trace for yourself the lineaments of your own nature. I have placed you at the very center of the world, so that from that vantage point you may with greater ease glance round about you on all that the world contains. We have made you a creature neither of heaven nor of earth, neither mortal nor immortal, in order that you may, as the free and proud shaper of your own being, fashion yourself in the form you may prefer. It will be in your power to descend to the lower, brutish forms of life; you will be able, through your own decision, to rise again to the superior orders whose life is divine.[43]

This is a bold precedent for Raphael's hypothesis that humans may not only ascend to angelic heights but also improve their very nature in the process. Like Milton and Boethius, Pico has great interest in the physicality of such a metamorphosis and the importance of free will. *The Oration* continues:

> But upon man, at the moment of his creation, God bestowed seeds pregnant with all possibilities, the germs of every form of life. Whichever of these a man shall cultivate, the same will mature and bear fruit in him. If vegetative, he will become a plant; if sensual, he will become brutish; if rational, he will reveal himself a heavenly being; if intellectual, he will be an angel and the son of God. And if, dissatisfied with the lot of all

creatures, he should recollect himself into the center of his own unity, he will there become one spirit with God, in the solitary darkness of the Father, Who is set above all things, himself transcend all creatures.[44]

Such a transformation, so nearly joining creature with creator, bears marks of the influence of Augustine, Neoplatonism, Aristotle, and Plato. Although Milton read Augustine directly, Pico della Mirandola's humanist treatise provides another link between Augustine and Milton, strengthening evidence for the influence and persistence of the idea that humans were created to physically return to God, and that, after the Fall, God became human so that humans might become gods. Milton warns his readers that biblical assertions that humans might become sharers in the divine nature (2 Pet. 1:4) refer to participation in the divine image rather than the essence of God (OW 8:33), but he also, as we have seen, asserts that all matter originates in God, and he writes of "complete glorification" and the "transformation of the living" at the last judgment (OW 8:879).

While *De doctrina Christiana* reserves ultimate human transformation for the time of the Second Coming of Christ, Pico provides a significant precedent for Milton in emphasizing Adam's potential to ascend the Great Chain. Granted, this metabolic power is in Pico the peculiar prerogative of humanity. We find the doctrine preserved in *The Courtier's Academy*, J. Kepers's Elizabethan translation (London, 1598) of Count Annibale Romei's *Discorsi* (1586):

> Live, O Adam, in what life pleaseth thee best and take unto thyself those gifts which thou esteemest most dear. From this so liberal a grant had our free will its original, so that it is in our power to live like a plant, living creature, like a man, and lastly like an angel: for if a man addict himself only to feeding and nourishment he becometh a plant, if to things sensual he is a brute beast, if to things reasonable and civil he growth a celestial creature; but if he exalt the beautiful gift of his mind to things invisible and divine he transformeth himself into an angel and, to conclude, becometh the son of God.[45]

While Raphael presents an all-inclusive vision of the cosmos ("if not deprav'd") returning to God "by gradual scale sublim'd," Adam's account provides evidence that, in conformity with the idea of humanity's special position found in Pico and in Romei, lower animals have less of a capacity to change (*PL* 5.471, 483). When Adam recounts the naming of the animals, he tells Raphael that the fish "pay [him] fealty" without a formal visit, "Not hither summon'd, since they cannot change / Thir Element, to draw the thinner Air" (8.344–48). This limitation may be presumed temporary, as is the human inability to find sustenance in angels' air and angels' food, but it does underscore the phenomenal importance Milton attaches to the gift of free will with its assistance ascending or descending the scale of nature.

"NOR DOTH THE MOON NO NOURISHMENT EXHALE"

Milton took extraordinary measures to explain the logistic possibilities of transformative ascent. Hypothetically, as unfallen Adam improves his nature, he will find himself in an intermediate state between his original position and that of the angels; that is, he will enter the earthly heavens, narrowing the formal and spatial gaps that distance him from the angels and ultimately from God. The moon represents one possible intermediate realm and an important liminal sphere — not for dichotomizing the mutable and the eternal, for heaven itself enjoys "grateful vicissitude," but for uniting the earthly and the ethereal. Milton also uses the moon to exemplify the role of celestial bodies as both consumers and suppliers of nourishment. The moon therefore both demonstrates how celestial bodies might actively participate in Milton's chain of eating and provides a transitional home for humans who might grow more rarefied with faithful eating over time.

Some of Milton's speculations on the moon's cosmic role are just that — speculative. In book 3, the narrator contrasts the Paradise of Fools, home of all things "abortive, monstrous, or unkindly mixt," with "the neighboring Moon": "Those argent Fields [of the moon] more likely habitants, / Translated Saints, or middle Spirits hold / Betwixt th' Angelical and Human kind" (3.456, 459–62). The oddest feature of this passage is that its viewpoint can be interpreted as none other than that of the poet speaking to his modern reader. Within the drama of the poem, there can yet be no "Translated Saints" because Adam and Eve are the only humans alive.[46] Considering the moon as land for "Translated Saints" and "middle Spirits," Milton proposes a bold hypothesis for postlapsarian humanity. Yet the passage is padded with indefinite and qualifying phrases: it is "more likely" that the moon holds these saints and spirits than the underdeveloped figures of Limbo, but it is by no means certain from the poem that such intermediary creatures even exist. In fact, within the context of the poem, because Milton tells his reader that Limbo is definitely *not* on the moon, the prospect of translated saints inhabiting the moon is only more likely than that which is certainly untrue. What first appeared a potentiality for human transcendence becomes a rather obeisant nod to indeterminacy — or simply a rhetorical maneuver that ensures the poem's durability and adaptability in light of the revolutionary changes to the scientific conception of the cosmos in Milton's day. Although the Copernican revolution had strong scientific support when Milton was writing *Paradise Lost*, the philosophical, theological, and imaginative implications of a heliocentric universe were still hotly debated, and so Dennis Danielson refers to "the not-yet-triumphant new astronomy of Milton's age."[47] While bold in the hypotheses he entertains, Milton is guarded in all of his astronomical observations.

Nevertheless, influenced by classical thought, Milton consistently depicts the moon as an important transitional space, the liminal celestial body between the earthly and the ethereal, having elements of both worlds. It, like Satan's shield, is of "ethereal temper," but it is also "terrestrial," the uncharted space where Galileo seeks "to descry new Lands, / Rivers or Mountains" (1.285, 290–91; 8.142). In book 5, a simile comparing Raphael's sight of earth from the heavens to Galileo's sight of the moon from earth suggests a certain correspondence and even a potential interchangeability between heaven and earth:

> From hence, no cloud, or, to obstruct his sight,
> Star interpos'd, however small he sees,
> Not unconform to other shining Globes,

Earth and the Gard'n of God, with Cedars crown'd
Above all Hills. As when by night the Glass
Of *Galileo*, less assur'd, observes
Imagin'd Lands and Regions in the Moon.   (5.257–63)

This correspondence and reciprocity is implicit in Galileo's discussion
of "earthshine" in *Siderius Nuncius*, and in Raphael's discussion of the
same in *Paradise Lost*:

What if that light [from earth],
Sent from her through the wide transpicuous air,
To the terrestrial Moon be as a Star,
Enlight'ning her by Day, as she by Night
This Earth? reciprocal, if Land be there,
Fields and Inhabitants.[48]   (8.140–45)

Galileo is "less assur'd" than Raphael in his knowledge of the cosmos as
the astronomer "observes / Imagin'd Lands and Regions in the Moon,"
but the limitations of science do not preclude life there — at least, not in
the world of *Paradise Lost*. Galileo may be uncertain and the bard may
have his speculative doubts, but Raphael is more confident in the potential for human aspiration, suggesting "every Star perhaps a World /
Of destin'd habitation" (7.621–22). Though Raphael does not name
the moon as the primary residence for humans aspiring to angels'
status, he does suggest to Adam the formulaic possibility of life there:

Her spots thou seest
As Clouds, and Clouds may rain, and Rain produce
Fruits in her soft'n'd Soil, for some to eat
Allotted there.   (8.145–48)

The spots on the moon are so important as representative features of
the cosmic chain of eating and excretion that Raphael mentions them
in two separate contexts. In the above passage, the spots are clouds that
water the moon, soften its soil, and produce food for its inhabitants.
In book 5, Raphael identifies these spots on the moon as unabsorbed
exhalations of the earth that will become food for the moon itself.

Earth's exhalations provide nourishment for the moon and higher celestial bodies:

> For know, whatever was created, needs
> To be sustain'd and fed; of Elements
> The grosser feeds the purer, Earth the Sea,
> Earth and the Sea feed Air, the Air those Fires
> Ethereal, and as lowest first the Moon;
> Whence in her visage round those spots, unpurg'd
> Vapors not yet into her substance turn'd.
> Nor doth the Moon no nourishment exhale
> From her moist Continent to higher Orbs.
> The Sun that light imparts to all, receives
> From all his alimental recompense
> In humid exhalations, and at Even
> Sups with the Ocean.   (5.414–26)

In a hierarchical system where "the grosser feeds the purer" by "nour-ishment" in the form of "humid exhalations," superfluities provide an important substitute for flesh in a nonpredatory food chain, allowing survival of both the provider and the recipient of food. For the system to work, both excretion and consumption are necessary: Milton curi-ously emphasizes this when referencing the "unpurg'd / Vapors" of the moon — "unpurg'd" not, as one might expect, because they have yet to be excreted, but because they have yet to be consumed, turned into the substance of the moon. This is a radical twist on humoral theory, asserting the goodness not only of expurgating superfluous matter but also of what one might call in-purgation, a qualitative, ameliorative change in one's food, not dissimilar to Galen's *alteration* (*alloiōsis*). In Raphael's theory, particles of matter become refined as they ascend, purged from one being and into another, with the prospect of com-plete bodily transformation for the eater as well as the eaten.[49] In this way Milton reworks the idea of the Great Chain of Being into a Great Chain of Eating, or, in Michael Schoenfeldt's term, a "Great Chain of Digestion and Secretion."[50]

Generosity and gratitude preserve this chain from being more than the self-serving "ideology of an elite," as some scholars have declared the hierarchical Great Chain of Being to be.[51] Rather than an ideological power ladder, Milton saw this chain, as it was earlier seen in the Neoplatonic and the Christian mystic traditions, as a ladder of love. Generosity, grace, and gratitude characterize the interactions and movement of creatures up and down the links of Milton's version of this chain. Raphael's gracious condescension and Adam's deference to his angel guest set an example of creatures benevolently giving of themselves or expressing gratitude in acknowledgment of Nature's gifts within a hierarchical cosmos. This dynamic of generosity, grace, and gratitude, of symbiotic giving and receiving, stands at the extreme opposite of predatory food chains or self-promoting power ladders. Among celestial bodies, the moon provides an important example of a created body gratefully accepting nourishment, becoming fruitful to the benefit of those most closely associated with her, and then gracefully passing on nourishment to others. The bard's and Raphael's comments about the moon uncover a precise formulation of the itinerant perfection of the cosmos, and of the first step upward in Adam's journey toward godhood and toward God.

Moreover, a hospitable, habitable moon is part of Milton's theodicy, for it supports the real possibility of obedience without overpopulation, of life without death, and proliferation without decay. Had the world continued obedient, fruitful, multiplying, and untainted by death and decay until the present day — or even until the day Milton completed *Paradise Lost* — the earth would not have sufficed to entertain all created things and their countless progeny. Milton considered this, and so he explicitly laid out an alternative plan for human growth and migration that did not require disobedience, death, and decay. For the success of his poetic enterprise, humankind must be sufficient to stand in all respects. Even Satan is aware of the potential for the overpopulation of earth, and in perverse hospitality proposes hell as a solution against cramped quarters: "there will be room, / Not like these narrow limits, to receive / Your numerous offspring" (4.383–85). Eventually, the human race must either fall down or move up. The references to life on the moon are critical to Milton's justification of God and his presentation of the importance of transubstantiating, grateful eating throughout the spectrum of created life. They provide a snapshot of eating and digestion as experienced by celestial bodies. They propose a resource-stashed base camp for other created beings on their way up to God. Most important, with all these provisions made for creatures not yet in need of them, Milton's moon instructs the reader that the Fall was not inevitable.

GRACE, MERIT, AND "THE WAY UP"

The stories of the creation of humans in books 7 and 8 support the innate potential for ascent. According to Adam's account, his first instinct is upward. He lifts his eyes to heaven and stands up "by quick instinctive motion...As thitherward endeavoring" (8.259–61). Adam's first address is made to the sun; his first request is to know his maker; in his first dream, the first voice to address him — the divine presence — tells him to rise, takes him by the hand, and guides him upward to the plateau of the garden of Eden (8.273, 295). The higher ground is such that by comparison "what [Adam] saw / Of earth before scarce pleasant seem'd" (8.305–06). He wakes to find that he truly has ascended, and what he sees "all real, as the dream / Had lively shadow'd" (8.310–11). His creation and the place where he was created were "entirely good," but there is still room for growth and ascent (7.549). The air Adam first breathes is pure but, as Satan or any other being entering the garden might experience, "Of pure now purer air" he breathes (4.153).

This aspiration appears to be part of God's original plan for humanity and part of his ultimate vision for Creation. God explains this plan to the Son and the faithful angels in the aftermath of the War in Heaven:

> [I] will create
> Another World, out of one man a Race
> Of men innumerable, there to dwell,

Not here, till by degrees of merit rais'd
They open to themselves at length the way
Up hither, under long obedience tri'd,
And Earth be chang'd to Heav'n, and Heav'n to Earth,
One Kingdom, Joy and Union without end.   (7.154–61)

At first God emphasizes that humans are not exact substitutions for the fallen angels — "there to dwell, / Not here" — but soon he reveals that earth and heaven are destined to be united, as humans access "the way / Up" through "degrees of merit" and "under long obedience." This is a rather un-Calvinistic rendering of the perseverance of the saints, and these hardly seem the words of the same narrator who describes the bridge from earth to hell as "a Monument / Of merit" and whose soteriology requires the Son's intervention in all human deeds, "Good or not good," through perfection of the former and atonement for the latter (10.258–59, 11.35). God's words in the book 7 passage reflect the Arminian quality of Milton's theology.[52] Also suggested by God's comments in this speech is the doctrine of dispensationalism, of progressively revealed truth. God's words to the angels before the creation of the world reveal a plan appropriate to the prelapsarian human who keeps the law, but this plan is insufficient to explain justification or sanctification after the Fall, which require grace beyond merit.

Free will and freely chosen obedience remain vital parts of Milton's system of Christian doctrine, whether before or after the Fall. The interworking of free will and predestination in *Paradise Lost* is complexly portrayed, and as Julia Walker argues, using Milton's phrase to describe the substance and shadow of Death, "each seem'd either."[53] Stephen Fallon examines how "an apparent residue of Calvinist teaching on election disturbs the otherwise Arminian and libertarian doctrine of the mature Milton, resulting in a tension between claims for different and incompatible forms of distinction."[54] Milton, Fallon explains, wants to be both specially elected by God (a Calvinistic rendering of "peculiar grace") and praised (in Arminian fashion) on the merit of his own labor and freely willed action. Yet Fallon sees in Milton "a need for recognition that the Arminian economy cannot satisfy." This leads to a "combination of security and anxiety or the related combination of confident virtue and intimations of frailty. If Milton did not think of himself as uniquely gifted with prophecy, he could never have written *Paradise Lost*; if he did not have more empathy for human frailty than he showed earlier in his career, we could not read it."[55] Confidence and anxiety, virtue and frailty, moral striving and rest in divine grace are all connected to Milton's experience and understanding of the faithful laborer.[56]

Paradise Lost carries a preponderance of evidence for Milton's belief in the necessity of grace and the insufficiency of good works for salvation, but, much more than Luther or Calvin, Milton also emphasizes the need for genuine faith to be demonstrated through good works. Significantly, *De doctrina Christiana* opens with a reminder that the teachings of faith and the actions of worship are "inseparable in practice" (OW 8:21). Later, paraphrasing and citing Romans 3:28, "that a person is justified by faith apart from the works of the law" and James 2:24, "that a person is justified on the basis of works, and not on the basis of faith only," Milton facilely resolves an apparent contradiction by noting that there can be good works apart from the *works of the law*—actions that he names the *works of faith*—and that these are a necessary part of justification: "We are justified, therefore, by faith, but by a living faith not a dead one.... So we are justified by faith apart from the works of the law, not apart from works of faith, because works cannot be absent from a living, true faith" (OW 8:623). Accordingly, God calls fallen humanity to "faith and faithful works" in *Paradise Lost* (11.64). However, Milton ultimately credits any such works of faith to God himself: "Good works are those which we do when God's spirit is working within us, through true faith, to the glory of God, to the sure hope of our salvation, and to the upbuilding of our neighbor" (OW 8:907). Insofar as these good deeds can be considered our own, they yet can never be supererogatory. They are no more than what humans are obliged to do under the twofold law of loving God and one's neighbor and can never outweigh the gifts God offers to humanity: "And hence the emptiness of our merits, too, is easily discerned, since neither do our right actions belong to ourselves—rather, they belong to God acting in us — nor, even granted they are our own, do they nevertheless cease to be obligations, nor can any calculation whatever of our duty in any respect equal the greatness of the reward held out [to us]" (OW 8:919).[57]

Further complicating this is the matter of free will, which for Milton must exist in matters of morality and religion: "Even in good works, or at least attempts, freedom is not absolutely non-existent, at least after the grace of God who calls us, but [it is] so meagre, and of so very little influence, that it simply and solely takes away from us any excuse for doing absolutely nothing, and brings us not even minimal matter for boasting" (OW 8:435). This freedom, "meagre" and of "very little influence," is nonetheless critical to justifying the ways of God to humanity: "Surely, in order to vindicate the justice of God, especially God who calls us, it is much more appropriate that some element of free will — either as a relic from man's first state or as a restoration of the caller's grace — be allowed to man in good works, or at least attempts, rather than in things indifferent" (OW 8:437). We have already noted how Milton defines freedom as "precisely the same as to be pious, wise, just, and temperate, careful of one's property, aloof from another's, and thus finally to be magnanimous and brave" (YP 4:684). In sum, then, Milton argues that humans have free will, and this free will has a dignifying but incriminating effect, rendering humans responsible for their faults. Merit is necessary for salvation, but ultimately all human merit is accredited to God, who gives grace to humankind. While *works of the law* are fruitless to earn salvation, the faithful are responsible for *works of faith*. Good works include the practice of piety, wisdom, justice, and temperance, and these moral actions in turn have a liberating effect on the soul. Whatever our conclusions about Milton's peculiar brand of soteriology — and Milton writes enough on grace and good works to suggest complicated paradox — in *Paradise Lost* humans were created to ascend to the heavens by merit and sustained obedience substantially exemplified in decisions made about eating.

Raphael's hypothesis leads to the questions of whether the eating of more rarefied viands is a means of ascent as well as a result of ascent, and whether or not Adam and Eve in fact initially have access to the food of the gods. Adam and Eve have the physical organs needed to eat the fruit of the Tree of Knowledge of Good and Evil, but God instructs them not to do so; they have no such interdict against eating typical angel fare, but such fare is presumably inaccessible and indigestible — a permissible but "inconvenient diet." Certainly the Tree of Life, "high eminent blooming ambrosial fruit / of vegetable gold," resembles the "trees / of life [that] ambrosial fruitage bear" in heaven; perhaps this fruit more than that of any other tree would initiate the process of aspiration Raphael suggests. As this tree is no longer accessible to humans after the Fall, eventually we must ask whether any plans for Adam expressed before the Fall remain relevant to Milton, to his readers, or even to "our grand parents," as Milton portrays them after the Fall. Although Michael's revelation in *Paradise Lost* includes the destruction of Eden at the Flood, in *Paradise Regain'd* Milton, following John the Evangelist's vision of the Apocalypse, suggests that the Tree of Life has been removed from Eden and preserved in heaven (*PL* 11.829–39; Rev. 22:2, 14, 19): after the final temptation in the wilderness, angels refresh the Son of God with "Celestial Food, Divine, / Ambrosial, Fruits fetcht from the tree of life" (*PR* 4.588–89). The angels' access to this tree further intimates the similarity between it and the ambrosial trees of heaven in *Paradise Lost*. Presumably such a tree of paradise is capable of being transplanted to higher ground.

The loss or removal of the Tree of Life contributes to the nostalgia and wistfulness of the poem. Even Satan perched as a gluttonous cormorant on the Tree of Life introduces a heavy sense of lost opportunity. Exile from Eden cuts Adam and Eve off from the Tree of Life and from further transgression by eating from the Tree of Knowledge of Good and Evil. Nonetheless, the effects of both peculiar trees were available to humankind regardless of their eating or not eating from these trees. Not knowing death, unfallen Adam and Eve thrive in Eden with no determinate time limit, and they live out the benefits of the Tree of Life. And even as the Tree of Knowledge of Good and Evil is taboo, unfallen Adam and Eve practice a natural moral knowledge, a simplified and nonexperiential understanding of good and evil, certainly, but still the ability to know the difference between right and wrong. Divine instruction helps them understand what an act of dis-obedience might look like, and Raphael's narration of the fall of Satan adds the knowledge gained from vicarious experience to their moral arsenal. Eve's dream further increases her moral knowledge, even giv-ing her a new awareness of evil in an imaginative sense, and occasioning Adam's assertion that "Evil into the mind of God or Man / May come and go, so unapprov'd, and leave / No spot or blame behind" (5.117–19). Before Eve covets the fruit, before Adam tastes, they already have a kind of knowledge of good and evil.

The prospect of humans becoming as the angels suggests that, in addition to their immortality (the effect of the Tree of Life), Adam and Eve might develop angelic intelligence (even beyond that promised by the Tree of Knowledge of Good and Evil). Angels already have the advantages signified by these two trees. After the Fall, God tells his angels, "O Sons, like one of us Man is become / To know both Good and Evil, since his taste / Of that defended Fruit" (11.84–86). This reference to Genesis 3:22, a passage where God's first-person plural pronoun is usually interpreted by Christians as a Trinitarian soliloquy, becomes instead in Milton an indication of the angels' knowledge of good and evil. What the angels know through intellect, intuition, and memory Adam and Eve learn through "sad experiment" (10.967). The twofold irony here is that Adam and Eve already had demonstrable moral knowledge before the Fall and there is every indication that their knowledge would have reached angelic heights over time. The benefits of the Tree of Knowledge of Good and Evil were available without its deleterious effects. Satan's temptation, then, offers Eve a deceptive shortcut, encouraging a particularly impatient kind of intemperance.

Satan again employs this strategy against the Son in *Paradise Regain'd* when, in accordance with the fourth chapter of Luke, Satan offers the Son all the kingdoms of the world without the torments of the Crucifixion. Like eating of the Tree of Knowledge of Good and Evil, what looks like a shortcut is really a trap. To Satan's offer, "Reign then," the Son replies, "All things are best fulfill'd in their due time, / And time there is for all things" (*PR* 3.180, 182–83). This brings up once again the connection between temperance and patience, and the tradition that eating *praepropere*, too soon, is a species of gluttony. Eve's intemperate desire to hasten the process of acquiring angelic knowledge, and to bypass the long trial of obedience, is an attempt to experience time as only God does, whose acts are "immediate" (*PL* 7.176). As odd as it may be to say of a *locus amoenus*, timing (and the patience it requires) is critical in Milton's Eden. As one might anticipate from the author of the sonnets "How soon hath Time, the subtle thief of youth" and "When I consider how my light is spent," patient reliance on God is key to Milton's idea of temperance and of virtue in general.

EXCESS AND EXCREMENT IN PARADISE

The ideal, temperate plan of gradual ascension through the "tract of time," however, is not without a kind of excess. As Adam and Eve eat temperately in the garden, their bodies assimilate the nutritive materials they consume, but there is also excess and excrement. Like the angels, who eat "secure / Of surfeit" while "what redounds, transpires," Adam and Eve's prelapsarian meals "suffic't, / Not burd'n'd Nature," while still producing "temperate vapors bland" (5.638–39, 438, 451–52, 5). These "temperate vapors bland" are, in the words of Gordon Teskey, "a discreet answer to the perennial question of Edenic excretion."[58] They are the exhalations that conclude a perfect human's digestion, and they contrast with the "exhilarating vapor bland" that arises in Adam and Eve after they eat forbidden fruit (9.1047). The latter is "exhilarating" not simply because of the euphoria experienced just after their disobedience but also because true joy has left them (L., *ex* + *hilaritas*). By contrast, the earlier innocent transpiration of "temperate vapors bland" does not indicate a personal, ethical excess but rather a finely honed physical system that can moderate the bounties of nature. Although unfallen humans and angels may have different staple foods, and though the physics of their respective digestive systems may differ greatly, the conclusions to their digestion are analogous. Both end in transpiring vapors rather than ordure, indicating the ideal assimilation of nutrients into the body, and allowing for the consumption of excess without necessarily incorporating it. This one detail of *Paradise Lost*, the transpiration of alimentary excess, shapes the teleological significance of eating, vitally contributing to a system of cosmic synthesis and heavenly ascent.

Any study of the natural philosophy of *Paradise Lost*, including its philosophy of eating, must include some observations on the rudiments of Greek physiology that prevailed in medieval and early modern thought on nutrition. Although Milton had access to ancient ideas on nutrition and humoral physiology through the Greek and Latin texts themselves, he also had recourse to early modern medical and philosophical works indebted to these ancient texts, including Robert Burton's *Anatomy of Melancholy* (1621).

In Burton's compendium the division of the parts of the human body follows Hippocrates through Laurentius: first, there is a simple division into *parts contained* (humours or spirits) and *parts containing*. The parts containing are divided into *homogeneal* (skin, bones, nerves, veins, arteries), and *heterogeneal*, the latter of which are divided into outward (head, shoulders, knees, toes, etc.) and inward, which inward parts are again divided (following Laurentius) into noble and ignoble parts. Here we get to the heart of the matter: "Of the noble there be three principal parts, to which all the rest belong, and whom they serve — brain, heart, liver; according to which site, three regions, or a threefold division, is made of the whole body." The brain is "privy counselor and chancellor to the heart"; the "heart as king keeps his court, and by his arteries communicates life to the whole body"; the liver resides in the lower third as "*Legat à latere* . . . serving for concoction, nourishment, expelling of excrements."[59] From here, Burton's organization seems to slip. He describes lower, middle, and upper parts of the body in turn, but only the lower and middle regions have subheadings, his description of the brain serving more as a commendatory preface to his anatomy of the soul in the next subsection.

His interest in the lower region of the body focuses on digestion, which, as Burton exemplifies, was often explained as cooking, and as a series of concoctions and extractions occurring in various parts of the body, each with its own system of waste management. According to Burton, the stomach, working for the commonweal of the body, is "the kitchen (as it were) of the first concoction," turning masticated food into *chylus*, and excreting any useless residue through the intestines as feces.[60]

The second concoction then occurs in the liver, the noble governor of the lower body, which turns the chylus into blood for the nourishment of the entire body.[61] Burton describes blood as "a hot, sweet, temperate, red humour, prepared in the *meseraick* veins, and made of the most temperate parts of the chylus in the liver, whose office is to nourish the whole body, to give it strength and colour, being dispersed by the veins through every part of it."[62] The ancient concept of blood as, in the words of A. Rupert Hall, "a warm nourishing soup" derived from digestion, was, as David J. Furley remarks, "an *idée fixe* among Greek thinkers, and was probably more than anything else responsible for their failure to understand that the blood circulates through the body and returns to its starting point."[63] This second concoction or *sanguinification* also produces waste residue, more refined, and expelled by the kidneys as urine.[64]

The next step, assimilation, is that whereby the individual organs draw from the blood the particular nutrients they need. This process works in accordance with the assumptions behind the law of sympathies and antipathies, in which an object is attracted to the elements that constitute it; each bodily organ draws from the blood the nutrients suitable to it, "as iron is attracted by the lodestone."[65] This stage also has its methods for the expurgation of waste. Because blood was considered to be food, and the respiratory and digestive systems interrelated, the last, most refined residue of the digestive process was expelled through the skin as "those excrementitious humours of the third concoction, sweat and tears."[66]

The third concoction concluded digestion by converting blood into the animal "*spirits . . .* first begotten in the heart, which afterwards by the *arteries* are communicated to the other parts," not least of which was the brain. For Burton, "Spirit is a most subtle vapour, which is expressed from the blood, and the instrument of the soul, to perform all his actions; a common tie or medium betwixt the body and the soul, as some will have it. ... Of these spirits there be three kinds, according to the three principal parts, brain, heart, liver; natural, vital, animal."[67] This "subtle vapour" connecting soul and body, or "the mind and the organs of sense and motion," grounds Raphael's theories of digestion ending in rarefaction in a prevalent physiology of early modernity.[68]

Recall that Raphael contrasts his description of angelic maneuvering in the War in Heaven with a description of "frail man" as having "Entrails, Heart or Head, Liver or Reins," each with their unique function (*PL* 6.345–46). This triad of body parts — entrails, heart/ head, and liver/reins — should give us pause, for it fails to conform to the expected medieval and early modern categorization of the three noble governors of the body: head (governing judgment), heart (governing sentiments), and liver (governing the passions). So, for example, Shakespeare's Duke Orsino itemizes the parts of the Countess Olivia: "liver, brain and heart, / These sovereign thrones" (*Twelfth Night* 1.1.43–44).[69] Instead, we find a division of the body according to the three stages of digestion as presented in Burton's *Anatomy of Melancholy*: the stomach and intestines governing the first concoction (turning food to chylus), the liver and kidneys governing the second concoction (turning chylus into blood), and the third concoction (turning blood into animal spirits) belonging to the heart and received by the head. Rejecting the conventional division of the body into head, heart, and liver, Milton instead lists the parts of the body according to their roles in the stages of digestion (entrails, liver and reins, head and heart), reinforcing Raphael's message that one's identity and potential depend on one's eating. The consequence of this is that, as a tree is known by its fruit, so a man is known by his excretions.

As reference books of the era attest, "excrement" could refer to any solid, liquid, or gas that naturally proceeds from the body. Thomas Cooper's 1565 *Thesaurus* defines *excrementum* as "the dregges or excrementes of digestion made in the bodie; as fleume, choler, melancholie, urine, sweate, snivell, spittel, milke, ordure."[70] When in *Hamlet* the Danish prince fixates on the apparition of his father, Gertrude observes of her wild-eyed son, "Your bedded hairs like life in excrements start up and stand on end."[71] What surprises her is not that Hamlet's hair is excremental, but that it seems alive. In *The Anatomy of Melancholy*, Burton writes that the body "expels all superfluous excrements, and reliques of meat and drink, by the guts, bladder, pores; as by purging, vomiting, spitting, sweating, urine, hairs, nails, &c."[72] Ephraim Chambers's 1728 *Cyclopaedia* registers little change from the concept that *excrement* includes any bodily secretions, including those that are useful to the body. In addition to urine, feces, and perspiration, "Among Excrements are likewise ordinarily rank'd, divers Humours and Matters, separated from the blood by the several Strainers, or Emunctories of the Body, tho' far from being useless, and serving divers valuable purposes of the OEconomy. Such are...earwax...mucus... tears; saliva, bile, lympha, menses, lochia, &c." One infers from these lists that not all excrements are alike. In *The Generation of Animals*, Aristotle divides excess (*perittōma*) in animal consumption into serviceable (*chrēsimon*) and useless (*achrēston*) nutriment (*trophē*). The former contributes to inert parts of the animal body (hair, nails, bones, and sinews), is stored as fat, or forms generative secretions, whereas the latter is more properly waste material, "that which is given off from the tissues by an unnatural decomposition."[73] Whether the excess is serviceable or useless to the body generating it, it is categorized as *trophē*, nutriment. This implies that the condition of the consuming body (and not just the kind of food consumed) will affect whether the residue of digestion is useful or not. According to humoral theory beginning with Hippocrates, excretions are not cast off by the body because they in themselves are noxious; they are merely superfluous, with the potential to toxify if collected and unused. Thus they flow out of the healthy body, while many excrements (e.g., hair, tears, saliva, wax, mucus, etc.) even serve the body by virtue of their being excreted.[74]

Excretion, of which the most refined example was the release of digested vapors through the pores, was critical to early modern medicine. As Schoenfeldt has shown in *Bodies and Selves in Early Modern England*, only the sick body fails to secrete excess. Qualifying Bakhtin's reading of the Renaissance ideal of the impermeable classical body, Schoenfeldt cites Tobias Venner's respected medical treatise *Via recta ad vitam longam*, first published in 1620: "They that have their belly naturally loose and open...are not easily affected with sicknesse: whereas of the contrary, they that have the same bound up...have for the most part, often conflicts with sickness."[75] Schoenfeldt explains, "This physiology demands not the seamless corporeal enclosure that Bakhtin identifies with the classical body, but rather the routine excretory processes that he displaces into lower-class festivity."[76] While there is a long and sensible tradition of reserving scatological talk for corrective ridicule, a reader of early modern literature need not invest these "routine excretory processes," so critical to health, with derogatory connotations. In *The Anatomy of Melancholy*, Robert Burton confirms that "costiveness, and keeping in of our ordinary excrements...as it often causes other diseases, so [causes] this of Melancholy in particular."[77] As Rebecca Totaro has shown, Margaret Cavendish describes the plague in *The World's Olio* (1655) as a summer disease caused by the warming of "Corrupted Humours that the Winter hath bred by Obstructions, like Houses that are musty...for want of Vent to Purge them, for Winter shuts up all the Windows and Dores, which are the Pores."[78] Totaro explains that respiration was vital to early modern notions of bodily temperance: "Breathing in allowed cool air to prevent the innate heat of the body from growing beyond measure. Exhalation expelled the hot breath tainted with excess heat."[79] Thus, as Tobias Venner relates, healthy excretion includes the release of vapors through sweating, or *transpiration*, the final and most refined stage of digestion: "For in every concoction some excrements are engendered, which residing in the body condense and oppilate, and so become the roots of divers diseases. Now the thicker sort of excrements which arise from the first and second concoction of the stomack and liver, are avoided by sensible evacuation, as by Stoole and urine; but the thinner that come of the third concoction in the limbs are wasted by transpiration, and purged forth by exercise, which causeth sweat in those which wish to live in health."[80]

So in *Of Education* Milton offers advice not only on the best forms of exercise for young scholars (swordplay and wrestling, beginning at 10:30 a.m.) but also on the best use of "the interim of unsweating" and "rest before meat" (listening to or practicing music). After a noon meal, further music would "assist and cherish nature in her first concoction,

and send their minds back to study in good tune and satisfaction"
(YP 2:409, 411). Harmonious music would thus help with the first and
final stages of digestion, supporting the mind preparing for renewed
study. Moreover, the "institution of Physick" was to be taught, that the
young men might learn "the tempers, the humors, the seasons, and how
to manage a crudity" (YP 2:392–93). Recommendations for assisting
digestion and transpiration were important enough to be included in
Milton's "right path of a virtuous and noble education" — one that, of
course, was designed to "repair the ruins of our first parents" by joining
knowledge, love, and virtue to "the heavenly grace of faith" (YP 2:366–
67). The concerns of the body have a part to play in this moral and
spiritual enterprise, for body and spirit are inextricable.

Transpiration was so important to early modern medicine that even
unnatural openness of the body was considered to prevent and cure
disease, or release toxic substances. In Anglo Saxon medicine, externally introduced poisons were to be released through odd methods:
Bald's Leechbook advises, "If a man eat wolf's bane, let him eat and
drink butter, the poison will go off in the butter. Again for that, let
him stand upon his head, let someone strike him many scarifications on
the shanks, then the venom departs out through the incisions."[81] Even
after William Harvey and the advent of modern medicine, Hippocratic
methods of controlling one's health through removing *discrasiae*,
"excess" bodily fluids, remained popular: bloodletting, for example, was
prevalent into the nineteenth century. Burton offers a curious anecdote
of a mentally unstable man, "one wounded in the head, who, as long as
the sore was open, was well; but when it was stopped his melancholy fit
seized on him again."[82] Bodily openness and excretion were considered
essential to health.

Incidentally, "dimnesse of the sight" is among the list of ailments
Venner says the body is susceptible to if it fails to excrete its excesses.
In a significant personal letter (1654) to an Athenian friend, Leonard
Philaras, Milton reveals his fears that his own loss of sight is due to
the collection of vapors arising from indigestion (YP 4:867–70).[83] In a
late effort to restore his vision, Milton underwent setoning (or seaton-
ing), a procedure also based on the principle of opening up passageways

for excess humors to escape. As Barbara Lewalski explains, it "involved piercing the skin just below the hairline, passing through the holes a hot cautery with a diamond point and then a needle with thread dipped in egg white and rose oil."[84] It did not work, but it provides evidence that, whatever the artistic picture of the ideal body, Milton accepted the dominant medical version extolling porosity and excretion. As Gail Kern Paster reminds us, the extent to which humoral theory is empirically inaccurate "is a matter entirely separate from its ideological efficacy and meaning."[85] Regardless of current medical opinions on bloodletting, setoning, and the like, Milton's prelapsarian universe and the bodies therein operate on the principle of beneficent excretion.

Excretions may be useful not only to the secreting body itself but also to other beings. Such is the case, of course, with the nourishing and generative secretions of milk and semen.[86] In examining relations between the sexes in *The Doctrine and Discipline of Divorce*, Milton compares the outpourings of the healthy mind to those of the healthy body, extolling the former but not depreciating the latter when he writes of "the minde from whence must flow the acts of peace and love, a far more precious mixture then the quintessence of an excrement" (YP 2:248). James Turner points to this passage as registering Milton's misogyny, and Barbara Lewalski considers it indicative of Milton's "disgust... for some of his sexual experiences," the act of coition reduced to the "release [of] waste products of the distempered and overheated body."[87] However supported or unsupported these interpretations may be in the context of Milton's personal life, they needlessly invest "quintessence of an excrement" with a negative connotation — as if Milton's disappointment in his relationship with Mary Powell led him to despise his own semen. More likely, Milton recognized something precious — though peace and love are admittedly "far more precious" — in this generative secretion. In the same tract, Milton repeats commonplace reproductive theories of his day when describing the male sexual act as the expenditure of "the best substance of his body, and of his soul too, as some think" (YP 2:271). In *De doctrina Christiana*, Milton counterintuitively appeals to the doctrine of original sin in order to argue for the soul as present in reproductive excretions rather than directly implanted by

God, for "if we have received a soul directly from God, surely it is pure: for who would dare to call it impure? But if it is pure, how, by receiving a pure one, which would tend rather to sanctify an impure body, are we conceived in sin? By what deserts of its own has a pure soul become guilty of bodily sin?" (OW 8:305–07). Milton believes the human soul is impure from conception, but the idea that original sin is transmitted with the soul from father to child via the semen does not register contempt for the generation of life. Referencing an Aristotelian argument, Milton reflects, "If the soul is wholly within the whole body, and wholly in whatever part of it, how can that inmost and noblest part — the human seed, I mean — be understood as bereft and devoid of its parents', or at least its father's, soul at the time when it is imparted to the child by generation?" (OW 8:307). As preformationist theories of the homunculus were prevalent well into the seventeenth century, bodily excrement could be considered of inestimable worth. That which the body may not need for its own exclusive purposes is not thereby useless to others, and may in fact be life-engendering.

Of Aristotle's two types of bodily excess, only the serviceable (*chrēsimon*) exists in Milton's prelapsarian Eden. Fruit in *Paradise Lost* is a prime example of serviceable excess — if consumed wisely. As we have seen, prudent eating in the garden involves timeliness, especially since mistimed eating is a species of gluttony. Conversely, Milton connects patience to nourishment. In his work *On the Properties of Foodstuffs*, Galen remarks that fruit from trees, particularly moist fruit, tends to be digested quickly through the skin; the moister the fruit, the faster it digested, and the less nutritive it was held to be.[88] Perhaps Milton had Galen in mind when he wrote of the "superfluous moist" of the harvested fruit which "by frugal storing firmness gains / To nourish" (5.324–25); this would underscore the benefits of the particularly patient species of temperance — waiting for the opportune time to eat a particular comestible can enhance its nutritional value.

Even if one disregards the fruit of the Tree of Knowledge, paradisal fruits are significant not solely because they are the staple of Adam and Eve's diet, and not only because they remind us of both the ease of Edenic living and the benefits of timeliness, but also because Milton follows Aristotle in describing fruit itself as plant excrement. In *Parts of Animals*, Aristotle describes fruit as not only contributing to, but also being analogous to, the most basic animal functions:

> For in all animals, at least in all the perfect kinds, there are two parts more essential than the rest, namely the part which serves for the inges-tion of food, and the part which serves for the discharge of its residue [*perittōmatos*]. For without food growth and even existence is impos-sible.... As for plants, though they also are included by us among things that have life, yet are they without any part for the discharge of waste residue [*to achrēstou perittōmatos*]. For the food which they absorb from the ground is already concocted, and they give off as its equivalent their seeds and fruits.[89]

Following Plato, Aristotle thought of the earth as an external "stom-ach" for plants, completing the first stages of digestion by breaking down substances into nutrients for plants to absorb.[90] The seeds and fruit that sustain the eater and ensure the propagation of the plant are serviceable excesses, the counterparts to useful animal excretions. And while fruit may be the most palpable example of plant excrescence, there are others. Even in the eighteenth century, Chambers's *Cyclopae-dia* notes that "Gums, diverse juices, balms, &c. issuing spontaneously from their respective trees, are sometimes called excrements." When the spicy fragrance of Eden entertains Satan in book 4 of *Paradise Lost*, and when Adam exhorts Eve to observe "What drops the Myrrh, and what the balmy Reed" in book 5, we encounter a delicious paradise of excrements (5.23, 292–3). The spice-laden air of Eden carries the vege-table equivalent to animal transpiration, the superfluity of the ultimate, most refined concoction of the body. This correlation between plant and animal excrement achieves further significance in *Paradise Lost* when Raphael explains how the superfluities of animals are absorbed by higher creatures, just as animals enjoy the superfluities and excre-tions of plants.

Milton's concept of excretion provides a framework both for under-standing the heavens and for accounting for what is lower than human beings. Raphael describes the process of rarefaction first with reference to the celestial bodies, with special attention given to the moon, and then a second time by offering the simple plant analogy as a synecdochic representation of cosmic aspiration.[91] The Great Chain of Eating assigns import to both food and fragrance from plants, and helps to explain why heavy fruit is not an illogical last step in the process of plant rarefaction. The process of creaturely growth and improvement, described as a flower's development from root to fragrant blossom, results in the secretion of excess, culminating in a ripe fruit, mature not only for death but also for sublimation. Raphael's description of a plant's progression from body to spirit, "from the root" all the way to "flow'rs and their fruit / Man's nourishment," is a metaphor for human ascent and rarefaction, but the plant itself is also literally "sublim'd" in two ways: through its natural growth upward, it develops from the anchoring root to delicately scented flowers, from fundamental material to rarefied perfume; through its nutritive excretion, it offers its ripening fruit as sustenance to a higher being and depends on this higher being for its fruit to be transformed through the process of digestion. One being's superfluity provides sustaining nutriment for a higher being, uniting all creation through a system of symbiotic giving.

WORSHIP AND THE FOOD OF THE GODS

This plant analogy, however, does not entirely explain our own serviceable excess; as we proceed up the chain to consider higher beings, it becomes less clear how excrement of a lower order can sustain celestial beings, or how celestial beings can be said to depend upon nourishment from below. Remarkable as it may be that Adam offers Raphael the food of humans, the plant analogy even more remarkably suggests that, as plant growth results in flowers and fruit for our enjoyment, our bodily excretions provide a service to superior beings, to the nostrils, if not to the taste buds.

In prelapsarian Eden, this is accomplished through perspiration rather than defecation, or in accordance with the plant metaphor, fragrance rather than fruit. As one ascends above the plants in the Great Chain, the analogs for flowery fragrance and fruit, vapors and food, become indistinguishable. The Sun, above much of the created world, receives "From all his alimental recompense / In humid exhalations" (*PL* 5.424–25). At Adam's first awakening, he finds himself "laid / In Balmy Sweat, which with his Beams the Sun / Soon dri'd, and on the reeking moisture fed" (8.254–56). ("Reeking" here holds no unpleasant connotation.) In the context of Raphael's description of the Great Chain, it seems improper to limit this to a metaphoric feeding: Adam's sweat nourishes the sun. As Schoenfeldt remarks, "It is deeply significant to Milton's alimental vision that the first thing the first human does, even prior to consciousness, is sweat. It is as if in a poem obsessed with firsts, the primal corporeal activity is excretion."[92] Schoenfeldt emphasizes the health benefits of this excretion to the excreting body; my larger purpose is to emphasize that this excretion becomes pleasing and serviceable both to other parts of creation — the sun, after all, is dining on Adam's sweat — and to God. From his first day of existence, Adam moves, speaks, and willfully seeks a creator to worship, but before all this, his sweat may be a natural and involuntary sort of cosmic participation and worship. While sweat and toil are united in the curse of the Fall, perspiration and rest cooperate in prelapsarian Eden. After Adam and Eve's first observed meal, the idyllic "Supper Fruits" of book 4, digestion results in perspiration during sleep (4.331). In fact, these excretions in some way perfect Adam's sleep, which is "Aery light, from pure digestion bred, / And temperate vapors bland, which.../ *Aurora's* fan / Lightly dispers'd" (5.4–7).[93] Awake, Adam voluntarily works to prune back the extra vegetative growth; asleep, his body involuntarily expels any excess warmth and moisture. Consciously he tends the garden while, often unconsciously, he demonstrates his body's natural tempering powers even while offering something valuable to others. Similarly, Eve's meal preparation and the internal "cooking" that follows consumption provide a parallel instance of human art initiating and imitating the natural tempering impulses of the body. Voluntary labor is wed to involuntary bodily processes; selection, preparation, and consumption lead to digestion and, ultimately, transpiration. As this process occurs in the angelic body, transpired excesses of digestion provide one of the most pleasing luxuries of heaven — its perfume.

The union of fragrance and food is available in the Homeric concept of ambrosia, which is not only the food of the ancient Greek gods but also their unguent and perfume. The uncertain etymology of this delicacy points to these two functions. Some classical philologists dissect *ambrosios* into the privative prefix *α-* and the root *brotos*, "mortal," thereby making the word cognate with *ambrotos*, "immortal" (and corresponding to the Sanskrit *amrita*, "that which is immortal"); others believe the similarities between *ambrotos* and *ambrosios* to be simply coincidental, the latter word derived instead from *ambar*, a Semitic word for "fragrance," from which we receive the English words "amber" and "ambergris."[94] At least one scholar has suggested the root for "ambrosia" derives from *drosos*, cognate with the Latin *ros*, meaning "dew."[95] As a land-derived food of the gods, ambrosia becomes a link between heaven and earth, suggested in the *Odyssey* when Circe mentions "the tremulous doves, which carry ambrosia to Zeus the father."[96] Mentioning this myth, citing instances in ancient Greek texts in which ambrosia is a liquid, and uniting the fragrant and eternizing properties of ambrosia in accordance with its ambiguous etymology, F. A. Wright suggested in 1917 that the Greek word for ambrosia originally referred to a sweet-smelling exhalation of the earth: "Ambrosia, then, is something produced on earth and taken up by birds to heaven, magic dew."[97] Ambrosia also figuratively links heaven and earth through art and the Muses, whose voices and songs are said to be ambrosial.[98] As a substance, ambrosia not only sustains the gods; it also purifies — in the *Iliad* Hera "from her body washed away all stains / with ambrosia" — and perfumes:

> Next [she] anointed herself with ambrosial
> sweet olive oil, which stood there in its fragrance beside her,
> and from which, stirred in the house of Zeus by the golden pavement,
> a fragrance was shaken forever forth, on earth and in heaven.[99]

Ambrosia is at once a luxury of the gods and their most basic provender. Even the warhorses of Ares and Hera enjoy ambrosial fodder on Mount Olympus.[100] On special occasions where divinities interact with mortals, mortals too may enjoy the sustaining attributes of ambrosia. In the *Iliad*, Thetis anoints the body of Patroclus with ambrosia to prevent its decay, and Athena sustains the living body of Achilles with the same; in the *Odyssey*, when Menelaus and his men ambush Proteus, Eidothea applies ambrosia under the noses of the mortals to mask the foul smell of the seal carcasses under which they hide.[101] Sometimes night was called "ambrosial"; even battle-torn Troy experienced grateful evenings mild.[102] For Homer, ambrosia is not just the food, perfume, and cleansing agent of the gods; it may sustain godlike heroes and divine horses; it is the gods' gift to humans, and especially to their chosen ones.

Milton's mythology derives from Jerusalem as well as from Athens, and so I would like to point out the Hebraic correspondent to Hellenic ambrosia: manna, the bread of angels. While in one tradition ambrosia is "magic dew" exhaled by the earth and carried upward to feed the gods, manna descends from heaven with the dew and provides a supernatural food for human beings. In the haggadic section of Midrash *Sifré to Numbers*, manna is described as the perfect food, completely assimilated into the body so that no excrement results.[103] It took the flavor desired by the consumer, and it was so adaptable that it even supplied the Hebrew women with perfume during their desert wanderings.[104] Within the Christian tradition, the Deuterocanonical book of Wisdom reinforces this understanding of the protean, ambrosial properties of manna. Looking back to the Israelite desert wanderings, the author praises God for the versatile gift of manna: "You nourished your people with food of angels and furnished them with bread from heaven, ready to hand, untoiled-for, endowed with all delights and conforming to every taste."[105] Within early modern poetry, line 74 of the Countess of Pembroke's ottava rima translation of Psalm 78 (c. 1595) praises God who "bade the cloudes Ambrosian Manna rain," proving that the similarities between ambrosia and manna did not go unnoticed in Elizabethan England.

In *Paradise Lost*, Milton develops the importance of ambrosia in his conception of heaven and earth, and not without a reference to manna:

> In Heav'n the Trees
> Of life ambrosial fruitage bear, and vines
> Yield Nectar, though from off the boughs each Morn
> We brush mellifluous Dews, and find the ground
> Cover'd with pearly grain.   (5.426–30)

While Raphael is specifically talking of divine food here, there are variant instances in which ambrosia perfumes heaven — through the spoken word of God, through the natural scent of the fruit itself, and through the consumption and transpiration of heavenly food. Almost all of these instances are contextually related to the themes of offering or of sacrifice. In book 3, God's prophetic words of mercy for humankind through the Son's sacrificial volunteerism provide a pleasure that unites the rational, the sensual, and the spiritual: "Thus while God spake, ambrosial fragrance fill'd / All Heav'n, and in the blessed Spirits elect / Sense of new joy ineffable diffus'd" (3.135–37). What joy the angels experience at hearing God speak of human redemption through the Son's sacrifice is far superior to anything they can return to him, but their worship is also marked by the scent of ambrosia, pleasing to God.

As Milton joins God's speech to ambrosial fragrance, one might investigate whether other beings are capable of breathing out heavenly scented words. David Reid tentatively suggests this: "It is not impossible indeed that the angels actually exhale ambrosia as they do halleluiahs. It may be then, that the ambrosial fragrance that fills heaven in Book 3 comes as much from the angels' responding to God's promises as from God. The ambiguous syntax of the lines allows both readings."[106] Does the ambrosial fragrance from God diffuse ineffable joy among the angels, or does the sense of joy diffuse in the angels whose praises release an ambrosial fragrance? Either way, Reid suggests, the ultimate origin is God, and, "Given the great monistic circulation that Raphael explains to Adam and Eve, the two interpretations run into each other."[107]

The correlation between eating and desire raises certain questions about angelic aspiration. When in *The Anatomy of Melancholy* Burton considers if and how angels eat, he cites Michael Psellus's statement that angels "are nourished and have excrements" along with Scaliger's rebuttal ("if they feed on air, why do they not strive for air more pure?").[108] The assumption is that all creatures seek improvement in their food sources. The Raphael discourse seems in part to answer Scaliger, presenting a way humans and angels may, through a well-attended diet, "strive for air more pure" without following the satanic example of destructive aspiration and consumption.

If there is a connection between digestion and worship, we can expect that angels who no longer willfully participate in an attitude of service will begin to show signs of moral corruption in their very bodies. At the Stygian council, Mammon begrudges God "Ambrosial Odors and Ambrosial Flowers, / Our servile offerings" (PL 2.245–46). These ambrosial odors come from more than the crowns of amaranth the angels lay at God's throne; they proceed from the angels' very being as a product of their eating, and are a concentrated effect of their attitude of service. Such a fragrance results from the natural, effortless bodily process of worshiping in accordance with one's desire. Mammon, a traditionally intemperate villain, resents the "Forc't Halleluiahs," without considering that he has become a sick body, begrudging the release of excess (2.243). The "least erected Spirit," Mammon generally glories in the stuff of the world and of his own body, without accepting the purpose of its existence — to direct his gaze and his gratitude upward to the Creator (1.679). He exemplifies intemperance not by the excretion of excess but by the retention of it. No longer transpiring with ease, the rebel angels' bodies are stopped up, dooming them to waste away, rot, or explode; in the interim they feign halleluiahs, hypocritically imitating what once came naturally (6.744). This hypocrisy, not their prefall praise, is "forc't." Contrariwise, gratefulness in Paradise Lost is easy and mobile, involved in both worship and in gracious condescension. The purest of angels may find ease in worship as well as "No ingrateful food" among earthly viands. Thankfulness and pleasure — the OED shows that "grateful" carried both senses since the mid-sixteenth century — are naturally part of Edenic and heavenly meal-taking and are naturally promoted through the culmination of the digestive process.

Satan cunningly capitalizes on his detailed knowledge of the healthy angel in the dream he inspires in Eve, a dream all the more troubling to her because it has elements of truth in it. Oddly, Eve can smell in her dream, and she relates that "the pleasant savory smell [of forbidden fruit] / So quick'n'd appetite" that she "Could not but taste" it (5.84–86). This smell is presumably ambrosial, a descriptor assigned to the Tree of Knowledge as well as the Tree of Life and the fount that "through veins / Of porous Earth with kindly thirst up-drawn... with many a rill / Water'd the Garden" (4.219, 227–230; 9.852; 11.279). Significantly, Eve's seducer in the dream also smells like the food of the gods; Eve describes him as "One shap'd and wing'd like one of those from Heav'n / By us oft seen; his dewy locks distill'd / *Ambrosia.*" (5.55–57). Like other dreams, Eve's dream mixes the usual and the unusual (cf. *PL* 5.114–16). That ambrosia-scented angel hair is part of the usual experienced by Eve is suggested not only by her revelation that such angels were "oft seen" in Eden but also by the coming of the similarly scented Raphael: "Like *Maia's* son he stood, / And shook his Plumes, that Heav'nly fragrance fill'd / The circuit wide" (5.285–87). Reid concedes the fragrance could be merely a superficially applied perfume, although he "should like to think" that the aroma is biological: "It may be that Raphael has put something on his feathers and that Eve thinks that Satan has done the same with his hair.... But perhaps they themselves secrete the scents," he surmises.[109] "Good smells are part of the divine metabolism of the unfallen world," Reid reminds us, but he is troubled by Milton's tendency to associate smells with angels and devils without ever saying they make those smells, and he finds no precedent in Neoplatonic and hermetic writings for angels making their presence known by giving off perfumes, neither in Augustine nor John Dee nor Marsilio Ficino nor Henry More. He finds nothing on this in Robert West's *Milton and the Angels*. He invites further inquiry into smell in angelologies, but, as Kent Lehnhof mentions, "his ensuing plea for assistance has gone unanswered."[110]

Lehnhof concludes that the concept of odorous angels appears to be unique to Milton. Two years later, without directly addressing Reid or Lehnhof, Joad Raymond drew attention to the angelophanies

experienced by the Behmenist John Pordage and his family, documented in *Innocencie Appearing* (1655). In that account, as Raymond
relates, "the eyewitnesses smell heavenly perfume, and eat the food of
angels"; Raymond also quotes Richard Baxter's relation and dismissal
of the claim: "They pretend to hold visible and sensible Communion
with Angels, whom they sometime see, and sometime smell."[111] Burton
acknowledges angel-caused smells in his section on angels and demons
in *The Anatomy of Melancholy*: Angels are corporeal, have aerial bodies,
feel pain; the cut body of an angel will come together again, and angels
can transform into whichever shape they please; they move swiftly, represent "castles in the air" and other visions, cause smells, deceive the
senses, foretell the future, and "in their fall their bodies were changed
into a more aerial and gross substance."[112] This list quite nicely suggests
the *Anatomy* as a primary source for Milton's own depiction of angels
in *Paradise Lost*.[113] I have not been able to find direct mention of angel
smells in Burton's main source, Psellus's *On the Operation of Daemons*,
but there are hints in Psellus's interest in both daemonic and human
secretions. Psellus records the opinion that porosity was a sign of freedom from demonic possession: "[Demons] gladly attach themselves to
the moisture of animals, as being congenial to their nature, but especially to that of man, as being most congenial of all; and when infused
into them they occasion no small uproar, the pores in which the animal
spirit resides being clogged, and the spirit confined and displaced by the
bulk of their bodies, which is the cause of their agitating men's persons,
and injuring their faculties, and obstructing their motions."[114] Psellus's
character Thracian insists that these symptoms are not due to an imbalance of humors, as physicians would persuade one to think, but are
signs of supernatural influence.[115] Nevertheless, the spirits' sphere of
influence is remarkably bodily. Thracian also declares that spirits eat
by "drawing nourishment from the extraneous moisture lying around
them, and they afterwards void a spermatic substance."[116] Implicit in this,
perhaps, is the suggestion of odor, but nowhere in the copy of Psellus
I accessed was there a direct indication of spirits producing smells.

In his study of early Christian monasticism and demonology, David
Brakke notes several works that refer to demons producing bad smells.

The sources he mentions come from the tradition of the fourth century Egyptian desert fathers, including the works of Evagrius of Pontus, whose list of eight tempting thoughts (with gluttony listed first) was examined in chapter 1. Evagrius connects the unpleasant odor of demons with emotional and psychic disturbance. Thus in Evagrius's *Praktikos*: "The soul usually flares up against thoughts at the bad smell that prevails among the demons, when it perceives their approach upon being affected by the passion of the one who torments it"; and in the *Kephalaia Gnostica*: "Bodies of demons neither grow nor diminish and a strong stench accompanies them, by which they also put our passions into motion; and they are easily known by those who have received from the Lord the power to perceive this odor."[117] Brakke also cites an episode in Athanasius of Alexandria's *Life of Antony*, where that saint discovers a demon by its stench.[118] The theology of Milton's *De doctrina Christiana* squarely opposes the Trinitarian and anti-Arian theology of Athanasius, but as Thomas N. Corns points out, Athanasius's "status among western theologians of Milton's own age was high," and the very embroilment of fourth century Alexandria in the Arian controversy is evidence enough that the writings of Athanasius would be of particular interest to the poet.[119] Brakke's study indirectly answers Reid's and Lehnhof's queries about sources for Milton's odorous spirits.

One might turn from the hermetic tradition of Psellus and the writings of or about the desert fathers to consider two poetic precedents that Milton would certainly have known, and which may have influenced Eve's dream of the heavenly scented tempter-angel. Once again, Dante and Chaucer inform us. The tempter-angel's "locks distilling ambrosia" mimic those of Hera in the *Iliad*, but Milton's curious insistence on dream smells may be indebted to Dante's dream of the Siren in *Purgatorio*, 19.7–33. Dante's Siren, like Milton's Sin, is at first unappealing but then is transformed by the viewer's gaze. The Siren's allure is interrupted by the appearance of "an alert and saintly woman" (*una donna santa e presta*) who scolds Virgil (probably in his allegorical role as human reason), inciting him to tear the Siren's clothes, revealing her belly ['*l ventre*]. The stench of the exposed Siren wakes up the dreaming pilgrim. In Eve's dream, the seducing angel and fruit deceptively give a pleasing fragrance, unexposed by a divinely motivated Virgilian voice of reason (and reason's sleep becomes an important part of Adam's exonerating commentary on Eve's dream).

The second possible source for angel smells is Chaucer's Second Nun's Tale, a hagiography of Cecilia, patron saint of music. Cecilia tells her husband, Valerian, on their wedding night that if he ever touches or uses her sexually an angel will kill him. Valerian, reasonably demanding confirmation of this threat, is sent to Pope Urban I, who converts him to Christianity. This conversion enables Valerian to see the angel guarding Cecilia, who gives the couple two sweet-smelling crowns made of roses and lilies brought from paradise, invisible to the unchaste. Valerian's brother Tiberce initially cannot see the angel or the flower crowns but nonetheless registers the sweet token of the angel's visit, the aroma of the heavenly scented flowers:

> I wonder, this tyme of the yeer,
> Whennes that soote savour someth so
> Of rose and lilies that I smelle heer.
> For though I hadde hem in myne hands two,
> The savour myghte in me no depper go.
> The sweet smel that in myn herte I fynde
> Hath changed me al in another kynde.[120]

Although Milton would have thought the "Second Nun's Tale" filled with bad medieval theology regarding sex within marriage, surely the peculiarities of the angel visitation marked by the sweet aroma of paradisal flowers would have perked his imagination.

Adopting the concept of ambrosia as both food and perfume of the gods, Milton has his angels smell like what they eat.[121] This has led Lehnhof to propose that "Raphael's pleasant odor might be related to the manner by which he easily transpires his digestive excess," to explain at length the physiological implications of angelic digestion and the demonic stoppage of praise, and to attend to the relationship between ambrosia and praise.[122] Lehnhof's interest in angel smells and digestion extends to consider God's own evacuative motions: "God's involvement in the operations of elimination and evacuation do not occasion disgust but rather incite adulation. Milton corroborates the goodness of God not by distancing him from the eliminative functions of the lower bodily stratum but rather by asserting the ease with which he participates in them."[123] I would only emphasize that, although Milton unabashedly mentions the functions of "the lower bodily stratum" in his epic, he customarily reserves defecation as a fit analogy for demonic action or the heavenly response to evil, while excretion as transpiration, a process involving every pore of the body, not just the lower body, is the more refined counterpart found in angelic worship. Critically, this worship is natural, not forced, and the result of healthy digestion. As Milton's angels digest ambrosial fruits, "what redounds, transpires," and what transpires is likely to emit a sweet-smelling fragrance. This fragrance is part of the "Ambrosial Odors" and "servile offerings" Mammon begrudges God; when given freely, this superfluity is serviceable excess, honoring to God and pleasing to all. Ideal eating in this way serves a dual purpose, of worship and of ministry.

Following Augustine in the *City of God*, Milton has his angels truly, not "seemingly," eat human food, and both Augustine and Milton understand this angelic condescension as a form of ministry. There is, however, one key difference in Augustine:

> [Angels appearing to humans] took food not because they had any need of it, but because they wished to perform their service to men in an appropriately human fashion, and had the power to do this; for we are not to believe that, when men receive them as guests, the angels ate only in appearance. Indeed, to any who did not know them to be angels, it might seem that they ate from a necessity similar to our own. This is why the angel said in the book of Tobit, "You saw me eat, but it was with your eyes that you saw": that is, You thought that I, like you, took food for the sake of restoring my body.[124]

Instead of eating for nourishment, Augustine's angels eat with humans as an act of service, as part of their mission to restore humans, not themselves. The Augustinian passage contains several similarities with Milton's poem: it highlights the bodies of angels and their capacity to eat, it addresses whether or not Raphael eats with humans in the book of Tobit, and in context it argues that, after bodily resurrection, humans might become like the angels. While Augustine's angels eat out of delight, not necessity, Milton's angel eats "with keen dispatch / Of real hunger," as a created being that "needs / To be sustain'd and fed" (*PL* 5.436–37, 414–15). Ideal eating in Milton then is a means of connecting with other beings: an (inward) action inextricable from self-interest also becomes a form of gracious ministry (condescension) and an action united with effortless offering through the (upward) transpiration of excess, as the exhalations of the lower creatures sustain the life of the higher as fragrance and fruit, breath, and bread. Thus the air of paradise is compared to "*Sabean* odors" that please the northwest winds while "Cheer'd with the grateful smell Old Ocean smiles" (4.162, 165). At the top of this chain, the all-sufficient God enjoys not sustenance, but praise:

> sacred Light began to dawn
> In *Eden* on the humid Flow'rs, that breath'd
> Thir morning incense, when all things that breathe,
> From th' Earth's great Altar send up silent praise
> To the Creator, and his Nostrils fill
> With grateful Smell.   (9.192–97)

The myth of the dove-carried ambrosia corresponds to Milton's idea of fragrant earthly exhalations and to the natural simplicity of worship. What sublimes the plant also benefits higher beings and pleases with "grateful Smell."

Even Adam's excretions are fragrant. The "bland" vapors produced by his digestion could be described as "soft; mild, pleasing to the senses; gentle, genial, balming, soothing."[125] It now becomes apparent that when Adam first awakes with "Balmy Sweat" upon him, he has been naturally, spontaneously sending "silent praise" to God by a delicately and deliciously fragrant perspiration (*PL* 8.255).[126] His balmy sweat has the same delicious and sacrificial undertones as the spicy sap of the trees of Eden, "What drops the Myrrh, and what the balmy Reed"

(5.23). Prelapsarian human digestion, then, is a model not only of temperance, but of praising God — the one action that a creature may participate in with no danger of "excess / That reaches blame" (3.696–97). The systole and diastole of the cosmos is an indicator of its health and of its right order in relation to God. In Rebecca Totaro's eloquent words, "In *Paradise Lost* every breath of life, every exhalation of foulness, every comet, every perfumed prayer, every inspiration, and every aspiration speaks of the importance of the respiratory process in creation and in destruction."[127] God breathes life into Adam's nostrils, and, with a humble measure of reciprocity, Adam's exhalations become part of a vast system of creation that results in a superfluity of praise, pleasing to the nostrils of God himself (7.525–26; 9.195–96). Raphael says that all things come from God and up to him return. Similarly, aromatic offerings and incense to Yahweh are required in the Jewish religious tradition, expounded by Pauline theology as a sacrifice of praise and of bodily dedication to God, and preserved in early modern England. For example, in a plague sermon Lancelot Andrewes recommends cleansing infected air with the sweet odors and incense of prayer, exemplifying that systems of thought connecting exhalation and worship in perfumed prayers extended beyond paradisal contexts.[128]

Adam and Eve may not demonstrate the patience and consistent obedience required for their ascent to angelic status, but they can see, smell, and taste what it is like to participate in the divinely ordained, free, and natural system of incorporation, excretion, worshipful aspiration, and transformative giving that attends every meal in paradise. The emphasis on eating in Eden is perfect synecdoche for the entire prelapsarian experience, not only providing the occasion for enjoyment of the variety of foods and the routine of mealtimes that help to characterize "Grateful vicissitude," but also illustrating the transformative power of natural participation (both involuntary and freely willed) in the Great Chain of Eating.

5

The Food of Love, the Paradise Within, Augustinian Triads, and the Body Resurrected

This is what it is to go aright, or be led by another, into the mystery of Love: one goes always upward for the sake of the Beauty, starting out from beautiful things and using them like rising stairs...so that in the end he comes to know just what it is to be beautiful.... The love of the gods belongs to anyone who has given birth to true virtue and nourished it, and if any human being could become immortal, it would be he.

—Plato, *Symposium*, 211c–212b

After the Fall Adam and Eve are dispossessed of Eden, and presumably of the means of radical transformation through tract of time. One might doubt that any vestige of the divine plan of sanctified eating still exists, for the poem concludes with an impulse not upward but outward from Eden, downward to the plains below, and inward to the recesses of the soul. As Adam and Eve leave the garden to seek a "paradise within," Milton suggests that their prelapsarian state of inner peace may be partially recovered through natural, rational, and moral philosophy. These three branches of philosophy correlate with three sustaining "foods" given to Adam and Eve, and with the poem's three descriptions of creation's scale from earth to the heavens. Yet because return to an inner, mental paradise need not occlude return to an external, physical one, this chapter will also examine just how *Paradise Lost* ultimately engages the Christian doctrine of the resurrection of the body. To this end, this chapter presents a fuller case for Milton's dependence on Augustine — a connection that has already been mentioned in several contexts throughout this book. In this chapter, particular attention will be given to new evidence for how Augustinian triads provide a structural framework for the world of *Paradise Lost*.

After the Fall, the evidence for a residual potential to rise to God appears ambiguously bleak. Wild beasts leering at Adam "with count'nance grim" signal an inversion of the Great Chain of Eating such that humans might become prey for lower creatures instead of naturally offering food to higher ones (10.713). Predation and the will to power rather than generosity and love now link each creature in the food chain. Concern for one's young only intensifies the pangs of knowledge that the sins of the parent will be visited on the child; so Adam laments, "All that I eat or drink, or shall beget, / Is propagated curse" (10.728–29). Eve separately reaches the same conclusion, adding the observation that the human race has now become food for Death:

> If care of our descent perplex us most,
> Which must be born to certain woe, devour'd
> By Death at last, and miserable it is
> To be to others cause of misery,
> Our own begott'n, and of our Loins to bring
> Into this cursed World a woeful Race,
> That after wretched Life must be at last
> Food for so foul a Monster, in thy power
> It lies, yet ere Conception to prevent
> The Race unblest, to being yet unbegot.   (10.979–88)

Ironically, Adam and Eve's eating has made them a meal for Death and has disturbed their natural prospects for ascending the Great Chain along the lines of Raphael's hypothesis. Adam and Eve are grounded, and their inability to sustain themselves on rarefied matter becomes increasingly apparent when Adam converses with Michael after the Fall. At their expulsion from the garden, Adam and Eve are denied access to ambrosial fruits. God and angels insist and humans lament that there must be a change of soil, flowers, and fruits (11.98, 262, 273–74, 285). The most obvious Judaic and Christian examples of divine food available to fallen humanity — the sending of manna and the distribution of the Last Supper — are curiously absent from Michael's revelation of the world to come, and at first glance no vestige of the original plan of spiritually transformative eating appears after the Fall.[1]

Instead of becoming a means of radical ascent, the need for food pins Adam and his progeny to the ground. In book 12, Michael reveals to Adam a failed attempt at postlapsarian ascent in the vision of Nimrod and the Tower of Babel. Adam acknowledges the impaired potential of the human race in his excoriation of Nimrod's efforts to build his way to heaven:

> what food
> Will he convey up thither to sustain
> Himself and his rash Army, where thin Air
> Above the Clouds will pine his entrails gross,
> And famish him of breath, if not of Bread?   (12.74–78)

Rather than recapitulate Raphael's hypothesis of improved eating and metabolic potential, Adam sees in the vision of the Tower of Babel the limitations of breath and bread. Whatever is eaten during ascent, Adam assumes, must be brought from below and "convey[ed] up."

Interpreting the vision as a cautionary tale against asserting unnatural dominion over one's equals or superiors, Adam first asserts that humans were not created to rule over men, and then he more sternly objects that "this usurper his encroachment proud / Stays not on Man; to God his Tower intends / Siege and defiance" (72–74). Confident of the failure of any such enterprise, Michael approves of Adam's assessment of human limitations, but comments on the political rather than the theological:

> Justly thou abhorr'st
> That Son, who on the quiet state of men
> Such trouble brought, affecting to subdue
> Rational Liberty.   (12.79–82)

Instead of emphasizing the hubristic impiety in Nimrod's aspiring to reach the heavens with his tower building, Michael focuses on Nimrod's tyranny over other humans. Civil equality becomes increasingly important after the Fall. Monarchy works in heaven because God and the angels are without sin; the tendency toward corruption renders dangerous an imitation of heaven's regime on earth. Even if the appeal to republicanism is predictable, Michael's deflection of theme from theological to political relations prevents the reader from knowing the angel's exact opinion on human aspirations to more rarefied environs.

Michael's silence on the Raphael hypothesis is intensified, and becomes more significant, by an omission of a detail in the biblical account. Genesis 11:6 suggests that Yahweh recognized the potential success of the Tower of Babel scheme: "And the LORD said, Behold, the people is one, and they have all one language; and this they begin to do: and now nothing will be restrained from them, which they have imagined to do" (AV). This verse legitimizes the tower as a potential threat to the sovereignty of God. Within *Paradise Lost*, however, the hint of divine insecurity is absent. Where silence offers less than an iota of evidence for man's inability to reach God's throne through his own efforts, the laughter in heaven that Michael subsequently relates dismisses Nimrod's attempt as false jeopardy. If Milton's God can comfortably laugh with the Son at Lucifer's attempted coup d'état, certainly humans can pose no genuine threat to the throne of God. Michael presumably finds Nimrod's plans as ridiculous as do the heavens in the vision he imparts to Adam: God "in derision" confuses the tongues of the builders, at which "great laughter was in Heav'n," and "the building left / Ridiculous" (*PL* 12.52, 59, 61–62). Commander of angels, war veteran, and eyewitness of Satan's defeat, Michael will not seriously entertain any human plot to besiege heaven, and to Adam's imagination Nimrod's power-aggrandizing aspirations could only result in asphyxiation and starvation, not adaptation and metamorphosis. And while the human desire to ascend to God may be removed from the desire to dominate one's own or to become one's own God, Michael ignores, rejects, or is ignorant of Raphael's detailed understanding of

God's original plan for humankind, his supposition that humans could aspire to the heavens by ascending the scale of Nature.

In lieu of the Raphael hypothesis, Michael offers his own supposition — that Eden would have been Adam's "Capital Seat" had he remained obedient (11.343). In Michael's version — the narrative's last extended speculation into the destiny of humanity — what Adam has lost is not the potential to rise but the position of preeminence among his children; susceptible to acting tyrannically as well as uxoriously, Adam is sentenced "to dwell on even ground now with [his] Sons" (11.348). Unfallen humanity's highest possible station plateaus into an unmiraculous dignity; imagining the horizontal growth of the species rather than the vertical ascent of the individual, Michael even supposes the future of sinless humans would have included a paradoxical growth downward, as Adam's progeny leave Eden to populate the plains below. Michael's severe, plain, and leveling words spoken in a postlapsarian context temper Raphael's cavalier optimism regarding prelapsarian upward mobility within a hierarchical cosmos, flatly suggesting that the potential for increased communion with the angels as expressed by Raphael is now and may ever have been a false dream. Then again, Michael's retrospective, counterfactual hypothesis may be tainted by his present knowledge of human failure. Michael does not necessarily confirm Adam's statement that the mountain air is too thin for Nimrod, nor does he directly contradict Raphael. As all Milton's angels and humans learn from the War in Heaven, besieging God is not beseeching him, and the futility of approaching God's throne through the former method does not bespeak the futility of the latter.

MODES OF ASPIRATION AND ASCENT

In the previous chapter I argued, following Kent Lehnhof, that the Great Chain of Eating is a means to worship, resulting in a naturally fragrant offering to God that also proves gratifying to the giver. In this way active participation in the scale of nature takes the form of beseeching God, even as it enacts a physical change in the beseecher.

Eating well results in transpiration of excess, which contributes to the "grateful Smell" of creation, so-called both because it carries the gratitude of Creation and because it is pleasing to the Creator (9.197). One indication of the perversion of this system, and of the effect of the Fall on Nature, is a vulturelike Death sniffing out "the smell / Of mortal change on Earth" from the gates of hell (10.272–73). The smell of mortality portends new evils and losses. When in the final book of the poem Adam questions the availability of breath and bread for those who, like Nimrod, assault heaven, he continues to associate eating and breathing, but notes new limitations for humanity and radical changes to the symbiotic system of grateful eating and exhalation. Nevertheless, the concept of the pleasingly fragrant offering is not lost to history; it becomes a key part of the tradition of sacrificial worship, beginning with the "grateful steam" of Abel's sacrifice (11.442). Even while yet in Eden, fallen Adam and Eve continue to connect with God through the customary, physical means of exhalation. The most pervasive indication of their repentance and desire for reparation with God is their sighing, which itself is only made possible by prevenient grace:

> Thus they, in lowliest plight, repentant stood
> Praying, for from the Mercy-seat above
> Prevenient Grace descending had remov'd
> The stony from thir hearts, and made new flesh
> Regenerate grow instead, that sighs now breath'd
> Unutterable, which the Spirit of prayer
> Inspir'd, and wing'd for Heav'n with speedier flight
> Than loudest Oratory.
>
> ....
>
>   To Heav'n thir prayers
> Flew up, nor miss'd the way, by envious winds
> Blown vagabond or frustrate: in they pass'd
> Dimensionless through Heav'nly doors: then clad
> With incense, where the Golden Altar fum'd,
> By thir great Intercessor, came in sight
> Before the Father's Throne.
>
> (11.1–8, 14–20; cf. 10.1090, 1102, 11.31)

Unvoiced, these sighs are breathed from the regenerate and contrite heart, and are themselves inspired by the "Spirit of prayer," breath within breath. The prayers and sighs are dimensionless but literally fly upward, "wing'd for Heav'n," and, "clad / With incense," through the Son's mediation they become the substance of supplication. Initiated by "implanted Grace" and presented to God as "Fruits of…pleasing savor" carrying the "smell of peace," they retain aspects of the physical scale of nature and the Chain of Eating (11.22–39). While the sighs fly up, tears of contrition drop to water the ground, a sign of the continued human task to cultivate the now-fallen earth and their now-fallen earthly lives. Milton's cosmos remains material and sensory even at the throne of heaven, and the path of ascent remains distinctly physical. The offering renews possibility for Adam and Eve's own ascent, for the Son petitions God to show mercy on them during their earthly lives and strengthens the hope that, beyond death, the "redeem'd may dwell in joy and bliss, / Made one," as the Son says to the Father, "with me as I with thee am one" (11.43–44). This promise of union with God remains consistent with Raphael's assertion that created things proceeding from God "up to him return," and with his account of God's proclamation that ultimately earth and heaven will form "One Kingdom, Joy and Union without end" (5.470, 7.161). A mediator is now necessary for humans to ascend, but God's ultimate and unshakeable purpose for humankind, as expressed before the Fall — even before the creation of earth — still involves the bodily, material, physical world.

There are yet other ways to understand this path of ascent. From the beginning, the scale of nature has had philosophical and moral counterparts. After Raphael gives his physiological explanation for the order of the cosmos, Adam responds,

> Well hast thou taught the way that might direct
> Our knowledge, and the scale of Nature set
> From centre to circumference, whereon
> In contemplation of created things
> By steps we may ascend to God.   (5.508–12)

Adam's turn to contemplation succeeds Raphael's most explicit defense of the materialism of the cosmos, and one might well surmise that Adam has misheard Raphael, quite failing to grasp his overt point about faithful eating. Adam's superimposition of the intellectual activity of contemplating onto Raphael's exposition of the physical activity of eating is certainly in accord with his tendency to philosophize (observable, for example, in his evening conversation with Eve in *Paradise Lost* 4.660–88). Perhaps Adam intuits the analogy between food and knowledge that Raphael later explicitly makes: "But Knowledge is as food, and needs no less / Her Temperance over Appetite" (7.126–27). At the same time that the knowledge/food analogy warns against an intellectual equivalent to gluttonous consumption of physical food, the analogy also suggests that well-governed knowledge might, as nature does, form a scale to heaven, ascended by patient effort and obedience. As Raphael divides the "scale of Nature" into "various degrees / Of substance," so he acknowledges a scale of knowledge of sorts, angelic (intuitive) and human (discursive) reason differing "but in degree, of kind the same" (5.473–74, 490). But when Adam defines "contemplation of created things" as the means to ascend this scale of Nature, his opinion is tempered by Raphael's warnings against excessive speculative knowledge: "Solicit not thy thoughts with matters hid.... be lowly wise," the angel cautions (8.167, 173). After the Fall, expulsion from the garden, demotion to lower soil, and the deleterious effects of sin on climate and the human body severely limit the possibilities of self-elevation through eating; similarly, the impairment of reason after the Fall hampers ascent to God through intellectual means. In the physical realm, divine grace must initiate and support temperance to enable ascent; in intellectual matters, Milton insists, divine revelation must direct and govern prudence in those seeking the heights of knowledge.

Before concluding his discourse with Adam, Raphael presents yet a third account of the scale to heaven, and in doing so he extends the "Knowledge is as food" analogy to include the correlative of love. Adam interprets the scale of nature or the Great Chain of Eating as a ladder of contemplation; Raphael encourages Adam in this interpretation but at last describes it Neoplatonically as a ladder of love:

> Love refines
> The thoughts, and heart enlarges, hath his seat
> In Reason, and is judicious, is the scale
> By which to heav'nly Love thou may'st ascend,
> Not sunk in carnal pleasure.   (8.589–93)

This time, Adam's response suggests no further analogy: "To Love thou blam'st me not, for Love thou say'st / Leads up to Heav'n, is both the way and guide" (8.612–13). Love is both ladder and leader, "the way and guide"; its prominence and pervasiveness, however, does not refute, disparage, or ignore the previous scales, the regions of the self they represent (body and intellect), or their corresponding virtues (temperance and prudence). It is "Charity, the soul / Of all the rest" of the virtues, that preserves, motivates, and inspires these virtues in the pursuit of godliness (12.584–85).

Of course, Milton's depiction of the scale from earth to God as one of love is no innovation. The idea is at least as old as Plato's *Symposium*, which joins the occasion of banqueting and the method of philosophy with the subject of love. At the climax of the discourse, as presented in the epigraph to this chapter, Socrates recounts Diotima's description of the mystery of love as vertical stages in appreciating beauty, beginning with the love of a single beautiful person or object.[2] Nearing the top of this ladder, the love of the beauty of knowledge comes just before the ultimate stage of loving divine Beauty itself.[3] The concept of the ladder of love found popular expression in the early modern era with Pietro Bembo's description of the *scala amoris* in the conclusion to Castiglione's *Book of the Courtier* (1528), and by this time this philosophy of love had been for centuries adapted by Christian Neoplatonists, theologians, and religious mystics to describe the soul's ascent to God. Ambrose of Milan, Augustine of Hippo, Benedict of Nursia, Gregory the Great, Bernard of Clairvaux, Bonaventure, Thomas Aquinas, the Flemish mystic John of Ruysbroeck, the English mystic Walter Hilton, and the Spanish mystic John of the Cross all envision the path to God as a ladder, often characterized by or culminating in love.[4]

Perhaps the most eloquent articulation of this sublimation (John of the Cross's poem *The Dark Night of the Soul* is a pithy and beautiful alternative) is found in Dante's *Divine Comedy*, where love is the ordering principle of the cosmos, *l'amor che move il sole e l'altre stelle*.[5] There is some evidence that Milton alludes to Dante's love-motivated cosmos when Satan, standing on the lower stair of the scale to heaven, looks down to earth through the planets and stars. The pilgrim Dante does this twice in *Paradiso*, once directly after having ascended the scale of contemplation from Saturn to the sphere of the fixed stars, and once as Beatrice prepares him to ascend to the Primum Mobile.[6] From Saturn, which holds the contemplatives, a ladder marks the movement beyond the intelligible toward the beatific vision, or, to put it in the context of the *Symposium*, from love of the beauty of knowledge to the love of divine Beauty itself. Interestingly, although all of creation may be perceived as a scale to God, Dante's and Milton's literal ladders seem to be similarly located in their respective poetic worlds, with the bottom step just above the planets. Both are associated with the contemplative and mystic traditions: "Each Stair mysteriously was meant" (*PL* 3.516). That Milton is engaging Dante rather than any other Christian poet, theologian, or mystic's imagination of the scale to God is suggested by an acrostic in the relevant passage from *Paradise Lost*:

> Such wonder seiz'd, though after Heaven seen,
> The Spirit malign, but much more envy seiz'd
> At sight of all this World beheld so fair.
> Round he surveys, and well might, where he stood
> So high above the Circling Canopy.   (3.552–56; emphasis added)

It is probable that this fanciful passage plays on Dante's own word-play in ending all three canticles of his *Divine Comedy* with *stelle*, the stars.[7] The allusion carries a certain irony in that Milton's cosmic traveler is cut off from all but a destructive and perverse self-love. One can only surmise what Milton is doing in having his Satan imitate Dante the pilgrim while his story and style imitate that of Dante the poet (demonizing his Catholic literary forbear? following the epic convention of authorial one-upmanship? revealing his anxiety of influence?); nonetheless, one may reasonably interpret the descriptions of the scale to heaven in *Paradise Lost* as Milton engaging Dante. Like Dante, Milton proclaims love's supremacy.

Like Milton's use of the Aristotelian concept of nesting faculties of the soul, the higher subsumes the lower. Raphael knows there is "without Love no happiness" (*PL* 8.621), and Michael acknowledges love "By name to come call'd Charity, the soul / Of all the rest" of virtues (12.584–85). The supremacy of love or charity, so central to the assertion of eternal providence in *Paradise Lost*, so integral to the Augustinian influence pervading the poem, can be neglected or overlooked by readers, either because the theme is well worn, or because it fails to convince in light of satanic grandeur or Divine authority. From Satan's perspective, position in the cosmos is a matter of power and its attendant splendor; the Great Chain is a matter of competition and rank. Yet, as it is for Dante, for Milton love is not only the means by which one may ascend to God, but also the means by which one may bring another to beatitude. So Adam and Eve first appear "hand in hand..., the loveliest pair / That ever since in love's imbraces met" (4.321–22); so they are "Imparadis't in one another's arms / The happier *Eden*" (4.506–07). Divine love is consummately expressed in the Son's sacrificial offering of himself, as the angel choir celebrates: "O unexampl'd love, / Love nowhere to be found less than Divine!" (3.410–11) — and Michael promises Adam that "through love" the Spirit will write the "Law of Faith" on the hearts of all Christians (12.488–89).

For the sake of comparison, consider Henry Vaughan's portrait of the contemplative pilgrim looking at eternity and time in "The World" (published in *Silex scintillans* in 1650). Vaughan, who was introduced to hermetic philosophy through his twin brother, Thomas, describes eternity as a great ring of light, beneath which he receives a vision of the world in time. In hermetic Neoplatonic philosophy, the world can be escaped through ascending the eight spheres of the cosmos, with songs of praise preliminary to entrance into the substance of God.[8] Henry Vaughan's poem takes comfort in this upward mobility toward light,

> The way which from this dead and dark abode
>   Leads up to God,
>   A way where you might tread the sun and be
>   More bright than he.   (53–56)

The ring of eternal light ultimately becomes a symbol of the marriage feast of Christ and the church: "This ring the Bridegroom did for none provide / But for his bride" (59–60). The poem's optimism, however, is darkened by the exclusion of those who prefer the world over this cosmic journey. The poem's coda quotes 1 John 2:16–17, and reference to the lust of the flesh, the lust of the eyes, and the pride of life suggests the characters described in each of the poem's three stanzas (the doting lover, the darksome statesman, and the fearful miser) respectively and collectively represent the sins of the world in toto. Granted, here are Christian (and distinctively Augustinian) commonplaces, and evidence for Milton being particularly influenced by Vaughan's "The World" is unnecessary for this argument; what is important are the ideas shared: The trifold division of the world's sin according to 1 John, the contemplative's ascent to God, a change in one's nature through this ascent, and an eternal banquet for the loving faithful. For Milton as for Vaughan, the world may be divided into the Johannine categories of the lust of the flesh, the lust of the eyes, and the pride of life, but Milton insists that this world may be an integral part of an avenue to God, variously envisioned as a scale of nature, of contemplation, and of love.

Nature, the intellect, and the will to love emphasize interrelated aspects of the same cosmic ordering in *Paradise Lost*. To become more like the angels is to improve in each of these interconnected areas of eating, knowing, and loving, and although the narrative progression reveals the hierarchical cosmos progressively as a scale of nature, then of contemplation, and finally of love, the movement toward God involves all three. Unlike Plato's scale, Milton's never leaves the material world behind. First, Milton interrelates knowledge and nature. Rational potential is a part of human nature, and reason looks in part to nature for its subject matter, and it is important that this includes thoughtful eating. Recently, David B. Goldstein, Amy L. Tigner, and

Wendy Wall have addressed the Western bias disconnecting food and drink from the life of the mind: "Influenced by Platonic philosophy, Western society has often treated cuisine as a less than serious focus for discussion. We may enjoy it, we may acknowledge its necessity for our survival and happiness, but we shouldn't spend too much time talking about it lest we be marked as unthinking and intemperate gluttons."[9] Early modern food studies and new Shakespeare scholarship attending to the culinary and the commensal bring to light the vast difference between thoughtful eating and *gula studiose*, a difference Milton clearly depicts in *Paradise Lost*, where good philosophy is rooted in the earth, even if its seeds are heavenly in origin. "Contemplation of created things" unites the fundamental, material description of the Chain of Being with the concept of an intellectually organized cosmic hierarchy. Raphael's examination of knowledge reinforces the necessity of created things for the philosopher as well as the raconteur. "Things on Earth" must serve as metaphors in Raphael's spiritual tale, as they must serve as objects of study from which to derive higher wisdom (6.893).

Second, knowledge and love are related. Contemplation itself provides a link between knowledge and love, a link already present in the Latin *studium*: enthusiasm, devotion, and eagerness of the will attached to the rigor of the intellect. At the same time, the revelation of human love as the scale to heavenly love is not a movement away from the intellect, for such love is "Founded in Reason" (4.755). Though right reason must rule over the passions, authentic love exceeds and governs reason: "Love unlibidinous reign'd" (5.449); love "refines / The thoughts" (8.589–90); love "hath his seat / In Reason, and is judicious" (8.590–91). In fact, there is some sense in which love apart from the intellect ceases to be love at all, for one cannot truly love without knowing something of the beloved; although divine love is not entirely intelligible to the human mind, the human love for God, expressed through worship, demands some knowledge of God. This is apparent in the very organization of *De doctrina Christiana* and of many systematic theologies preceding Milton's, including those of Reformed theologians Amandus Polanus, William Ames, and Johannes Wollebius (the last being Milton's closest model). Each of these is divided into two parts, on faith (and thereby devoted to explaining doctrine) and love or charity (devoted to the practice of faith, and therefore to worship or ethics).[10] In the opening chapter to De doctrina Christiana Milton avers that faith (fides), defined as "knowledge of God," and love (charitas), defined as "the worship of God," are inseparable in practice. While knowledge enables love, love supports knowledge, for "obedience and charity are always the best guides to knowledge" (OW 8:21). This correspondence is fundamental to Paradise Lost.

Finally, love and nature are also intertwined. Love itself has its grounding in ontology, for love without an object and without action cannot be realized. In insisting on the ontological value of earth and its creatures Milton diverges significantly from the characteristically Neoplatonic turn from the material world and the pleasures of the body. For Plotinus, "What else is Sophrosyny, rightly-so-called, but to take no part in the pleasures of the body, to break away from them as unclean and unworthy of the clean?"[11] Milton famously argues the opposite in Areopagitica, insisting that passions and pleasures "rightly temper'd are the very ingredients of vertu" (YP 2:527). In Paradise Lost, the demonstration of love depends on a certain materiality, even if rarefied. As Raphael explains, the human body was created pure, and angelic expressions of love are physical, even though they are perfected from bodily obstruction:

> Whatever pure thou in the body enjoy'st
> (And pure thou wert created) we enjoy
> In eminence, and obstacle find none
> Of membrane, joint, or limb, exclusive bars:
> Easier than Air with Air, if Spirits embrace,
> Total they mix, Union of Pure with Pure
> Desiring.   (8.622–28)

The angels eat better food than humans, are pure intelligences, and embrace without bar, but their "intelligential substances" still require food, and their felicity depends on the expression of love (5.407–08; 8.621, 633–34). As "incorporeal spirits" engaged in divine service, these angels illustrate what Milton imagines a perfect human might look like if he improved his nature: not leaving behind the physical world or rational sphere, but perfected by love.

AUGUSTINIAN TRIADS

Nature, knowledge, and love: these three variations of the scale of the cosmos correspond to an Augustinian tripartition so exactly that the correspondence deserves careful examination. In book 11, chapters 24 and 25 of the *City of God*, Augustine argues from the Trinity and from Creation to divide all philosophy into three branches. Book 11 marks a significant new beginning for Augustine's tome, for this is where the second part begins and where the city of God is introduced (chapter 1). The book is also of particular relevance to *Paradise Lost*; its chapters ponder the role of the Son of God as mediator leading humans to divine knowledge (chapter 2), the dangers and futility of trying to comprehend the time before the creation of the world and the infinite realms of outer space (chapter 5),[12] the six days of Creation and the day of rest (chapters 7 and 8), the question of whether the angels were indeed created by God (chapter 9), the free will of the angels at their fall (chapters 11 and 13), the comparison of pre-Fall paradise with the future blessedness promised to fallen humankind (chapter 12), the punishment and degradation of Satan (chapter 15), the gradations and hierarchy of beings in the created world (chapter 16), the pleasing vicissitudes of creation (chapter 18), and in chapter 23, the fallen angels' retention of beautiful bodies (contra Origen, who argued that fallen bodies became gross by sinning). In this context one may find the rather long passage quoted below, which, despite its Trinitarianism and origin in Platonic thought, bears directly on the structure and purpose of Milton's *cosmopoiesis*:

> But if the divine goodness is nothing other than holiness, then certainly it is a careful use of reason, and not a presumptuous boldness, to see a suggestion of the Trinity expressed in the works of God as if by a veiled mode of speech: a mode intended to develop our understanding when we ask, of anything whatsoever that God has created, Who made it? By what means did He make it? And, Why did He make it? For it is the

Father of the Word Who said, Let it be. And that which was made when He spoke was beyond doubt made by means of the Word. Again, when it is said, "God saw that it was good," it is thereby sufficiently signified that God made what He made not from any necessity, not because He had need of any benefit, but simply from His own goodness: that is, so that it might be good.... And if this goodness is rightly understood to be the Holy Spirit, then the whole Trinity is revealed to us in the works of God. In this Trinity is the origin, the instruction and the blessedness of the holy City which is on high, among the holy angels. For if we ask, whence comes it? God founded it; or Whence comes its wisdom? God enlightened it; or Where lies its happiness? In the enjoyment of God. It has its form by subsisting in Him; its enlightenment by contemplating Him; its joy by abiding in Him. It is; it sees; it loves. Its strength is in the *eternity* of God; its light is in God's *truth*; in God's *goodness* is its joy.[13]

Augustine asserts that every created thing by virtue of its peculiar being, wisdom, and happiness reveals essential attributes of the tri-une God: God's eternity (and Augustine names God the Father as the source of all creation and being), his truth (associated with the Son as Logos), and his goodness (manifest in the Holy Spirit as Paraclete, and as appraiser of the virtue of creation). He then extends the analogy to explain how these three divine attributes account for three key philosophical categories, which he finds in classical (and thus non-Trinitarian) as well as Christian thought:

So far as one is given to understand, it is for the same reason that the philosophers have wished to divide their discipline into three parts (or rather, were enabled to see that there is such a threefold division; for they did not invent it, but only discovered it): of which one part is called *physical*, another *logical* and the third *ethical*. In the writings of many authors, these divisions are called by the Latin terms *natural*, *rational* and *moral* philosophy....

It does not follow from this threefold division that these philosophers had any notion of a Trinity in God. Plato, however, is said to have been the first to discover and recommend this division, and he saw that only God could be the author of nature, the giver of intelligence and the inspirer of the love by which life is made good and blessed. Also, it is certain that, though opinions differ as to the nature of things, and the method of investigating truth, and the good to which we ought to refer all that we do, it is to these three great and general questions that all the efforts of the philosophers are devoted.[14]

In Augustine's synthesizing theology, God's eternity, truth, and goodness correspond to the natural, rational, and moral aspects of all knowledge, to the philosophical branches of ontology, epistemology, and ethics. Moreover, Augustine continues, anyone who imitates the Creator in fashioning a work of art demonstrates three corresponding attributes: "natural aptitude, education, and practice."[15] Finally, humans as humans contain within themselves a similar tripartition:

> And we indeed recognize in ourselves the image of God: that is, of the supreme Trinity. This image is not equal to God. Indeed, it is very far removed from Him; for it is neither co-eternal with him, nor, to express the whole matter briefly, is it of the same substance as God. It is however, nearer to God in nature than anything else made by Him, even though it still requires to be reformed and perfected in order to be a still closer likeness. For we *exist,* and *know* that we exist, and we *take delight* in our existence and our knowledge of it.[16]

In summary, the Augustinian analogy develops as follows:

Father: Son: Spirit::
Eternity: Truth: Goodness::
Physical: Logical: Ethical::
Natural: Rational: Moral::
Ontology: Epistemology: Ethics::
Natural Aptitude: Education: Practice::
Being: Knowledge: Love::
Body: Intellect: Will.

These groupings are not merely analogous, of course. Many are nearly synonymous expressions of a triplicity that Augustine saw in his God, in nature, in all philosophy, and in human psychology. The most surprising connection is perhaps that between morality and love, but in *De doctrina Christiana* Milton reinforces this by filling the section on love with ethical matters, and in *Paradise Lost* Raphael reinforces such a connection when he asserts that to love God is to obey him (*PL* 5.501–02, 529–40). And in Augustine, although the perversion of the will, rather than any single action, becomes the fulcrum of the Fall, love and virtue are similarly united, for human desire necessarily influences human action. For Augustine, our weight is our love, drawing us toward God, or toward whatever we desire more than God.[17] Augustine's triadic structure thus neatly corresponds to Milton's three articulations of the scale from earth to heaven, beginning with the fundamentally physical one of eating, proceeding to rational contemplation, and thence to active love.

An equally intriguing correspondence may be observed between these partitions and the three direct invocations opening books 1, 3, and 7 of *Paradise Lost*. Stevie Davies and William B. Hunter Jr. in "Milton's Urania" made a claim similar to what I am arguing, but the structure they observed has been overlooked or dismissed by many Milton scholars, in part due to Hunter's use of this perceived structure to support arguments for Milton's orthodoxy, or at least for Milton holding a subordinationist position that could still be described as Trinitarian, a position in which the Son and the Holy Spirit are considered inferior persons of the Trinity but still sharing in the Godhead.

The Kerrigan, Rumrich, and Fallon edition of Milton's *Complete Poetry and Essential Prose* provides an example of recent strong reactions against such attempts to smooth out Milton's heterodoxies; its introduction to *Paradise Lost* describes arguments such as Hunter's for Milton's "alleged orthodoxy" as "complicated, recondite, and to the embarrassment of Milton scholarship, highly successful," especially in the 1970s and 1980s. The editors note that after Hunter's arguments Milton scholars had used the term *subordinationism* in confusing and misleading ways, but at least one thing is clear: "The subordinationism attributed to Milton is in short, per Michael Bauman's definitive formulation, 'not orthodox, and Milton does not teach it.'"[18] Much strong scholarship has recently attended to Milton's many heresies and heterodoxies (heretical at least for the seventeenth century Church of England) and has consequently raised a flag against any readings wedding Milton to mere Christianity. I am aware that I may lose readers here in reproducing parts of Davies and Hunter's argument, but I think it deserves another look, regardless of its Trinitarian strains, for reasons to be made clear in due course.

Hunter had argued in 1959 that the figurative expressions of the Son in the book 3 invocation suggest a subordinationist trinity in *Paradise Lost*, one not unrelated to the Neoplatonic trinity of One-Mind-Soul.[19] Almost 30 years later, Davies and Hunter argued that a Trinitarian motif runs through the invocations of *Paradise Lost*, with the "Heav'nly Muse" of book 1 progressively identified as God the Father, the Son, and the Holy Spirit in "lines 6 to 10a, 10b to 16, and 17 to 22a," respectively.[20] In book 3, the argument runs, the invocation of "holy Light" refers particularly to the Son as Logos, described both as a stream derived from an inexpressible fountain and as an effluence of light derived from a "bright essence," suggesting also the Father's role as the superior source of the Son (6–8). Hunter and Davies identify the "heav'nly Muse" in line 19 of book 3 as the Holy Spirit. In book 7, Davies and Hunter assert, the Holy Spirit corresponds to Urania not primarily as the muse of astronomy but as Aphrodite Urania, or heavenly love. The Holy Spirit is more readily associated with this female source of inspiration through the description of the Spirit's maternal brooding over the waters of Creation and in accordance with the feminine Hebrew substantive *ruah* (spirit, breath, that which God breathes into Adam to give him life).[21] Finally, in book 9, the reference to a "Celestial Patroness" is indirect, Davies and Hunter explain, because by this point in the poem "Milton had attained such profound assurance of the continuity and audibility of his inspiration as to have reached a condition identifiable as the state of (poetic) Grace," and consequently did not need to invoke a muse that comes "unimplor'd" (*PL* 9.22). Davies and Hunter go so far as to claim, "The distinctions between the persons of the Trinity are not experienced as discrete boundaries, but as subtle transitions mysteriously integrating the perception of the Godhead, as the narrator's vision pauses on each in turn."[22]

While the heterodox views of the Son and the Holy Spirit in *De doctrina Christiana* should make readers wary of any Trinitarian interpretations of *Paradise Lost*, they need not prevent us from interpreting the three direct invocations as expressive of distinct attributes or aspects of God, variously expressed in the Father, the Son, and the Spirit.[23] Such a reading helps reconcile this understanding of *Paradise Lost* with some otherwise incongruent statements in *De doctrina Christiana*: that the Son of God is not equivalent to the character of Wisdom in Proverbs 8, for example, or that the Holy Spirit should not be an object of invocation, or that the Spirit of God or Holy Spirit could simply mean "that divine breath or influence by which everything is created and nourished" (YP 6:304, 295, 282).[24] Hunter further notes that Milton describes God as unapproachable without mediation, and this limit perhaps suggests that the invoking of "the meaning, not the Name" of Urania reveals not mere dissatisfaction with classical sources of inspiration but also humble reverence in approaching God (*PL* 7.5).

In general, Davies and Hunter's reading of the invocations of *Paradise Lost* demonstrates familiarity with various traditional associations of divine attributes with specific persons of the Trinity. The assigning of these attributes holds whether or not Father, Son, and Holy Spirit are thought to share in the total essence of the Godhead.[25] As anti-Trinitarian as *De doctrina* is, in confronting orthodox Trinitarianism in book 1 Milton includes separate sections on God (esp. chapter 2), on the Son (chapter 5), and on the Holy Spirit (chapter 6). One need not accept the argument for Milton being a non-Arian subordinationist to argue that Milton's invocations meditate on various aspects and attributes of God, brought to light by turns in particular association with God the Father, with the Son, and with the Spirit of God. To this extent I agree with Hunter and Davies's argument for structure within the invocations of *Paradise Lost*, only suggesting that, while the book 1 invocation introduces God, the Son, and the Holy Spirit, per Hunter and Davies's argument, it especially emphasizes the attri-butes of the Father. This would well coincide with their argument that book 3 refers to Father, Son, and Spirit but focuses particularly on the Son. (Milton's third invocation, of Urania, will receive extended con-sideration in chapter 6.)

I further propose that Milton conscientiously organizes his three direct invocations in accord with Augustinian triads. Milton, like Augustine, asserts that "God the Father is the first efficient cause of all things" and "the first, absolute and sole cause of all things" (OW 8:287, 291). Although the Son as "Omnific Word" and the "brood-ing...Spirit of God" have direct roles to play in fashioning the universe, God's responsibility for creation is in *Paradise Lost* primarily attached to his fatherhood, especially as Milton also makes God the material cause of creation (*PL* 7.217, 235; OW 8:291–93). The "great Father" presides over creation as the "Author and end of all things," the "sovran Planter" and "our Nourisher" (*PL* 7.588, 591; 4.691; 5.398). In *De doctrina Christiana* Milton thinks it "readily intelligible" from sacred Scripture that the works of God, even those ascribed to the Son, "all ought principally and properly to be ascribed to the father alone" (OW 8:165). The Father, or the creative power associated with him, becomes the logical source of inspiration for the beginning of a Christian epic poem dealing with the beginnings of creation. The first invocation fitly corresponds to the physical and ontological attributes of Augustine's first third to his triad (*PL* 1.6–10). The parallels are intensified when one considers Milton's expectation that even his detractors would iden-tify God as superlatively associated with being ("the *ens* of [all] *entia*") (OW 8:151–53).

In the second invocation, the poet implores Holy Light, or the power of God demonstrated in the Son as Logos (reason or wisdom) to "Shine inward, and the mind through all her powers / Irradiate" (3.52–53). Here the poet seeks mental and spiritual illumination from God, accessible through the Son as the sole "word...wisdom, and effectual might" of God (3.171). The Son specifically acts as God's "effectual might" in the creation of the cosmos, just as in book 3 Holy Light is said to be present at and involved with Creation (3.9–12). This corresponds with Milton's description of the Son as Word in *De doctrina Christiana* (OW 8:128–29, 170–71).

Finally, if Milton has the myth of Urania as heavenly love in mind, the last direct invocation of *Paradise Lost* may be readily associated with the Holy Spirit.[26] Love is the aspect of the Godhead that is traditionally matched with the Holy Spirit in particular, as expressed by Augustine, Peter Lombard, and Aquinas, among others.[27] Despite this tidy correspondence, none of Milton's invocations need be read as addressing a single person of the Trinity; as Augustine avers of Plato, Milton could use triads without strict Trinitarianism. In fact, when Milton lists the attributes of God that "show his divine strength and power," he has three in mind: "Life, or intelligence, or will" (OW 8:42–43). Invoking three aspects of God that accord with nature, reason, and love, Milton employs Augustine's triadic structuring to emphasize the comprehensiveness of his poetic task and of his inspiration.

At the end of book 7, as Raphael concludes his Creation narrative with a benediction, the reader encounters yet another triadic structure:

> Thrice happy men,
> And sons of men, whom God hath thus advanc't,
> Created in his Image, there to dwell
> And worship him, and in reward to rule
> Over his Works, on Earth, in Sea, or Air,
> And multiply a Race of Worshippers
> Holy and just: thrice happy if they know
> Thir happiness, and persevere upright.   (7.625–32)

"Thrice-happy" is an ancient idiom, but Milton's passage contains two noteworthy groupings of three, both of which correspond to the triads found in Augustine.[28] Raphael sees humans as blessed in three ways: naturally, because they are created by God; rationally, because they may exercise self-government through reason, and with this advantage are further suited to hold dominion over creation; and morally, because they are called to worship God and, in love, "multiply a Race of Worshippers." This blessing provides yet another correspondence to Augustine's triad of being, knowledge, and love, especially when one remembers Milton's definition of love of God as active worship, and that the second book of Milton's *De doctrina Christiana*, dedicated to the love or worship of God, contains Milton's ethics, or analysis of virtue (OW 8:21, 905–07). With this in mind, it becomes clear that the Augustinian triad is again expressed at the conclusion of the passage: Adam and Eve are happy (a natural condition), doubly happy if they know they are happy (a rational condition), and triply happy if they persevere upright (a moral condition). Their very existence depends upon their Creator, but the call to perseverance gives them a measure of responsibility, as Raphael advises: "That thou art happy, owe to God; / That thou continu'st such, owe to thyself" (*PL* 5.520–21). Be grateful; be virtuous. Certainly, Adam and Eve's felicity depends upon their maintenance and development of these three areas of being, knowledge of being, and love in response to their knowledge of their felicitous state of being — the three areas by which one might approach God according to the Raphael discourse — the three areas in which a human being comes closest to, as Augustine says, a representation of God, and, as Milton intimates, a "paradise within." Adam and Eve's relationship and Raphael's advice affirm Augustine's question in book 11, chapter 28 of *The City of God*: "Whether We Ought to Love the Love Itself with Which We Love Our Existence and Our Knowledge of It, So that We May Come to Resemble More Closely the Image of the Divine Trinity." Excepting, of course, the affirmation of the Trinity, Milton's answer follows Augustine's query with a resounding yes.

The argument for Milton's adaptation of this Augustinian structure to the series of invocations in *Paradise Lost* and to his presentations of the scale between heaven and earth is supported by his interest in gluttony and temperance. Eating becomes the literal basis for participation in philosophic discourse and in love. Even the very name of the Tree of Knowledge of Good and Evil fortuitously supports this structure, beginning with a physical object (a tree), proceeding to the intellectual (knowledge), and thence to the ethical (good and evil). Chapter 2 has already mentioned how Adam tells Eve of three sorts of sustenance: food proper, food of the mind, and food of love, each corresponding (it is now obvious) to a member of the Augustinian triad (*PL* 9.235–41). Adam notes that each of these "foods" are allotted refreshment, and so even though the curious concept of eating one's way to heaven draws attention to human action in the physical world, it also paradoxically emphasizes the importance of resting in grace with gratitude. Deciding what and when and how to eat becomes an exercise of temperance, but eating in Eden is also an occasion for thanksgiving, for Adam and Eve's prelapsarian meals all show the ease, felicity, and naturally transformative experiences that characterize life in the garden of Eden. This, then, is Milton's philosophy of eating — the need for active virtue on one hand and for grateful acknowledgment of God's gifts on the other. This, for Milton, is the true *eucharist* (from the Greek word for "thanksgiving"): the earthy and mystic sacrament of gratitude celebrated in communion with others and with God, resulting in virtuous action, and in response to his gracious provision and exceeding love. In a small way Eve's fear is justifiable: the hour of eating will always come unearned, as long as one is trying to earn it, without acknowledgment of or gratitude for the parts God and Nature play in the invitation to eat. The best meals, conversations, and tokens of love are those one recognizes as gifts that surpass the expected rewards of fruitful labor — unless, of course, one feels the satanic burden of pursuing autonomy, where gifts become obligations, "So burdensome, still paying, still to owe" (4.53). If, as Adam suggests, the refreshments punctuating one's work can be indulged in gratefully, these very refreshments can become the means for spiritual transformation. Conversely, as Satan knows, if gratitude is begrudged, it burdens the soul. There is a profound connection between gratefulness and grace in *Paradise Lost*, and both are necessary for beatitude. And gratitude is a safeguard against physical, intellectual, and moral gluttony, or the lust of the flesh, the lust of the eyes, and the pride of life. Gratitude encourages mindfulness of the sacrifices others have made so that we may eat, learn, and enjoy love. It causes one to be more deliberate and careful with what is done with those gifts. It keeps one alert to recognize grace and the providence of God.

The three aspects of the scale to heaven in *Paradise Lost* — nature, contemplation of created things, and love — each have their perversions.

Gluttonous eating, a particular representation of an excessive indulgence in or overemphasis on nature, observable both in overeating and
in undue fastidiousness in diet, is a danger even in a cosmos where
all derives from "one first matter" (5.472). The dangers of gluttonous
knowledge (or folly) are similarly manifest both in the *curiositas* of
indiscriminate information junkies as well as in the *superbia* of smug
pundits of human wisdom. Just as not eating — and William Ian Miller
labels anorexia as a species of gluttony under patristic and medieval tax-
onomies — is also a perversion of the scale of nature, willful ignorance
itself can be a perversion of the scale of contemplation; doing nothing
is hardly a means to avoid physical and intellectual excess.[29] Would it
surprise us, then, to discover that the scale of love has its own perversions as well? Complete apathy, ignorance, and self-starvation are the
negatives of charity, prudence, and (the narrowly defined, physically
concerned virtue of) temperance, respectively. But can one love excessively? Does the knowledge/food analogy extend to love in this respect,
or, like God's glory, does it have no proper limits? The ultimate appearance of the scale to heaven is devotion to an infinite Being. With a "debt
immense of endless gratitude," Satan realizes that at best a worshiper is
"at once / indebted and discharg'd" by a grateful mind (4.52–57). Such
love could never become excessive.

Yet loves could be misplaced and misprioritized, and in Christian
thought there is a danger of excessively loving a secondary good
to the detriment of one's love of God, which is the idea behind the
Augustinian and Thomistic warnings against inordinate desire. Thus
Milton warns against "inordinate charity" in *De doctrina Christiana*,
citing Samuel's persistent love for King Saul after God had rejected
him (1 Sam. 2:29, 16:2) and Jesus's warning to his disciples against
loving their parents more than they loved him (Matt. 10:37; OW
8:1113). Love requires knowledge of the true worth of the beloved, and
in inordinate, disproportionate love there exists an unhealthy excess:
"*Philautia*, or extravagant self-love" is the vice "by which one either
loves oneself more than God, or despises one's neighbor by comparison with oneself" (OW 8:1063); "Love should be so governed that we
love most those things which are most worthy of love, [and] likewise

correspondingly hate each individual thing which is worthy of most hate" (OW 8:1065); "Joy should be so governed that we rejoice about good things in proportion to the excellence of each, [and] about the rest so far as is reasonable; similarly sadness about evil and indifferent things should be regulated" (OW 8:1067).

In *Paradise Lost*, Adam exemplifies this unhealthy and inordinate excess in his uxoriousness (10.145–56).[30] In Raphael's mind, Adam's susceptibility to the passions is an indication of disordered love, not excessive love: "In loving thou dost well, in passion not" (8.588). Perhaps the most dangerous example of excessive love is directed toward oneself, but that too is excessive only in proportion to one's love for God and others. Conversely, Milton's definition of the love of God in *De doctrina Christiana* depends on having other loves in proportion: "Love of God is that whereby we love God above all other affections, and are eager for his glory" (OW 8:945). This insistence upon ordering one's loves correctly is very Augustinian; Augustine's own *De doctrina Christiana* repeatedly insists that God must be loved supremely, and that only God is to be loved for his own sake.[31] Raphael recommends self-esteem (one of Milton's coinages), but when disordered this self-esteem is twisted into the sin of pride. *Superbia*, though it may reveal itself as intellectual pride, is more fundamentally a perversion of love. The three main perversions of the Great Chain of Eating, then, may be considered gluttonous involvement in the more bodily aspects of the material world, the gluttonous pursuit of knowledge, and gluttonous love of anything other than God, most formidably expressed in *superbia*. Expressed another way by Augustine, these moral failures are the lust of the flesh, the lust of the eyes, and the pride of life — the sins of 1 John 2:16.[32]

This Augustinian triadic structuring certainly is Johannine in influence, but its roots may also be traced further back to the Hellenistic philosophy of Stoicism, and to the philosophic culture of fifth and fourth century BCE Athens from which it arose. The book of John, with its doctrine of Jesus as Logos, derives from Stoic teachings, most likely through Philo of Alexandria, who synthesized Judaism with Greek philosophy.[33] Augustine names Platonism the foundation for the scale of love, and Plato's philosophy was the "first to discover and recommend" the threefold division, but he was certainly also influenced by Stoic thought as transmuted through the writings of John the Evangelist, and through the direct influence of Ambrose, the bishop of Milan well reputed for his harmonizing of Stoic philosophy with Christian doctrine.[34] Because Stoicism divides reality into three divisions corresponding to the ones Augustine makes in the *City of God*—physics, logic, and ethics—and because Milton himself adhered to certain Stoic principles, the philosophy deserves some consideration here.

Even though the Son famously rejects Stoicism in *Paradise Regain'd*, several Stoic concepts resonate in Miltonic thought:

- A monistic, material cosmos (*PL* 5.472)
- The four elements of earth, water, air, and fire, with the higher elements (air and fire) nourished by the exhalations of the lower (5.416)
- The corporeality of the mind or soul (5.472)
- The idea that all things emanate from God and will return to him (5.469–70)
- The foreknowledge of God (defined by the Stoics as fate) (3.117, 7.173)
- Happiness found in virtuous living (12.581–87)
- The need for humility in the face of the universe (8.172–73)
- An eschatology expecting a conflagration of the universe (12.548)
- An epistemology grounded in the senses (5.104)
- The mind receiving information through fancy or *phantasia*, surveyed by reason, and then admitted as knowledge or opinion (5.100–08)
- Reason as law (9.654)
- Body and soul as indivisible but qualitatively different, with the penetrability of matter as explanation of the soul's total permeation of the body (OW 8:303)
- The soul described as divine fire, rational but tenuously material, breathed into the first human and then passed down from parent to child (OW 8:305).[35]

Nevertheless, Milton's thought departs from Stoicism in a few crucial ways. Deterministic tenets of Stoicism are certainly incongruent with Milton's insistent defense of human free will, and if not for the preponderance of correlations listed above, this alone might discourage our inquiry into Miltonic Stoicism. Moreover, I contend that Stoic asceticism, disregard for pleasure, and suppression of the passions cannot achieve the exultant, liberating perspective on temperance so often appearing in Milton's corpus. Merritt Y. Hughes has insistently argued against readings of Milton's Stoicism, pointing to a passage in *De doctrina Christiana* in which Milton opposes "the Stoic *apatheia*" to the virtue of patience, "for sensibility to feelings of pain, and complaints or lamentations, are not inconsistent with [true] patience, as may be clearly seen in Job and the other holy people when bearing adversity" (OW 8:1107). Hughes also mentions the Son's words in *Paradise Regain'd* against the Stoic's "Philosophic pride, / By him call'd virtue," and the Stoic contempt of both pleasure and pain, which "For all his tedious talk is but vain boast, / Or subtle shifts conviction to evade" (*PR* 4.300–308).[36] But even Hughes mentions Stoic influences on Christian humanism in general and on Milton's work in particular.[37]

In *Paradise Lost* pleasure and change are good, manifest in heaven and earth as grateful (i.e., gratifying) vicissitude; yet no respectable argument in defense of delight and of occasional, appropriate excess in *Paradise Lost* can ignore the part that excess and the passions play in the Fall. *Areopagitica* mentions that God created passions to be the "ingredients of vertu" once "rightly temper'd" (YP 2:527); *Paradise Lost* maintains this idea but also retains the negative connotations Stoics heard in the word "passion," which the Stoics contemned and defined as the tumultuous result of allowing oneself to be affected by one's circumstances. None of the 17 occurrences of "passion," "passions," or "impassion'd" in *Paradise Lost* hold positive connotations (although "compassion" is beneficently used once of the Son and once of Adam); many references include qualifying descriptions such as "wanton passions" (1.454), "passions foul" (4.571), "fit / Of Passion" (10.626–27), "troubl'd Sea of passion" (10.718), and "upstart Passions" (12.88). And, of course, Raphael advises Adam, "In loving thou dost well, in passion not" (8.588). When describing the pleasurable, virtuous, and intelligent response to goodness or beauty in *Paradise Lost*, Milton prefers to use the words "delight," "delectable," and "delicious." Thus paradise and its features are repeatedly described as delicious (4.132, 729; 7.537, 9.439; 10.746); Eve's creation is a response to Adam's request for a consort "fit to participate / All rational delight" (8.390–91), and Adam instructs Eve "to delight / He made us, and delight to Reason join'd" (9.242–43). In this Milton follows Augustine's defense of the word *dilectio* against Stoic misgivings, showing its use in the Vulgate interchangeable with that of *amor*.[38] Yet there is no discrepancy between Milton's apparent Stoic disregard for the Greek-derived "passion" and his Augustinian defense of "delight." In fact, the distinction between licit and approved feelings with near-synonyms is itself Stoic. Known by their opponents for paradoxes and inconsistencies, Stoics distinguished the passions from *eupatheiai*, the "good feelings" that became the reward of the morally and intellectually perfect sage, and which included *chara* (joy, delight) but not its dangerous counterpart, *hēdonē* (delight, pleasure).

Finding a consistent, narrowly defined understanding of the passions in Milton proves controversial, as attested by the criticism and commentary on the last line of Milton's last poetic work — with a variety of conflicting readings, *Samson Agonistes* may be said to end with "calm of mind, all passion spent" (*SA* 1758). Generally, Milton's ideas of passion side with Augustine, who, like Aristotle, and in opposition to the Stoics, defended a proper place for passions under the governance of reason. Yet in the idea of *eupatheiai* even the Stoics may be said to join Milton, Augustine, and Aristotle in asserting that reason wisely used results in proper delight.[39] Thus the austere, virginal voice of the Lady in *A Maske* claims freedom and pleasure for the temperate: "Thou canst not touch the freedom of my mind with all thy charms," she tells Comus, and "that which is not good, is not delicious / To a well-governed and wise appetite" (*Maske*, 663–64, 704–05).

Furthermore, Milton endorses a Stoic concept — one to which Augustine does not entirely assent — in his description of an interior paradise achievable on earth. For the Stoics, this interior paradise was only available to the very few; with some doubt, they pointed to Socrates and Diogenes as exemplars. The difficulty of attainment did not devalue the attempt. For Milton, as for the Stoics, this inner paradise is a mental and psychic state achievable through virtuous living. Milton's version involves temperance as a preliminary but is ultimately governed by charity and supported by a grace-infused process of sanctification in this life that Milton calls *inchoata,* "incomplete" or "unfinished" glorification; simultaneously, as a Christian looking forward to the Second Coming of Jesus and the resurrection of the dead, Milton waits for a complete, physical glorification at the eschaton (OW 8:650–51; YP 6:503). In the "paradise within" he nods to Athens and promotes *sophrosynē;* in the expectation of the life to come, and in the prospect of being imparadised through communion with others, he looks toward the New Jerusalem and its law of *caritas.* Thus Milton in *De doctrina Christiana* promotes temperance as the first of the "special virtues relating to a person's duty toward himself" (OW 8:1075) and charity as the first duty toward God and others (OW 8:909, 945, 1061). But the roles of temperance and charity in attaining delight, both morally and spiritually, on earth and in the life to come, are internecine. Together temperance and charity oppose gluttony, curbing the self and involving others through gratitude and grace.

VIRTUOUS STRIVING AND THE PARADISE WITHIN

When in *Paradise Lost* Milton fuses classical Greek philosophy (particularly aspects of Platonism and Stoicism) with Christianity, he concludes that prelapsarian conditions of human nature, the intellect, and the will are partly recoverable through physics, logic, and ethics, or bodily, intellectual, and moral discipline — philosophy as Augustine defined it in its three parts. Let us especially consider the third of these triads, and the connections Milton saw among virtue, human effort, grace, gratitude, obedience, and love. The ambitious enterprise of the paradise within is not limited to Milton's poetry. In his 1644 treatise *Of Education,* Milton famously defined the purpose of education as the reparation of "the ruins of our first parents by regaining to know God aright, and out of that knowledge to love him, to imitate him, to be like him, as we may the neerest by possessing our souls of true vertue, which being united to the heavenly grace of faith makes up the highest perfection" (YP 2:366–67). The cultivation of "true vertue" corresponds to the third category of Augustine's triads, and it supports a high view of the dignity of humankind. The moral depends on the intellectual ("out of that knowledge...love") and the physical. Acknowledging that "our understanding cannot in this body found it selfe but on sensible things," Milton proposes a regimen of instruction that includes physical education and improvement as well as intellectual and moral growth (YP 2:368). Exercise and diet are two of three components constituting the prescribed "daies work," while the third, devoted to studies, focuses on practical sciences, "things usefull to be known," including "the institution of Physick; that they may know the tempers, the humors, the seasons, and how to manage a crudity [a digestive problem]" (YP 2:381, 369, 392–93). This pragmatism is not quite the utilitarian vocational training proposed by Comenian educational reformers like Samuel Hartlib, the addressee in *Of Education*, but neither does Milton's portrait of the ideal humanist education, which seeks to achieve "the highest perfection" through moral knowledge "united to the heavenly grace of faith," conform entirely to Calvinist perspectives on human action and potential.[40]

Milton believes that grace is always necessary, but also that humans have a practical role to play in "repair[ing] the ruins of our first parents," and this includes both moral and soteriological matters. In *De doctrina Christiana*, Milton states more clearly than he does in *Paradise Lost* that "in man there are certain remnants of the divine image...out of whose combination this person becomes more fit and, as it were, more ordered for the kingdom of God than that one" (OW 8:93; cf. *PL* 11.511–25). Since "indeed we are clearly not pawns," he continues, "As to why...some people embrace and others rebuff this grace, some cause at least is to be sought in man's very nature" (OW 8:93). Speaking of a Christian's life on earth, Milton further argues that "when God had decided to restore humankind, he also indubitably decreed (for what was fairer?) to restore lost freedom to the will, in some measure at least"

(OW 8:95). In asserting the freedom of the will and the power to resist grace, Milton departs from Lutheran and Calvinist theology, respectively, emphasizing the gift of Christian liberty and taking an Arminian position on human ability and responsibility.[41] As Maurice Kelley explains, Milton ultimately accepts the Arminian doctrine that "God's plan is neither Pelagian nor Augustinian, but rather synergistic: to attain salvation the restored free will of man cooperates with the initial and continuing grace of God."[42] The insistence on a more elevated will naturally lends itself to an emphasis on morality, especially temperance infused with charity. Although Milton asserts that God is "the primary efficient cause of good works," the "proximate causes of good works are naturally, as a rule, good habits, which are called virtues; in this is contained the whole rationale of our duty both towards God and towards humankind" (OW 8:925). And as we have observed, Milton lists temperance as the first of man's duties toward himself (OW 8:1075).

For Augustine, temperance is a proper response to the Fall, but not a means of solace. Instead, suffering itself is instructive and "found to be marvellous; for it teaches us to live soberly and to understand that … all the promises of the new covenant refer only to our new inheritance of which it is a pledge."[43] Milton likewise finds hope in the afterlife, and recommends sober living on earth, temperance in demeanor as well as diet. Under the heading of temperance in *De doctrina Christiana*, citing 1 Peter 5:8 ("Be sober, be vigilant…"), Milton defines sobriety as "self-restraint from immoderate eating and drinking," but also allies it to watchfulness (OW 8:1076). This definition of sobriety is yet one more indication of the union of matters of body and intellect, and of the importance of patient waiting, in Miltonic thought.

Where Milton differs from Augustine is in his insistence that education and sober living can partially repair the detriment of the Fall in this life. Literal ascent along the threefold scale of nature, contemplation, and love was a poetic possibility for Milton's Adam, but even after the Fall, temperate eating in opposition to gluttony, learning untainted by *superbia* or *curiositas*, and love apart from "passions foul" grant partial access to elevated living and to an interior paradise. Yet Augustine also entertains the idea of humans approaching the heavens in the sense that Milton develops. While in counteracting the Pelagian heresy Augustine wrote forcefully on the corruption of the will, he also argued that God created man "a creature of earth, indeed, yet worthy of heaven if he clung to his Maker."[44] Augustine even encourages his fallen readers that they may yet become like the angels by "resembling them in good will; for by this means, we are able to be with them, to live with them, and to worship with them the God whom they worship."[45]

For comparison, Augustine's older contemporary Evagrius of Pontus also mentions that humans are better able to resemble the angels in psychology than in physiology. His ascetic ideas carry a Stoic tenor: "Passionlessness [*apatheian*] is what we shall call the soul's health, and the soul's food is knowledge, which is the only means by which we shall ordinarily be united with the holy powers, seeing that the natural basis for our union with incorporeal beings is the similarity of our disposition to theirs."[46] Augustine's exhortation, more sympathetic to the emotional or desiring part of the human soul, is reminiscent of his early work in defense of human free will in *De libero arbitrio* (popular enough to make it into the Nun's Priest's digression on foreknowledge and free will in *The Canterbury Tales*); it is Augustine who prepares us for Milton's paradoxical or compatibilist acknowledgment of both free will and predestination.[47] This residual possibility for transformation is appropriated into and intensified in *Paradise Lost*. The stairs are yet let down to humankind, not to dare us by easy ascent, nor to aggravate our sad exclusion from the doors of bliss, but to guide us in the initial stages of our journey to beatitude (cf. 3.523–25). In accordance with his Arminian theology, Milton presents this ascent at once as miraculous and as naturally accomplished in part through human effort. Like a child that slowly, over time, grows accustomed to increasingly substantial food, the adult seeking the paradise within might, through alert, temperate feeding of the body, mind, and will, grow increasingly in stature, wisdom, and favor with God and humans.

The effect of temperance, however, is indisputably incomplete. As Michael explains, temperance, the course he proposes to "lead / Safest thy life," may extend a mortal's years, but even then life concludes in old age, the blunting of the senses, and easy but melancholy death, described as dropping "like a ripe Fruit.../ Into thy Mother's lap" (11.364–65, 535–46). Attention to the human body reveals the limits of temperance and physiological regulation. The processes of consumption and defecation, and death and decomposition, destroy one body to sustain another or perpetuate the species at the expense of the individual. One animal consumes and assimilates the flesh of another. Feces and corpses fertilize the earth. All this perpetuates the cycles of earthly life, but when one considers that a man may fish with the worm that hath eat of a king, and eat of the fish that hath fed of that worm, it is hard to attribute any dignity or propriety to one's material being. Galenic digestive theories optimistically suggest on some small level a possibility for ameliorative alteration of both eater and eaten, yet Milton reminds us that the vertical ascent of the individual requires special grace. What may be evident from scatology — that a fallen human in a fallen world can never eat perfectly and must of nature expel ordure rather than ambrosial offering — reinforces the need for a radical transformation to achieve the kind of natural worship that Milton presents as a product of prelapsarian eating. Virtuous living, though strongly emphasized at the conclusion to Milton's poem, does not even fulfill the requirements for the incomplete glorification that Milton acknowledges is possible in earthly life unless it is attended by "regeneration, growth and preservation, considered as proximate causes on God's part" (OW 8:653). Moreover (though this does not negate the benefits of virtuous living), Milton affirms that "the emptiness of our merits [in terms of earning salvation] is easily discerned, since neither do our right actions belong to ourselves — rather, they belong to God acting in us — nor, even granted they are our own, do they nevertheless cease to be obligations, nor can any calculation whatever of our duty in any respect equal the greatness of the reward held out [to us]" (OW 8:919). While Milton attributes to God the goodness in humanity, this attribution does not free humankind from virtuous striving. The disproportionate "greatness of the reward" God extends to the virtuous further emphasizes divine generosity over human merit. Milton's belief in "our duty" to live virtuously is clear in Michael's repeated exhortations to "Faith and faithful works," to "Faith not void of works" (PL 11.64, 12.427). But beyond the earthly benefits of virtue, in the matter of soteriology, Milton avers that virtue is worthless without grace, without the intercession of a mediator; so the Son proclaims, "all [universal man's] works on mee / Good or not good ingraft, my Merit those / Shall perfet, and for these my Death shall pay" (PL 11.34–36). For Milton, grace is the means to God by which our pursuit of temperance must itself be tempered, while paradoxically it is also the means by which the physical sphere is retained at the end of time. Although temperance and good works can reach only so far, grace and faith anticipate the glorification of the physical, with eating becoming the metaphor for ultimate communion with God.

RADICAL GRACE AND THE RESURRECTION OF THE BODY

This ultimate amelioration, what Milton calls complete glorification, looks to eschatology and the doctrine of the resurrection of the body (OW 8:868–99). This complete glorification firstly must be accomplished by grace, and secondly, it must involve the body. Augustine describes this transformation as far superior to Adam's original unfallen condition in paradise: "But as for present delight, our first father in Paradise was more blessed than any just man of the world: but as for his hope, every man in the miseries of his body, is more blessed: as one to whom truth (not opinion) has said that he shall be rid of all molestation, and partake with the angels in that Great God, whereas the man that lived in Paradise in all that felicity, was uncertain of his fall or continuance therein."[48] For Augustine, the paradise far happier than Eden is eschatological, not available until humanity might "partake with the angels in that Great God." It is this eschatological hope that makes the fallen more blessed than Adam in the garden (but this hope would not distinguish fallen humans from prelapsarian humans in Milton's Paradise Lost, for Raphael's message shows that the unfallen also might fulfill this hope). Augustine points to the changes after the Fall as unexpected evidence for the possibility of positive changes at the end of time: "Man's body before his fall was of such a nature that it could not suffer death: and yet in his fall was altered unto that mortal misery wherein now all mankind lives, to die at length: and therefore at the resurrection it may undergo such another alteration, unknown to us as yet."[49]

Similarly, in *De doctrina Christiana* Milton considers the principles of generation with regard to the doctrine of original sin, also pointing to an eventual glorification of the body: "Nor is it less credible that a corporeal power can issue from a spiritual substance than that anything spiritual can be made out of a body, which is what we hope will also happen to our own bodies at last, at the Resurrection" (OW 8:295). Milton understands the glorification of the body as transformation rather than replacement: "Now the resurrection takes place either by the resuscitation of the dead or by sudden transformation of the living. Each person, it seems, will rise again as one and the same.... If this be not so, we shall not be conformed to Christ, who, himself too, in his own body, in his own flesh and blood — the same, of course, in which he died and rose again — also entered into glory" (OW 8:879). As a millennialist, Milton imagined the conclusion of history as a thousand-year reign of Christ, culminating in the judgment of all, the punishment of the wicked and the complete glorification of the righteous (OW 8:885–87). Concerning the conflagration of the world, Milton avers, "whether it will lead to the abolition of its substance or only to the changing of its qualities, we are taught as much as it is useful for us to know" (OW 8:889); nevertheless, "our glorification will have as its companion the renewal and possession of heaven and earth and of the things created in them, those at least which could be of use or delight to us" (OW 8:887). If Milton's idea of heaven is anything like his earthly paradise, it appears there will even be room for the "unwieldy Elephant" and his mirth-making "Lithe Proboscis"; perhaps even the innocuous "Serpent sly" with his Gordian motions will be reinstated and elevated beyond his status before the Fall (*PL* 4.345–49).

Most importantly, under the section dedicated to the renovation of useful and delightful created things, Milton's scriptural citations include the promise of the enjoyment of physical food at an eternal banquet:

"Luke 14:15: *one of those who were reclining together at table said to him* [i.e., Jesus], *Blessed is he who eats bread in the kingdom of God* — nor is he reproved by Christ; and 22:30: [*I confer on you a kingdom...*] so *that you may eat and drink at my table in my kingdom;* Rom. 8, from v. 19 to [v.] 24" (OW 8:897). There is a possibility that Milton understands, as almost all Christians do, that the eternal banquet is to be understood as a metaphor. But because Milton cites Luke 14:15, 22:30, and Romans 8:19–21 as support for his belief in the eventual "renewal and possession of heaven and earth"; because Milton notes in Luke 14:15 that the speaker is not reproved by Christ, as if to confirm on Jesus's authority that humans will once again eat the bread of heaven, and because the passage from Romans refers both to the detrimental effects of the Fall on the natural world and to the hope of eventual restoration of the created world, I think it fair to state that, metaphor or not, Milton envisions the afterlife to be a physically enjoyed, eternal banquet, even if the means by which that physicality is enjoyed are radically transformed. If it is a metaphor, one might still apply the theory of accommodation, which Milton defends in the beginning of *De doctrina Christiana*. Even if God does not have hands, who are we to question that picture of himself that he has presented to us? Even if glorified humans do not have stomachs, if God presents heaven as an eternal banquet, and the highest vision as a shared meal where God is host, who is man to question this? (OW 8:29–33).[50]

In a sense, the mature Milton's description of ultimate beatitude in his theological treatise looks back to the highly sensual heavenly delights he envisions, for example, at the conclusion of *Epitaphium Damonis*: "Festa Sionaeo bacchantur & Orgia Thyrso." Only, the sensual, heavenly delights are not worth mentioning if not sustained by love. Milton insists that complete glorification required the Christian to be rooted and grounded in love (OW 8:651, Eph. 3:18) and to "persist in faith and charity" (OW 8:655). Milton associates this persistence with the reward promised to the faithful of the church of Pergamos in Revelation 2:17: "*to him who conquers I shall grant* [the right] *to eat of that hidden manna*" (OW 8:655–57).[51] He also reinforces the importance of love using Christ's words to the Church of Ephesus, known for its good works, but straying from God as its first love. Milton was apparently moved by the promise to the faithful that they would be rewarded with the privilege of eating from the Tree of Life (Rev. 2:7), a promise he cites four times in *De doctrina Christiana* (OW 8:191, 361, 609, 839). While he also quotes Romans 14:17, "*for God's kingdom is not food and drink, but righteousness, peace, and joy through the holy spirit,*" when he wants to describe "joy unspeakable," he envisions a share in the food of the gods (OW 8:657). There is no gluttony here, and Milton's speculations about an eternal banquet correspond to the description in *Paradise Lost* of feasting angels before the War in Heaven:

> They eat, they drink, and in communion sweet
> Quaff immortality and joy, secure
> Of surfeit where full measure only bounds
> Excess, before th' all bounteous King, who show'r'd
> With copious hand, rejoicing in thir joy.   (5.637–41)

Concluding book 1 of *De doctrina Christiana*, Milton posits from Scripture that, at the end of time, "after all things have been subjected to him, then will the son himself also be subjected to him who subjected all things to him, so that God may be all in all" (OW 8:889). This ultimate vision does not disregard cosmic hierarchy, for it depends on creation's subjection to the Son's authority and on the Son's subjection of himself to the Father; but the consequence is the incorporation of all into a joyful, unanimous communion.

In *Paradise Lost* the Father remarks that, notwithstanding human sin, ultimately "God shall be All in All," so the Son prophesies, "in the end / Thou shalt be All in All, and I in thee / For ever, and in me all whom thou lov'st" (*PL* 3.341, 6.731–33). In this manner Raphael's prelapsarian vision of the return of all creation to God remains a steadfast tenet of Milton's theology. This eschatological statement corresponds well with the original plan of the Father in Milton's poem, to create the human race to live on earth until

> by degrees of merit rais'd
> They open to themselves at length the way

Up hither, under long obedience tri'd,
And Earth be chang'd to Heav'n, and Heav'n to Earth,
One Kingdom, Joy and Union without end.   (7.157–61)

Ultimately, Michael's closing vision does not negate Raphael's message but presents its eschatological fulfillment, at once the gift of grace and the reward of the faithful, "Whether in Heav'n or Earth, for then the Earth / Shall all be Paradise, far happier place / Than this of *Eden*, and far happier days" (12.463–65). Both the paradise within and the ultimate consolidation of heaven and earth remind us that God "attributes to place / No sanctity, if none be thither brought" by those who dwell in faith and righteousness (11.836–37). At this point it would become apparent that the three scales by which humanity may ascend to God not only have had Providence as a guide, but they are ultimately consummated in God. As Augustine anticipates, "In Him, our being will have no death, our knowledge will have no error, and our love will know no check."[52] In the rapturous vision of Augustine, our worship will result in the most radically transformative experience of eating yet imagined: "Eternal Truth, true Love, beloved Eternity — all this, my God, you are.... I realized that I was far away from you. It was as though I were in a land where all is different from your own and I heard your voice calling from on high, saying 'I am the food of full-grown men. Grow and you shall feed on me. But you shall not change me into your own substance, as you do with the food of your body. Instead you shall be changed into me.'"[53] Only in God can such excess and such satiety be found.

In *both* his ethics and in his religious doctrine, Milton sees a need for *both* physical bodily action and extraordinary, divine grace. In *Paradise Lost*, the final goals of these ethical and religious exhortations are, respectively, the paradise within and the beatific communion that includes a banquet made all the more significant by the doctrine of the resurrection of the body. The conclusion promised is happiness and beneficent satiety, but not stasis. In book 5 of *Paradise Lost*, Raphael commands Adam, "enjoy / Your fill what happiness this happy state / Can comprehend, incapable of more" (503–05). In book 9, Adam jeopardizes that happiness by "Eating his fill" from the Tree of Knowledge of Good and Evil (1005). As a remedy, Michael reveals to Adam the hope found in the oracle, along with guidelines for self-government, to which Adam gratefully replies, "Greatly instructed I shall hence depart, / ...and have my fill / Of knowledge, what this Vessel can contain" (12.557–59). What had left Adam unsatisfied in his conversation with Raphael has now satiated him, although it has come after the advent of evil. Yet soon enough Adam will hunger again. As expressed in the gustatory theme throughout *Paradise Lost,* the whetting of one's appetite is an occasion for the exercise of temperance. Nature, reason, and love each have a part in humankind's pursuit of God. Following Augustine, with moments of Dantean influence, Milton suggests that with sufficient grace this endeavor can prove ultimately satisfying, concluding in unspeakable delight.

6

The Temperate Poet and
"This Flying Steed Unrein'd"

"And the soul," he said, "my dear friend, is cured by means of certain charms, and these charms consist of beautiful words. It is the result of such words that temperance arises in the soul, and when the soul acquires and possesses temperance, it is easy to provide health both for the head and for the rest of the body."

— Plato, *Charmides* 157a[1]

There is a time-honored belief that poets are mad, and that poesy results from ecstasy, but Milton casts aside this tradition in favor of a staid alternative connecting temperance and poetic inspiration.[2] Even in his invocations, Milton represents the art of poesy as fundamentally a matter of order and control, even if that control is attributed to divine help. The poet's role and responsibility are brought to the forefront: the bard is the one to command the heavenly muse to sing in book 1, to hail holy light in book 3, and to soar beyond Olympus in book 7. The poet brags in book 9 that his celestial patroness visits him unimplored, but he also affirms that he has chosen his own subject for heroic song. Yet in inserting and asserting himself as poet in *Paradise Lost*, Milton also weds successful poetic action to caution and reverence. After each intrepid beginning to his invocations, the poet checks his confidence: in book 1 he is tentative in locating the source of his inspiration; in book 3 he wonders if he can express holy light without blame; and in book 7 he admits his presumption in merely following the muse into the heavens and turns back to humbler ground. The poet's reserve is mingled with confessions of vulnerability as he struggles with bodily and circumstantial checks on his talent. Granted, the poet's admission of all-too-human shortcomings may appear conventional and affected, and his consideration of his situation, with "wisdom at one entrance quite shut out," and having "fall'n on evil days ... In darkness, and with dangers compast round," may serve as a foil to set off the brilliance of his achievements — but these statements also carry the real burden and the honest cry of a man dispossessed of eyesight and of patriotic dream (3.50, 7.25, 27). This chapter proposes that Milton's very wavering between confidence and reserve is integral to his model of poem making. Over the course of his oeuvre Milton crafts a persona that is also an image of the ideal bard, one elected by God, yet never out of his mind, whose pen and thoughts are inspired by divine grace but solicited by careful study and, in some respects, careful eating. Milton's philosophy of eating extends to the poetic process, where delicious words are best served with a temperate mind and a grateful spirit.

Consider the poetic implications of Milton's philosophy of eating as presented thus far. Milton makes gluttony a foundational sin of the Fall, opposing this vice with temperance and charity. He experiments with a definition of gluttony that is medieval in its broad scope, inclusive of verbal sins of the mouth as well as mental attitudes inordinately feeding the appetite, if not the belly; he also participates in a tradition (also medieval) in which gracious words and grateful speech can counteract gluttony. He marks the descent of the rebel angels with gluttony, crudities, and scatological metaphor, and envisions a prelapsarian condition where, when graciousness and gratitude attend the table, perfect digestion naturally results in ambrosial offerings that praise the Creator. He develops correspondences between mind and body, where gluttony serves both as analog and portal to folly and selfish, inordinate love, as temperance does to prudence and charity, thereby insisting that the choices we make in tending our bodies influence not only our physical well-being but also our thoughts and desires. Finally, he insists that, whether in worship or in eating (itself a potential mode of reverence), we are called to act upon our free will responsibly even as we paradoxically acknowledge our continual indebtedness to divine grace. Given these claims, we might conclude Milton envisions a role for temperance — including but not limited to the narrowly defined, mundane regulation of the appetite for food — in shaping his poetry, and that Milton's poem is itself a deliberate if partial attempt to repair the ruins of the Fall, to counter gluttony with eloquence.

This chapter begins by examining two strains of inspiration in Western literature, what I will call the jovial and pensive muses, and reflects upon these strains as they influence Milton's *Elegia sexta* and the companion poems *L'Allegro* and *Il Penseroso*. It finds correlative duality in Milton's opposition of genius and technique, or "easy numbers" and "slow-endeavoring art" in Milton's "On Shakespeare." From this the argument turns to examine Urania as Milton's muse invoked in book 7, and to consider several relevant meanings of Urania (muse of astronomy, of temperance, of love), and how these meanings are developed in Plato's *Symposium*, Dante's *Commedia*, and Milton's *Paradise Lost*. Milton asks his muse not only to descend to help him, but also to help him descend safely, reminding the reader that the poet needs temperance just as much as Adam and Eve do. In sum, this chapter examines how Milton follows a convention associating temperate diet with sober poetics, and where this convention's powers to explain inspiration may cease. Defending poetic agency even while pursuing divine favor, Milton remains cautious against presumption even as he grows bold to acknowledge a celestial patroness. While the poet seeks with the muse's help to become a better version of the mythic Bellerophon, the final books of the poem guide the reader and Adam toward the new sort of temperance needed after the Fall, one that must temper joy with sorrow, as well as human virtue with divine grace. Turning to consider Milton's writings on temperance, his assessment of his own temperance, and the opinions of Milton's biographers on the same topic, we recall that temperance is lifeless without charity, the soul of all the rest of the virtues. Considered together, however, it becomes apparent how vigorous temperance can be and how extravagant love can be as well. Together, with the gratitude and grace they support, vigorous temperance and extravagant charity emerge as the great themes of *Paradise*

Lost, and charity-infused temperance the happy remedy for one of its great problems: gluttony. Insofar as *Paradise Lost* proclaims divine charity and promotes human gratitude and active virtue in response to eternal providence, it represents an attempt to counter the Fall. Milton's poetry is itself a response to and remedy for gluttony.

THE JOVIAL AND THE PENSIVE MUSES

Hesiod's *Theogony* offers two different strains connecting consumption and inspiration. The work describes the muses joining the Graces and Desire in feasting (*en thaliēs,* a phrase particularly associated with Thalia, muse of comedy) but also shaming those shepherds who attend to their bellies alone (*kak' elenchea gasteres oion*).[3] From the beginning of one of the earliest extant works of Western literature, then, there are two different representations of the relationship between art and feasting, from which we derive two distinct perspectives of these daughters of Zeus and of Memory, whom one might call either the jovial or the pensive muses. This double tradition continues today, as artists variously envision their work as the effect of an inspired and elevated genius, or as the technical product of arduous deliberation. To ignore one or the other of these strains is but to half understand poetry, just as, I believe Milton would say, to deny either divine grace or human responsibility is but to half understand God's dealings with humanity. But could one's choices in eating affect one's poetics?

For Hesiod — a shepherd who taught how the world rose out of chaos — poetry is something to be both imbibed and emitted.[4] Even as the muses may scorn the shepherds whose god is their belly, they visit Hesiod as he tends his lambs on Mount Helicon, teaching him the art of song. Their gift of eloquence is described with food metaphors:

> He whom the daughters of great Zeus honor
> Of the kings cherished by Zeus and watched over from birth,
> Upon him, on his tongue, they pour sweet dew [*glukerēn eērsen*],
> And from him, out of his mouth, flow honeyed words.[5]

Zeus, Hesiod proceeds to relate, is responsible for making prudent kings, but anyone who receives the favor of the Muses is truly blessed, for from his lips flows honey-sweet speech.[6] Mellifluous words are the natural result of inspiration, which is described as the imbibing of divinely offered dews. If Hesiod thought the root of *ambrosia* to be, as F. A. Wright determines, the same for *drosos, eersē,* "dew," then the food of the gods is not just an earthly offering to the gods, but it is also, at least metaphorically, the muses' gift to humanity. But can what a poet does with the mundane meals readily available to him prepare him for such morsels of eloquence?

Milton distinguishes between Thalia, the pleasure-loving muse of comedy, and the more solemn and sober muse of epic poetry, the unnamed Calliope, in *Elegia sexta.* In this Latin verse letter to Charles Diodati, the young Milton demonstrates his awareness and acceptance of a tradition associating lofty poetry with abstemious diet. As Milton explains in the headnote to his elegiac poem, Diodati had sent a letter begging excuse if his verses were not as good as usual, for the festive hospitality he enjoyed while visiting friends in the country during Christmastide hampered the successful solicitation of the muses. Milton begins his response to his friend with stark contrast: "On an empty stomach I send you a wish for the good health of which you, with a full one, may perhaps feel the lack. But why does your Muse provoke mine, instead of permitting her to seek the obscurity that she craves?"[7] This opposition between the muses, however, is soon genially re-expressed as alternate modes to inspiration: "But why do you complain that poetry is a fugitive from wine and feasting? Song loves Bacchus and Bacchus loves songs" (13–14). Milton lists Ovid, Anacreon, Pindar, and Horace as poets inspired by wine and feasting. "In your case also," Milton assures Diodati, "the sumptuous board with its generous provision gives strength to your mind and fire to your genius" (29–30). Bacchus, Ceres, and Thalia (i.e., wine, grain, and the comic muse) are united in poetic revelry and in the leisurely compositions of Charles Diodati, but as for the poet who seeks the inspiration of Calliope, the young Milton claims,

> he whose theme is wars and heaven under Jupiter in his prime, and
> pious heroes and chieftains half-divine, and he who sings now of the
> sacred counsels of the gods on high, and now of the infernal realms

where the fierce dog howls, let him live sparingly, like the Samian teacher [Pythagoras]; and let herbs furnish his innocent diet. Let the purest water stand beside him in a bowl of beech and let him drink sober draughts from the pure spring.... So Homer the spare eater and the water-drinker carried Ulysses through vast stretches of ocean.... For truly the bard is sacred to the gods and is their priest. His hidden heart and his lips alike breathe out Jove. (55–62, 71–72, 77–78)

The epic poet, with his loftier themes and his nobler, even sacerdotal vocation, should imitate the reputed temperance of Pythagoras and Homer. What goes into his mouth affects what his lips breathe out, sometimes in unexpected ways. The fantastical feasting of Odysseus, Milton seems to imply, could only be exalted into epic by a temperate and serious "spare eater" and "water-drinker." Milton concludes *Elegia sexta* with reference to his recently composed Nativity ode, "these simple strains that have been meditated on my native pipes," and while that poem is certainly not an epic, Milton links his own serious, meditative Christian poetry to his exalted view of the epic form, further distinguishing himself from Diodati's Saturnalian festivities and their correlative lighthearted and profane verse (89).[8]

The association Milton makes between temperate diet and lofty poetry is conventional; it was undoubtedly in the mind of Giovanni Boccaccio when he took care to mention Dante's temperate fare in *Vita di Dante*. Boccaccio's description of Dante's eating habits methodically seems to clear him of all five of Gregory's branches of gluttony: "In food and drink [Dante] was most temperate, both in partaking of them at the appointed hours and in not passing the limits of necessity. Nor did he show more epicurism in respect of one thing than another. He praised delicate viands, but ate chiefly of plain dishes, and censured beyond measure those who bestow a great part of their attention upon possessing choice things, and upon extremely careful preparation of the same, affirming that such persons do not eat to live, but rather live to eat."[9] Both Dante in fashioning his authorial persona in his divine *Commedia* and Boccaccio in his *Vita di Dante* adhere to the convention of the temperate epic poet. Milton probably had both Boccaccio and Dante in mind when composing *Elegia sexta*. Boccaccio in the *Genealogy of the Gods* writes of Homer's ascetic habits while composing the *Odyssey*. To my knowledge, Merritt Hughes was first to indicate this correspondence between *Genealogy of the Gods* and *Elegia sexta;* the significance of this link is increased if, following E. M. W. Tillyard's opinion, we read *Elegia sexta* as Milton's early declaration of his grand poetic intentions, "a personal self-dedication" to epic poetry.[10] To do so leads to the inference that from his youth Milton intentionally associated himself in diet with the best epic poets of the past and cultivated the hope that he might in time share in their renown by writing serious poetry of the first rank. As he wrote *Paradise Lost*, all too aware of his shared fate with "Blind *Thamyris* and blind *Maeonides*," the expression of this desire only intensified (*PL* 3.35). While he often avoids naming Dante as a poetic influence, in as early a work as *Elegia sexta* Milton does not avoid imitating and alluding to him, along with Pythagoras, Hesiod, Homer, Virgil, and others whose wisdom was partly attributed to their reputedly modest response to pleasures of the flesh.[11] Eventually Milton, who would own the first copy of Dante's *Convivio* (*The Banquet*) in England, who read Boccaccio's *Vita di Dante* while at Horton, and who was demonstrably interested in matters of diet and the poetic process, could not have failed to be aware of this association of temperate consumption and inspiration.[12]

We have yet to consider how boldly the line should be drawn between the young author of *Elegia sexta* and the mature poet of *Paradise Lost*, and how clearly one can see a temperate poet behind either of these works. Tillyard's suggestion that *Elegia sexta* is a deliberate commitment to the writing of epic poetry is not uncontested; other critics easily dismiss *Elegia sexta* as a youthful letter that had no effect on the mature Milton, or that even the young Milton did not take seriously or personally. E. K. Rand argues that *Elegia sexta* is simply a playful exercise with a bland ethics in accordance with Renaissance theory.[13] William Riley Parker interprets the elegiac verse as a "flippant, gay, bantering," "semi-serious" debate in the style of the Prolusions, on whether or not feasting is "favourable to poetry."[14] Parker argues that Milton presents both sides of the issue and that there is no serious commitment to epic poetry, nor is there proof of Milton's temperate lifestyle. While Diodati is the model for conviviality, the vegetarian Pythagoras is the model for temperance, not Milton himself; Milton is not *Il Penseroso*, for the style of the poem itself is a "gay elegy."[15] Such an interpretation does not do much to explain the obvious (even if playful) dichotomy Milton introduces in the beginning of his poem between his friend's muse and his own muse, nor does it account for the possibility that a serious poet might adjust his tone to suit a more jocular addressee. Nevertheless, Parker's reading fairly accepts Diodati's loose definition of moderation — "Live, laugh, make the most of Youth and the hours as they pass" — as partly representative of the young Milton's own perspective.[16]

Where Parker fails to find autobiography or a statement of intent, Stephen M. Fallon has more recently observed early signs of a characteristically Miltonic fashioning of the self: "*Elegy* 6 foreshadows the explicit self-representations in the *Apology* and the *Reason of Church-Government*. Milton may not be firmly settled on his path in December 1629, as Parker suggests, but in the Elegy he is, nevertheless, trying on a self-construction."[17] Young Milton is playing dress-up in the garb of a serious poet. The convivial tone of this elegy does not exclude the sober implications of such play. Testing possible modes of self-representation, the young Milton associates the highest sort of *poiesis* with the deliberately temperate diet.

Milton's pairing of Diodati with Thalia experiments with the alternative convention that wine and feasting are excellent incitements to song. As Robert Herrick wrote in "His Farewell to Sack,"

> 'Tis not Apollo can, or those thrice three
> Castalian sisters, sing, if wanting thee.
> Horace, Anacreon, both had lost their fame,
> Hads't thou not fill'd them with thy fire and flame.[18]

This is a more jubilant, albeit less sober, recourse to inspiration, one that Milton does not ignore, and that has enjoyed long prosperity. Homer has the honor of being claimed by this tradition as well as its counterpart. The Roman poet Horace in his Epistle 19 suggests that "no verses which are written by water-drinkers can please, or be long-lived." Horace then alleges that "Homer, by his excessive praises of wine, is convicted as a boozer: father Ennius himself never sallied forth to sing of arms, unless in drink."[19] Centuries later, Rabelais's persona Alcofribas jocosely concurs in the Author's Prologue to Gargantua: "For I never spent — or wasted — any more — or other — time in the composing of this lordly book, than that fixed for the taking of my bodily refreshment, that is to say for eating and drinking. Indeed, this is the proper time for writing of such high matters and abstruse sciences; as Homer, who was the paragon of all philologers, very well knew, and Ennius, the father of Latin poets too, as Horace testifies, although a certain imbecile declared that his verses smack rather of wine than of oil."[20] The slight against Ennius reverses a remark made about Demosthenes, whose labored orations reputedly carried the scent of dirty lamp oil.[21] Of course, despite Rabelais's comparison of his own writing to a Silenus box externally adorned with grotesque curiosities but enclosing valuable medicines within, the "lordly book" and "high matters" of Rabelais are of a different sort than those of Homer or Milton. But this is not to conclude that Milton ignored the tradition of the playfully self-gratifying and well-sated poet.

The connection between bodily regulation and poetic output was an easy one for satirists, and Milton addresses this connection both satirically and seriously. Michael Lieb sees in Paradise Lost's infernal image of Mount Aetna a satirical juncture of digestive imagery and absurd, sputtering attempts at creation, and notes Milton's participation in a tradition that plays upon the correlation between healthy consumption (or lack of it) and the imagination (or lack of it).[22] In Eikonoklastes (1649), Milton excoriates "bad Poets; who sit and starve themselves with a delusive hope to win immortality by thir bad lines" (YP 3:502). In the Second Defense (1654), he attacks the poetasters who write "without choice, without discrimination, judgment, or measure...according as they are puffed up and swept away by the bottle, by the hope of a halfpenny, or by that empty frenzy of theirs" (YP 4:593). In contradistinction, Milton joins himself to Homer and Demosthenes (the water drinker and the lamp oil burner), both once of uncertain fame, as Salmasius had claimed of his opponent. Milton attests that he has awaited not fame but the opportune moment for publication and that he "had learned to hold [his] peace," having "mastered the art of not writing" — a fascinating self-assessment given the extent of personal vitriol and polemic in the *Second Defense* (YP 4:608). Milton elaborates, describing himself as almost the patient hero of *Paradise Regain'd*, unsolicitous of political office, keeping himself "at home for the most part," giving to Caesar more than was "entirely just," and maintaining, as he testifies, his "frugal way of life" (YP 4:627). In the immediate context of this account of his own self-restraint, Milton ironically appears unable to practice "the art of not writing," fed up with the libel of *The Cry of the Royal Blood to Heaven, against the English Parricides*: "Hold your tongue, I say! For the more you abuse me, the more copiously will you compel me to account for my conduct. From such accounting you can gain nothing save the reproach, already most severe, of telling lies, while for me you open the door to still higher praise of my own integrity" (YP 4:629). The high praise, of course, comes from Milton's own lips here.

Milton's self-representations, as Fallon, Campbell and Corns, and others have warned us, may be self-sustaining illusions or may be incompatible with other Miltonic self-representations, and so the dish he serves us in the *Second Defense* should be taken with a grain or two of salt.[23] As we shall consider later, Milton is not the only biographer recording his domestic frugality, but even these may serve as his Boccaccio, promoting the image of the temperate poet in accordance with convention. What is more important than any biographical authentication here is that Milton paints a self-portrait of modesty and restraint even as he seems to have lost the ability to restrain his own pen. And no wonder he felt compelled to respond — the author of *The Cry* had written that Milton's pages were dusted with sesame and poppy, the emetic and the soporific, inducing two expected outcomes of gluttonous nimiety (YP 4:653).

Nevertheless, Milton considered personal temperance only one of the conditions promoting *poiesis*, and not the most indispensible one, either. In his autobiographical preface to book 2 of *The Reason of*

Church-Government (1642), Milton aligns himself and his poetic aspirations with temperate, seasoned impulses as well as divine favor:

> Neither doe I think it shame to covnant with any knowing reader, that for some few yeers yet I may go on trust with him toward the payment of what I am now indebted, as being a work not to be rays'd from the heat of youth, or the vapours of wine, like that which flows at wast from the pen of some vulgar Amorist…but by devout prayer to that eternall Spirit who can enrich with all utterance and knowledge, and sends out his Seraphim with the hallow'd fire of his Altar to touch and purify the lips of whom he pleases: to this must be added industrious and select reading, steddy observation, insight into all seemly and generous arts and affaires, till which in some measure be compast, at mine own peril and cost I refuse not to sustain this expectation from as many as are not loath to hazard so much credulity upon the best pledges I can give them. (YP 1:820–21)

Milton imagines his best poetry will result from both conscientious self-dedication and divine election. He attributes any future artistic success not to the "vapours of wine" but to a God who, like Hesiod's muses, can "touch and purify the lips of whom he pleases." Nevertheless, Milton argues that even if a poet is called by God to write, "to this must be added" studious, selective, steady, and seemly preparation. Divine inspiration is critical to Milton's self-presentation, but he also wants some credit for his years of preparation and for the long expected fruits of his labors. There are Virgilian echoes in this self-presentation. Milton does not quite begin his epic poem with *Pomum virumque cano*, but neither does he let his reader forget the human singer behind the song.

Milton's self-representation in *The Reason of Church-Government* more readily aligns him with the pensive over the jovial muses, and with *Il Penseroso* over *L'Allegro*, despite William Riley Parker's objections. As the Kerrigan, Rumrich, and Fallon edition observes, "The gifts of Melancholy are those of a life of planned accomplishment similar to Milton's."[24] Certainly there is charm in the description of the country comestibles of *L'Allegro*, where "Spicy Nut-brown Ale" is paired with tales of goblin cream-bowls and Queen Mab eating junkets (100–06); *L'Allegro* celebrates both the "savory dinner" of "Herbs, and other Country Messes" (84–85), as well as the urban pleasures of "pomp, and feast, and revelry" (127). Such jovial delights may move the mind of the youthful poet (129), but it is the sage and solemn speaker of *Il Penseroso* who enjoys the "dim religious light" so welcome to Milton's self-representation (160). The muse of *Il Penseroso* is a "pensive Nun, devout and pure, / Sober, steadfast, and demure" (31–32), and the speaker seeks "Spare Fast, that oft with gods doth diet, / And hears the Muses in a ring, / Ay round about Jove's Altar sing" (46–48). The connection between restraint and creation is iterated as the speaker calls on the sober and virginal spirit of Melancholy to "raise Musaeus from his bower" (104). The anticipated result of such inspiration is not stories of fairies feasting but divine insight based on contemplation of created things:

> And may at last my weary age
> Find out the peaceful hermitage,
> The Hairy Gown and Mossy Cell,
> Where I may sit and rightly spell,
> Of every Star that Heav'n doth shew,
> And every Herb that sips the dew;
> Till old experience do attain
> To something like Prophetic strain.   (167–74)

Dew is the only aliment that enters the poem, and ambrosial as it may be, it is only savored by the herbs. The sweetness in *Il Penseroso* is enjoyed through the ear and by the eye, not the mouth (164–66). Granted, the sounds are not purely melancholic to all ears. Michael Schmidt writes of *Il Penseroso* being "a little silly, with the gentle self-mockery we hear in Chaucer, an unusual note in Milton."[25] The point is that, in poetry and prose, when his style supports his message and even when it contradicts it, Milton never seems to forget the spiritual, scholarly, and even artistic advantages of melancholy, isolation, restraint, and fasting. If one must choose (as Milton does for himself in *The Reason of Church-Government*), Milton's verses smack of oil rather than wine.

GENIUS, SLOW-ENDEAVORING ART, AND DIVINE CALLING

The duality of the jovial and the pensive muses, or the carefree and the striving poet, may also be described as the difference between *phuē* (genius, nature) and *technē* (art, skill).[26] The division is noted in Pindar, who primarily attributes artistic success to the former element. Gilbert Norwood interprets Pindar's corpus as generally proposing three conditions required for success, poetic or otherwise: *phuē, technē,* and *tucha theōn* (divine fortune).[27] Milton frequently draws a line separating the first from the last two; he presents his own work not as the product of easy, natural genius but of labored artistry and divine calling. In Sonnet 7, "How soon hath time the subtle thief of youth" (1632), the speaker can but depend upon the will of God and "strictest measure ev'n" for his eventual poetic success, in the face of "more-timely-happy spirits" who have published at a younger age (8, 10). Two decades later, Sonnet 19, "When I consider how my light is spent" (1652), reveals Milton's persistent preoccupation with the struggle to write even as the sonnet endorses patience in serving God.

Excepting those early instances when sad occasion compels him to pluck the unripe berries and leaves of Apollo, Milton consistently presents his poetry as "slow-endeavoring art," in contrast, most notably, with the work of Shakespeare, whose "easy numbers flow" as proof of his genius.[28] But with divine favor purportedly on his side, Milton finds ways of distinguishing himself from Shakespeare to his own advantage. Shakespeare bereaves "our fancy of itself" and "Dost make us Marble with too much conceiving" (13–14). In *L'Allegro*, "sweetest *Shakespeare*, fancy's child, / Warble[s] his native Wood-notes wild" (133–34); in *Il Penseroso*, featuring the artistic disposition arguably more suited to the epic poet, Shakespeare is unnamed, and worthwhile "later age" tragedies beyond the classical period are deemed "rare" (101). Milton's distinguishing of his own painstaking, deliberate, divinely influenced poetry from the genius of Shakespeare survives in the criticism of William Hazlitt, if not to Milton's favor among those Romantics who highly prized both genius and nature. Quoting Milton's contempt for poetry inspired by the "vapours of wine" in the preface to book 2 of *The Reason of Church Government*, Hazlitt concludes, "Milton, therefore, does not write from casual impulse, but after a severe examination of his own strength, and with a resolution to leave nothing undone which it was in his power to do. He always labours, and almost always succeeds.... In Milton, there is always an appearance of effort: in Shakespeare, scarcely any."[29] But perhaps a little common sense can prevent false dichotomizing. There has been much good work to underscore the *companionship* of Milton's companion poems: *Il Penseroso* and *L'Allegro* might make incompatible roommates, but the poems dedicated to these characters work hand in hand beautifully. Horace's *Ars poetica* resolves the dispute between genius (*ingenium*) and art (*ars*) by refusing to choose one over the other: "People like to ask whether a good poem comes natural or is produced by craft. So far as I can see, neither book-learning without a lot of inspiration nor unimproved genius can get very far. The two things work together and need each other."[30] And while Hazlitt follows Milton's sonnet in opposing Shakespeare's easy numbers and apparent effortlessness with Milton's triumphant labors, Coleridge disagrees. The two poets are compeers, not rivals, and Shakespeare must have, like Milton, cultivated his talent and his success through patient study and prolonged meditation.[31] Ben Jonson gives Shakespeare a similar tribute (somewhat begrudged if we accept the gossip of John Aubrey in his *Brief Lives*): "Yet must I not give nature all; thy art, / My gentle Shakespeare, must enjoy a part.../ For a good poet's made as well as born.[32] Labored art can lead to ease in writing, and the bard in *Paradise Lost* wants his readers to believe that his labors have been rewarded with poetic facility. He was long in choosing his heroic subject, but now his muse visits him "unimplor'd," inspiring "easie [his] unpremeditated Verse" (*PL* 9.20–26). And so Milton's anonymous biographer (probably Cyriack Skinner) attributes Milton's success to a combination of *phuē, technē,* and *tucha theōn,* or natural ability, diligent study, and the good fortune of a divine calling: "He had a naturally sharp wit, and steady judgment; which helps toward attaining learning he improved by an indefatigable attention to his study; and was supported in that by a temperance always observed by him, but in his youth even with great nicety. Yet did he not reckon this talent but as entrusted with him; and therefore dedicated all his labors to the glory of God and some public good: neither binding himself to any of the gainful professions, nor having any worldly interest for aim in what he taught."[33] Milton never denies an illogical element — whether we call it Pindar's *tucha theōn* or "supernal Grace" — to successful poem making (*PL* 11.359). The making of an epic poet may have a conventional trajectory — short lyric, pastoral, georgic, epic — but the solicitation of the muses itself is not mere formula. Homer, the supposed "spare eater and the water-drinker," did not create the *Iliad* or the *Odyssey* by spare eating and water drinking alone. And Milton's perception of himself as *stylus Dei* combined his sense of his own talents with a deep awareness of the obligation of active gratitude: "Yet did he not reckon this talent but as entrusted with him." And so Milton's poetry invokes "that eternall Spirit who can enrich with all utterance and knowledge," but "to this must be added industrious and select reading, steddy observation, insight into all seemly and generous arts and affaires" — no trivial program of study (YP 1:820–21).

A parallel may be drawn between Pindaric *phuē*, nature defined as genius, or innate creative ability, and the Nature that, profuse and boon, adorns Milton's Eden. In *Paradise Lost*, the natural world is "not nice Art" — but it wildly invites, indeed requires, sweet labor (*PL* 4.241, 436–39, 625). So also *phuē* must be dressed and tilled; the word may signify *fine growth, noble stature, the flower of age,* and *produce* or *harvest,* as well as *nature, genius.*[34] In light of the conventional debate on the topic of poetic inspiration, the common sense observation deserves iteration: any natural proclivity to poetry must be cultivated before it produces a masterpiece.

By implication temperance, whether bodily, intellectual, or ethical, supports poetry in several ways. Bodily temperance constructs the right conditions for writing; wherever there is "More than anough, that temperance may be tri'd," a careful regimen prevents both distracting hunger pangs and the lethargy of overconsumption (*PL* 11.805). Temperance also trains the mind, as it demands and supports, especially in Milton's understanding of the virtue, not stagnant mediocrity or habituated complaisance, but rational deliberation, delightful sensitivity, and active virtue. Furthermore, temperance strengthens through acknowledgment and reconciliation of difference, just as any great argument may be strengthened by acknowledging and incorporating potential objections. The result of tempering is increased strength and stability; like "the sword / Of Michael . . . / . . . temper'd so, that neither keen / Nor solid might resist that edge," a gleaming, newly forged weapon is sounder once it is plunged into cool water (*PL* 6.320–23).[35] Finally, Miltonic temperance also permits grateful vicissitude, the variety and indulgence that bring pleasure while simultaneously moderating the extremes that ignore either the practicality of human responsibility or the unpredictable and wondrous quality of undeserved grace.

URANIA, MUSE OF TEMPERANCE

When in *Paradiso* Dante the poet expresses his desire to return to Florence and earn there the laureate crown, he knows such a prize would be greatly due to "this sacred poem — / This work so shared by heaven and by earth / that it has made me lean through these long years" (*Paradiso*, 25.1–3). This leanness is more elaborately considered in an earlier invocation of the muses, where Urania is given special status. Dante's request for poetic assistance precedes the description of Beatrice's stately, allegorical progress in the earthly paradise atop Mount Purgatory. The poet implores,

> O Virgins, sacrosanct, if I have ever,
> For your sake, suffered vigils, cold, and hunger,
> Great need makes me entreat my recompense.
> Now Helicon must pour its fountains for me,
> Urania must help me with her choir
> To put in verse things hard to conceive.   (*Purgatorio*, 29.37–42)

Dante attributes his physical suffering, including his hunger, not to his political exile but to the poetic process. He has hungered for the muses' sake, and he asks them for recompense. The prominence of Urania in this invocation is exquisitely apposite, suited not only to Dante's imminent ascent to the stars, since Urania is the muse of astronomy, but also (and more immediately) to Dante's peculiar reference to the ascetic conditions under which he writes his poetry, for Urania is also the muse of temperance. The reference to Urania's choir reminds us that her patronage of astronomy and temperance are related in the music of the spheres: the sixteenth-century Italian mythographer Natale Conti quotes Callimachus in identifying Urania as the muse who first discovered harmony in the stars; thus she presides over the temperance achieved by combining the different musical notes made by each planet in the Pythagorean universe.[36] Dante hereby unites the temperance that suffers present hunger for future reward with the temperance that seeks harmonious balance in the universe and in art. And since Urania is also an epithet for Aphrodite in her role as goddess of heavenly love, the invocation of this name serves as fit harbinger to the long-awaited arrival of Beatrice. When Dante invokes Urania, then, he invokes notes of temperance in diet, celestial harmony, and heavenly love.

Dante is certainly not the first to associate temperate eating with this muse of harmony. The connection exists in the words of Eryximachus, the physician attending Agathon's banquet in Plato's *Symposium*. Eryximachus's medical advice to the guests is as indulgent as they might hope for; he advises against heavy drinking but agrees that each should drink as much as pleases him.[37] But it is the theme of temperance that governs Eryximachus's speech on love, in which he conflates Aphrodite Urania as heavenly love with Urania the muse of temperance, drawing an analogy between the task of moderating and satisfying erotic desire with his own practical art of moderating and gratifying the taste of the epicure:

> But the moment you consider, in their turn, the effects of rhythm and harmony on their audience…complications arise directly, and they require the treatment of a good practitioner. Ultimately, the identical argument applies once again: the love felt by good people or by those whom such love might improve in this regard must be encouraged and protected. This is the honorable, heavenly species of Love, produced by the melodies of Urania, the Heavenly Muse. The other, produced by Polyhymnia, the muse of many songs, is common and vulgar. Extreme caution is indicated here: we must be careful to enjoy [Love's] pleasures

without slipping into debauchery — this case, I might add, is strictly parallel to a serious issue in my own field, namely, the problem of regulating appetite so as to be able to enjoy a fine meal without unhealthy aftereffects.[38]

For this physician, achieving temperance in love and in dining means experiencing the delight of indulgence without the insalubrious side effects of excess or poor taste. The banqueters must conform to the rules of temperance and to the "honorable species of heavenly love," lest the enjoyment of delicacies result in a crudity. Eryximachus prescribes a temperance in eating and in love that, rather than condoning stagnant mediocrity, enables a refined gratification of the senses. This exquisite and wholesome art is the correlative of Eve's culinary ability to introduce "taste after taste upheld with kindliest change." The physician's contrasting of Urania, "the Heavenly Muse," with "common and vulgar" Polyhymnia emphasizes that this artistry is not common nor always appreciated; Milton must have had this very passage in mind when he asks his muse in book 7, "Still govern thou my Song, / *Urania*, and fit audience find, though few" (7.30–31). Eryximachus and Milton know not everyone has a taste for the best food, the purest love, the finest words.

Poetic temperance requires not only cautious solicitation of the muses but also careful moderation of imaginative flight once inspiration is achieved. In the opening invocation of *Paradise Lost*, Milton introduces his "advent'rous Song / That with no middle flight intends to soar / Above th' *Aonian* mount" (1.13–15). The tone exudes confidence and self-composure. Milton states that Mount Parnassus, the source of inspiration for the poetry of ancient Greece, is inadequate for the writer of a Christian poem. In fact, by identifying the gods of the Greek pantheon as fallen angels who "on the Snowy top / Of cold *Olympus* rul'd the middle Air, / Thir highest Heav'n," Milton raises the stakes for his poem — not to surmount the middle air is to achieve demonic, not celestial, inspiration (1.515–17).[39] In the book 7 invocation, the bard again asserts his superior position to the Greek poets:

"above th' *Olympian* Hill I soar, / Above the flight of *Pegasean* wing" (7.3–4). However, there is an apparent tension between this opening metaphor of poetic soaring and the poem's pervading themes of temperance, restraint, and humility, further supported by mythographers' ethical interpretations of legendary ambitious soarers, including Icarus, Phaethon, and Bellerophon. Each of these fell through excess. And so, in his last direct invocation in *Paradise Lost*, Milton invokes Urania, opposes himself and his writing to Bacchus, the god of wine and revelry, and envisions the dangerous heights of poetic soaring while acknowledging the need for restraint. Milton specifies that he calls "The meaning, not the Name" of Urania, partly because he wants a Christian source of inspiration rather than one of the nine classical Muses (7.5). But the meaning of Urania does not end there.

Urania signifies an ideal patroness for Milton. As we have seen, Dante set a precedent when he invoked her as he prepared to describe Beatrice and the earthly paradise in his Christian epic. The muse shares her name with Aphrodite Urania, the goddess of heavenly beauty, by analogy linked to the Holy Spirit and the third division of Augustinian triads. She is the muse of astronomy, and her invocation introduces books 7 and 8 (together composing book 7 in the 1667 edition), which feature both Raphael's account of the creation of heavens and earth and Raphael's warnings against cosmological speculation. Finally, Urania is the muse of temperance and harmony. Fittingly, Milton includes in this invocation the importance of returning to earth, presumably to a position even lower than that of Olympus. When Milton implores, "Descend from Heav'n, *Urania*," he knows that the telling of the story of the War in Heaven, which he has just narrated, and which is also Raphael's story for Adam and Eve, is prudent only if tempered by a return to earthly matters (*PL* 7.1). So Adam humbly responds to Raphael's admonitions regarding cosmic speculation: "from this high pitch let us descend / A lower flight, and speak of things at hand" (8.198–99). As Adam's "high pitch" of imagination was made possible by Raphael's story, the poet in the invocation to book 7 also relies on celestial conveyance. The ascent itself was a result of divine tempering:

> Up led by thee [Urania]
> Into the Heav'n of Heav'ns I have presum'd,
> An Earthly Guest, and drawn Empyreal Air,
> Thy temp'ring; with like safety guided down
> Return me to my Native Element:
> Lest from this flying Steed unrein'd, (as once
> *Bellerophon*, though from a lower Clime)
> Dismounted, on th'*Aleian* Field I fall
> Erroneous there to wander and forlorn.
> Half yet remains unsung, but narrower bound
> Within the visible Diurnal Sphere;
> Standing on Earth, not rapt above the Pole,
> More safe I Sing with mortal voice...
>   ...still govern thou my Song,
> *Urania*, and fit audience find, though few.   (7.12–24, 30–31)

This introduction to the second half of the poem is notable for delimiting the poet's flight. The poet mounts Jerusalem's correlative to Athens's Pegasus, that ancient symbol for inspiration. Yet he is merely a "Guest" when he soars the heavens; his "Native Element" is earth. It appears then that Milton depicts his inspiration, or his poetic art in portraying the heavens, as a temporary ability, one furthermore dependent on the muse's "temp'ring" of "Empyreal Air" to accommodate human lungs. After revelation of the War in Heaven, the poet's song is now "narrower bound" and will focus on Adam and Eve in the garden of Eden, or on the cosmology of the earthly heavens from a more limited and subdued perspective. Yet this change in emphasis from soaring to descent does not simply mark a change in setting — it also provides the needed counterpart to Milton's previous display of unchecked poetic ambition. In turn, this descent contributes to the greater harmony of his poem. It is just as necessary as silence is to heavenly music, as grateful evening to the brilliance of light, or as rest to fruitful activity in Milton's prelapsarian spaces.

Milton's concept of grateful vicissitude is essentially the active temperance of creation, and the creative act of God is comparable to the creative act of writing poetry. As Miltonic as this concept is, it is yet again distinctly Augustinian. Turning once more to book 11 of Augustine's *City of God*, we find in chapter 18 a meditation on "the beauty of the universe, which, by the disposition of God, is made all the more magnificent by the opposition of contraries." Contextually Augustine is pondering the Falls of angels and of men; in preparing to consider the Genesis Creation account, he begins with assurances of the happy ending: "For God would never have created any men, much less any angels, whose future wickedness He foreknew, unless He had equally known to what uses He could put them on behalf of the good, thereby adorning the course of the ages like a most beautiful poem set off with antitheses."[40] The rules of rhetoric carry a hint of theology: "Just as the opposition of contraries bestows beauty upon language, so is the beauty of this world enhanced by the opposition of contraries, composed, as it were, by an eloquence not of words but of things. This is quite clearly explained in the Book of Ecclesiasticus, in this way: 'Good is set against evil, and life against death: so is the sinner against the godly. So look upon all the works of the Most High, and these are two and two, one against another.'"[41] For Milton, as for Augustine, the story of God's action in creation throughout time and space is poetic. To this we have added a converse observation, that Milton views his poem and even the very act of poem making as morally responsive to the story of the Fall. The active role he accepts and promotes includes good speaking, the creative art of poetry, and the self-fashioning art of cultivating the virtuous, temperate soul, of becoming "a true Poem, that is, a composition, and patterne of the best and honourablest things" (YP 1:890). Milton's poetry tempers joy with sorrow, and human action with divine grace. We should expect to hear good with bad in this story, but ultimately to see how both are in the control of God the artist. This is all part of Milton's poetic harmonizing, and all part of his attempt to justify the ways of God to humanity. Finally, poetically and religiously, Milton's project requires confidence as well as humility. The "highth of this great Argument" is made all the more relevant by descending "to compare / Great things with small" and to contemplate created "things at hand" (1.24, 2.921–22, 8.199). Thus in the book 7 invocation Milton prepares for a controlled descent, positioning himself as a better version of Bellerophon.

A BETTER BELLEROPHON

From the ancient Greek myth of Bellerophon, Renaissance mythographers extracted two moral lessons: the praiseworthiness of the hero who is modestly temperate with regard to physical pleasures, and the dangers when that same hero seeks to gratify an overreaching ambition. Bellerophon's story is told in part in book 6 of the *Iliad* by his descendent, Glaucus.[42] He is "Bellerophontes the blameless" when he turns down the advances of Proitos's wife, but the spurned Anteia vengefully and falsely accuses him of offending her honor to her husband.[43] The code of guest-friendship prevents Proitos from directly punishing Bellerophon, so he sends his guest to his father-in-law in Lycia with a sealed letter containing "murderous symbols."[44] Bellerophon's death is again prevented when Proitos's father-in-law Iobates delays in reading the letter until he has entertained his guest for several days, thereby making it also an unjust breach of the hospitality code for him to kill Bellerophon. Instead King Iobates sends his guest on a succession of dangerous ventures. The gods in sympathy give Bellerophon the winged horse Pegasus to accomplish his tasks, with which he kills the Chimera and defeats the Solymoi, the Amazons, and the Lycian men set in ambush against him. At his return to Lycia, the evident favor of the gods results in the welcoming of the hero, who enjoys some measure of success before his hubristic attempt to soar on Pegasus to the abode of the gods. Zeus sends a gadfly, Pegasus bucks, and Bellerophon falls into a thicket on the plains of Aleios, is blinded by thorns, and wanders alone for the rest of his life, hated by the gods and — figuratively, we presume, although he may have starved to death — "eating his heart out."[45] The man who initially receives the favor of the gods and the gift of Pegasus for his bodily temperance and moral probity is ultimately cast down from his high-flying horse because of his excessive pride.

From this myth Milton finds support for the temperance his poem endorses, but in context he alludes to Bellerophon not to encourage restrained contentment in Adam and Eve, as might be expected, but to consider the divine "temp'ring" needed to guide his own poetic ambition (*PL* 7.15). In a poem concerned about the fruit of the Tree of Knowledge of Good and Evil, it is no surprise that Milton's Adam and Eve are exhorted to show discretion in their diet and restraint in their intellectual aspirations. What is most intriguing about the reference to Urania and Bellerophon is that bodily regulation and checked hubris may also be a prescriptive ethics for the poet.

Without temperance, the poet risks being dismounted from the back of his "flying Steed unrein'd." In his essay on "Milton on Himself" in *Milton in Context*, Stephen M. Fallon notes that "Plutarch (*Concerning the Virtues of Women*, 9) and Horace (*Odes* 3.7) echo Homer on Bellerophon's chastity and heroism"; in *Milton's Peculiar Grace*, Fallon expands his analysis of variations of the Bellerophon myth in Hesiod, Pindar, and Plutarch as well as Homer, with the proposition that the varying characterizations of the classical hero serve as "an echo chamber for the self-referential dialogue that Milton had been having with himself and with his readers for many years."[46] The complexity of the Bellerophon myth fitly reinforces the complexity of Milton's self-representation as a temperate, intrepid, divinely appointed, and virtuously heroic poet. Fallon understands Miltonic self-representation in the proems of *Paradise Lost* as revealing the bard's bipolarity, "veering between confident assertions of inspired status and dark intimations of exclusion and abandonment," even as temperance is advocated and partially represented (if not exercised) in the narrative: "A balanced self-understanding on Milton's part would place him between Abdiel and Satan, neither as heroically virtuous as the one nor as degraded as the other. And although Milton's temperament seems to lead him more often to extremes than to balance, he places as much of himself in flawed Adam (and Eve) as he does in the faithful and faithless angels."[47] Certainly the poet is fallen, and has fallen on evil times, but he presents both the ascent and controlled descent of his poetic flight as a sign of strength. The reader is left to decide if these artistic and self-representational undulations indeed point to appropriately modulated excesses or if they have been protracted into hellish extremes.

Milton suggests that the success of his poetic project depends on his imaginative flight reaching air higher than Bellerophon could on Pegasus (beyond the pagan limits of inspiration) and yet descending to fly lower than Bellerophon did (lest in unchecked ambition he lose control of the narrative, or of his own moral self). This flight is not limited to straight lines at a single altitude; he may soar upward and downward, as the sun rises and sets, and still model temperance. Put another way, the poet with the most elevated spiritual thoughts still must descend to consider the stuff of the natural world. To use a simile from John Cassian, even the ascetic monk most successful in his struggle against gluttony is like an eagle — able to soar into heavens of contemplation, but still needing to descend to eat.[48] Odysseus, that excellent man of many ways, still is plagued by the needs of the belly.

Darker dangers lurk for the epic poet in the company of Bacchus. In *Elegia sexta*, the young Milton positioned Bacchus beside his own sober muse as an alternative if subordinate mode of inspiration. In *Paradise Lost*, however, the bard depicts Bacchus as inimical and life-threatening:

> But drive far off the barbarous dissonance
> Of *Bacchus* and his Revellers, the Race
> Of that wild Rout that tore the *Thracian* Bard
> In *Rhodope*, where Woods and Rocks had Ears
> To rapture, till the savage clamor drown'd
> Both Harp and Voice; nor could the Muse defend
> Her Son. So fail not thou, who thee implores:
> For thou art Heav'nly, shee an empty dream. (7.32–39)

Commentators and critics frequently point to this passage, as well as the accompanying complaint against "evil days … and evil tongues; / In darkness, and with dangers compast round," as registering Milton's disappointment with England after the Restoration, and perhaps more specifically his antipathy toward cavalier court poets attending Charles II (7.25–28).[49] The passage positions Milton in the role of Orpheus, the poet who could charm nature but suffered dismemberment by the Maenads, in part for his neglect of Bacchus, in part for his condemnation of his tormentors' sexual promiscuity. Like Bellerophon, Orpheus was known for a certain chaste temperance; however, as Fallon notes, while some versions of the myth "credited Orpheus with chastity for spurning the Bacchantes[,] Ovid, on the other hand, implies that Orpheus angered the Bacchantes by his practice and advocacy of sodomy" (a footnote points to *Metamorphoses*, 10.78–85 and 11.6–7, and acknowledges John Rumrich for the observation).[50] While Bellerophon falls due to his own intemperance, Orpheus's demise involves his suffering at the hands of others, whose actions he cannot control. Calliope fails to protect Orpheus, but Urania ("The meaning, not the Name") might better assist Milton, not only because she is "Heav'nly" but also because he, an "Earthly Guest," has sought a temperate descent to safety. Yet it is the myth of the death of Orpheus, Alistair Fowler observes, that "seems to have focused some of Milton's deepest fears."[51] And it is this myth that addresses the possibility that even the temperate, successful poet may suffer evil for his temperance as well as for his artistic success, or that he might encounter opposing forces beyond his capacity to control.

TEMPERATE MILTON?

We have seen how Milton promotes the convention of the temperate epic poet, but the complicated matter of Milton's own temperance still lies before us. Various early *Lives* of Milton characterize the poet as a temperate man, and one sufficiently charitable to allow exceptions to his general rules of conduct. John Aubrey writes that Milton was "a spare man" and "temperate, rarely dranke between meales. Extreme pleasant in his conversation, & at dinner, supper, &c: but Satyricall."[52] The comment is platitudinous, but Aubrey relates that Milton's "harmonicall, and ingeniose soule did lodge in a beautifull & well proportioned body."[53] Independent of Aubrey, John Toland wrote that Milton was "extraordinarily temperate in his diet, which was anything most in season or the easiest procured, and was no friend to sharp or strong liquors."[54] Milton had good taste; his granddaughter Elizabeth Foster told Thomas Newton that the poet "always loved to have of the best," and so Elizabeth Milton prepared his favorite dishes in accordance with a prenuptial promise, but Jonathan Richardson remarks that he was "not nice" and "took what was set before him."[55] We have already noted the description of Milton's temperance, "always observed by him, but in his youth even with great nicety," in the anonymous *Life of Milton* usually attributed to Cyriack Skinner.[56] Parker notes "two exceptions to [Milton's] rule of economy," according to the anonymous biographer: "'he was not sparing to buy good books' and he 'was generous in relieving the wants of his friends.'"[57] Edward Phillips attributes the chief reason for Milton's move from St. Bride's Church-yard to Aldersgate the necessity of finding a place to house his books, and names Milton's "studies and curious search into knowledge, the grand affair perpetually of his life."[58] Phillips confirms his uncle's "hard study and spare diet," but also admits, "only this advantage he had, that once in three weeks or a month, he would drop into the society of some young sparks of his acquaintance...the beaux of those times, but nothing near so bad as those now-a-days; with these gentlemen he would so far make bold with his body as now and then to keep a gawdy-day."[59] And so the composite portrait of Milton painted by his early biographers and relations suggests a man of moderation, generally industrious and frugal, but with no compunction against maintaining social ties with more frivolous characters, occasionally gratifying his taste for delicacies, and habitually indulging his desire for intellectual stimulation, even with regard to curiosities.

When David Masson considers Edward Phillips's account of Milton's hard study and spare diet, and the nephew's special interest in Milton's gaudy days, the biographer dismisses the significance of these outings, suggesting that "the beaux of those times" — identified by Masson as Thomas Alfray of Catsfield, Sussex, and John Miller of Litton, Middlesex — did not represent Milton's preferred companions; they simply "made a greater impression upon the two boys than more important men."[60] In the late months of 1640, Masson remarks, Milton "is in the habit of seeing Young, Calamy, and others of the Root-and-Branch Puritan ministers in London. He sees *them*, I should say, more frequently than the two Gray's Inn beaux, Messrs. Miller and Alphry" [sic].[61] Similarly, when Masson waxes poetical on the natural splendors of Italy while covering Milton's grand tour, he checks his eloquence to pay tribute to the more somber side of Milton's character, the side he customarily sees as predominant: "But in Milton the sensuous poet was merged in the poet of larger cares; nor did the poet in him exclude the historian and the scholar."[62] Masson presents Milton not only as temperate, but also as eminently serious. Yet, as Barbara Lewalski points out, the sustained friendships Milton formed with the Florentine *Apatisti* Carlo Dati and Antonio Francini reveal a personable side to the principled traveler: "The warmth of their praise indicates that they liked him and found him amiable, sociable, and eager for new cultural experiences; an austere or defensive mien would not elicit such comment."[63]

It would be unnecessary and unwise to assume from these remarks, and from the conventional duality of poetic inspiration, that Milton must either be temperate and sober or charitable and companionable. Parker is the biographer most interested in the question of Milton's temperance, which he presents as paradoxical. Quoting Edward Phillips, Parker paints a domestic scene familiar to Milton's nephews: "On suitable occasions Milton chatted informally and memorably with his impressionable charges, but for the most part the routine was strict and vigorous, the teacher setting an example to his pupils of hard study and a temperate diet."[64] His example put into practice the temperance he argued for as a youth in his Cambridge *Oratio pro Arte* (his Seventh Prolusion): "But if we were to set ourselves to live modestly and temperately, and to tame the first impulses of headstrong youth by reason and steady devotion to study, keeping the divine vigour of our minds unstained and uncontaminated by any impurity or pollution, we should be astonished to find, gentlemen, looking back over a period of years, how great a distance we had covered and across how wide a sea of learning we had sailed, without a check on our voyage" (YP 1:300).

One of temperance's greatest attractions for the young Milton was the enhanced prospect of great intellectual advancement. Milton's own intemperate thirst for knowledge was an inducement to his pursuit of bodily temperance. Later, he also argues that temperance supports the virtue of chastity, an unsurprising claim when we remember the corresponding belief that gluttony provokes lust. In *The Doctrine and Discipline of Divorce*, arguing that "the flesh hath...naturall and easie curbes which are in the power of any temperate man," Milton recommends "frugal diet" to "remedy a sublunary and bestial burning" (YP 2:252, 296). The example Milton set for his nephews evidently also followed his terse recommendation for the scholars' diet in *Of Education:* "that it should be plain, healthfull, and moderat I suppose is out of controversie" (YP 2:414).

What is controversial, however, is the extent to which Milton can be described as temperate, especially in thought and language, given his vast capacity for learning and his penchant for vitriolic rhetoric. As Parker expounds, "Within Milton was the vast, ruthless energy of what we call the Renaissance, an energy which could and did shift its direction from time to time, but whichever way it moved, bowed everything before it. He probably wrote so much about the virtues of temperance because, in some respects, he had so little. He was an extremist, a perfectionist; he had a one-track mind. He also had a genuine talent (God-given, he sincerely believed) for the vigorous, vituperative give-and-take of controversy." Milton had, Parker concludes, "a nature over-strong in combativeness."[65] Despite Milton maintaining long-standing friendships and engaging in amicable private correspondence with some whose religious and political views he opposed, his combative temperament was subject to censure. In 1787, Sir John Hawkins suspected Milton's temperament made him practically intolerable: "[Milton's] style in controversy was sarcastic and bitter, and not consistent with Christian charity...nor does he seem in his private character to have possessed many of those qualities that most endear men to each other...and there is reason to suspect, from the sternness of his temper, and the rigid discipline of his family, that his domestic manners were far from amiable, and that he was neither a kind husband nor an indulgent parent."[66] Even so, Hawkins concludes, Samuel Johnson's censure of *Samson Agonistes* was unwarranted, seemingly "prompted by no better a motive, than that of hatred of the author for his political principles."

Milton's polemical writings reveal that his most bitter and intemperate remarks were expended against the excesses and intemperance of his rhetorical opponents. For example, when Milton wrote *Of Reformation*, Parker remarks, "he lavishly and intemperately lashed out at all that his frugal and temperate soul despised," including the "worldly prelates" who delighted in eating exquisite dishes — to satisfy their "unctuous, and epicurean paunches," as Milton writes — rather than offering spiritual nourishment to the church (YP 1:611).[67] In the words of *Lycidas*, these false pastors were "Blind mouths" inattentive to their ministry: "The hungry Sheep look up, and are not fed, / But swoln with wind" (119, 125–26). So also Dante excoriates the hypocritical ecclesiastics who offer false comfort and idle tales to their flocks, "so that the wretched sheep, in ignorance, / return from pasture, having fed on wind — / but to be blind to harm does not excuse them."[68] Demanding more of leaders than of followers, Milton focuses on the blindness of the greedy prelates rather than the blindness of their hungry sheep.

His censure is intensified and extended in *The Reason of Church-Government*, where clergy ambitious for preferment are condemned and compared to Lucifer, "the first prelat Angel"; both he and Adam "for aspiring above their orders were miserably degraded" (YP 1:762). This disordered aspiration is condemned through extended food metaphors: those touting themselves to be God's ministers are guilty of "a grave and reverent gluttony"; they are "fat and fleshly, swoln with high thoughts and mischievous designs," vexing the church under their "Egyptian tyranny" (YP 1:792, 793). Milton paints a grim, ravenous, Deathly picture of liberty enthralled "under the swelling mood of a proud Clergy, who will not serve or feed your soules with spirituall food," doubting if "their ingratefull bodies,... those open sepulchers should ever be glutted" (YP 1:851). As expected, Sloth attends Gluttony as security encourages more open violence: "They snore in their luxurious excesse. Openly proclaiming themselvs now in the sight of all men to be those which for a while they sought to cover under sheeps cloathing, ravenous and savage wolves threatning inroads and bloody incursions upon the flock of Christ, which they took upon them to feed, but now clame to devour as their prey" (YP 1:856–57). The clergy, who "should be to us a pattern of temperance and frugal mediocrity," are wolves who have discarded their sheep's clothing, ignoring their pastoral commission and openly preying upon those they should be feeding (YP 1:856). This all-too-common observation gave rise to the popular early modern English pun on *bishop / bite-sheep*. There was often in Milton's mind a connection not only between temperate eating and poetics, but also between temperate eating and readiness to offer words of spiritual nourishment. Like Hesiod's muses, Milton abhorred shepherds whose primary concern was their own belly. Milton was ever ready to ridicule corruption and to defend a proper use of obscene, seemingly intemperate language, for "Christ himselfe speaking of unsavory traditions, scruples not to name the Dunghill and the Jakes" (YP 1:895).[69] As Sin and Death inadvertently serve divine purposes in *Paradise Lost* by "lick[ing] up the draff and filth" of the fallen world, described as "suckt and glutted offal," there is a role for impolite, indecorous expressions in Milton's rhetoric; these are the hellhounds of his language (*PL* 10.630, 633).

We sense the irony of Milton's brag in the *Second Defense* that he "learned to hold [his] peace," having "mastered the art of not writing" (YP 4:608), and wonder if there has ever been a greater gap between person and persona. The awkward disconnect between the convention of the temperate poet and the intemperate lashings of the polemicist even makes its way into editorial notes on *De doctrina Christiana*. Milton's chapter on duties to be performed toward humankind culminates in a long reflection on control of the tongue. Hale and Cullington note the passage's peculiarity: "The final paragraph is especially abundant in citations, as if Milton himself was being aroused by this topic (control of tongue, and failure to control it)" (OW 8:1073 note xiv). This section incorporates several quotations that advance the analogy Milton makes between knowledge (especially spoken knowledge) and food — for example, Proverbs 12:14: "from the fruit of his mouth, a good man is sated"; Proverbs 15:23: "O, how good is a word in its proper season!" — as well as metaphors of unfavorable consumption and indigestion — for example, Proverbs 15:2: "the mouth of dolts belches out folly"; Proverbs 15:28: "the mouth of the wicked belches out evil things"; Proverbs 19:28: "iniquity engulf[s] the mouth of the wicked" (OW 8:1069). Milton was undoubtedly intrigued by bodily images of healthy and unhealthy speaking. The same paragraph cites Proverbs 15:4: "A wholesome tongue is a tree of life" (AV); one may recollect Dante's gluttons in purgatory, running past the offshoot of the Tree of Knowledge and combating their hunger with words of praise. The space Milton dedicates to controlling the tongue, or temperance in speech, indicates that this was a subject close enough to him that he could write much about it.

Despite accounts of Milton's temperate diet and records of his opinion on the poetic and spiritual consequences of intemperate eating, Milton attributed his blindness on one occasion to digestive problems, on others to unrestrained commitment to scholarly and political tasks. While his political enemies pointed to his blindness as divine punishment for his support of the regicide, Milton would explain his blindness in Sonnet 22 as personal sacrifice, having lost the use of his eyes "overplied / In liberty's defense." In 1654, two years after Milton became completely blind, he wrote in the *Second Defense* that his failing sight was probably first caused by frequent reading by candlelight until midnight as a child (YP 4:612). Milton suspected that his indefatigable commitment to studying, and later to writing, had brought about the greatest physical setback of his life. His commitment to the cause of liberty, he asserts, is what made him continue to deny his eyes the rest that could have delayed total loss of vision. The Campbell and Corns biography dismisses this claim as "a sustaining illusion": "The aetiology of his blindness was unconnected with working too hard. But Milton needed the comfort of such fictions to assure himself that he was 'content though blind.'"[70]

On September 28 of the same year in which he wrote of his blindness in the *Second Defense*, Milton describes the onset of his blindness in a familiar letter to Leonard Philaras, an Athenian friend residing in Paris. Here, Milton suspects a more physical and less glorious cause: indigestion. Philaras's desire to explain Milton's case to a prominent

Parisian physician (most likely Louis XIV's oculist Dr. Francois Thevenin, though Milton names an unknown Dr. Thevenot), results in Milton's famous self-diagnosis:

> It is ten years, I think, more or less, since I noticed my sight becoming weak and growing dim, and at the same time my spleen and all my viscera burdened and shaken with flatulence.... Certain permanent vapors seem to have settled upon my entire forehead and temples, which press and oppress my eyes with a sort of sleepy heaviness, especially from mealtime to evening.... But if, as it is written, man shall not live by bread alone, but by every word that proceedeth out of the mouth of God, why should one not likewise find comfort in believing that he cannot see by the eyes alone, but by the guidance and wisdom of God. Indeed while He himself looks out for me and provides for me, which He does, and takes me as if by the hand and leads me throughout life, surely, since it has pleased Him, I shall be pleased to grant my eyes a holiday. (YP 4:867–70)[71]

Milton's meditations on the limits of temperance in diet in preserving the body must have been shaped by the onset of his blindness, one of his most intimate and obvious encounters with the effects of the Fall and the need for resting in divine grace.

In *De doctrina Christiana*, Milton's position on temperance itself was tempered. In fact, all virtues were to be moderated and subjected to charity. Thus in his definition of good works at the beginning of book 2, Milton explains that "though [good works] are never contrary to the love of God and of our neighbor, which is the whole sum of the law, [these works] can nevertheless sometimes deviate from the letter even of gospel commands...through a supreme regard for charity" (OW 8:909). This subordination of the other virtues, including temperance, to charity is often touched upon in subsequent definitions. For example, the virtue of frugality, Milton explains, is shown when one "spares expense, *so far as is seemly*, and [spares] things to be kept for a suitable use" (OW 8:1089; my italics). Sometimes, Milton implies, decency demands extravagance. The counterpart of *frugalitas* is *lautitia*, the virtue "by which we temperately enjoy honourably acquired possessions for food and clothing and all refinements of life" (OW 8:1091). *Lautitia* (Sumner's "liberality," Carey's "elegance," Hale and Cullington's "orderliness") holds widely varying connotations for Milton's translators, some diverging from the path of restraint. Lewis and Short's *Latin Dictionary* defines *lautitia* as "*elegance, splendor, magnificence* in one's style of living, in one's house, furniture, food, etc." Hale and Cullington note the more restrained etymological root: "Since Milton uses *lautitia* to mean something less luxurious than 'elegance,' we translate it as 'orderliness' (derived as it is from *lautus*, ('washed' or 'well-turned-out')" (OW 8:1101, note xv). Yet it is worth remembering both that *elegance* itself depends on tasteful choice (derived from L. *elego*, "I choose"), and that Milton supports a virtuous enjoyment of "refinements of life" that does not fall into *luxus* (OW 8:1090–91, which Hale and Cullington translate as "dissipation"). Fallon has shown that, in a list of virtues that follow John Wolleb's *Compendium theologiae* (including *contentment, frugality,* and *industry*), the Miltonic addition of *lautitia* is an idiosyncratic and revealing reflection of "Milton's refined taste and his hostility toward asceticism."[72] At the same time, Fallon notes that the nearby definition of modesty (*verecundia*) is also peculiarly Miltonic: "abstinence...from anything that fails to conform with the strictest standards of personal or sexual conduct" (YP 6:727). Even so, all told, Milton's final view of temperance rests a comfortable distance from the severe asceticism to be found in, for example, Tertullian's *De jejuniis* or Jerome's Letter 22.

Milton's writings provide evidence that his personal standards of conduct were not so strict as to debar pleasure and recreation. Beyond the playful academic exercise of Prolusion 6, "That Sportive Exercises are Occasionally Not Adverse to Philosophic Studies," which describes itself as a "serious speech in praise of buffoonery," Milton more seriously advocates rest and recreation in *Tetrachordon*: "No mortal nature can endure, either in the actions of religion or study of wisdom, without some time slackening the cords of intense thought and labor.... No worthy enterprise can be done by us without continual plodding and wearisomeness to our faint and sensitive abilities. We cannot, therefore, always be contemplative, or pragmatical abroad, but have need to some delightful intermissions wherein the enlarged soul may leave off awhile her severe schooling, and like a glad youth in wandering vacancy, may keep her holidays to joy and harmless pastime" (YP 3:331). A diligent scholar whose writings resulted from extended and repeated periods of "continual plodding," and a poet who made bold as to "keep a gawdy-day" occasionally, Milton also defended leisure. He wrote two conviviality sonnets, "Lawrence, of virtuous father" and "Cyriack, whose grandsire." The former of these invites the addressee to fine music, food, and friendship:

> What neat repast shall feast us, light and choice,
> Of Attic taste, with Wine, whence we may rise
> To hear the Lute well toucht, or artful voice
> Warble immortal Notes and *Tuscan* air?
> He who of those delights can judge and spare
> To interpose them oft, is not unwise.   (9–14)

"To interpose them oft" — The sonnet endorses wise and delightful indulgences as frequent respite from the speaker's and addressee's normal activities. Similarly, the second conviviality sonnet begs a break from studying the classics or talking politics, reproving (on divine authority) those who avoid seasonable recreation:

> For other things mild Heav'n a time ordains,
> And disapproves that care, though wise in show,
> That with superfluous burden loads the day,
> And when God sends a cheerful hour, refrains.   (11–14)

Campbell and Corns describe the sonnet addressed to Cyriack Skinner as "an invitation to enjoy hospitality and leisure with Milton," and note that the two sonnets "appear in the Trinity Manuscript in what seems to be Cyriack Skinner's hand, which may mean that Milton dictated them to the person to whom they are addressed."[73] The sonnet to Edward Lawrence contains "Horatian echoes" that "cascade through the poem in its celebration of friendship and *otium*." In fact, Milton's repeated defense of his professional choice to deny the life of business (*negotium*), which is itself a denial of leisure, may be seen as an ongoing defense of the vigorous yet delightful and satisfying exercise of scholarship. Yet the conviviality sonnets qualify even the scholar's task with the praise of hospitality, friendship, alimental recompense, and rest.

Both frugality and elegance, and both restraint and liberality are necessary. Milton's Comus argues,

> If all the world
> Should in a pet of temperance feed on Pulse,
> Drink the clear stream, and nothing wear but Frieze,
> Th'all-giver would be unthank't, would be unprais'd,
> Not half his riches known, and yet despis'd.   (*Maske* 720–24)

The rhetoric here may be "o'erfraught," as Louis Schwartz has observed, but the satyr's message is only half-reasonable (732).[74] As the Lady counters,

> swinish gluttony
> Ne'er looks to Heav'n amidst his gorgeous feast,
> But with besotted base ingratitude
> Crams, and blasphemes his feeder.   (776–79)

The implication throughout Milton's works is that the temptation to "Be wise, and taste" must first of all be changed to "Choose wisely what you taste, and when you taste, taste wisely" (813). Second, the choice to taste must be attended by gratitude and generosity lest we become like Mammon at the altar of God. The bounties set before us become the occasion for virtue, for companionship, for gratitude, and for praise. He who does well with little, to him will be given more, and the decisions made with the body are not void of effect on the soul. "What would be endlessly suggestive, but perhaps futile to dispute," Denise Gigante remarks, "is whether Milton viewed his own digestive processes as responsible for his poetic creation."[75] But if Milton's anonymous biographer is Cyriack Skinner, it is the recipient of one of Milton's charming conviviality sonnets who records that Milton intentionally regulated his studies, and described his poetry not only as nourishment to others, but also as something he simply had to excrete: "He rendered his studies and various works more easy and pleasant by allotting them their several portions of the day. Of these the time friendly to the Muses fell to his poetry; and he, waking early (as is the use of temperate men) had commonly a good stock of verses ready against his amanuensis came; which if it happened to be later than ordinary, he would complain, saying he wanted to be milked."[76] At his most gracious, Milton found shared needs and obligations by looking both above and below his imagined position on the Great Chain of Eating. Like a cow, he would consume, ruminate, digest, transform, collect, and secrete thoughts and language. Like a good angel, he gratefully accepted the gifts of heaven, digested these, and returned them as ambrosial offerings.

THE STORY OF EVERYTHING

In the 1674 edition of *Paradise Lost*, a commendatory poem in Latin began, "You who read *Paradise Lost*, the magnificent poem by the great Milton, what do you read but the story of everything?"[77] Indeed, the poem stretches to encompass heaven, earth, and hell, past, present, and future, and a variety of perspectives and possible readings. It includes multiple themes, and my foray into the role of gluttony in the poem seeks to add rather than replace.

In 1917, Edwin Greenlaw contended that Milton's theme was temperance, an argument that recent scholarship on Milton's interest in the body has deemed worth further inquiry.[78] In 1963, Christopher Ricks argued, "Certainly ingratitude is the great theme of the poem. Adam, Eve, and Satan are all guilty of it, and it occasions some of the most moving passages in the poem."[79] For John T. Shawcross and others, love or charity is undoubtedly the great theme of *Paradise Lost*.[80] In fact, as this study of gluttony in *Paradise Lost* has shown, the themes of temperance, (in)gratitude, and charity are interwoven. These themes are prominently supported by Milton's prose. In the beginning of the *Second Defense*, Milton asserts, "In the whole life and estate of man the first duty is to be grateful to God and mindful of his blessings, and to offer particular and solemn thanks without delay when his benefits have exceeded hope and prayer" (YP 4:548). As we have seen, in *De doctrina Christiana* Milton lists temperance as the first of the "special virtues relating to a person's duty toward himself" (OW 8:1075). And ultimately, temperance and gratitude in response to grace may be subsumed into the divine mandate to love. Curiously, Milton argues in *De doctrina Christiana* that the power to perform this duty originates in God the Father, and in the Son, and in the Holy Spirit: "Charity is a general virtue infused in the faithful by God the father in Christ through the spirit; it embraces the whole duty of love, that is, each person's duty both toward himself and toward his neighbor" (OW 8:1061).

Whether Milton thinks about eating, philosophizing, writing poetry, or seeking divine favor, he advocates a temperance that, if cognizant of grace and of gratitude, permits indulgence and grateful vicissitude. Milton enjoyed fine foods, read with extraordinary curiosity, tackled what he considered to be the highest of literary genres, and acted on the assumption that he was influenced by special grace, called by God to write the great Christian epic poem of the English language. But he also ate sparingly, promoted the principle of usefulness in educational reform, trained his poetic hand with slow, arduous deliberation, and named God the efficient cause of all human success and goodness. While assuming the Son must transform all human action, atoning for the bad and perfecting the good, he nevertheless insisted that humans are responsible for living temperate lives seasoned with gratitude and motivated by charity — by love that invites excess in generosity of spirit, and in hospitality and good cheer at table.

In *sophrosynē*, we see just how crucial self-knowledge is to Milton's socio-ethical, religio-spiritual, self-formative, and poetic enterprises. Temperance requires an understanding of oneself and one's relation to God, other humans, and the world. It involves gratitude and graciousness. It permits, even requires, fit excess in accordance with self-knowledge and in relation to others. Intimately connected to the materiality of the cosmos, temperance examines both the needs of the body and the resources that are at hand, which the temperate person will use with humility, gratitude, and justice. Thus, "Temperance includes not only sobriety and chastity but also respectfulness and decency" (OW 8:1075).

For Milton, gluttony is weighed not on a scale but in the heart. Temperance is ultimately not a matter of self-denial, calorie counting, or strict balance, but an attitude toward God and his providence — that is, to the provisions available to humankind, provisions that have their origin *de Deo*. Not contemptuous of lower creatures and lower bodily functions, but seeking to regain — if only through metaphor — what he described in his poem as paradisal, pure digestion, Milton fashioned a poem of praise in response to eternal providence. Only after great suffering and great striving does Milton say his muse comes unimplored. For Milton, "knowing thyself" means both being grounded in practicalities and cognizant of human limits, and being aware of rapturous possibilities for metamorphosis. He makes love the ladder to radical spiritual transformation, never forgetting the soil of earth and the dark materials of creation. He writes of Padan-Aram and Bethel as well as heaven. He writes of love descending as grace, and of love ascending as gratitude. He makes love the inspiring, animating force charging the material world to participate in the sustained climb. He envisions virtuous action and worthy enterprise, including his own poetry, following the path shown by faith up to joy and bliss, and led on by love to the place where works are dressed in angel garments, and the good worker is rewarded with rest and repast — no inconvenient diet, nor too light fare, but an invitation to enjoy manna and the fruit of the Tree of Life, and to drink one's fill from pure immortal streams.

NOTES

NOTES TO INTRODUCTION

1. Mulryan, introduction to *Milton and the Middle Ages*, 15–16.

2. Temperance (*sophrosynē*) is pleasant restraint, distinct from the difficult task of continence or self-control (*enkrateia*), because temperance is the achievement of an orderly soul at ease with virtue, whereas self-control requires the effort of subjugating the passions to reason. Aristotle argues this in the *Nicomachean Ethics* 1119a11–20; Plutarch reproduces the distinction between temperance and self-control in his *Moralia* 445b–c. See also Reiss, *Mirages of the Selfe*, 213.

3. Aristotle, *Nicomachean Ethics*, 1106a30–1107, 1109a–b; cf. 1104a1–5.

4. Ibid., 1119b11–18.

5. Aristotle, *Politics* 1253a.

6. For Augustine's opposition of *caritas* (defined as love of God for his own sake and love of self and others in subordinate relation to God) and *cupiditas* (defined as selfish love without reference to God), see Augustine's *De doctrina Christiana*, 3.10.15–16.

7. *OED* s.v. "dear" (adj.), def. A.I.2.a, II.6.a, A.I.1.a.

8. Shakespeare, *Troilus and Cressida* 5.3.26–28, First Folio text as printed in *The Norton Shakespeare*.

9. Langland, *Piers Plowman* (B text), passus 16, ll. 1–17.

10. See Summers, *Muse's Method*, 71–86.

NOTES TO CHAPTER 1

1. Tertullian, *De jejuniis*, chap. 3, trans. S. Thelwall.

2. Ibid.

3. The late antique patristic belief that bodily abstinence could regain paradise also appears in Jerome's Letter 22, "To Eustochium" (384 AD):

There are, in the Scriptures, countless divine answers condemning gluttony and approving simple food. But as fasting is not my present theme and an adequate discussion of it would require a treatise to itself, these few observations must suffice of the many which the subject suggests. By them you will understand why the first man, obeying his belly and not God, was cast down from paradise into this vale of tears; and why Satan used hunger to tempt the Lord Himself in the wilderness [Matt. 4:2–3]; and why the apostle cries: "Meats for the belly and the belly for meats, but God shall destroy both it and them" [1 Cor. 6:13]; and why he speaks of the self-indulgent as men "whose God is their belly" [Phil. 3:19]. For men invariably worship what they like best. Care must be taken, therefore, that abstinence may bring back to Paradise those whom satiety once drove out. (sec. 10)

Jerome's Letter 22, perhaps the most well known of his epistles for its extraordinary defense of virginity — "I praise wedlock, I praise marriage, but it is because they give me virgins. I gather the rosebud from the thorns" — could hardly agree with the man who hailed wedded love and viewed marriage as much more than procreative copulation (sec. 20). But there are more fascinating similarities between Jerome and the mature Milton. Jerome, like Tertullian, supposed that one might repair the ruins of our first parents and "bring [them] back to Paradise" — perhaps cultivating a paradise within the soul — through alimentary abstinence. Simultaneously, the Jerome passage offers a hint of the idea that because Jesus succeeded where Adam failed, he thereby offered humanity a way to regain paradise.

4. Tertullian, *De jejuniis*, chap. 17.

5. Ibid., chap. 6.

6. See, for example, Milton's *Epitaphium Damonis* and "Elegia sexta."

7. *Milton, Commonplace Book*, ed. Horwood; cf. Tertullian, *De jejuniis*, chap. 3. The translation of Milton's entry is my own.

8. Roebuck, "Milton and the Confessionalization," 55.

9. In the Columbia edition, Nelson Glenn McCrea translates *eleganter* as "with nicety of phrase" (CM 18:131). For further reference to Milton's punning on *sapience*, see Gigante, "Milton's Aesthetics of Eating," 89; and Schoenfeldt, *Bodies and Selves*, 194n18. For a related analysis of the ethical import of

literary *ruminatio*, the concept of *ruminating* on a text, see Carruthers, *Book of Memory*, 205–06.

10. Dante, *Purgatorio*, in *Divine Comedy*, 23.10–15, 64–66.

11. Evagrius of Pontus, *Praktikos*. For a concise essay on the history of gluttony within Christendom, see Miller, "Gluttony," 92–112. For Miller's more comprehensive source, see Bloomfield, *Seven Deadly Sins*.

12. See Cassian, *Conferences*, bk. 1, conf. 5, chaps. 2, 10, and 26.

13. In time, *acedia* was restored to the list, replacing *tristia*, and — *super-bia* still first — adjustments in the late medieval period created the popular mnemonic acronym *saligia* and its whimsical corresponding verb, *saligiare*, to commit a mortal sin (see Kraus, *Les sept péchés mortels*, 4).

14. The older sequence with gluttony listed first persisted. For example, Eutropius of Valencia (d. 610), in a letter to Bishop Peter, depends on and replicates Cassian's list in his discussion of eight deadly sins. The highly popular *Summa de vitiis et virtutibus* of William Peraldus (c. 1190–1271 AD), reprinted in France and Italy through the fifteenth, sixteenth, and seventeenth centuries, also lists gluttony first. Peraldus's ordering of vices served as the basis for the list in Henry of Langenstein's Middle High German peniten-tial manual, *Erchantnuzz der sund* (Knowledge of sin), a work William C. MacDonald identifies as the "crown jewel of the Viennese School" of four-teenth century theology. This text also places gluttony first. Of course, glut-tony's position as first in a list of deadly sins does not ensure that it is the gravest: one might even assume that Evagrius of Pontus's and Cassian's lists were intentionally ordered from least severe (gluttony) to most severe (pride). But there are other reasons for giving gluttony top billing, as this chapter will explain. See MacDonald, "Singing Sin: Michel Beheim's 'Little Book of the Seven Deadly Sins,'" in Newhauser and Ridyard, *Sin in Medieval*, 288; cf. Newhauser, "Parson's Tale," 45–76.

15. Cassian, *Conferences*, bk. 1, conf. 5, chap. 6.

16. Ibid., bk. 1, conf. 5, chap. 26.

17. Ibid., bk. 1, conf. 5, chaps. 4 and 10. Tertullian (c. 155–225) and Gregory the Great (c. 540–604) also point to the body as evidence of the part-nership between lust and gluttony: lust follows gluttony because the stomach is directly above the genitals. See Gregory, *Moralia in Job*, 31.45, para. 89, and Tertullian's *De jejuniis*, chap. 3.

18. Cassian, *Conferences*, bk. 1, conf. 5, chap. 10; cf. Gregory, *Moralia in Job*, 30.18.

19. Ibid., bk. 1, conf. 2, chap. 16, and bk. 1, conf. 5, chap. 18.

20. Ibid., bk. 1, conf. 5, chap. 11.

21. Miller, "Gluttony," 105–06.

22. See, for example, Chrysostom, *Homily 13 on Matthew*, sec. 2, and Gower, *Confessio Amantis*, 6.1.15, 608.

23. Cassian, *Conferences*, bk. 1, conf. 5, chap. 11; see also bk. 1, conf. 2, chap. 17.

24. The triad was later reproduced by Alcuin of York, *De virtutibus et vitiis liber*, chap. 28, sec. 35.

25. Cassian, *Conferences*, bk. 1, conf. 2, chap. 24.

26. Gregory, *Moralia in Job*, 30.18.

27. Caesarius of Heisterbach, *Dialogus miraculorum*, vol. 1, chap. 73; Wright, *Gesta Romanorum*, 390–91; Raymond of Peñafort, *Summa de poenitentia*, bk. 3, chap. 4, sec. 2; Aquinas, *Summa theologica*, 2a.2ae.148.4. While maintaining Gregory's five branches, Thomas Aquinas's definition of gluttony favors a duality in which the first division is marked by eating the wrong thing in terms of substance, quality, or quantity, and the second division is marked by eating in the wrong way, either by consuming before need prompts the satisfaction of appetite, or by consuming too greedily:

> Now two things are to be considered in eating, namely the food we eat, and the eating thereof. Accordingly, the inordinate concupiscence may be considered in two ways. First, with regard to the food consumed: and thus, as regards the substance or species of food a man seeks "sumptuous" — i.e. costly food; as regards its quality, he seeks food prepared too nicely — i.e. "daintily"; and as regards quantity, he exceeds by eating "too much."
>
> Secondly, the inordinate concupiscence is considered as to the consumption of food: either because one forestalls the proper time for eating, which is to eat "hastily," or one fails to observe the due manner of eating, by eating "greedily." (*Summa theologica*, 2a.2ae.148.4)

We may be gluttons in *what* we eat (which for Aquinas includes matters of quantity, expense, and fastidiousness, implicating shovelers, snobs, and finicky eaters) and in *how* we eat (the fault of impatient or obsessive consumers).

28. Cassian, *Conferences*, bk. 1, conf. 5, chap. 16.

29. Gregory, *Moralia in Job*, 31.45; Caesarius of Heisterbach, *Dialogus miraculorum*, vol. 1, chap. 73; Raymond of Peñafort, *Summa de poenitentiae*, bk. 3, sec. 31; Aquinas, *Summa theologica*, 2a2ae.148.6; Wright, *Gesta Romanorum*, 390–93.

30. Aquinas, *Summa theologica*, 2a2ae.148.3. His source is Chrysostom's *Homily 13 on Matthew*, sec. 2, on Matt. 4:1.

31. Caesarius of Heisterbach, Aquinas, and the Elizabethan homilies record this interpretation of Sodom's doom; Tertullian suggests that fasting would have saved the city. See Caesarius of Heisterbach, *Dialogus miraculorum*, vol. 1, chap. 73; Aquinas, *Summa theologica*, 2a2ae.148.3; Tertullian, *De jejuniis*, chap. 7; and the Elizabethan homily "Agaynst Gluttony and Drunkennesse," with a marginal reference to Ezekiel 16: "What was the cause that God so horribly punished Sodom and Gomorrha? was it not their proud banquetting and continuall idlenesse, which caused them to bee so lewde of life, and so vnmercifull towards the poore?" Lancashire, *Elizabethan Homilies*, 2.5.164–166.

32. Caesarius, *Dialogus miraculorum*, vol. 1, chap. 73; Raymond of Peñafort, *Summa de casibus poenitentiae*, bk. 3, chap. 4, sec. 2; Gregory, *Moralia in Job*, 30.18.

33. Cassian, *Conferences*, bk. 1, conf. 5, chap. 26.

34. Ibid., bk. 1, conf. 5, chaps. 19–21.

35. Ibid., bk. 1, conf. 2, chap. 17; see also bk. 1, conf. 2, chaps. 2 and 16.

36. Caesarius of Heisterbach, *Dialogus miraculorum*, vol. 1, chap. 73, appeals to Jerome to explain broadly the correlation between Adam's Fall and Jesus's temptation. In his *Conferences*, Cassian lists the three sins of the Fall and the equivalent three temptations of Christ as gluttony, vainglory, and pride (bk. 1, conf. 5, chap. 6). The fifth homily of Pseudo-Chrysostom's *Opus imperfectum in Mattheum* (a work quoted extensively in Aquinas's *Catena Aurea*) correlatively identifies these three temptations or sins as gluttony (*spiritu gulae*), avarice (*spiritu avaritiae*), and pride (*spiritu superbiae*). Aquinas cites Ambrose's declaration that the three sins of the Fall are overturned by Christ in the same order in the fourth chapter of Luke (*Summa theologica*, 2a2ae.163.1).

37. Augustine, "Homily 2," para. 14.

38. Augustine, *Confessions*, bk. 10, chap 31.

39. Ibid., bk. 10, chap 35.

40. Augustine, "Psalm 8," para. 13, in *Exposition on the Book of Psalms.*

41. The regaining of paradise is symbolic not only because the "fairer paradise" recovered is not the geographic region of Eden but also because the Son's resisting of temptation is exercise for the larger task of the Passion and Resurrection. As God explains to Gabriel, the Son will win

> by Conquest what the first man lost
> by fallacy surpris'd. But first I mean
> To exercise him in the Wilderness;
> There he shall first lay down the rudiments
> Of his great warfare, ere I send him forth
> to conquer Sin and Death the two grand foes,
> By Humiliation and strong Sufferance." (*PR* 1.154–60)

42. See Kermode, *Shakespeare, Spenser, Donne,* 69–70. See also Roy Flannagan's entry on gluttony in Hunter, *Milton Encyclopedia,* vol. 3, 130.

43. Cassian, *Conferences,* conf. 5, chap. 6; Augustine, *Confessions,* bk. 10, chaps. 31–33.

44. Cassian, *Conferences,* conf. 5, chap. 18.

45. Augustine, *Confessions,* 10.31. Similarly, objecting to the proposition that gluttony is "the greatest sin," Aquinas thought "the sin of gluttony is diminished rather than aggravated, both on account of the necessity of taking food, and on account of the difficulty of proper discretion and moderation in such matters." Nevertheless, citing Gregory the Great, Aquinas warns that gluttony remains a capital sin because of its propensity to lead to other vices. See Aquinas, *Summa theologica,* 2a2ae.148.3, 5, and Gregory, *Moralia in Job,* 31.45, para. 88. Also compare Augustine with Origen's discussion of overindulgence in *On First Principles,* quoted and analyzed in light of Milton's treatment of the patristic question of satiety by Poole, "With Such Joy Surcharg'd," esp. 4.

46. Augustine, *Confessions,* 10.37.

47. Augustine, "Homily 2," para. 14.

48. Although Aquinas follows Gregory the Great in concluding that pride, not gluttony, was the first man and woman's first sin, he is compelled, citing Ambrose, to consider the influential tradition of a gluttonous Fall and to acknowledge gluttony both as a result of pride and as, like pride, a sin opposite

charity. For Aquinas on gluttony and pride, see *Summa theologica*, 2a2ae.163.1. Aquinas refers to Gregory's *Moralia in Job*, bk. 33, sec. 12, para. 25, and sec. 33, para. 57, and to Ambrose's gloss of Luke 4 in his *Exposition on the Gospel of Luke*. The force of the tradition of the gluttonous Fall is acknowledged by Aquinas's very insertion of his argument for pride as the principal sin of Adam and Eve's fall into the section of the *Summa theologica* dedicated to temperance and its opposite vice, gluttony (2a2ae.141–70). In response to the objection that gluttony cannot be a mortal sin since it is not opposed to charity, neither to the love of God nor to the love of one's neighbor, Aquinas replies, "In so far as gluttony turns man away from his last end, gluttony is opposed to the love of God, who is to be loved, as our last end, above all things: and only in this respect is gluttony a mortal sin" (2a2ae.148.2.2 and Reply to Objection 2; cf. 2a2ae.132.3). Not even the voice of Aquinas could eradicate the tradition of gluttony's infamy within Christendom.

49. Augustine, *Confessions* 10.31, sec. 46.

50. Augustine, *On Christian Doctrine* 3.12, sec. 19.

51. Shakespeare, *King Lear*, 2.4.262–64.

52. Dante, *Purgatorio*, 24.123, 125.

53. Ibid., 24.52–53, 62–63.

54. Abrams, "Inspiration and Gluttony." Milton also opposes poetics to gluttony in his Elegy 6, where he argues that an abstemious diet is a necessity for the epic poet. See chapter 6.

55. Kilgour, *From Communion to Cannibalism*, 56, referring to Augustine's *Confessions*, bk. 1, chaps. 7–9.

56. Ibid., 72.

57. Samuel, *Dante and Milton*, 246. The argument for Milton's familiarity with Dante is concisely articulated in Kuhns, "Dante's Influence on Milton." Samuel's *Dante and Milton* provides a more comprehensive comparison. More recently, this has been a subject of interest in Hollander, "Milton's Elusive Response."

58. Dante, *Paradiso*, in *Divine Comedy*, 26.115–17.

59. Yeager cites a fourteenth century English translation of Friar Laurens's thirteenth century religious manual *Somme le roi*, which divides the "synne of mouth" into "the synne of glotonye, that is in mete and drynke, and…the synne of wikkede tonge, that is to speke folye" ("Aspects of Gluttony," 48).

60. Gower, *Confessio Amantis*, 6.1.1, 5, 9–10.

61. There is another intriguing parallel between Milton and Gower in their descriptions of the genealogy of Sin and Death in *Paradise Lost* and in Gower's *Mirour de l'omme*, the Anglo-Norman French poem also known as *Speculum meditantis*. In Gower's work, the Devil impregnates his daughter, Sin, who gives birth to their son, Death. Death then engenders upon his mother the Seven Deadly Vices, which the Devil sends into the world to defeat the plans of Providence for the salvation of humankind. Man is then subjected to temptation. The summary of the rest of this poem of nearly 30,000 lines as presented in the *Cambridge History of English and American and Literature* (vol. 2, chap. 6, sec. 4) reveals other parallels between Gower's and Milton's stories, but the temptation to read a direct connection between *Mirour de l'omme* and *Paradise Lost* must be approached cautiously, since, as Boswell warns in *Milton's Library*, "The only manuscript [of Gower's *Mirour de l'omme*] known... was published first in 1899, and there is no evidence that Milton ever knew it or owned it" (115). Gower's work was long presumed lost, and the only extant manuscript is in Anglo-Norman French, discovered in the Cambridge University Library in 1895. The similarity between Gower's and Milton's accounts of Sin, Death, and Satan was presented by Tatlock, "Milton's Sin and Death."

62. Gower, *Confessio Amantis*, 6.1.15, 608. Chrysostom also divides gluttony into drunkenness and delicacy in his *Homily 13 on Matthew*, sec. 2, and these divisions correspond to Cassian's division of gluttony into the belly (which cries for more) and the palate (which cries for better).

63. Gower, *Confessio Amantis*, 6.1.39, 45–50.

64. Ibid., 6.1.307.

65. Ibid., 6.1.169.

66. Ibid., 6.1.178–83.

67. Ibid., 6.1.207, 209–210.

68. Ibid., 6.1.629.

69. Ibid., 6.1.653–74.

70. Ibid., 6.1.940, 954–961.

71. Ibid. 6, epigraph; translation by Andrew Galloway.

72. See Lewis and Short, *Latin Dictionary*, s.v. *vetito*, def. 2.a, and *pomus*, def. 1.

73. I am indebted to Lesleigh Balkum Jones for identifying these syntactical options for translation.

74. For example, see Ambrose, *Apologia prophetae David* 11.56–57; Augustine, *De gratia Christi* 1.53–55, 2.47; Aquinas, *Summa theologica,* 1a2ae.86.2, 87.6.

75. Lewis and Short, *Latin Dictionary,* s.v. *crassus,* def. 1.

76. Chaucer, "Pardoner's Tale," in *Canterbury Tales,* 498–504. All citations to the *Canterbury Tales* are from the *Riverside Chaucer.*

77. Augustine, *De doctrina Christiana,* 3.10.15–16; Aquinas, *Summa theologica,* 2a2ae.148.4; For *gula concupiscientia,* see Burn, *Preces Privatae of Lancelot Andrewes,* 320.

78. Chaucer, "Pardoner's Tale," 481–82.

79. Chaucer, "Physician's Tale," 59–60.

80. Chaucer, "Summoner's Tale," 1911–17.

81. "Parson's Tale," 817–18.

82. Ibid., 820.

83. Ibid., 827, 828, 833–35.

84. Cf. Magoun, "Chaucer of Spenser and Milton"; Christopher Baker, "Chaucer, Geoffrey," in Corns, *Milton Encyclopedia,* 62–63; Boswell, *Milton's Library,* s.v. "Chaucer, Geoffrey," 55–56.

85. Lancashire, *Elizabethan Homilies,* 2.5.90–9.

86. Ibid., 2.5.176.

87. Ibid., 2.5.30, 32–36; a marginal gloss points to Galatians 5.

88. Ibid., 2.5.206, 215–19.

89. Ibid., 2.5.191–93, 208–12.

90. Byles, introduction to *Book of Chivalry,* 29, 97; Fallows, *Book of Chivalry,* 81; originally published in Catalan.

91. Gilbert of the Haye's Prose MS, ed. J. H. Stevenson, vol. 2, p. 54, l. 34, to p. 55, l. 9; qtd. in Byles, introduction to *Book of Chivalry,* 37.

92. Spenser, *Faerie Queene,* 1.4.21–23.

93. Ibid., 1.4.43. For comparison, when the Seven Deadly Sins go to shrift in Passus 5 of William Langland's *Piers Plowman,* Sir Glotoun is penultimate, after Coveytise and just before Sleuthe. Gluttony's gross excesses and its especially close link to sloth are apparent as Glotoun describes the aftermath of one of his binges and articulates the commonly perceived consequences of his

lifestyle, excess leading to acedia (*Piers Plowman* 5.340–77). When he makes his confession to Repentance, he admits to eating and drinking himself into a stupor: "I slepe and ete at ones." He then recounts his wasteful habits, including wine-spilling, spending too much money on food, and eating "Overdelicatly." His sins are also those of timing: he rushes to eat before noon on fasting days. "I have trespassed with my tonge," he confesses, linking the palate and the belly with the tongue as articulator, lamenting both his habit of swearing and his weakness for tavern tales. Yet Glotoun's oral confession is itself a corrective measure, as Repentance instructs, "As thow with wordes and werkes hast wroughte yvel in thi lyve, / Shryve the and be shamed therof, and shewe it with thi mouth" (5.365–66). Sin of the mouth is fought with the mouth, and the shriving of Glotoun depends on his oral confession. *Piers Plowman* also draws attention to the role of food in the Fall, with special reference made to Adam's complaint and dissatisfaction with both his permitted diet and the knowledge available to him in Eden (11.417–19).

94. Spenser, *Faerie Queene*, 2.7.51–66.

95. Sirluck, "Milton Revises *The Faerie Queene*." Virtues are "mean conditions,…active conditions,…willing things,…in the way that right reason would dictate" (Aristotle, *Nicomachean Ethics*, 1114b25). The virtue of temperance is "in a mean condition" concerning pleasure (1119a12). Despite Sirluck's understanding of the ethical importance Aristotle assigns to habit, Joe Sachs successfully argues that Aristotle's understanding of virtue depends less on habit than is commonly supposed. The difficulty arises with the misleading (but appropriate) translation of the Greek word *hexis* as the Latin *habitus,* and thence to (the inappropriate) *habit.* See Sachs's introduction to his edition of the *Nicomachean Ethics.* As a further irony, Sirluck seems not to find applicable Milton's assertion in *De doctrina Christiana* that good deeds are most often the result of good habits (YP 6:647).

96. Qtd. in Greenlaw, "'Better Teacher than Aquinas,'" 197.

97. Ibid., 198. The comment derives from Aubrey's *Collections for the Life of Milton* (CPMP 1023).

98. Sirluck, "Milton Revises *The Faerie Queene*," 95.

NOTES TO CHAPTER 2

1. *CPMP* 7. Masson briefly states that "Apologus de rustico et hero" was "written at some uncertain date after 1645" (*Life of John Milton*, 6:689).

2. Lewis and Short, *Latin Dictionary*, s.v. *degusto*.

3. "Venial" here means "allowable, permissible; blameless" (*OED*, def. 3).

4. In this passage Eve is also compared to Pales, the Roman goddess of shepherds, responsible for the fertility of the flock. In these images of fruition, Milton once again unites metaphors of birth with those of consumption.

5. For the strengthened connection between Eve and Circe through their shared ability to know the nature and virtues of plants, see Ovid, *Metamorphoses*, 14.306–13, and *PL* 5.331–36, 11.273–79.

6. For a comparison of the Ovidian and Homeric Circe in Renaissance literature and mythography as they pertain to *Paradise Lost*, see Browning, "Sin, Eve, and Circe," and Brodwin, "Milton and the Renaissance Circe." For Milton's use of the tradition of bacchic gluttony, especially in *A Maske Presented at Ludlow Castle*, see Klein, "Demonic Bacchus." An argument identifying moly, haemony, and rue as the same plant for Milton (building on scholarship connecting moly and haemony by Edward S. Le Comte and Thomas P. Harrison Jr.) may be found in Otten's "Homer's Moly and Milton's Rue."

7. Homer, *Odyssey* 10.329. A popular Renaissance reading of this episode opposes Circe's sensually seductive magic against Odysseus's rational powers. From another early modern perspective, natural knowledge is itself worthy of the name "magic," for the hermetic philosopher Thomas Vaughan attests in *Magia Adamica*, "Magic is nothing else but the wisdom of The Creator revealed and planted in the creature" (87).

8. The same point has been made by Friedman, "Divisions on a Ground," 204n4, and by Schoenfeldt, *Bodies and Selves*, 147.

9. Aristotle, *Politics*, 1.1253a3ff. For the connection between this passage and the Circean temptation to which Eve succumbs, see Segal, *Tragedy and Civilization*, 61.

10. Aristotle, *Nichomachean Ethics*, 1118a25.

11. Poole, "'With Such Joy Surcharg'd,'" 5.

12. Lieb, *Dialectics of Creation*, 197.

13. McCluskey, "Winds of Folly," 227–238. For McCluskey, there is a pun on "seat" when, at Eve's crucial act of disobedience, "Nature from her seat / Sighing through all her Works gave signs of woe" (*PL* 9.782–83; McCluskey, 234). Then Nature's act of "gently breaking wind" leads to "a more forceful display of flatulence" when, at Adam's participation, "Earth trembl'd from her entrails, as again / In pangs, and Nature gave a second groan" (235; *PL* 9.1000–01). Alternatively, Richard DuRocher finds in this passage a more philosophical tone, as "terms associated with pathos ('[s]ighing,' 'woe') reinforce emotions proper to Aristotelian tragedy" (*Milton among the Romans*, 131). Whether or not Milton intended Nature's display of pathetic flatulence or catharsis here, Earth's trembling represents yet another instance of Milton's motif of the inner workings of the embodied soul. Milton's use of (in)digestive and scatological metaphors, especially in relation to sin, receives special consideration in chapter 3.

14. Poole, "'With Such Joy Surcharg'd,'" 12.

15. Davis, "Technique of Guilt," 31; *PL* 9.1024–26.

16. Bentley, ed., *Milton's Paradise Lost*, 44.

17. So John Kelly, nineteenth century rector of St. Joseph's, Birkdale, writes in his sermon on gluttony: "[Gluttony] is a vice ruling alike in the *gourmand* and the *gourmet*, in the man who overloads his stomach, and the man who aims at gratifying his palate with dainties.... [Adam and Eve's eating of forbidden fruit] was the sin of pride, along with the sin of the *Gourmet* — gluttony" (Kelly, *Sermons*, 102–03).

18. Schoenfeldt, *Bodies and Selves*, 157.

19. See Gilbert, "Milton's Defense of Bawdry."

20. The *OED* heading to the entry on "sensuous" states that the word was "Apparently invented by Milton, to avoid certain associations of the existing word 'sensual,' and from him adopted by Coleridge; evidence of its use in the intervening period is wanting. Coleridge seems to have been mistaken in saying that it occurs in 'many others of our elder writers.'" The *OED* attributes the first two recorded uses of this word to Milton, the third to Coleridge referring to Milton:

> *Reform*.I.3 The Soule...finding the ease she had from her visible, and sensuous collegue the body in performance of Religious duties...shifted off from her selfe the labour of high soaring any more.

1644 *Educ.* 6 To which Poetry would be made subsequent, or indeed rather precedent, as being lesse suttle and fine, but more simple, sensuous, and passionate.

1814 Coleridge *Princ. Gen.Crit.* iii. in *Farley's Bristol Jrnl.* Aug., Thus, to express in one word what belongs to the senses, or the recipient and more passive faculty of the soul, I have reintroduced the word *sensuous*, used, among many others of our elder writers, by Milton.

21. Fallon, *Milton among the Philosophers*, 203–06.

22. Augustine, *City of God*, 14.13.

23. Sumner's translation alternately reads: "It was called the tree of knowledge of good and evil *from the event*; for since Adam tasted it, we not only know evil, but we know good by means of evil" (*CPMP* 993). John Gill's commentary on Genesis 3:3 in his *Exposition of the Old Testament* (1748–63) develops this idea: "[Eve] does not give [the interdicted tree] any name, which perhaps was not as yet given it; or she was not acquainted with it, its name in the preceding chapter being given by anticipation; and most likely it is, it had its name *from the event*, and as yet was without one" (emphasis added). Although in *Paradise Lost* both Adam and Eve use the formal name of the tree before the Fall, Adam and God remark that knowledge of good and evil is the "work" or "operation" of the tree, in accordance with Augustinian teaching (*PL* 4.423–24, 5.51–52, 7.542–43, 8.323–24).

24. Lewis, *Preface to "Paradise Lost,"* 70–71. Recently, David Urban and Peter C. Herman have redebated this idea, Herman arguing that the importance of the apple is "vastly more complex" than Lewis's summation allows. The debate itself is complex. Herman notes that God tells Adam the forbidden fruit "'*works* knowledge of good and evil' (7.543, [Herman's emphasis]) . . . suggesting that there might very well be, contra Lewis, something 'intrinsic' to the fruit itself" (261). Yet this very passage could also support Urban and Lewis, for the *work* of the tree may mean the *effect* of eating. It is the *act* of tasting that brings death; it is the "consequence" that God warns will be "bitter," not the taste (*PL* 8.328). This is reinforced by God as quoted by Adam in book 8, who interdicts "the tree whose operation brings / Knowledge of good and ill" (*PL* 9. 323–24). The Latin *opus* may mean "any result of labor" (Lewis and Short, *Latin Dictionary*, s.v. "opus"), a definition that does not necessitate intrinsic power in the apple but instead suggests the power is in the *operation*

of the tree. But is it the tree that operates, or is it operated *upon*, when Adam eats the forbidden fruit? Both meanings are possible. The burden of proof lies with Lewis and those who might speak for him, for it is currently a much bolder claim to insist Milton's message is "dazzlingly simple" than to point to inconsistencies, problems, and indeterminate cruxes within Milton's text. See Urban, "Speaking for the Dead," esp. 99; Herman, "C. S. Lewis," esp. 261–62.

25. Aquinas, *Summa theologica*, 2a2ae q. 15, a. 2, 3. He cites Gregory, *Moralia in Job*, 31.45, twice on this subject.

26. Kerrigan, *Sacred Complex*, 204, 245.

27. Lewis, *Preface to "Paradise Lost*," 129.

28. Edward Phillips, *The Life of Milton* (*CPMP* 1034). Milton's anonymous biographer also mentioned the "issues and seatons, made use of to save or retrieve" the poet's eyesight, and while John Aubrey's *Life of Milton* promotes the image of a hale man who "Seldom took any physic," attempts to preserve his eyesight are presumably excepted. See *An Anonymous Life of Milton* (*CPMP* 1042) and Aubrey, "Life of Milton" (*CPMP* 1022). Cf. Lewalski, *Life of John Milton*, 259–60; Campbell and Corns, *John Milton*, 211–12, 231–32.

29. Gloss from the Fowler and Carey edition of *Poems of John Milton*.

30. For the key observation that through homophonic possibility "euphrasy" could denote poetry, I am indebted to David Oliver Davies, University of Dallas. See also the *OED* entry for "euphrasy." My own argument for this reading is developed in "Euphrasy, Rue, Polysemy, and Repairing the Ruins," prepared for the forthcoming volume of conference proceedings from the 2015 Conference on John Milton in Murfreesboro, Tennessee.

31. For the "rule of not too much," its physiological benefits and its limits for Milton and his audience, see Schoenfeldt, *Bodies and Selves*, 160–61.

32. Milton is also perhaps remembering the Roman *vomitoria*, passages below or behind tiered seating in amphitheaters or theaters efficiently designed for expeditious ushering of crowds (Lewis and Short, *Latin Dictionary*). This is another example of a place being given the emetic apparatus of a body. (The *vomitoria* have been mistakenly conceived to be rooms designated for purges after binging at Roman banquets. See *OED*, def. 2.)

33. In his explication of *PL* 11.50–57, Schoenfeldt mentions a similar passage, Leviticus 18:25 (not 28:25 as printed on page 154 of *Bodies and Selves*). Also cf. Virgil's description of vomiting Aetna mentioned in the section on

"Infernal Eructations" in chapter 3 of this book, and Milton's anger in the *Second Defense* at an anonymous accusation of his being "vomited out" of Cambridge (YP 1:884–85).

34. Cassian, *Conferences*, conf. 5, chaps. 16–19, esp. chap. 18.

35. Aquinas, *Summa theologica*, 2a2ae.148.3. The biblical passage to which Aquinas refers is Psalm 135:10 in the Roman Catholic enumeration of the Psalms, and Psalm 136:10 in the Jewish and Protestant enumerations.

36. Campbell and Corns, *John Milton*, 353.

37. For previous examples of the gluttony of warfare, see Ariosto's *Orlando Furioso*, Shakespeare's *Troilus and Cressida*, 1.3.119–24, Petrarch's letter "Italia Mia," and Eumolpius's poem on the glut of Roman luxury and warfare in Petronius's *Satyricon*, secs. 119–20.

38. See Luke 16:19–31; Lupton, *All for Money*; and Langland, *Piers Plowman*, 14.71–72. For eating as a "zero-sum game," see Miller, "Gluttony," 97. For an examination of how Menenius's belly fable in *Coriolanus* informs Shakespeare's representation of the body politic in light of early modern food insecurity, scarcity, and famine, and in the play turns "the citizens' hunger to ideological and psychological dependency," see Ernst Gerhardt, "Feeding on the Body Politic," in Goldstein and Tigner, *Culinary Shakespeare*, 97–111.

39. Jordan, *Quiet Hero*, 2. Jordan does mention the long-standing allegorization of Odysseus as a model for prudence, but this, he insists, is a misreading of Homer, while to "Homer and to those earliest readers of Homer who published their own views of Odysseus, he was anything but a quiet hero" (ibid.). Jordan's view should be qualified in light of the years and intense moments of patient restraint that climactically result in the killing of the suitors in Ithaca; the characterization of Odysseus in the Myth of Er in book 10 of the *Republic* and Socrates's calling into question the unscrupulousness of Odysseus as a liar in the *Lesser Hippias* also deserve attention. Milton himself expressed a qualified hope to be compared with the Greek hero: "For although I should like to be Ulysses — should like, that is, to have deserved as well as possible of my country — yet I do not covet the arms of Achilles" (YP 4:595).

40. Jordan, *Quiet Hero*, 1.

41. Knoppers, *Complete Works of John Milton*, 2:142n549.

42. Plato, *Symposium*, 186b, in *Complete Works*; Aristotle, *Nichomachean Ethics*, 1145b10.

43. Cicero, *Tusculan Disputations*, 4.11, p. 138; Juvenal, *Satires*, 10.356.

44. Reiss, *Mirages of the Selfe*, esp. 212–17.

45. Stephen Pender, introduction to Pender and Struever, *Rhetoric and Medicine*, 25–6. Pender quotes the aphorism from Everard Digby, *Theoria Analytica* (London, 1579), 374.

46. Pender, introduction to *Rhetoric and Medicine*, 8, 35.

47. Qtd. in Prose, *Gluttony*, 52.

48. Shakespeare, *Timon of Athens*, 4.3.220–22. For an analysis of Timon of Athens as "the most extended consideration of humanist banqueting ideology and its latter-day corruption in the Shakespearean canon," see Douglas M. Lanier, "Cynical Dining in *Timon of Athens*," in Goldstein and Tigner, *Culinary Shakespeare*, 142.

49. Shakespeare, *Love's Labour's Lost*, 1.1.26–27. Biron later extends the metaphor to provide a much-desired rationale for tempering oaths of asceticism: "Say, can you fast? Your stomachs are too young; / And abstinence engenders maladies" (4.3.288–89).

50. Michael Schoenfeldt argues that Raphael's reference to the wind of indigestion indicates that "intestinal gas is neither an exclusively postlapsarian nor an exclusively terrestrial experience, or the comparison has no meaning for either party," but he does admit that "there seems to be no defecation in Paradise" (*Bodies and Selves*, 138, 142). Milton sometimes nods or intentionally presents his reader with information that the characters could not empirically understand. Gordon Teskey sees these occasions in the narrative not as mistakes but as "fold[s] in the poem's frames of reference." Cf. Teskey's note on Raphael's anticipation of the "three different motions" of the earth in his edition of *Paradise Lost*, 8.130. We need not think of unfallen Adam or of angels as flatulent in our understanding of the term, nor "oppress[ed]" with the "surfeit" mentioned in Raphael's analogy (*PL* 7.129).

51. So Dennis Danielson examines in Psalm 8 "an almost paradoxical sense of being at once humbled and exalted," a "significance/insignificance paradox" repeated in the cosmological hymn in chapter 43 of the Deuterocanonical book of Sirach (200–175 BCE) (Danielson, *Book of the Cosmos*, 7, 9). While Danielson writes of "the persistent myth that ancient and medieval geocentrism placed the earth and humankind in a position of supreme importance

in the universe," he draws attention to Galileo's contrary avowal in *Siderius nuncius*: "I will prove that earth does have motion, that it surpasses the moon in brightness, and that it is not the sump where the universe's filth and ephemera collect" (Danielson, *Book of the Cosmos*, 150). Galileo's assumption of the metaphysical repercussions of geocentrism has medieval precedent in the diablocentric portrait of earth in Dante's *Inferno*, although the pilgrim's perspective of the cosmos is radically altered in *Paradiso* (see Danielson, *Book of the Cosmos*, 90–91).

52. *Bald's Leechbook*, book 1, chap. 35, p. 85; Cf. book 2, chap. 27.

53. Merchant, *Death of Nature*, 84–85.

54. Ibid., 94–95.

55. Tommaso Campanella, *Apologia pro Galileo*, qtd. in Danielson, *Book of the Cosmos*, 175.

56. Dodds, *Literary Invention of Margaret Cavendish*, 123, 143. Dodds offers a helpful distinction between utopia and paradise in the Christian tradition: "If paradise was given, and then taken, from Adam by God, utopia, by contrast, is an attempt to discover and represent human solutions to the collective problem that, though currently restricted to the no-place of fiction, may one day be enacted in time" (132). Quoting passages where Marmaduke Carver and Sir Walter Raleigh insist that the paradise of Genesis is *not* utopia (133), Dodds summarizes, "Utopia flourishes in fiction and impossibility, while paradise requires reality and certainty" (134).

57. Ibid., 146.

58. Ibid.

59. Ibid., 147.

60. Cf. 1 Cor. 6:12 and 10:23. Because "everything is permissible," it does not follow that eating is inconsequential, though Paul may seem to say this in 1 Cor. 8:8: "But meat commendeth us not to God: for neither, if we eat, are we the better; neither, if we eat not, are we the worse" (AV). Milton is aware of this passage, yet the one place in *De doctrina Christiana* where he quotes it, and others like it, is a paragraph not disprizing eating but discouraging the taking of vows against eating (OW 8:991–93). Furthermore, Paul's statement in 1 Cor. 8:8 is qualified by his exhortation in 1 Cor. 10:31: "Whether therefore ye eat, or drink, or whatsoever ye do, do all to the glory of God."

61. And so in *Paradise Lost* Milton leaves indeterminate the manner in which the Son clothes the naked Adam and Eve "with Skins of Beasts, or slain, / Or as the Snake with youthful Coat repaid" (*PL* 10.217–18).

62. Aristotle, *Nicomachean Ethics*, 1106b4.

63. In Plato's dialogue *Charmides*, 164e (in *Complete Works*), Critias equates the two inscriptions.

64. Compare this passage with 2 Peter 1:5–7: "And beside this, giving all diligence, add to your faith virtue; and to virtue knowledge; And to knowledge temperance; and to temperance patience; and to patience godliness; And to godliness brotherly kindness; and to brotherly kindness charity" (AV). Curiously, what is missing from Milton's list is godliness and brotherly kindness. Perhaps "brotherly" kindness may not be pertinent yet given that Adam has no fraternal relationships, and the absence of an exhortation to godliness may indirectly support the theme of knowing (and staying within) one's natural human limits. Perhaps, with the Seven Deadly Sins in mind, Milton had numerological reasons for reducing the number of worthy qualities to seven.

65. Schoenfeldt, *Bodies and Selves*, 162.

66. Ibid., 60.

67. Eden's perfection is destroyed not only by the advent of death but by the "brandish'd Sword of God" that "began to parch that temperate Clime" after the expulsion (*PL* 12.633, 636). The motion of the heavens is disturbed as a consequence of human sin, the earth's axis is tilted, and in an intriguing metaphor of repulsion after cannibalistic gluttony, "the Sun, as from Thyestean Banquet, turn'd / His course intended" (10.688–89). All vestiges of physical Eden are lost in Noah's Flood, and though the earth retains some of the goodness of its creation, the paradise within is "happier far."

NOTES TO CHAPTER 3

1. Voss, "Debris from Heaven."

2. See Hebrews 10:1–14, a passage Milton frequently cites in *De doctrina Christiana* (OW 8:161, 475, 485, 487, 495, 503, 521, 529, 565, 609, 761).

3. Prometheus is bound with adamantine chains for stealing divine fire and bringing (what is often interpreted as that which the fire symbolizes) divine knowledge to humanity. Thus Might says in his opening speech of Aeschylus's

Prometheus Bound, "Hephaestus, it is you that must heed the commands the Father laid upon you to nail this malefactor to the high craggy rocks in fetters unbreakable of adamantine chain. For it was your flower, the brightness of fire that devises all, that he stole and gave to mortal men" (65). Prometheus associates fire with learning: "I myself gave them fire...and from it they shall learn many crafts" (75); "I found them mindless and gave them minds, made them masters of their wits. I will tell you this is not as reproaching man, but to set forth the goodwill of my gifts.... And numbering as well, preeminent of subtle device, and letter combinations that hold all in memory, the Muses' mother skilled in craft, I found for them" (82). One of the most famous associations of Promethean fire with forbidden knowledge can be found in the frontispiece to Rousseau's *First Discourse* (1750).

4. Virgil, *Aeneid*, 3.570–77, trans. Gordon Teskey, as appearing in his comparison of this passage with *PL* 1:230–37 in his edition of *Paradise Lost* (p. 9).

5. For example, "If anyone does not raise his voice loud and clear enough, I shall swear that his breath is so foul and poisonous that the fumes of Etna or Avernus could not be more noisome" (YP 1:278).

6. Plummer, introduction to *Summoner's Tale*, 6–7.

7. Link, *Devil*, 90–91.

8. Warrick, "Medieval Theatrical Hell-Mouth."

9. Chaucer, *Romaunt of the Rose*, lines 7575–76 and "Summoner's Tale," 1694, in *Riverside Chaucer*; cf. Kolve's reference to the medieval cycle plays in "Chaucer's Wheel of False Religion," 268–70.

10. *Inferno* 21.139, trans. John Ciardi. Ciardi's note on this passage explains medieval expectations of obscene devils on religious grounds: "It is worth pointing out that the mention of bodily function is likely to be more shocking in a Protestant than in a Catholic culture. It has often seemed to me that the offensive language of Protestantism is obscenity; the offensive language of Catholicism is profanity or blasphemy: one offends on a scale of unmentionable words for bodily function, the other on a scale of disrespect for the sacred.... The difference is not, I think, national but religious. Chaucer, as a man of Catholic England, took exactly Dante's view in the matter of what was and was not shocking language."

11. *Vision of Tundale*, 895–902.

12. Mechthild of Magdeburg, *Selections*, 65–66.

13. Ibid., 66–67.

14. King, *Milton and Religious Controversy*, 13.

15. Lupton, *All for Money*.

16. The symbol is readily evident from Phineas Fletcher's *Locustae, vel Pietas Jesuitica* (1627). For early modern Protestant polemic associating Catholic priests with locusts, see King, *Milton and Religious Controversy*, 46–50.

17. Yet Gabriel mentions that Satan once was a fawning sycophant: "Who more than thou / Once fawn'd, and cring'd, and servilely ador'd / Heav'n's awful Monarch?" (*PL* 4.958–60).

18. Compare Milton's portrayal of Mammon and violent digging with Guyon's speech to Mammon in the *Faerie Queene* (2.7.12–17). For an Enlightenment perspective on the evils of metallurgy, see Rousseau's *Second Discourse*, 152–56. For a survey of descriptions of mining as violating an animate or anthropomorphized Earth, with connections to Pliny's *Natural History*, 2.63.158; Ovid's *Metamorphoses*, 1.125–42; Seneca's *Natural Questions*, 5.15; Henry Cornelius Agrippa's *The Vanity of Arts and Sciences*; Spenser's *Faerie Queene*; Milton's *Paradise Lost*; and poems by John Donne, see Merchant's ecofeminist classic *The Death of Nature* (28–41); see also DuRocher's *Milton among the Romans*, 159–164.

19. Qtd. in Teskey's edition of *Paradise Lost*, 396.

20. See Joseph Addison's characterization of the pun as "false wit" in *The Spectator* 62 (May 11, 1711). See also Alderson, "Augustan Attack on the Pun," 1–19.

21. If this pun was intentional, Milton is not the first to joke that women are the cause of all human woe. Eve is a Pandora of sorts, and she plays a critical role in the Fall, but Milton is more measured in distributing blame than many of the conventional misogynistic glosses on Eve that he may allude to here. See *PL* 11.632–34 and 1.27–34. See Tertullian's *De cultu feminarum* for an early example of a particularly hostile denunciation of women on account of Eve: "Do you not know that you are each an Eve? . . . You are the devil's gateway. You are the unsealer of that (forbidden) tree" (bk. 1, chap. 1). For an early modern effort to correct this misogynistic convention, see Lanyer, "Eve's Apology," where Eve's "only fault was too much love / which made her give [forbidden fruit] to her Dear" (801–02). Milton's Eve also claims that

love informs her decision to involve Adam in her fall, but her preference for Adam's death over loss of his company betrays her declared love as selfish and speciously rationalized (*PL* 9.830–33, 857–59).

22. Lieb, *Dialectics of Creation*, 116–20; *PL* 6.482–90, 552–52.

23. King, *Milton and Religious Controversy*, 125–26; *PL* 6.582–84.

24. Ibid., 126n29. See also Lehnhof, "Scatology and the Sacred," 432.

25. Lehnhof, "Scatology and the Sacred," 432.

26. Watkins, *Anatomy of Milton's Verse*, 10.

27. The havoc experienced by the environment of heaven is a celestial variation of the infernal plight of Sin — raped by Death, with her brood gnawing at her insides, entering and exiting her at will and without her permission. The importance of consent, and thereby of the will, is apparent when considering an alternative expression of this violent interruption: the angelic embrace, a consensual expression of love resulting in the temporary commingling of bodies. As free will requires individuation, doing violence to bodily boundaries without consent or restoration destroys both form and freedom. The rebellion is more self-destructive than self-assertive.

28. For this use of "exonerate," see *OED*, def. 2; see also Hobbes's *Leviathan*, 1.6.4.

29. Lehnhof, "Scatology and the Sacred," 432, 438.

30. Lehnhof, "'Intestine War,'" 431, 288, 289, 292.

31. I choose the former word not only because its etymology signifies the expulsion of feces or dregs (i.e., solid crudities rather than gaseous or vaporous matter), but also because the adjective "defecate" in the seventeenth century could describe something (usually a liquid, spirit, or air) that had been clarified and purified. See *Oxford English Dictionary*, s.v. "defecate," adj. def. 1, obsolete. Thus, Burton writes of "defecate and clear" rivers in the *Anatomy of Melancholy*, II.ii.I.i.223.

32. Lieb, *Dialectics of Creation*, 86–87, 22–25. On the coextensive character of generation and consumption, cf. Aristotle, *On the Soul*, 2.4. Reproduction is a logical extension of the self-sustenance and growth sought through nutrition and is a reaching for the eternal and the divine insofar as nature allows.

33. Ibid., 22.

34. *OED*, def. 1; Gigante, "Milton's Aesthetics of Eating," 99n20. Also the Latin *venter*, *ventris* (masc.) could mean stomach, womb, or belly. This carries over into Anglo-Saxon: see s.v. "venter," "wamb," and "womb" in Bosworth,

Dictionary of Anglo-Saxon Language. Book 2 of *Bald's Leechbook*, dedicated to medical treatments or "leechdoms" for a variety of internal ailments, is filled with references to the *wamb* as a locus of digestion.

35. Lieb, *Dialectics of Creation*, 87.

36. The Augustinian doctrine of evil as a privation of good begins with the idea of existence as inherently good, as Milton summarizes in *De doctrina Christiana*: "Every entity is good; a non-entity is not good" (OW 8:295). For Milton's Augustinian depiction of the Fall, see the chapter on Milton and Augustine in Lewis, *Preface to "Paradise Lost,"* 66–72; see also Fiore, *Milton and Augustine.*

37. Lehnhof, "Scatology and the Sacred," 432; Gigante, "Milton's Aesthetics of Eating," 94.

38. Gigante, "Milton's Aesthetics of Eating," 94.

39. Rogers, *Matter of Revolution*, 133–34. Three years later, Schoenfeldt also recognized a tension between the discriminative sorting necessary for digestion and the monist materialist synthesis of the universe, for a system where all things come from and return to a good God cannot easily account for the infernal dregs. This discrepancy forms "perhaps the central ontological paradox in Milton's thought" (*Bodies and Selves*, 145).

40. Rogers, *Matter of Revolution*, 137.

41. Marlowe, *Tamburlaine the Great*, part 2, 2.3, 4.1 (twice), 5.1. For an extended consideration of Milton's reference to the Tartar people, see "The Strange Fire of the Tartars," chapter 1 of Song's *Dominion Undeserved*, 17–44.

42. Compare with Wolfram Schmidgen's discussion of Galenic mixture, where "healthful and diseased states are associated with balanced and unbalanced mixtures," disease not arising from the humors themselves, but from their proportions within the body (*Exquisite Mixture*, 25).

43. Gigante, "Milton's Aesthetics of Eating," 103.

44. Rumrich, *Matter of Glory*, 99.

45. Gigante, "Milton's Aesthetics of Eating," 95.

46. Ibid., 95; cf. Hunter, "Milton's Arianism Reconsidered," 37.

47. Augustine, *City of God* 21.8.

48. Chaucer, *Parliament of Fowls*, in *Riverside Chaucer*, 362; Shakespeare, *Love's Labour's Lost*, 1.1, *Richard II*, 2.1.38, and *Coriolanus*, 1.1.119, in *Riverside Shakespeare*. Cf. OED, s.v. "cormorant," def. 2. See also notes on *PL*

4.196 in *CPMP*, *CPEP*, and the Teskey *Paradise Lost*. In medieval heraldry, cormorants were also symbols of indulgence and bounty. Alternatively, the cormorant, which spreads its wings to dry after diving, was considered in this posture to imitate the shape of the Christian cross. The association of this bird with Satan, who on the Tree of Life "not true Life / Thereby regain'd," would then be ironic (*PL* 4.196–97). The cormorant then is like the pelican in its use as a Renaissance emblem of both selfish voracity (as in Lear's railing against his "pelican daughters" in *King Lear*, 3.4) and self-sacrifice (as in the famous "pelican" portrait of Queen Elizabeth I).

49. Miller, "Gluttony," 92.

50. Davis, "Technique of Guilt," 29–34.

51. Conti, *Natali Conti's Mythologiae*, 7.12, 750–51.

52. Ibid., 3.5, 173.

53. Bede, *Letter to Egbert*, 154–55. Bede's Latin for "covetousness" varies between *avaritia* and *concupiscentia*.

54. Augustine, *City of God*, 4.7.18.

55. Lieb notes in Eve's proposal a dangerous substitute for creation and birth (*Dialectics of Creation*, 209).

56. Sin is subject to herself as allegory, to the complex nature of sin as choice, action, and condition. According to her account, she is agent and sufferer, her story featuring both active and passive voices, where she is both subject and object. Recent readings of Sin as an innocent rape victim often neglect her allegorical role. There is also the possibility that Sin is like Francesca da Rimini in Dante's circle of the Lustful: doing her best to seduce and evoke sympathy, but inexact and self-serving in her storytelling.

57. Summers, *Muse's Method*, 72.

58. After the Fall, pleasure becomes separable from and subordinate to higher objects of desire. Consider Adam's postlapsarian understanding of pleasure: "Eve, thy contempt of life and pleasure seems / To argue in thee something more sublime / And excellent, than what thy mind contemns" (*PL* 10.994–96). So, too, does Aristotle position pleasure as the most puerile object of desire, subordinate to the advantageous and the beautiful: "For children too live in accordance with desire, and the desire for what is pleasant is greatest in them" (*Nicomachean Ethics*, 1119b7). The separation of the pleasant and the sublimely beautiful may be understood particularly as a

product of the corruption of the will. Milton writes in accord with the idea that where sin yet taints the soul, we cannot say as Virgil to Dante, "let pleasure be your guide.... your will is free, erect, and whole" (*Purgatorio*, 27.131, 140). Thus Michael warns Adam, "Judge not what is best / By pleasure, though to Nature seeming meet" (*PL* 11.603–04).

59. See Regina Schwartz's chapter on "Chaos vs. Creation" in *Remembering and Repeating*, in which she not only presents her case for the antagonism of *Paradise Lost*'s chaos despite Milton's opinion of its goodness in *De doctrina Christiana* but also summarizes the opinions of Robert M. Adams (Chaos is neutral but with an inclination to evil), Michael Lieb (Chaos is neutral), A. B. Chambers (Chaos is an "exemplar of hell"), and A. S. P. Woodhouse (reservedly admitting in a footnote the difficulty of escaping the inference of an evil Chaos in *Paradise Lost*).

60. For Chaos as a place of nonbeing or lost identity, see Lieb, *Dialectics of Creation*, 21–25.

61. The act of creating out of the "dark materials" of Chaos may suggest the tainted mixture of good and evil, but the four contraries are not bad in themselves (*PL* 2.916). The contingency and intensity of such "fierce extremes" is what occasions the chaos. In the medieval worldview, when these four contraries are mixed appropriately, they become the four elements (earth is cold and dry, air is hot and moist, fire is hot and dry, water is cold and moist). Within the human body, the mixing of the contraries comprises the four humors (melancholy or black bile is cold and dry, blood is hot and moist, choler or yellow bile is hot and dry, phlegm is cold and moist). These humors, when intermixed within the body, account for one's temperament. See Lewis, *Discarded Image*, 94–95, 169–74.

62. For the emphasis in Jewish philosophy on separation as an initial and necessary action of creation, see, for example, Strauss, *Jewish Philosophy*, 363–65.

63. See Dante, *Inferno*, 32.1–8.

64. Lewis, *Preface to "Paradise Lost,"* 94–103.

65. Frederick L. Taft directs the reader to Luke 14:35; Mark 7:15, 19–23; and Matthew 15:17 (YP 1:895n146).

NOTES TO CHAPTER 4

1. See Aristotle's *Physics*, 3.4.203a–b, and Milton's schoolboy prolusion, "On the Harmony of the Spheres" (YP 1:234–39). In *De doctrina Christiana*, while arguing for the normal invisibility of angels to human sight, Milton suggests that the wings of angels are merely figurative depictions of their great swiftness (*OW* 8:299). At one point, Adam surmises the "incorporeal speed" of the planets, but Raphael corrects this to "speed almost spiritual," a correction that suggests a key difference between the denizens of the earthly and the celestial heavens (*PL* 8.37, 110).

2. For plant bodies in Milton, see especially Milton's vivid contribution to the vine and elm topos in *PL* 5.215–19, and the flowering plants' sensitive response to Eve's touch in *PL* 8.40–47. For the anthropomorphic natural sympathies of Eden and Egypt with their inhabitants, see chapter 4.

3. Qtd. in Danielson, *Book of the Cosmos*, 15–17.

4. Qtd. in ibid., 15–16.

5. For a concise examination of Milton's indebtedness to the Jewish philosopher Avencebrol's concept of *materia universalis*, see Curry, *Milton's Ontology, Cosmology, and Physics*, 166.

6. Gigante, "Milton's Aesthetics of Eating," also notes the alimentary connotations of Milton's *indigesta* and *digessit*.

7. Donnelly, "'Matter' versus Body," 79–85; Hart, "Matter, Monism, and Narrative," 16–27.

8. Curry, *Milton's Ontology, Cosmology, and Physics*, 166.

9. Ibid., 168–70.

10. Ibid., 223n25.

11. Ibid., 170.

12. For Milton's complicated debt to Aristotle, see, for example, Fallon, *Milton among the Philosophers*, 99–105. The word *ylem* has been used since the 1940s to name primordial substance associated with the Big Bang theory, but its roots are much earlier than the twentieth century. *Ylem* is only mentioned in the *OED* in one earlier instance: in book 3 of John Gower's *Confessio Amantis* (line 91), but it is derived from the Greek *hylē* (wood, material, matter), found again in the *OED* under the entry for the obsolete English word "hyle," and discernible in the philosophical term "hylozoism."

13. See also Pitt Harding's chapter on Milton's philosophy in Dobranski, *Milton in Context*, 444–45.

14. Milton's views of transformative eating do not extend to the doctrine of Eucharistic transubstantiation: "The mass drags Christ's holy body — after it has completed all its sufferings and miseries — back to the earth from its supreme point of exaltation [and] from the right hand of God the father, to a state of humiliation much more wretched and undeserved than before, [and] exposes it to be once more broken, crushed, and ground up, even by the fangs of brutes; [and] finally, when it has been thoroughly digested through all the filthy channels of the guts, [the mass] — shocking as this is to tell — ejects it into the latrine" (OW 8:763). Milton here follows the conventional rhetoric of some Protestants who restrict the Lord's Supper to a memorial meal. His doctrine of the Eucharist is Paracelsan, but his poetic representation of the possibility of transformative eating is implicitly Galenic and Augustinian (see chapters 4 and 5, below, and *City of God*, 8.25 and 12.22). For an excellent discussion of criticism examining Milton's view of the Eucharist, and an original reading of Milton's nonteleological appreciation for the sacrament as a sign to be desired in and of itself, which in turn becomes a model for devotional desire and for reading characterized by love and lack of need or self-interest, see Netzley, *Reading, Desire, and the Eucharist*, esp. 149–65.

15. Of the most influential book-length works that have treated the subject of Milton's materialist monism, the earliest to my knowledge is Saurat's *Milton: Man and Thinker*, which tracks Milton's indebtedness to philosophical concepts of creation in the *Zohar*. Lewis's *Preface to "Paradise Lost"* acknowledges a scholar's debt to Saurat but believes that in presenting the case for Milton's heterodox materialism, Saurat "with the enthusiasm incident to a pioneer…pressed his case too far" (82). Nevertheless, Lewis has a section dedicated to Milton's depiction of the material omnipresence of God as a safeguard (itself unorthodox) against the dualism of, for example, Plato's *Timaeus* (89–90). For Platonic dualism in opposition to the monism of the Genesis account, see Danielson, *Book of the Cosmos*, 34. He also dedicates an entire chapter, "The Mistake about Milton's Angels," to the corporeality of Milton's angels. Curry discusses dualism, monism, chaos, and the scale of nature in *Milton's Ontology, Cosmogony, and Physics*. Lieb's *Dialectics of Creation* analyzes Milton's description of matter, chaos, Creation, and the falls of Satan

and of humanity in generative vocabulary, with an important appendix exploring Milton's use of an alchemical vocabulary to explain transubstantiative eating and the scale of nature in *Paradise Lost*. Kerrigan's Freudian reading in *Sacred Complex* spends a good portion of its argument inquiring into Milton's monism. Rumrich's *Matter of Glory* challenges "the implicit assumption of the same orthodox horizon for *Paradise Lost* that Lewis explicitly proposes" and seeks to develop "the surprising consequences of Milton's heretical theology, his material monism in particular" (8; Rumrich does not here mention Lewis's admissions in his *Preface* of Milton's potentially heterodox views). Schwartz's *Remembering and Repeating* deals adroitly with Milton's theology and depiction of Chaos, and Fallon's *Milton among the Philosophers* posits that Milton worked out an original philosophy of "animist materialism" in response to the mind-body debates of his contemporaries. In *Matter of Revolution*, Rogers explores a complication to Milton's monism by noting Milton's use of Paracelsan "tartareous dregs" that, resisting assimilation into the cosmos, must be separated and purged. In 1997, Fish entered the monistic argument in the opening pages of his preface to the second edition of *Surprised by Sin*, compelled to respond to Rumrich's criticism of Fish as assigning an "anticarnal bias" to the poem (see Rumrich, "Uninventing Milton"). Schoenfeldt devotes an influential, monist-driven chapter to temperance and the "alimental vision" of *Paradise Lost* in *Bodies and Selves*. At the turn of the twenty-first century, the critical consensus, generally accepted without question, was that Milton is a monist, a materialist, and a mortalist.

Nevertheless, the critical pendulum has begun to question the consensus regarding Milton's monism or animist materialism. We have already seen how Rogers and Gigante each drew attention to the dualism implicit in the expulsion of the fallen angels and the separation of tartareous dregs from the matter of creation. Sugimura's *"Matter of Glorious Trial"* questions the extent to which we can literally accept Raphael's monistic cosmology, given his need to accommodate an angelic message to a human audience through analogy. Song's *Dominion Undeserved* also disturbs the image of Milton's monism through inquiry into Milton's anti-universalism and into the necessary and dynamic conflict between creativity and original unruliness, or chaos. Monism is a misleading term for Milton's natural philosophy if it obscures the distinctions Milton makes between humans and angels, between body and spirit, and between the corporeal and what Milton's narrator calls the incorporeal (*PL* 1.789, 5.413). Granted, in certain passages these distinctions may be read to be nominal and rhetorical; thus, glossing the passage on angelic digestion, Fallon asserts, "The turning of the corporeal to the incorporeal must be taken as relative" (*Milton among the Philosophers*, 107). In other passages (as in the creation of light and later of the celestial bodies to house it), the narrative requires the reader to treat these distinctions more literally. In *De doctrina Christiana*, Milton's defense of his heretical view of the Son reveals his insistence on the essential difference between God and the rest of the world, even when this rest is created *ex Deo* (OW 8:33). In *Paradise Lost*, Raphael mentions that angelic and human rational powers differ only "in degree, of kind the same," but this is not to say that angels and humans share the same nature, form, or substance; there are "various forms" as well as "various degrees / Of substance," "Each in their several active spheres assigned," each mobile but positioned "in bounds / Proportioned to each kind" (5.471–72, 486–88, 490).

16. Adam's disposition may be comparable to that of the seventeenth century English reader, who was likely to believe in angels and to hold them in reverence. For early modern assertions of the existence of angels, including the opinions of Henry More, Johannes Wier, Robert Burton, and Niccolo Machiavelli, see Lewis's chapter, "The Mistake about Milton's Angels," in his *Preface to "Paradise Lost,"* and see Burton's *Anatomy of Melancholy*, 1.2.1.2.

17. Lewis, *Preface to "Paradise Lost,"* 88.

18. Curry, *Milton's Ontology, Cosmology, and Physics*, 162. The idea of ether as attenuated matter, a mixture of air and fire, is related to the Stoic understanding of pneuma. Cf. Furley and Wilkie, *Galen*, 37.

19. Compare this to Augustine's teaching on the fallen angels' retention of bodily beauty and excellence in *City of God*, book 11, chap. 23.

20. Aristotle, *On the Soul*, 2.2–3.

21. See Reynolds, "Milton's Adam and the Angels," 175–76.

22. Burton, *Anatomy of Melancholy*, 1.1.2.5:135; cf. Aristotle, *On the Soul*, 2.3. For Milton's invention of intellectual spirits, see John Rumrich's "Critical Responses, Early," in Dobranski, *Milton in Context*, 119. For a recent compendium of early modern physiology, including the role of the animal spirits, see Babb, "Physiology and Psychology," 749–63.

23. Kass, *Hungry Soul*, gives a modern biological and philosophical analysis of the "you are what you eat" conundrum, increasing the relevance of this aspect of *Paradise Lost* to today's readers. Using common sense and simple terms, Kass looks at eating to examine how materiality is insufficient to explain human nature:

> At first glance there is some reason to believe that one *is* just *what* one eats. We begin life as a single cell, barely visible to the naked eye. To reach our adult size, we must increase our bulk 120 billionfold. We acquire this extra mass entirely from without, by ingestion. In addition, it seems that — no matter how diligently we search — we will never find any immaterial something that enters our bodies along with that stuff. We are, from head to toe, altogether stuff-y. To be sure, we don't *look* like the food we eat. But appearance is deceiving. At bottom we are proteins, carbohydrates, fats, vitamins, minerals, and nucleic acids — and so is our food. No wonder food is so important to survival: Where it goes, there I am; where it goes not, there I am not; what it is, that too am I. We are identical, I and my stuff.
>
> This plausible explanation of what I am with what I eat, by means of the intermediate and even more plausible identification of me and my stuff and of my stuff with my food, requires closer scrutiny. An obvious difficulty confronts us. Chicken embryos digest egg yolk and grow into egg-laying chickens; calves drink milk and grow into milk-giving cows; human children eat egg yolks and drink cows' milk but grow up only human. Yolk taken by the chicken becomes chicken; the same yolk taken by the child is humanized. How can this be, if one is what one eats? (20–21)

Arguing for the "necessary supremacy of living form," Kass asserts, "because of our constant need to eat and to replenish our bodily stuff, the living animal has a unity and a self-identity that in fact outlast its ever-shifting material" (34, 41). Kass proceeds to demonstrate the insufficiency of a "corporealistic ontology" to explain consumption and, turning to Aristotle's four causes, concludes that biology itself shows us there is some aspect of our being (our form) that cannot be explained through strict materialism (59). Though there is good precedent for labeling Milton a materialistic monist, the portrait of eating as transubstantiation in *Paradise Lost,* following Galen's concept of *alteration,* also suggests an ontology insufficiently explained by materialism alone.

24. Galen, *On the Natural Faculties,* 29.9, p. 31; see also Brock's introduction, xxixn1.

25. Ibid., 11.

26. Ibid., 1.2, p. 9.

27. Pagel, *Paracelsus,* 323. For information on how theories of digestion could be condemned as "pestilential heresy," see Rudolph, "Hohenheim's Anthropology," 187–92.

28. Rumrich, *Matter of Glory,* 76.

29. Ibid., 189n23; cf. Empson, *Milton's God,* 169–72.

30. Lieb, *Dialectics of Creation,* 229, 232, 234. Lieb quotes Evelyn Underhill, *Mysticism: A Study in the Nature and Development of Man's Spiritual Consciousness* (Cleveland: World Publishing, 1955), 143.

31. Lieb, *Dialectics of Creation,* 239.

32. Rogers, *Matter of Revolution,* 130–38.

33. Galen, *On the Natural Faculties,* 1.6, p. 15.

34. Galen, *On Habits,* as quoted in the introduction to his *On the Natural Faculties,* xxxi.

35. Suetonius, "Divus Vespasian," secs. 23–24, in *Twelve Caesars,* 287.

36. Virgil, *Aeneid,* 8.475, 480–85.

37. Irenaeus, *Against Heresies,* preface to book 5; Clement of Alexandria, *Exhortation to the Heathen,* chap. 1; Athanasius of Alexandria, *Against the Arians,* discourse 1, para. 39 and discourse 3, para. 34, and *On the Incarnation,* sec. 54; Gregory of Nyssa, *The Great Catechism,* 37, and *On Christian Perfection.* For more on the relationship between Milton's thought and the patristic doctrine of *theosis,* see Jefferey H. and Leslie A. Taylor's *The Influence of Boethius' "De consolatione philosophiae" on John Milton's "Paradise Lost"* (Lewiston, NY: Edwin Mellen, 2017).

38. Augustine, "Psalm 50," para. 2, in *Exposition on the Book of Psalms.*

39. Augustine, *City of God,* 8.25, p. 353

40. Boethius, *Consolation of Philosophy,* 59.

41. Ibid., 78–79.

42. See Wittreich, "Pico and Milton."

43. Pico della Mirandola, *Oration*, 7–8.

44. Ibid., 8–9.

45. Quoted in Tillyard, *Elizabethan World Picture*, 68. See also *Cambridge History*, vol. 3, chap. 19, sec. 13.

46. Contrast this with *De doctrina Christiana*, which permits no "translated Saints" before the final judgment day: "Before the resurrection, therefore, [Christ] declares quite outspokenly, there is not even a living–place in heaven for the saints" (OW 8.445).

47. See Dennis Danielson, "Astronomy," in Dobranski, *Milton in Context*, 213–25.

48. See Danielson, *Book of the Cosmos*, 149–50.

49. While definitions of "purge" generally involve removal of moral or physical impurities, Milton appears to be using the word in *PL* 5.420 in a positive, transformative sense. The purification or purgation here seems to be the process of rarefaction rather than the removal of substantial matter. Definition 3b of "purge" in the *OED* is "to prune (a tree)," with citations dating from c. 1384 to 1717. If Milton also had this possible meaning in mind, there is yet another way Adam and Eve's work in the garden imitates the natural digestive processes as described by Raphael.

50. Schoenfeldt, *Bodies and Selves*, 140.

51. Citing Theodore Spencer, Herbert Howarth, Jonathan Dollimore, Stephen Greenblatt, and Louis Montrose, Todd Borlik notes the work of early modernists "to debunk this theory as the ideology of an elite, which served to naturalize the inequalities of the social hierarchy" (*Ecocriticism*, 27). The cosmic hierarchy is certainly a part of Milton's poiesis, but social hierarchies among humans are some of the most lamentable results of the Fall for Milton. Michael insists that human beings were not created to dominate one another, and Adam readily assents (12.24–32, 64–71). Adam and Eve are given dominion over the other creatures of paradise, but not without responsibility (*PL* 4. 427–37; 7.532–34). Recently, Borlik has labored to "scrape the rust from the Chain of Being" to reclaim it for twenty-first century ecocriticism. According to Borlik, "While [the Great Chain of Being's] spiritual taxonomy works to underwrite a belief in human exceptionalism, its holism also fostered an 'analogical habit of mind' that can be seen in some ways as intimating an ecological sensibility" (*Ecocriticism*, 27, quoting

W. R. Elton, "Shakespeare and the Thought of His Age," 17). The way forward, Borlik suggests, is to follow Jeanne Addison Roberts's lead in "horizontalizing" the Great Chain of Being, doing so upon a hint from S. K. Heninger Jr. and under the auspices of Pythagoras, Shakespeare, and, at times, Milton. Borlik, *Ecocriticism*, 28, citing Jeanne Addison Roberts, "Animals as Agents of Revelation: The Horizontalizing of the Great Chain of Being in Shakespeare's Comedies," in *Shakespearean Comedy*, ed. Maurice Charney (New York: New York Literary Forum, 1980), 79–96. Borlik also cites Heninger's pointed reference to Pythagorean (and Timaean) "variety on a horizontal scale," but Heninger (unlike Borlik) takes no issue with the Great Chain's hierarchical "variety on a vertical scale." In fact, Heninger argues, "in an ingenious way the horizontal scale of variety is interlocked with the vertical scale to provide a complex but coherent system" (*Touches of Sweet Harmony*, 328).

52. Assuming at least partial responsibility for one's own perseverance in faith is a concept pervading Milton's theology and is found in the doctrine of Arminian Remonstrants whom Milton praises in *De doctrina Christiana* in his discussion of the perseverance of the saints (OW 8:669). In Milton's soteriology, "regeneration, growth and preservation" are "proximate causes on God's part, and their effects such as faith, charity, and so on, [considered as proximate causes] on man's part or within man, produce the *assurance of salvation* and the *perseverance of the saints*" (OW 8:653). Although Milton dissents from the Calvinist doctrine of perseverance of the saints, his affirmation that faith and charity are the effects of God's motions and his addition of the concessive phrase "or which take place in man" reveal that Milton is still inclined to attribute human virtue to God's involvement even as he asserts its importance. See Danielson, "Milton's Arminianism and *Paradise Lost*," 47–73; Fallon, "Milton's Arminianism," 103–27; Stavely, "Satan and Arminianism," 125–39.

53. Walker, "For each seem'd either,'" 13–16. Cf. *PL* 2.670.

54. Fallon, *Milton's Peculiar Grace*, 184. Fallon later explains the incompatibility he sees: "Milton can have either the self-satisfaction of the self-made spiritual man or the self-satisfaction of the one chosen by God in a manner different from that by which others are chosen, but he cannot have both self-satisfactions at once" (201).

55. Ibid., 201, 210. Finding autobiographical echoes and "an authentic cry of pain" in the lover's complaint of *PL* 10.898–906, Fallon proposes, "If

marital woes are one of the first fruits of the fall in the epic, Milton's own marital woes may have been the shock that awoke him to his fallibility" (206).

56. See Milton's "Letter to a Friend" (*CPEP* 770–72); cf. Fallon on the parable of the workers in the vineyard and the parable of the talents (*Milton's Peculiar Grace*, 18–19).

57. In addition to the chapters "Of Predestination," "On Justification," and "On Good Works" in *De doctrina Christiana*, see *PL* 3.173–82, 290–92; 11.3, 34–36, 64; 12.402–04, 408–10, 427, 581–83.

58. *Paradise Lost*, ed. Teskey, 5.5n. See also the note for this line in *CPEP*.

59. Burton, *Anatomy of Melancholy*, 1.1.2.4. Note the Englishman's positioning of the papal delegate as lowest of the three governors.

60. Burton, *Anatomy of Melancholy*, 1.1.2.4, p. 132. In the opening scene of Shakespeare's *Coriolanus*, Menenius Agrippa gives a notable speech comparing the aristocracy to the belly as storehouse and distributor for the commonweal, and Spenser's famous allegory of the body as the House of Temperance depicts the stomach as a kitchen (*Faerie Queene* 2.9.27–32). In early modern thought, the stomach is both pantry and oven for the body.

61. So also in *Bald's Leechbook*, book 2, chap. 17: "The liver . . . is the material of the blood, and the house and the nourishment of the blood; when there is digestion and attenuation of the meats, they arrive at the liver, and then they change their hue, and turn into blood; and it casteth out the uncleannesses which be there, and collects the clean blood, and through four veins principally sendeth it to the heart, and also throughout all the body as far as the extremities of the limbs" (199).

62. Burton, *Anatomy of Melancholy*, 1.1.2.3, pp. 128–29. *Meseraick veins* is an obsolete term for the mesentery, the folded sheet of the peritoneum connecting the jejunum and ileum of the small intestine with the dorsal wall of the abdominal cavity (*OED*).

63. A. Rupert Hall, "Studies on the History of the Cardiovascular System," *Bulletin of the History of Medicine* 34 (1960): 404, qtd. in Furley and Wilkie, *Galen*, 8. Plato's *Timaeus* describes blood as the substance that "feeds our flesh and indeed our whole bodies" (in *Complete Works*, 80e5). Before Plato, as Furley notes in his introduction, the pre-Socratics Empedocles, Philistion, Diocles, and Diogenes of Apollonia developed theories associating blood with

respiration through the pores — a concept that led to related Hippocratic theories of excretion through transpiration, united by Galen's time into "a theory of some precision: the arteries draw in air through the skin in diastole and expel waste through the skin in systole, and this process is part of the system that maintains moderate heat in the body" (5).

64. Burton, *Anatomy of Melancholy*, 1.1.2.4, pp. 131–35.

65. Galen, *On the Natural Faculties*, 2.7, p. 106.

66. Burton, *Anatomy of Melancholy*, 1.1.2.2, p. 129.

67. Ibid.

68. Babb, "Cave of Spleen," 166.

69. See also Shakespeare, *Twelfe Night*, note to 1.1.43–44, pp. 19–20. See also Babb, "Physiology and Psychology," 749–64.

70. Cf. *OED*, s.v. "excrement."

71. *Hamlet* 3.4. There are a few fascinating studies of early modern thought about hair and its relationship to physiological, philosophical, religious, or political ideas. Edward James Geisweidt explains the shaken Hamlet's hair as follows: "Hamlet's spirits are making their way to the edge of his body, and perhaps even beyond it. In so doing, the spirits give a kind of life to Hamlet's hair, a body part that, as we shall see, is readily amenable to taking on life of its own in the early modern imagination." See Geisweidt, "Like Life in Excrements," 2; see also Dobranski, "Clustering and Curling Locks," 337–53.

72. Burton, *Anatomy of Melancholy*, 1.1.2.6, p. 136.

73. Aristotle, *Generation of Animals*, 1.18.724b26–28. Aristotle's distinction between useful and useless secretions or excretions is somewhat vague: "Every secretion or excretion is either of useless or useful nutriment; by 'useless' I mean that from which nothing further is contributed to natural growth, but which is particularly mischievous to the body if too much of it is consumed; by 'useful' I mean the opposite" (1.18.725a4–7). This imprecise definition suggests that it would not be particularly mischievous to the body if one had too much of a "useful excess": hair, nail growth, semen, or — what is perhaps most curious to the modern mind — fat.

74. Although Paracelsus differed from Galen in this by asserting that diseases were externally introduced, and not simply the result of an imbalance of the humors, Galenic physiology remained influential until the dissemination of the works of such sixteenth century anatomists as Vesalius, Michael

Servetus, and Andrea Cesalpino, and of William Harvey on the circulation of the heart in the first half of the seventeenth century (see introduction to the Loeb edition of Galen's *On the Natural Faculties*, xxii–xxiv.)

75. Qtd. in Schoenfeldt, *Bodies and Selves*, 14.

76. Venner, *Via recta ad vitam longam*, 321–22.

77. Burton, *Anatomy of Melancholy*, 1.2.2.4, pp. 203, 205.

78. Cavendish, *World's Olio*, 162. See Totaro, *Suffering in Paradise*, 146–48.

79. Totaro, *Suffering in Paradise*, 169.

80. Venner, *Via recta ad vitam longam*, 314.

81. *Bald's Leechbook*, bk. 1, chap. 84.

82. Burton, *Anatomy of Melancholy*, 1.2.2.4, pp. 203, 205.

83. For this letter's relevance to Milton's personal temperance, see chapter 6.

84. Lewalski, *Life of John Milton*, 260. For a more in-depth account of the procedure and others Milton may have undergone to prevent blindness, as well as some information on Milton's possible access to contemporary doctors like William Harvey, Francis Glisson, Thomas Sydenham, and their circles (in addition to his own physician, Dr. Nathan Paget), see Hanford, "John Milton Forswears Physic," 23–34. The anonymous biographer of Milton claims setoning may have even accelerated Milton's blindness: "And the issues and seatons, made use of to save or retrieve that [first failing eye], were thought by drawing away the spirits, which should have supplied the optic vessels, to have hastened the loss of the other" (qtd. in *CPMP* 1042).

85. Paster, *Body Embarrassed*, 7.

86. For Aristotle, semen is a useful "residue of the nutriment" rather than a waste product (*Generation of Animals*, 1.18.724b26–28), although one might argue that semen does not directly "contribute to natural growth" of the body from which it is secreted, but instead manifests its usefulness for another individual, or that its usefulness to the body generating it is limited to the gratification of its reproductive instincts and the perpetuation of the species. Instead, Aristotle argues that "the exhaustion consequent on the loss of even a very little of the semen is conspicuous because the body is deprived of the ultimate gain drawn from the nutriment" (1.18.725b6–8). See also *Generation of Animals*, 2.5.651a21, 2.6.744b23–25, 4.10689a8–13. For a succinct summary of the properties and uses of serviceable residue synthesizing these

passages and others, see William Ogle's note on the *Parts of Animals* 2.3.650a22 (in Aristotle's *Works*).

87. Turner, *One Flesh*, 229; Lewalski, *Life of John Milton*, 171. See also Shigeo Suzuki's coinciding interpretation of "a disgusting 'quintessence of an excrement'" in his essay on seventeenth century marriage and divorce in Dobranski, *Milton in Context*, 386.

88. Galen, *On the Properties of Foodstuffs*, 76. Galen does not consider food thus digested to be particularly nutritive:

> Generally speaking, then, you should understand, as a general principle regarding fruits edible for man, that the nutriment the moist ones produce and deliver to the body is moist and thin. From which it follows, absolutely, that such nutriment passes through the system and goes rapidly through the body as a whole, being quickly evacuated both in the urine and through the skin. This is why all such foods have been properly described by physicians as poorly nutritive. As against that, the contribution to the body in nutrient value of fruits that are solid in composition is greater, and the evacuations are slower, especially when the fruits contain within themselves any fluid, be it thick, viscid or astringent.

89. Aristotle, *Parts of Animals*, 2.10.655b, 29–37, in *Works*. Elsewhere in the *Parts of Animals*, Aristotle explains, "For plants get their food from the earth by means of their roots; and this food is already elaborated when taken in, which is the reason why plants produce no excrement, the earth and its heat serving them in the stead of a stomach" (2.3.650a20–23). In his treatise *On the Soul*, Aristotle compares the roots of plants to the mouths of animals, "both serving for the absorption of food" (2.1). Similarly, Richard DuRocher notes Seneca's comparison of earth's water and air passages to the veins and arteries of the human body in *Natural Questions*, 3.15.1–2, which he connects to "Milton's personified earth" (*Milton among the Romans*, 140–41). Carolyn Merchant digs even deeper to discover the roots of the Gaia hypothesis, citing Anaxagoras, Theophrastus, and Dionysius of Periegetes. If roots of plants were likened to the air and blood passages in animals, the metal veins in the earth were likened to the roots and branches of plants. Metals were believed to be a lower form of life than vegetables and animals, but alive nonetheless.

In the early modern era, there was a popular belief in a golden tree consisting of interconnected minerals and metallic vein networks originating at the center of the earth (29).

90. So Nicholas of Cusa relates: "And thus the earth, as Plato says, is like an animal whose bones are stones, whose arteries are rivers, whose hairs are trees; and animals feed among those hairs just as mites do among the hairs of the animals" (in Danielson, *Book of the Cosmos*, 100).

91. As Fallon argues in *Milton among the Philosophers*, "The relation of plant to the one first matter is synecdochic. The plant not only represents in its root and flowers the poles between grossly corporeal and relatively incorporeal matter, it also enacts the process of digestion by which individuals ascend the chain. The metabolism of the plant transforms matter from the gross to the tenuous" (103–04).

92. Schoenfeldt, *Bodies and Selves*, 142.

93. Burton's *Anatomy of Melancholy* explains that sleep results from "an inhibition of spirits" caused by "vapours arising out of the stomack, filling the nerves, by which the spirits should be conveyed" (1.1.2.8, p. 140). With characteristic detail and whimsy, Burton also argues that sleep perfects digestion:

> It moistens and fattens the body, concocts, and helps digestion.... The chiefest thing in all Physick, Paracelsus calls it, above every secret of precious stones and metals. The fittest time is two or three hours after supper, when as the meat is now settled at the bottom of the stomack, and 'tis good to lie on the right side first, because at that site the liver doth rest under the stomack, not molesting any way, but heating him as a fire doth a kettle, that is put to it. After the first sleep 'tis not amiss to lie on the left side, that the meat may better descend, and sometimes again on the belly, but never on the back. (2.2.5, pp. 464–65)

94. Ambergris (gray-amber), the fragrant but morbid excretion in the intestines of the sperm whale, used in perfumes and culinary dishes, was often confused with amber as fossilized tree resin (or yellow amber, Fr. *ambre jaune*), which was thought to emit a pleasant fragrance when burned (*OED*, def. II.3a). Milton seems to combine properties of both definitions in his use of "amber," properties that unite in "ambrosia." In *A Mask*, Sabrina has "amber-dropping hair" (863); in *Paradise Regain'd*, the banquet temptation includes meat dishes

"In pastry built, or from the spit, or boil'd, / Grisamber steam'd" (2.343–44). In *Paradise Lost*, the sweet scents of myrrh, tree balms, and ambrosial fruits intermingle.

95. F. A. Wright, "Food of the Gods," 6. Ambergris has been used as a symbol of resurrection or renewal. Herman Melville's chapter on "Ambergris" in *Moby Dick* nicely sermonizes on this fragrant excrement derived from the "inglorious bowels of a sick whale" (317), with reference to Saint Paul's and Paracelsus's comments on deriving the pleasing from the foul. In the *Archidoxies*, Paracelsus explains that ordure mixed with musk aids penetration of the fragrance into the body of the patient (*Hermetic and Alchemical Writings*, 61).

96. Homer, *Odyssey*, 12.62.

97. Cf. Homer, *Iliad*, 5.777, 14.170; Sappho, fr. 45; Euripedes's *Medea*, 982; all cited in Wright, "Food of the Gods," 5–6.

98. Hesiod, *Theogony*, 69, and Homeric Hymn 27, to Artemis, line 18.

99. Homer, *Iliad*, 14.170–74.

100. Ibid., 5.369, 8.434.

101. Ibid., 19.39, 348; Homer, *Odyssey*, 4.445.

102. Homer, *Iliad*, 24.363; cf. *PL* 5.642.

103. Consider Jacob Neusner's translation of and commentary on *Sifré to Numbers* 88:1:

> A. "'but now our strength is dried up and there is nothing at all but this manna to look at.' [Now the manna was like coriander seed and its appearance like that of bdellium. The people went about and gathered it, and ground it in mills or beat it in mortars and boiled it in pots, and with oil. When the dew fell upon the camp in the night, the manna fell with it]" (Num. 11:4–9):
>
> B. They said, "The manna is going to burst in our bellies and kill us. Is there a creature born of woman who does not excrete what he eats [while we do not excrete at all]!"
>
> C. They said to R. Simeon, "If so, how do you explain the verse, 'And you shall have a paddle with your weapons' (Deut. 23:14) [for burying excrement]?"
>
> D. He said to them, "What is excreted by them is what the merchants of the nations of the world sell to them, but manna never is excreted, as

it is said, 'and ate of the bread of angels [BYRYM]' (Ps. 78:25), bread that is absorbed in the limbs '[YBRYM].'"

What is explained is the statement that "our strength is dried up," interpreted to mean that the people did not excrete the manna. At the same time two contradictory verses are harmonized. (Neusner, *Sifré to Numbers*, 87)

104. Cf. *Sifré to Numbers*, 87.2, 89.2 (Neusner, 86, 90). For Milton's knowledge of midrashic texts, see Werman, *Milton and Midrash*, and Fletcher, *Milton's Rabbinical Readings*.

105. Wisdom 16:20, *New American Bible*. Though Milton did not consider the book of Wisdom canonical, he does cite it in defense of his theological views and considers "the Apocryphal writers...closest in authority to scripture" (OW 8:289). Adapting the tradition of the *symposium* in uniting philosophy and food, the Hellenistic text of the book of Wisdom draws a parallel between wisdom and manna, a precedent for Dante's description of wisdom as the bread of angels at the beginning of the *Convivio* and in *Paradiso*, 2.10–12. Manna and ambrosia have a further intriguing (even if incidental) similarity in that scientists have considered the stories of both to have originated in fungal growth. In *The World of Classical Myth*, Ruck and Staples explain that one of the legends of the naming of Mycenae involves the honoring of an entheogenic mushroom, the *amanita muscaria*, that grew there and was used in Indo-European shamanism, and eventually was imagined as the food of the gods: "The thunderbolt of Zeus was itself a mediation between the Father God's realm and earth, as the ethnomycologist R. Gordon Wasson has shown in demonstrating the wide-spread belief that mushrooms appear where lightning strikes the earth. Amanita was divine food, not something to be indulged in lightly, not something to be profaned. It was food of the gods, their ambrosia, and nectar was the pressed sap of its juices" (26).

At the same time, the manna that fed the wandering Israelites has been described as a plant lichen scraped from trees, or an entheogenic mushroom with mycelia resembling hoarfrost. Interestingly, explanations of manna as non–seed-bearing fungi or lichens would not render this "bread of angels" kosher according to Jewish law (cf. Gen. 1:29). As early as the turn of the fifteenth century, some have described manna as dried sap or gum of trees, and later, especially that of the manna ash, *Fraxinus ornus* (see *OED*, s.v. "manna," def. 2.3). Since the nineteenth century, another explanation attributes the phenomenon to the carbohydrate-rich excretion (honeydew) of scale insects that feed on the tamarisk tree (*OED*, def. II.3.d).

106. Reid, "Spirits Odorous," 141.

107. Ibid., 141.

108. Burton, *Anatomy of Melancholy*, 1.2.1.2, p. 159.

109. Reid, "Spirits Odorous," 140, 142.

110. Lehnhof, "Scatology and the Sacred," 441.

111. Raymond, *Milton's Angels*, 126.

112. Burton, *Anatomy of Melancholy* 1.2.1.2, pp. 159–60.

113. Cf. West, *Milton and the Angels*; Nicolson, *Reader's Guide to John Milton*, 53.

114. Psellus, *On the Operation of Daemons*, 34.

115. Ibid., 35.

116. Ibid., 29.

117. Evagrius, *Praktikos*, 39; *Kephalaia Gnostica*, 5.78, trans. Robert E. Sinkewicz, cited in Brakke, *Demons*, 281n64.

118. Athanasius of Alexandria, *Life of Anthony*:

> Afterwards, on another occasion, having descended to the outer cells, he was asked to enter a vessel and pray with the monks, and he alone perceived an exceedingly unpleasant smell. But those on board said that the stench arose from the fish and salt meat in the ship. He replied however, the smell was different from that; and while he was speaking, a youth with an evil spirit, who had come and hidden himself in the ship, cried out. But the demon being rebuked in the name of the Lord Jesus Christ departed from him, and the man became whole. And all knew that the evil smell arose from the demon. (63)

119. Corns, *Milton Encyclopedia*, s.v. "Athanasius," 22. In *Of Reformation*, Milton refers to the "faithfull and invincible Athanasius" (YP 1:555).

120. Chaucer, "Second Nun's Tale," 246–52.

121. The counterpart to the united smell and taste of life-giving ambrosia is the united smell and taste of death. So Satan tells Sin of the pleasant smell of the new world and immediately proceeds to say, "There ye shall be fed and filled" (*PL* 2.843). But Satan has an ambivalent opinion of the smells of

paradise: "So entertained those odorous sweets the Fiend / Who came their bane, though with them better pleased / Than Asmodeus with the fishy fume" (4.166–68).

122. Lehnhof, "Scatology and the Sacred," 441. In my research for this project I independently formed certain opinions on angelic digestion that were reinforced when reading Lehnhof's excellent article.

123. Ibid., 445.

124. Augustine, *City of God*, 13.22; cf. *PL* 5.434. Augustine's and Milton's references to the book of Tobit invite consideration of interesting contrasts between the story of Sarah in the book of Tobit and that of Saint Cecilia. Sarah wants to consummate her marriages, but the demon Asmodeus kills her husbands before she can have intercourse. An angel intervenes: Asmodeus the demon, repelled by the odor of burning fish liver and heart, flees to Egypt, where Raphael binds him. By contrast, Cecilia wants to keep her virginity after marriage, and an angel, smelling of paradisal flowers, promises to kill her husband Valerian if he touches her "carnally."

125. Cf. *OED*, s.v. "bland," def. 2.

126. Cf. *OED*, s.v. "balmy," def. 3.

127. Totaro, *Suffering in Paradise*, 175.

128. For the required aromatic offerings and incense to Yahweh in ancient Jewish religion, see Exodus 30:34–38 and Leviticus 1:15; 2:2, 9, 12; 3:5, 16; 4:31; 6:15, 21; 8:21, 28. For the Pauline adaptation of the fragrant offering, see Romans 12:1, Ephesians 5:2, and Philippians 4:18. For thoughts on Lancelot Andrewes's *A sermon of the pestilence Preached at Chiswick, 1603*, see Totaro, *Suffering in Paradise*, 181–82.

NOTES TO CHAPTER 5

1. Milton notes the typological ties between the Last Supper and the sending of manna in *De doctrina Christiana* (OW 8:749–51). In *Paradise Lost*, he merely mentions the movement from law to grace, "From shadowy Types to Truth, from Flesh to Spirit" (*PL* 12.303).

2. Plato, *Symposium*, 210a–212b, in *Works*.

3. Ibid., 211e.

4. In book 1 of his *De doctrina Christiana*, Augustine describes the order of love. In the sixth century, Gregory the Great glosses Jacob's ladder to explain

the active and contemplative aspects of the angels' lives (*Moralia in Job*, 2.3). Bernard of Clairvaux associates Jacob's ladder with Benedict of Nursia's Twelve Steps of Humility, which include loving God's will over our own (see Whiting, *Milton and This Pendant World*, 64–66). Ambrose of Milan considered Jacob's dream a prefiguration of Christ, and John Calvin also wrote of Christ as the stairs between humankind and God (ibid., 64, 72). Thomas Aquinas refers to Jacob's ladder as a symbol for contemplative and active lives (*Summa theologica*, 2.2ae.181.4, resp. 2). The ladder of love or mysticism is correlated to a ladder of speculation (described by Bonaventure) and a ladder of merit (described by Aquinas): "Nevertheless, for Aquinas, who was a Dominican, and Bonaventure, who was a Franciscan, and indeed virtually all Catholic thinkers, every ladder culminates in the mystical ascent. For as God is love and man perfects himself by loving God, all Christian aspiration leads into the ladder of love" (Singer, *Nature of Love*, 179–80). In the fourteenth century, the Flemish mystic John of Ruysbroeck wrote *Seven Steps of the Ladder of Spiritual Love*, and the English Augustinian mystic Walter Hilton wrote in *The Scale of Perfection*, "How Virtue beginneth in Reason and Will and is perfected in Love and Liking, or Affection" (16–17). The sixteenth century Spanish mystic John of the Cross wrote in *The Dark Night of the Soul* of the ten steps to the "ladder of love which the soul climbs, one by one, in her ascension to God" (225).

5. The prominent discourses on Love as the ordering principle of the cosmos in *The Divine Comedy* are found in *Inferno* 11, *Purgatorio* 17 and 18, and, of course, the last line of *Paradiso* (33.145).

6. *Paradiso* 22.124–53, 27.76–87.

7. For an exploration of Milton's interest in the stars and in ancient, medieval, and early modern texts on the influence of the stars, with special attention to Manilius's *Astronomica*, see DuRocher, *Milton among the Romans*, 106–11. While noting that Milton would deny the Stoically deterministic tenets of *Astronomica*, DuRocher draws out a connection between *Paradise Lost* and passages from Manilius's epic that provide "a flattering appeal to readers to use their heavenly gifts to rise to the stars" (110).

The use of acrostics to convey theological truths was not unprecedented; for example, Augustine analyzes a Christian mystical message (Iesous Chreistos THeou Uios Soter, the meaning of the ichthys symbol) purportedly hidden in an acrostic in a poem of the Erythraean Sibyl (*City of God*, 18.23). Dante also sets a precedent for introducing anagrams into epic poetry with the famous DXV (*dux*, leader) in *Purgatorio*, 33.43–44, and acrostics in *Purgatorio*, 12.25–63 (VOM, *uomo*, man) and in *Paradiso*, 19.115–41 (LVE, *lue*, plague), though only from the turn of the twentieth century have the acrostics received attention — and not always acceptance — from Dante scholars (see Robert Hollander's commentary on *Purgatorio*, 12.25–63).

Since an acrostic such as this in Milton may require others like it to strengthen the evidence for intentionality, it is perhaps worthwhile to cite the most noteworthy of these in this space. As Satan in the serpent slithers through Eden in book 9, the bard compares him in beauty to other mythic serpents, including the one that with Olympias

> bore
> **S**cipio the highth of Rome. With tract oblique
> **A**t first, as one who sought access, but fear'd
> **T**o interrupt, side-long he works his way.
> **A**s when a Ship by skilful Steersman wrought
> **N**igh River's mouth or Foreland.   (9.509–14; emphasis added)

With these lines, Milton "with tract oblique," "side-long," and perhaps even "fear[ing] to interrupt" his own poetry, visually replicates the slithering nefariousness of Satan in the written poem even as the preponderance of sibilants replicate the hissing snake on a sonorous level. For more on Milton's use of acrostics, see Partner, "Satanic Vision and Acrostics," and Vaughn, "'More than Meets the Eye.'"

8. See Rumrich and Chaplin, *Seventeenth-Century British Poetry*, 601n5.

9. Introduction to Goldstein and Tigner, *Culinary Shakespeare*, 2. Two other notable works on eating, ethics, and literature in early modern England are Goldstein's *Eating and Ethics* and Fitzpatrick's *Food in Shakespeare*.

10. See Maurice Kelley's comments in YP 6:128n9.

11. Plotinus, *Enneads*, 1.6.6.

12. Milton is often credited with the first astronomical use of the term "space" when his Satan speculates that "Space may produce new worlds" (*PL* 1.650); however, the *OED* cites two earlier instances of this use of the word in early modern English, and, more relevant to our inquiry, Milton is

probably indebted to Augustine in this use, for chapter 5 of book 11 of *The City of God* — "That We Ought Not to Seek to Comprehend the Infinite Ages of Time before the World, Nor the Infinite Realms of Space" — uses the Latin word *spatia* (as well as *locus*) in this sense repeatedly. Joined to the other correspondences, this becomes one more piece of evidence that Milton carefully reflected on and engaged with this particular section of Augustine's *City of God*, a section that, despite its Trinitarian motifs, becomes a model for Milton's own exploration of triads in nature, philosophy, and (attributes of) divinity.

13. Augustine, *City of God*, 11.24; emphases added.

14. Ibid., 11.25; emphases added.

15. Ibid., 11.25.

16. Ibid., 11.26. The chapter concludes, "just as there is no one who does not wish to be happy, so is there no one who does not wish to exist; for how can anyone be happy if he is nothing?" The thought is continued in the next chapter, considering "even those who seem to themselves to be completely miserable, and who clearly are so.... Suppose someone were to grant all these men an immortality in which their misery should never end, but with the condition that, if they did not wish to remain forever in this same misery, they might perish entirely and have no existence of any kind. Would they not surely jump for joy, and choose to remain miserable forever rather than not exist at all?" (485). *Paradise Lost* may allude to these exact passages at least twice: once, when Belial argues, "For who would lose, / Though full of pain, this intellectual being?" and again when God orders the expulsion: "I at first with two fair gifts / Created him endow'd, with Happiness / and Immortality: that fondly lost, / This other serv'd but to eternize woe" (2.146–47, 11.57–60).

17. Augustine, *City of God*, 11.28.

18. *CPEP* 262–63, citing Bauman, *Milton's Arianism*, 133.

19. Hunter, "Meaning of 'Holy Light.'"

20. Davies and Hunter, "Milton's Urania." The article revises Hunter's earlier association of Urania with the Son in his *SEL* essay, "Milton's Urania."

21. Davies and Hunter, "Milton's Urania," 103.

22. Ibid., 108, 97.

23. Milton's Arianism is most clearly expressed in the fourth and fifth chapters of the first book of *De doctrina Christiana*, dedicated to the Son of

God and the Holy Spirit, respectively (OW 8:126–273). The subject has been explained in detail by Michael Bauman in *Milton's Arianism*, and by John Rumrich in "Milton's Arianism: Why It Matters," in Dobranski and Rumrich, *Milton and Heresy*, 75–92. Barbara Lewalski explains the use of the term "Arian" to describe general anti-Trinitarian beliefs in seventeenth century England and the case for Milton's particular anti-Trinitarianism being closely aligned with the narrow definition of Arianism (*Life of John Milton*, 424–28); cf. Campbell and Corns, *John Milton*, 273, 368. The anti-Trinitarian elements of Milton's *De doctrina Christiana* cannot in themselves refute my claims about Milton's triadic structure, for Milton does not need to believe in the consubstantiality of God, Son of God, and Holy Spirit to write of the three successively in the same work (as he clearly does in *De doctrina Christiana*). In fact, the distinctions among Father, Son, and Holy Spirit are far more essential to my argument about Milton's triads than any reflection on consubstantiality, and these distinctions preoccupied most of Milton's discussion of the Son of God in chapter 5. While Milton states that biblical references to the spirit of God often refer to "the Father's virtue and power," he also insists that the spirit of God is "a person," "distinct from God both in fact and number" (OW 8:249, 253, 257).

24. Also acknowledged and cited in Hunter, "Milton's Urania," 35, 39, and in Davies and Hunter, "Milton's Urania," 100.

25. For Milton's distinction between substance (*substantia*) and total essence (*essentia tota*), see OW 8:134–37.

26. *Symposium*, 180d, 187e, in Aristotle, *Works*, 465, 471.

27. See especially Peter Lombard's *Sentences*, book 1, distinction 10, chap. 1, and distinction 17. In Augustine, "only caritas is true love: for only then does man desire an object worthy of devotion. In effect this [the difference between *caritas* and *cupiditas*] is the distinction between the heavenly and the earthly Aphrodite, inherited from Plato by the eros tradition" (Singer, *Nature of Love*, 178). For Aquinas on the Holy Spirit and love, see *Summa contra Gentiles*, 4.19–22; *Summa theologica*, 1.93.5–6.

28. Consider, for example, the familiar epithet "Thrice-great Hermes," or the formula for the distressed epic hero's mournful comparison of himself with luckier men (*Odyssey*, 5.306; *Aeneid*, 1.134).

29. Miller, "Gluttony," 110.

30. See also the argument to book 9 and Milton's assessment of the sins of the Fall (OW 8:413).

31. See, for example, Augustine, *De doctrina Christiana*, book 1, chaps. 3–5, 8, 22, 26–27, 33.

32. See Augustine's Homily 2 on 1 John and book 10 of the *Confessions* (secs. 30–39). See also Thomas à Kempis's *Imitation of Christ*, 3.20.4. See chapter 1 for how this Johannine triad may form the structure for *Paradise Regain'd* as well as *Paradise Lost*.

33. Cannon, *Gospel of John*, 14.

34. Although Augustine points to Plato as the first to recommend the threefold division of physics, logic, and ethics, the Stoics, who were more Aristotelian than Platonic, could have also found a similar triadic division in Aristotle, who states in the *Politics*, "There are admittedly three things by which men are made good and virtuous, and these three things are nature [*phusis*], habit [*ethos*] and reason [*logos*]" (7.1332a40). Though often conflated, *ethos* (habit) and *ēthos* (character, mores) are distinct in Aristotelian thought. See Joe Sachs's introduction to *Nicomachean Ethics* (xi–xvii) and his appended glossary s.v. "character" and "habit."

35. See Rubarth, "Stoic Philosophy of Mind"; "Stoicism," *Internet Encyclopedia of Philosophy*; and Stock, "Guide to Stoicism."

36. See Merritt Hughes's editorial notes in *Complete Poems and Major Prose*, 193n40, 217–18n255, 245n564, 444n504, 479–80nn23–24, 522nn300–08. In the Prolusion "That Sportive Exercises Are Occasionally Not Adverse to Philosophic Studies," Milton playfully derided "Stoic sternness" and the "too-too-rigid Cato," but the tone of the speech demands some skepticism of the author's earnestness (*CPMP* 615–16).

37. See *CPMP* 56nn2, 3; 193n40; 441n363; 635n52.

38. For Augustine on the unwarranted moral prejudice against the Latin word *amor* in favor of *dilectio*, see the *City of God*, 14.7. Augustine also draws attention in this place to the interchangeability of *amor* and *caritas* in Scripture, which Milton also joins in *PL* 12.583–84.

39. For Augustine on the difference between Stoicism and Christianity regarding the passions, see the *City of God*, 14.8–9. For the influence of Stoicism on John Milton, see Shifflett, *Stoicism, Politics and Literature*, and Baumgartner, "Milton and Patience," 203–13.

40. For Milton's response to Comenian reformers like Samuel Hartlib, see Gregory Chaplin's essay, "Education," in Dobranski, *Milton in Context*, 281–91.

41. See, for example, Maurice Kelley's comments in YP 6:538n31, and on pages 79–86 of his introduction to the volume, which explain Jacobus Arminius's views against the supralapsarianism of Calvin and Beza (the elect and the damned predestined before the predestined Fall) and against "the autonomous man of Pelagius, independently working out his own salvation"; Arminius replaces these doctrines with "a synergism wherein the human will cooperates with divine grace to attain an earned rather than a bestowed election to eternal life" (YP 6:80). Kelley argues that if "Milton had not consciously and openly accepted Remonstrant doctrines by the time of *Areopagitica* [1644], he had at least [by then] taken a position that would logically develop into the Arminianism advanced in the *Christian Doctrine*" (YP 6:82). Even so, Kelley may too strongly see election as earned rather than simply affected by human effort. Milton's *De doctrina* insists that virtue is a duty of humankind, but the credit for any goodness is ultimately returned to God.

42. YP 6:85.

43. Augustine, *City of God* 21.15.

44. Ibid., 22.1.

45. Ibid., 8.25.

46. Evagrius of Pontus, *Praktikos*, sec. 56.

47. *Nun's Priest's Tale*, ll. 468–84. In terms that will remind Miltonists of God's self-exonerating speech in *Paradise Lost* 3, Augustine directly explains the compatibility of free will and divine foreknowledge in Augustine's *De libero arbitrio*, 3.4.11. As Brandon R. Peterson ("Augustine") has cogently explained, divine predestination and human free will are theologically compatible if superficially at odds in Augustine's works. Although Augustine's thought developed over time to greater emphasis of divine grace, the pro–free will, anti-Manichean theses of *De libero arbitrio* (c. 395) and the pro–divine sovereignty, anti-Pelagian theses of the *Enchiridion* (c. 421–22) are not contradictory, and are in fact considered together in *City of God* (c. 415) and eloquently in *De gratia et libero arbitrio* (c. 427). This last work, written three years before his death, may be considered Augustine's authoritative final word on the seeming paradox.

48. Augustine, *City of God*, 10.13.

49. Ibid., 17.8.

50. N. K. Sugimura splendidly examines the difficulties inherent in this approach to accommodation in *De doctrina Christiana* and *Paradise Lost*, for "the accommodated picture remains distinct from what God truly is" (*"Matter of Glorious Trial,"* 217). In the *Second Defense*, Milton considers the banquet of the gods as a myth created by the poets to reward their heroes.

51. Rev. 2:17 is also cited in YP 6:255, although the corresponding section in OW 8:191 cites Rev. 2:7 in its place.

52. Augustine, *City of God*, 11.28, p. 488.

53. Augustine, *Confessions*, 7.10, qtd. in part in Kilgour, *From Communion to Cannibalism*, 51, and in Gigante, "Milton's Aesthetics of Eating," 100.

NOTES TO CHAPTER 6

1. Plato, *Works*, 643.

2. See, for example, *Ion* and *Phaedrus*, 244a–245b. Arguments for the ecstatic poet's role in establishing civilization are found both in Sidney's *An Apology for Poetry* and Shelley's *Defence of Poetry*.

3. Hesiod, *Theogony*, 26, 65. See also lines 915–17.

4. I am indebted to John Alvis for noting the correlation between Hesiod and Moses as Milton refers to him in *PL* 1.8–10. The correlation is also discussed by Northrup, "Milton's Hesiodic Cosmology."

5. Hesiod, *Theogony*, 81–84 (my translation).

6. Hesiod, *Theogony*, 97.

7. *CPMP* 50–53, lines 1–5.

8. For the subtle ways in which Milton associates Diodati with the pagan revelries of the Saturnalia and himself with the commemoration of the Nativity of Christ, see Thomas Luxon's notes for Elegy 6 in the Milton Reading Room, www.dartmouth.edu/~milton/reading_room/ elegiarum/ elegy_6/notes.shtml (accessed May 18, 2011).

9. Boccaccio, *Life of Dante*, 43.

10. Tillyard, *Miltonic Setting*, 33.

11. See Hollander, "Milton's Elusive Response." Milton refers to Dante directly in his sonnet "To Mr. Henry Lawes, on His Airs," and in *An Apology for*

Smectymnuus he records his esteem for "the two famous renowners of Beatrice and Laura, who never write but honor of them to whom they devote their verse, displaying sublime and pure thoughts without transgression" (*CPEP* 850).

12. See Catherine Gimelli's essay on Italy in Dobranski, *Milton in Context*, 318–27; Samuel, *Dante and Milton*, 33–34; and Parker, *Milton*, 1:145.

13. E. K. Rand, "Milton in Rustication," *Studies in Philology* 19 (1922): 111, cited in *CPMP* 50.

14. Parker, *Milton*, 1:67–68.

15. Ibid., 1:69.

16. Ibid., 1:70.

17. Fallon, *Milton's Peculiar Grace*, 53. Fallon quotes Parker's position from *Milton*, 1:70.

18. Herrick, *Hesperides*, 39.

19. Horace, Epistles.

20. Rabelais, *Histories of Gargantua and Pantagruel*, 39. For the popularity of Rabelais in Renaissance England, and especially the influence of *Gargantua and Pantagruel* on Robert Burton's *Anatomy of Melancholy*, see Prescott, *Imagining Rabelais*, 1–12. Milton also had indirect access to Rabelais through Burton's *Anatomy of Melancholy*.

21. See the Author's Prologue to Rabelais's *Gargantua* as well as Lucian's *Encomium on Demosthenes*.

22. Lieb, *Dialectics of Creation*, 30n17.

23. See, for example, Campbell and Corns, *John Milton*, 200–02.

24. *CPEP* 41.

25. Schmidt, *Lives of the Poets*, 234.

26. There are also obvious but inexact correspondences between what I call the jovial and the pensive muses and the two classical sources of inspiration that Nietzsche calls the "Dionysian" and the "Apollonian" in *The Birth of Tragedy*.

27. Norwood, *Pindar*, 49–52.

28. "On Shakespeare," 9, 10, in CPMP 63.

29. "On Shakespeare and Milton," in *English Romantic Writers*, ed. David Perkins (New York: Harcourt, Brace, 1967), 628. For later examples of Milton criticism emphasizing his art over his genius, see Wimsatt and Brooks, *Literary Criticism*, 9, 92.

30. Horace, *Ars poetica*, 408–11, in Wimsatt and Brooks, *Literary Criticism*, 93.

31. So Coleridge maintains in the *Biographia literaria*:

> What then shall we say? Even this; that Shakespeare, no mere child of nature; no automaton of genius; no passive vehicle of inspiration possessed by the spirit, not possessing it; first studied patiently, meditated deeply, understood minutely, till knowledge, become habitual and intuitive, wedded itself to his habitual feelings, and at length gave birth to that stupendous power, by which he stands alone, with no equal or second in his own class; to that power which seated him on one of the two glory-smitten summits of the poetic mountain, with Milton as his compeer, not rival. While the former darts himself forth, and passes into all the forms of human character and passion, the one Proteus of the fire and the flood; the other attracts all forms and things to himself, into the unity of his own IDEAL. All things and modes of action shape themselves anew in the being of Milton; while Shakespeare becomes all things, yet for ever remaining himself. (458)

Coleridge's comments prevent us from too quickly dividing genius from skilled labor and nature from art: Shakespeare's stupendous power was painstakingly developed, and the man who attracted and reshaped all things into a pattern of himself could hardly be said to lack genius. Whatever favor Milton might have lost among Romantics for privileging *technē* over *phuē* he must have regained by his extraordinary use of the self as poetic subject.

32. Ben Jonson, "To the Memory of My Beloved, The Author, Mr. William Shakespeare, and What He Hath Left Us," 55–56, 64.

33. *CPMP* 1042. As Hughes mentions, the case for Cyriack Skinner being the anonymous biographer is developed in Parker, *Milton*, 1:xiv–xv.

34. *A Greek- English Lexicon*, ed. Liddell, Scott, and Jones, s.v. *phuē*. In his introduction to *Pindar's Homer*, Gregory Nagy quotes Elroy Bundy's qualification of Pindar's imperative of *phuē* in poetry: "Pindar's phua [phuē] has nothing to do with the natural, unschooled, unconscious genius of the eighteenth and nineteenth centuries, but denotes schooling by experience in the truth of words and actions in a living tradition" (10).

35. *"Tempering"* a weapon is etymologically related to the virtue *"temper-ance"*: the words share the same Latin root, *temperare*. To temper a sword is to strengthen it through opposition, to put hot metal in cold water. This idea of temperance well supports Milton's understanding of virtue strengthened through trial, and of Truth growing stronger by grappling with Falsehood.

36. Conti quotes Callimachus's remark that "Urania discovered the pole and the dance of the stars of heaven" (*Natale Conti's Mythologiae*, 2:656).

37. Plato, *Symposium*, 176e, in *Complete Works*, 462.

38. Plato, *Symposium*, 187c–e, in *Complete Works*, 471. The division that Eryximachus makes between heavenly and common love was first delineated in the speech by Pausanias in *Symposium*, 180d.465, in *Complete Works*, 465.

39. I owe this observation to John Alvis.

40. Augustine, *City of God*, bk. 11, chap. 18.

41. Ibid., bk. 11, chap. 18.

42. Cf. Fallon, *Milton's Peculiar Grace*, 222–25, for a more comprehensive examination of variations of the Bellerophon myth in Hesiod, Pindar, and Plutarch as well as Homer, with the proposition that the varying characteriza-tions of the hero serve as "an echo chamber for the self-referential dialogue that Milton had been having with himself and with his readers for many years" (225).

43. *Iliad*, 6.155.

44. Ibid., 6.168.

45. The phrase in the *Iliad*, 6.202 is ὅν θυμὸν κατέδων.

46. Fallon, "Milton on Himself," in Dobranski, *Milton in Context*, 55, 56; Fallon, *Milton's Peculiar Grace*, 225.

47. Fallon, *Milton's Peculiar Grace*, 206.

48. Cassian, *Conferences*, conf. 5, chap. 20.

49. See, for examples, the notes for the invocation of book 7 in the editions of *Paradise Lost* by Richardson (1734), Vaughan (1894), Teskey (2005), and Kerrigan, Rumrich, and Fallon (2007). For Milton's (and England's) response to the court of Charles II, see Campbell and Corns, *John Milton*, 349.

50. See Rumrich, "Milton on Himself," in Dobranski, *Milton in Context*, 55, 56. See also Graves, *Greek Myths*, 1:113.

51. Fowler and Carey, *Poems of John Milton*, 777.

52. Darbishire, *Early Lives of Milton*, 6.

53. Ibid., 4.

54. Toland, 1.46, qtd. in Parker, *Milton*, 2:1096.

55. Parker, *Milton*, 2:1096.

56. "An Anonymous Life of Milton," in *CPMP* 1042.

57. Parker, *Milton*, 1:584.

58. *CPMP* 1030, 1033.

59. Ibid., 1030.

60. Masson, *Life of John Milton*, 2:209.

61. Ibid., 2:212.

62. Ibid., 1:761.

63. Lewalski, *Life of John Milton*, 103.

64. Parker, *Milton*, 1:194.

65. Ibid., 1:589.

66. Shawcross, *Critical Heritage*, 342.

67. Parker, *Milton* 1:198.

68. Dante, *Paradiso*, 29.106–08.

69. Frederick L. Taft's note directs the reader to Luke 14:35, Mark 7:15, 19–23, and Matt. 15:17 (YP 1:895n146).

70. Campbell and Corns, *John Milton*, 267. Compare Milton's sonnet "To Mr. Cyriack Skinner upon His Blindness" and his account of the onset of his blindness in the *Second Defense* (*CPEP* 1082).

71. For the identity of the Parisian physician, see Hanford, "John Milton Forswears Physic," 23–34. An earlier (June 1652) letter to Leonard Philaras may be found in YP 4:851–53. Regarding the vapors Milton claimed were affecting "spleen and all my viscera": *Bald's Leechbook* offers early remedies for "a windy distention of the milt [i.e., spleen] from eating of apples" and other foods (bk. 2, chap. 39, p. 247). Among the "leechdoms for mistiness of eyes," *Bald's Leechbook* recommends rue (bk. 1, chap. 2, p. 27). The book explains, "From the vapour and steam of ill juices and from nausea cometh mist of eyes and the sharpness and corrupt humour causes" (bk. 1, chap. 2, pp. 27–39).

72. Fallon, *Milton's Peculiar Grace*, 188–89.

73. Campbell and Corns, *John Milton*, 266.

74. Schwartz, *Milton and Maternal Mortality*, 146.

75. Gigante, "Milton's Aesthetics of Eating," 85n14.

76. *CPMP* 1043–44.

77. The poem is "In paradisum amissam summi poetae Johannis Miltoni," signed "S. B., M. D.," and attributed by John Toland to Samuel Barrow, a physician and Milton's friend. The translation used here is found in Kastan's edition of *Paradise Lost*, 2.

78. Greenlaw, "Better Teacher than Aquinas," esp. 211, 213, 215.

79. Ricks, *Milton's Grand Style*, 113.

80. Shawcross, *Self and the World*, 199, 237.

BIBLIOGRAPHY

Abrams, Richard. "Inspiration and Gluttony: The Moral Context of Dante's Poetics of the 'Sweet New Style.'" *Modern Language Notes* 91 (1976): 30–59.

Aeschylus. *Prometheus Bound*. In *Greek Tragedies*, 2nd ed., vol. 1, edited by David Grene and Richmond Lattimore, 61–106. Chicago: University of Chicago Press, 1991.

Alcuin of York. *De virtutibus et vitiis liber*. Translated by Rachel Stone. In *The Heroic Age: A Journal of Early Medieval Northwestern Europe* 16 (2015).

Alderson, Simon J. "'The Augustan Attack on the Pun." *Eighteenth-Century Life* 20, no. 3 (1996): 1–19.

Alvis, John. "Philosophy as Noblest Idolatry in *Paradise Lost*." *Interpretation* 16, no. 2 (1989): 263–84.

Ambrose. *Apologia prophetae David*. Edited and translated by Felix W. Heinrichs. Oberhausen: Karl Maria Laufen, 2013.

———. *Exposition on the Gospel of Luke*. https://sites.google.com/site/aquinasstudybible/home/luke-commentary/st-ambrose-on-luke — latin (in Latin). Accessed June 26, 2017.

Anderson, Judith H., and Jennifer C. Vaught, eds. *Shakespeare and Donne: Genetic Hybrids and the Cultural Imaginary*. New York: Fordham University Press, 2013.

Appelbaum, Robert. *Aguecheek's Beef, Belch's Hiccup, and Other Gastronomic Interjections: Literature, Culture, and Food among the Early Moderns*. Chicago: University of Chicago Press, 2006.

———. "Eve's and Adam's Apple: Horticulture, Taste, and the Flesh of the Forbidden Fruit in *Paradise Lost*." *Milton Quarterly* 36, no. 4 (2002): 221–39.

Aquinas, Thomas. *Summa theologica*. Rev. ed. Translated by the Fathers of the English Dominican Province. New York: Benziger, 1947–48. www.newadvent.org/summa. Accessed June 26, 2017.

Arendt, Hannah. *Love and Saint Augustine*. Edited by Joanna Vecchiarelli Scott and Judith Chelius Stark. Chicago: University of Chicago Press, 1996.

Aristotle. *Nicomachean Ethics*. Translated by Joe Sachs. Newburyport, MA: Focus, 2002.

———. *On the Generation of Animals*. Translated by Arthur Platt. In *Works*, vol. 5.

———. *On the Parts of Animals*. Translated by William Ogle. In *Works*, vol. 5.

———. *On the Soul*. Translated by J. A. Smith. In *Works*, vol. 3.

———. *The Politics*. Translated by H. Rackham. Cambridge, MA: Harvard University Press, 1944.

———. *Works*. 12 vols. Edited by William David Ross and John Alexander Smith. Oxford: Oxford University Press, 1908–52.

Athanasius of Alexandria. *Life of Anthony*. Translated by H. Ellershaw. In *Nicene and Post-Nicene Fathers*, 2nd ser., vol. 4, edited by Philip Schaff and Henry Wace. Buffalo, NY: Christian Literature Publishing, 1892.

Augustine of Hippo. *The City of God against the Pagans*. Translated by R. W. Dyson. Cambridge: Cambridge University Press, 2007.

———. *Confessions*. Translated by J. G. Pilkington. In *Nicene and Post-Nicene Fathers*, 1st ser., vol. 1, edited by Philip Schaff. Buffalo, NY: Christian Literature Publishing, 1887.

———. *De doctrina Christiana*. Ed Carl Hermann Bruder. Lipsiae: C. Tauchnitii, 1838.

———. *De gratia Christi et de peccato originali contra Pelagium*. www.augustinus.it/latino/grazia_cristo. Accessed June 26, 2017.

———. *Expositions on the Psalms*. In *Nicene and Post-Nicene Fathers*, 1st ser., vol. 1, edited by Philip Schaff. Buffalo, NY: Christian Literature Publishing, 1887.

———. "Homily 2 on the First Epistle of John." Translated by H. Browne. In *Nicene and Post-Nicene Fathers*, 1st ser., vol. 7, edited by Philip Schaff, 939–51. Buffalo, NY: Christian Literature Publishing, 1888.

———. *Nicene and Post-Nicene Fathers*. 1st ser., 14 vols. Edited by Philip Schaff. Buffalo, NY: Christian Literature Publishing, 1886–89.

———. *On Christian Doctrine*. Translated by James Shaw. In *Nicene and Post-Nicene Fathers*, 1st ser., vol. 2, edited by Philip Schaff. Buffalo, NY: Christian Literature Publishing, 1887.

———. *On Genesis: On Genesis: A Refutation of the Manichees; Unfinished Literal Commentary on Genesis; The Literal Meaning of Genesis*. Translated by Edmund Hill. New York: New City Press, 2002.

————. *On the Trinity: Books 8–15.* Edited by Gareth B. Matthews. Translated by Stephen McKenna. Cambridge: Cambridge University Press, 2002.

Babb, Lawrence. "The Cave of Spleen." *Review of English Studies* 12, no. 46 (1936): 165–76.

————. "The Physiology and Psychology of the Renaissance." In *Seventeenth-Century British Poetry, 1603–1660*, edited by John Rumrich and Gregory Chaplin, 749–63. New York: Norton, 2006.

Baker, Christopher. "'Greedily she ingorg'd': Eve and the Bread of Life." In *Milton Studies*, vol. 53, edited by Laura L. Knoppers, 95–110. Pittsburgh: Duquesne University Press, 2012.

Bakhtin, Mikhail M. *Rabelais and His World.* Translated by Helene Iswolsky. Bloomington: Indiana University Press, 1984.

Bald's Leechbook. Vol. 2 of *Leechdoms, Wortcunning, and Starcraft of Early England: Being a Collection of Documents, for the Most Part Never Before Printed Illustrating the History of Science in this Country before the Norman Conquest.* 3 vols. Edited by T. O. Cockayne. London: Rerum Britannicarum Medii Aevi Scriptores, 1864–66.

Bauman, Michael. *Milton's Arianism.* Frankfurt: Lang, 1987.

————. *A Scripture Index to John Milton's "De Doctrina Christiana."* Binghamton, NY: Medieval and Renaissance Texts and Studies, 1989.

Baumgartner, Paul R. "Milton and Patience." *Studies in Philology* 60, no. 2 (1963): 203–13.

Bede. *Letter to Egbert.* In *The Historical Works of the Venerable Bede*, vol. 2, *Biographical Writings, Letters and Chronology.* Edited by J. A. Giles, 154–55. London: 1845.

Bentley, Richard, ed. *Milton's "Paradise Lost": A New Edition.* 1732. In *Milton, 1732–1801: The Critical Heritage*, edited by John T. Shawcross. London: Routledge and Kegan Paul, 1972.

Bloomfield, Morton. *The Seven Deadly Sins.* Lansing: Michigan State College Press, 1952.

Boccaccio, Giovanni. *The Life of Dante.* Translated by James Robinson Smith. In *The Earliest Lives of Dante*, edited by Albert S. Cook, 8–78. New York: Holt, 1901.

Boethius. *The Consolation of Philosophy.* Translated by P. G. Walsh. Oxford: Oxford University Press, 2008.

Borlik, Todd A. *Ecocriticism and Early Modern English Literature*. New York: Routledge, 2011.

Boswell, Jackson C. *Milton's Library: A Catalogue of the Remains of John Milton's Library and an Annotated Reconstruction of Milton's Library and Ancillary Readings*. New York: Garland, 1975.

Bosworth, Joseph. *A Dictionary of the Anglo-Saxon Language*. London: Longman, 1838.

Bradley, S. A. J., trans. and ed. *Genesis*. In *Anglo-Saxon Poetry*, 10–48. London: J. M. Dent, 1982.

Brakke, David. *Demons and the Making of the Monk: Spiritual Combat in Early Christianity*. Cambridge, MA: Harvard University Press, 2006.

Brodwin, Leonora. "Milton and the Renaissance Circe." In *Milton Studies*, vol. 6, edited by James D. Simmonds, 21–83. Pittsburgh: University of Pittsburgh Press, 1974.

Browning, Judith E. "Sin, Eve, and Circe: *Paradise Lost* and the Ovidian Circe Tradition." In *Milton Studies*, vol. 26, edited by James D. Simmonds, 135–57. Pittsburgh: University of Pittsburgh Press, 1991.

Burn, A. E., ed. *The Preces Privatae of Lancelot Andrewes*. Translated by F. E. Brightman. London: Methuen, 1908.

Burton, Robert. *The Anatomy of Melancholy*. Edited by Floyd Dell and Paul Jordan-Smith. New York: Tudor, 1927.

Byles, Alfred T. P., ed. *The Book of the Order of Chivalry*. New York: Routledge, 2010.

Caesarius of Heisterbach. *Dialogus miraculorum, Textum ad quatuor codicum manuscriptorum editionisque principis fidem accurate recognovit Josephus Strange*. Coloniae: J. M. Heberle, 1851.

Campbell, Gordon, and Thomas N. Corns. *John Milton: Life, Work, and Thought*. Oxford: Oxford University Press, 2008.

Campbell, W. Gardner. "Paradisal Appetite and Cusan Food in *Paradise Lost*." In *Arenas of Conflict: Milton and the Unfettered Mind*, edited by Kristen Pruitt McColgan and Charles W. Durham, 239–50. Cranbury, NJ: Associated University Presses, 1997.

Cannon, William R. *The Gospel of John*. Nashville: Upper Room, 1985.

Carruthers, Mary. *The Book of Memory: A Study of Memory in Medieval Culture*. Cambridge: Cambridge University Press, 2008.

Cassian, St. John. *Conferences.* Translated by Edgar C. S. Gibson. In *A Select Library of Nicene and Post-Nicene Fathers of the Christian Church,* 2nd ser., vol. 11. Revised and edited by Kevin Knight. New York: Christian Literature Publishing, 1894. www.newadvent.org/fathers/3508.htm.

Cavendish, Margaret. *The World's Olio.* London, 1655.

Chaucer, Geoffery. *The Riverside Chaucer.* 3rd ed. Edited by Larry Benson. Boston: Houghton, 1987.

Cicero. *Tusculan Disputations.* Translated by C. D. Yonge. New York: Harper, 1877.

Coffin, Charles M., ed. *The Complete Poetry and Selected Prose of John Donne.* New York: Modern Library, 1994.

Coiro, Ann Baynes. "'To Repair the Ruins of Our First Parents': *Of Education* and Fallen Adam." *Studies in English Literature, 1500–1900* 28 (1988): 133–47.

Coleridge, Samuel Taylor. Excerpts from *Biographia Literaria.* In *English Romantic Writers,* edited by David Perkins, 448–91. New York: Harcourt, Brace, 1967.

Conti, Natale. *Natale Conti's Mythologiae.* 2 vols. Translated by John Mulryan and Stephen Brown. Tempe: Arizona Center for Medieval and Renaissance Studies, 2006.

Corns, Thomas N. "Obscenity, Slang and Indecorum in Milton's Prose." *Prose Studies* 3 (1980): 5–14.

Corns, Thomas N., ed. *The Milton Encyclopedia.* New Haven, CT: Yale University Press, 2012.

Cox, Lee Sheridan. "Food-Word Imagery in *Paradise Regained.*" *English Literary History* 28, no. 3 (1961): 225–43.

Curry, Walter Clyde. *Milton's Ontology, Cosmology, and Physics.* Lexington: University of Kentucky Press, 1957.

Dales, Douglas. "Introduction." In *Alcuin: His Life and Legacy,* 15–17. Cambridge: James Clark, 2012.

Danielson, Dennis. "Milton's Arminianism and *Paradise Lost.*" In *Milton Studies,* vol. 12, ed. James D. Simmonds, 47–73. Pittsburgh: University of Pittsburgh Press, 1979.

———. *Milton's Good God: A Study in Literary Theodicy.* Cambridge: Cambridge University Press, 1982.

Danielson, Dennis, ed. *The Book of the Cosmos: Imagining the Universe from Heraclitus to Hawking.* Cambridge, MA: Perseus, 2001.

———. *The Cambridge Companion to Milton*. 2nd ed. Cambridge: Cambridge University Press, 1999.

Dante Alighieri. *The Divine Comedy*. Translated by Allen Mandelbaum. New York: Knopf, 1995.

———. *The Inferno*. Translated by John Ciardi. New York: Signet Classics, 2009.

Darbishire, Helen, ed. *The Early Lives of Milton*. London: Constable, 1932.

Davies, Stevie, and William B. Hunter Jr. "Milton's Urania: 'The Meaning, not the Name I Call.'" *Studies in English Literature, 1500–1900* 28, no. 1 (1988): 95–111.

Davis, Donald M. "The Technique of Guilt by Association in *Paradise Lost*." *South Atlantic Bulletin* 37 (1972): 29–34.

Demetz, Peter. "The Elm and the Vine: Notes toward the History of a Marriage Topos." *PMLA* 73, no. 5 (1958): 521–32.

Dobranski, Stephen B. "Clustering and Curling Locks: The Matter of Hair in *Paradise Lost*." *PMLA* 125, no. 2 (2010): 337–53.

Dobranski, Stephen B., ed. *Milton in Context*. New York: Cambridge University Press, 2010.

Dobranski, Stephen B., and John P. Rumrich, eds. *Milton and Heresy*. Cambridge: Cambridge University Press, 2009.

Dodds, Lara. *The Literary Invention of Margaret Cavendish*. Pittsburgh: Duquesne University Press, 2013.

Donnelly, Phillip. "'Matter' versus Body: The Character of Milton's Monism." *Milton Quarterly* 33, no. 3 (1999): 79–85.

DuRocher, Richard J. *Milton among the Romans: The Pedagogy and Influence of Milton's Latin Curriculum*. Pittsburgh: Duquesne University Press, 2001.

Edwards, Karen. "Cormorant." *Milton Quarterly* 39, no. 4 (2005): 258–59.

Empson, William. *Milton's God*. Rev. ed. Cambridge: Cambridge University Press, 1981.

Evagrius of Pontus. *Praktikos*. www.earlychurchtexts.com. Accessed March 20, 2017.

Fallon, Robert T. "Milton's 'defenseless doors': The Limits of Irony." *Milton Quarterly* 13 (1979): 146–51.

Fallon, Stephen M. *Milton among the Philosophers: Poetry and Materialism in Seventeenth- Century England*. Ithaca, NY: Cornell University Press, 1991.

———. "Milton's Arminianism and the Authorship of *De Doctrina Christiana*." *Texas Studies in Literature and Language* 41, no. 2 (1999): 103–27.

———. *Milton's Peculiar Grace: Self-Representation and Authority.* Ithaca, NY: Cornell University Press, 2007.

Fallows, Noel. Translated by *The Book of the Order of Chivalry.* Woodbridge, UK: Boydell Press, 2013.

Fiore, Peter Amadeus. *Milton and Augustine: Patterns of Augustinian Thought in "Paradise Lost."* University Park: Pennsylvania State University Press, 1981.

Fish, Stanley. *Surprised by Sin.* 2nd ed. Cambridge, MA: Harvard University Press, 1998.

———. "Transmuting the Lump: *Paradise Lost,* 1942–79." In *Doing What Comes Naturally: Change, Rhetoric, and the Practice of Theory in Literary and Legal Studies,* 247–93. Durham, NC: Duke University Press, 1989.

Fitzpatrick, Joan. *Food in Shakespeare: Early Modern Dietaries and the Plays.* Burlington, VT: Ashgate, 2007.

Fletcher, Harris Francis. *Milton's Rabbinical Readings.* New York: Gordian Press, 1967.

Friedman, Donald M. "Divisions on a Ground: 'Sex' in *Paradise Lost.*" In *Of Poetry and Politics: New Essays on Milton and His World,* edited by Paul G. Stanwood, 203–19. Binghamton, NY: Medieval and Renaissance Texts and Studies, 1995.

Furley, David J., and J. S. Wilkie. *Galen: On Respiration and the Arteries.* Princeton, NJ: Princeton University Press, 1984.

Galen. *On the Natural Faculties.* Translated by A. J. Brock. Cambridge, MA: Harvard University Press, 1916.

———. *On the Properties of Foodstuffs.* Translated by Owen Powell. Cambridge: Cambridge University Press, 2003.

Geisweidt, Edward James. "'Like Life in Excrements': Natural Philosophy, Hair, and the Limits of the Body's Vitality in Early Modern England." PhD diss., University of Alabama, 2010.

Genesis Rabbah. 10 vols. Translated by H. Freedman and Maurice Simon. London: Soncino Press, 1961.

The Geneva Bible and Notes (1599). *The Reformed Reader.* www.reformed reader.org/gbn/en.htm. Accessed June 26, 2017.

Gigante, Denise. "Milton's Aesthetics of Eating." *Diacritics* 3, no. 2 (2000): 88–112.

———. *Taste: A Literary History.* New Haven, CT: Yale University Press, 2005.

Gilbert, Allan H. "Milton's Defense of Bawdry." In *South Atlantic Modern Language Association Studies in Milton*, edited by J. Max Patrick, 54–71. Gainesville: University of Florida Press, 1953.

Gill, John. *Exposition of the Old Testament*. www.freegrace.net/gill. Accessed May 18, 2011.

Goldman, Jack. "Perspectives of Raphael's Meal in *Paradise Lost*, Book V." *Milton Quarterly* 11, no. 2 (1977): 31–37.

Goldstein, David B. *Eating and Ethics in Shakespeare's England*. Cambridge: Cambridge University Press, 2013.

Goldstein, David B., and Amy L. Tigner, eds. *Culinary Shakespeare: Staging Food and Drink in Early Modern England*. Pittsburgh: Duquesne University Press, 2016.

Gower, John. *Confessio Amantis*. Vol. 3. Edited by Russell A. Peck. Translated by Andrew Galloway. Kalamazoo, MI: Medieval Institute Publications, 2004.

———. *Mirour de l'omme*. Translated by William Burton Wilson. PhD diss., University of Miami, 1970.

Graves, Robert. *The Greek Myths*. 2 vols. London: Folio Society, 1996.

Greenlaw, Edwin. "'A Better Teacher than Aquinas.'" *Studies in Philology* 14 (1917): 196–217.

Gregory the Great. *Moralia in Job*. Translated by John Henry Parker. London: J. G. F. and J. Rivington, 1844. www.lectionarycentral.com/Gregorymoraliaindex.html. Accessed June 26, 2017.

Grell, Ole Peter, ed. *Paracelsus: The Man and His Reputation, His Ideas and Their Transformation*. Leiden, Netherlands: Koninklijke Brill, 1998.

Grossman, Marshall. "Milton's 'Transubstantiate': Interpreting the Sacrament in *Paradise Lost*." *Milton Quarterly* 16, no. 2 (1982): 42–47.

Gulden, Ann Torday. "Milton's Eve and Wisdom: The 'Dinner-Party' Scene in *Paradise Lost*." *Milton Quarterly* 32, no. 4 (1998): 137–43.

Hale, John K., and J. Donald Cullington, eds. *The Complete Works of John Milton*. Vol. 8, *De Doctrina Christiana*. Oxford: Oxford University Press, 2012.

Hampton, Bryan Adam. *Fleshly Tabernacles: Milton and the Incarnational Poetics of Revolutionary England*. Notre Dame, IN: University of Notre Dame Press, 2012.

Hanford, James H. "John Milton Forswears Physic." *Bulletin of the Medical Library Association* 32 (1944): 23–34.

Hart, D. Bentley. "Matter, Monism, and Narrative: An Essay on the Metaphysics of *Paradise Lost.*" *Milton Quarterly* 30, no. 1 (1996): 16–27.

Hawkins, Sherman. "Samson's Catharsis." In *Milton Studies*, vol. 2, edited by James D. Simmonds, 211–30. Pittsburgh: University of Pittsburgh Press, 1970.

Hazlitt, William. "On Shakespeare and Milton." In *English Romantic Writers*. Edited by David Perkins, 620–33. New York: Harcourt, Brace, 1967.

Heninger, S. K., Jr. *Touches of Sweet Harmony: Pythagorean Cosmology and Renaissance Poetics*. Tacoma, WA: Angelico Press, 2013.

Henry, Matthew. *Commentary on the Whole Bible* (1706–1721). *Christian Classics Ethereal Library*. www.ccel.org/ccel/henry/mhc.i.html. Accessed May 18, 2011.

Hequembourg, Stephen. "Monism and Metaphor in *Paradise Lost.*" In *Milton Studies*, vol. 53, edited by Laura L. Knoppers, 139–67. Pittsburgh: Duquesne University Press, 2012.

Herman, Peter C. "C. S. Lewis and the New Milton Criticism." *Milton Quarterly* 45, no. 4 (2011): 258–66.

Herrick, Robert. *Hesperides, or, Works both Human and Divine of Robert Herrick*. Edited by Henry Morley. London: Routledge, 1884.

Hesiod. *Theogony*. Translated by M. L. West. Oxford: Oxford University Press, 1999.

Hiltner, Ken. *Milton and Ecology*. Cambridge: Cambridge University Press, 2003.

Hilton, Walter. *The Scale of Perfection*. Translated by Serenus Cressy. 1659. Reprint, London: John Philp, 1870.

Hobbes, Thomas. *Leviathan*. Edited by Edwin Curley. Indianapolis: Hackett, 1994.

Hodges, Horace Jeffery. "Fruit Uncropt and Fruit Cropt: Unnoticed Wordplay in *Paradise Lost?*" *Milton Quarterly* 45, no. 4 (2011): 252–57.

Hollander, Robert. "Milton's Elusive Response to Dante's *Divine Comedy.*" *Milton Quarterly* 45, no. 1 (2011): 1–24.

The Holy Bible. King James Version. 1611.

Homer. *The Iliad*. Translated by Richmond Lattimore. Chicago: University of Chicago Press, 1951.

———. *The Odyssey*. Translated by Richmond Lattimore. New York: HarperCollins, 1965.

Horace. *Epistles*. In *The Poetical Works of Christopher Smart*, vol. 5, *The Works of Horace, Translated into Verse*, edited by Karina Williamson. Oxford: Clarendon Press, 1996.

Hunt, Leigh. *Table Talk: To Which Are Added Imaginary Conversations of Pope and Swift*. New York: Appleton, 1879.

Hunter, William B., Jr. "The Meaning of 'Holy Light' in *Paradise Lost* III." *Modern Language Notes* 74 (1959): 589–92.

———. "Milton's Arianism Reconsidered." In *Bright Essence: Studies in Milton's Theology*, edited by William B. Hunter, C. A. Patrides, and J. H. Adamson. Salt Lake City: University of Utah Press, 1973.

———. "Milton's Urania." *Studies in English Literature, 1500–1900* 4, no. 1 (1964): 35–42.

Hunter, William B., Jr., gen. ed. *A Milton Encyclopedia*. 9 vols. Lewisburg, PA: Bucknell University Press, 1978–83.

Hunter, William B., C. A. Patrides, and J. H. Adamson. *Bright Essence: Studies in Milton's Theology*. Salt Lake City: University of Utah Press, 1973.

Huntley, John F. "Gourmet Cooking and the Vision of Paradise in *Paradise Lost*." *Xavier University Studies* 8, no. 2 (1969): 44–54.

Jerome. Letter 22, "To Eustochium." Translated by W. H. Fremantle, G. Lewis, and W. G. Martley. In *Nicene and Post-Nicene Fathers, Second Series*, vol. 6, edited by Philip Schaff and Henry Wace. Buffalo, NY: Christian Literature Publishing, 1893. Revised and edited for *New Advent Encyclopedia* by Kevin Knight.

John Chrysostom. "Homily 13 on Matthew." Translated by George Prevost. In *A Select Library of Nicene and Post-Nicene Fathers of the Christian Church*, 1st ser., vol. 10, edited by Philip Schaff. Buffalo, NY: Christian Literature Publishing, 1894. Revised and edited for *New Advent Encyclopedia* by Kevin Knight.

John of the Cross. *The Dark Night of the Soul*. Kila, MT: Kessinger, 1995.

Johnson, Kimberly. "Raphael's 'Potent Tongue': Power and Spectacle in *Paradise Lost*." *Milton Quarterly* 46, no. 4 (2012): 205–18.

Jones, Edward, ed. *Young Milton: The Emerging Author, 1620–1642*. Oxford: Oxford University Press, 2013.

Jonson, Ben. "To the Memory of My Beloved, the Author, Mr. William Shakespeare, and What He Hath Left Us." In *Seventeenth-Century British Poetry: 1603–1660*, edited by John P. Rumrich and Gregory Chaplin. New York: Norton, 2006.

Jordan, Richard Douglas. *The Quiet Hero: Figures of Temperance in Spenser, Donne, Milton, and Joyce.* Washington, DC: Catholic University of America Press, 1989.

Juvenal. *Satires.* Translated by G. G. Ramsay. Christian Classics Ethereal Library. www.ccel.org/ccel/pearse/morefathers/files/juvenal_satires_10.htm. Accessed May 18, 2011.

Kass, Leon. *The Hungry Soul: Eating and the Perfecting of our Nature.* Chicago: University of Chicago Press, 1999.

Kelley, Maurice. *This Great Argument: A Study of Milton's "De Doctrina Christiana" as a Gloss upon "Paradise Lost."* Gloucester, MA: Peter Smith, 1962.

Kelly, John. *Sermons.* Edited by T. Croskell. Manchester: Deschamps, 1897.

Kermode, Frank. *Shakespeare, Spenser, Donne.* London: Routledge, 1971.

Kerrigan, William. *The Sacred Complex: On the Psychogenesis of "Paradise Lost."* Cambridge: Harvard University Press, 1983.

Kilgour, Maggie. *From Communion to Cannibalism: An Anatomy of Metaphors of Incorporation.* Princeton, NJ: Princeton University Press, 1990.

King, John N. *Milton and Religious Controversy: Satire and Polemic in "Paradise Lost."* Cambridge: Cambridge University Press, 2000.

Klein, Joan L. "The Demonic Bacchus in Spenser and Milton." In *Milton Studies,* vol. 21, edited by James D. Simmonds, 93–118. Pittsburgh: University of Pittsburgh Press, 1985.

Knoppers, Laura, ed. *The Complete Works of John Milton.* Vol. 2, *The 1671 Poems: Paradise Regain'd and Samson Agonistes.* Oxford: Oxford University Press, 2008.

Kolbrener, William. "'Plainly Partial': The Liberal *Areopagitica.*" *English Literary History* 60, no. 1 (1993): 57–78.

Kolve, V. A. "Chaucer's Wheel of False Religion: Theology and Obscenity in *The Summoner's Tale.*" In *The Centre and Its Compass,* edited by Robert A. Taylor et al., 268–70. Kalamazoo, MI: Medieval Institute Publications, 1993.

Kraus, Stefen. *Les sept péchés mortels en référence au "Roman de la Rose."* Norderstedt, Germany: Druck und Bindung, 2006.

Kuhns, Oscar. "Dante's Influence on Milton." *Modern Language Notes* 13 (1898): 1–6.

Lancashire, Ian, ed. *Elizabethan Homilies (1603).* Toronto: University of Toronto Library, 1997. *Renaissance Electronic Texts.* www.library.utoronto.ca/utel/elizhom.html. Accessed June 26, 2017.

Langland, William. *Piers Plowman* (B Text). Edited by Elizabeth Robertson and Stephen H. A. Shepherd. Translated by E. Talbot Donaldson. New York: Norton, 2006.

Lanyer, Aemilia. "Eve's Apology in Defense of Women." In *Salve Deus Rex Judaeorum*. 1611.

Lehnhof, Kent. "'Intestine War' and 'The Smell of Mortal Change': Troping the Digestive Tract in Milton's *Paradise Lost*." In *Shared Space: Rethinking the Sacred and the Profane in English Renaissance Literature*, edited by Mary A. Papazian, 278–300. Newark: University of Delaware Press, 2008.

———. "Scatology and the Sacred in Milton's *Paradise Lost*." *English Literary Renaissance* 37 (2007): 429–49.

Leonard, John. *Faithful Labourers: A Reception History of "Paradise Lost."* 2 vols. Oxford: Oxford University Press, 2013.

Levi-Strauss, Claude. *The Origin of Table Manners*. Translated by John and Doreen Weightman. New York: Harper and Row, 1978.

———. *The Raw and the Cooked*. Translated by John and Doreen Weightman. New York: Harper and Row, 1969.

Lewalski, Barbara K. *The Life of John Milton*. Oxford: Blackwell, 2003.

———. "Structure and Symbolism of Vision in Michael's Prophecy, *Paradise Lost*, Books XI–XII." *Philological Quarterly* 42 (1963): 25–35.

Lewis, C. S. *The Discarded Image*. Cambridge: Cambridge University Press, 1964.

———. *A Preface to "Paradise Lost."* London: Oxford University Press, 1942.

———. *The Screwtape Letters*. New York: Harper Collins, 2001.

Lewis, Charlton T., and Charles Short. *A Latin Dictionary*. Oxford: Clarendon Press, 1879.

Liddell, Henry George, and Robert Scott. *A Greek-English Lexicon*. Revised and augmented by Henry Stuart Jones. Oxford: Clarendon Press, 1940.

Lieb, Michael. *The Dialectics of Creation: Patterns of Birth and Regeneration in "Paradise Lost."* Amherst: University of Massachusetts Press, 1970.

———. "Further Thoughts on Satan's Journey through Chaos." *Milton Quarterly* 12 (1978): 126–33.

Link, Luther. *The Devil: A Mask without a Face*. London: Reaktion Books, 1995.

Lombard, Peter. *The Sentences. Book 1: The Mystery of The Trinity*. Translated by Giulio Silano. Toronto: Pontifical Institute of Mediaeval Studies, 2007.

Low, Anthony. "Angels and Food in *Paradise Lost*." In *Milton Studies*, vol. 1, edited by James D. Simmonds, 135–45. Pittsburgh: University of Pittsburgh Press, 1969.

Lucian of Samosata. "Demosthenes: An Encomium." In *Works*, 4 vols., translated by H. W. Fowler and F. G. Fowler, 4:145–64. Oxford: Clarendon Press, 1905.

Lupton, Thomas. *All for Money*. Edited by John S. Farmer. Tudor Facsimile Texts, 1910. University of Toronto digital archives.

Luxon, Thomas. "Elegy 6 Notes." *Milton Reading Room*. www.dartmouth.edu/~milton/reading_room/elegiarum/elegy_6/text.shtml. Accessed June 26, 2017.

MacDonald, William C. "Singing Sin: Michel Beheim's 'Little Book of the Seven Deadly Sins,' a German Pre-Reformation Religious Text for the Laity." In *Sin in Medieval and Early Modern Culture: The Tradition of the Seven Deadly Sin*, edited by Richard G. Newhauser and Susan J. Ridyard, 282–303. Woodbridge: York Medieval Press, 2012.

Machacek, Gregory. *Milton and Homer: "Written to Aftertimes."* Pittsburgh: Duquesne University Press, 2011.

Magoun, F. P., Jr. "The Chaucer of Spenser and Milton." *Modern Philology* 25, no. 2 (1927): 129–36.

Marcus, Leah S. *The Politics of Mirth: Jonson, Herrick, Milton, Marvell, and the Defense of Old Holiday Pastimes*. Chicago: University of Chicago Press, 1986.

Martz, Louis L. *The Paradise Within: Studies in Vaughan, Traherne, and Milton*. New Haven, CT: Yale University Press, 1964.

Masson, David. *Life of John Milton*. 7 vols. 1858–94. Gloucester, MA: Peter Smith, 1965.

McCluskey, Peter. "Milton and the Winds of Folly." In *Arenas of Conflict: Milton and the Unfettered Mind*, edited by Kristen Pruitt McColgan and Charles W. Durham, 227–38. Selinsgrove, PA: Susquehanna University Press, 1997.

McColley, Diane. *A Gust for Paradise: Milton's Eden and the Visual Arts*. Urbana-Champaign: University of Illinois Press, 1993.

McDowell, Nicholas, and Nigel Smith, eds. *The Oxford Handbook of Milton*. Oxford: Oxford University Press, 2009.

Mechthild of Magdeburg. *The Flowing Light of the Godhead*. Edited by Frank Tobin. Mahwah, NJ: Paulist Press, 1998.

———. *Mechthild of Magdeburg: Selections from "The Flowing Light of the Godhead."* Translated by Elizabeth A. Anderson. Woodbridge: Boydell and Brewer, 2003.

Melville, Herman. "Ambergris." In *Moby-Dick*, 2nd ed., chap. 92. New York: Norton, 2002.

Merchant, Carolyn. *The Death of Nature: Women, Ecology, and the Scientific Revolution.* San Francisco: Harper and Row, 1980.

Miller, William Ian. "Gluttony." *Representations* 60 (1997): 92–112.

Milton, John. *A Commonplace Book.* Edited by Alfred J. Horwood. Cornell University Library Digital Collections, 1877.

———. *Complete Poems and Major Prose.* Edited Merritt Y. Hughes. New York: Odyssey, 1957.

———. *The Complete Poetry and Essential Prose of John Milton.* Edited by William Kerrigan, John P. Rumrich, and Stephen M. Fallon. New York: Random House, 2007.

———. *Complete Prose Works of John Milton.* Edited by Don M. Wolfe. 8 vols. New Haven: Yale University Press, 1953–82.

———. *The Complete Works of John Milton.* Vol. 2, *The 1671 Poems: Paradise Regain'd and Samson Agonistes.* Edited by Laura L. Knoppers. Oxford: Oxford University Press, 2008.

———. *Paradise Lost.* Edited by David Scott Kastan. Indianapolis: Hackett, 2005.

———. *Paradise Lost.* Edited by Jonathan Richardson. London: Knapton, 1734.

———. *Paradise Lost.* Edited by Gordon Teskey. New York: Norton, 2005.

———. *Paradise Lost.* Edited by Robert Vaughan. London: Cassell, 1894.

———. *The Poems of John Milton.* Edited by Alistair Fowler and John Carey. London: Longmans, 1968.

———. *The Works of John Milton.* Edited by F. A. Patterson et al. 20 vols. New York: Columbia University Press, 1931–40.

Mintz, Susannah B. "'On an empty stomach': Milton's Food Imagery and Disordered Eating." In *Reassembling Truth: Twenty-First Century Milton,* edited by Charles W. Durham and Kristen A. Pruitt, 145–72. Selinsgrove, PA: Susquehanna University Press, 2003.

Morkan, Joel. "Wrath and Laughter: Milton's Ideas on Satire." *Studies in Philology* 69 (1972): 475–95.

Mulryan, John, ed. *Milton and the Middle Ages.* Lewisburg, PA: Bucknell University Press, 1982.

Nagy, Gregory. *Pindar's Homer.* Baltimore: Johns Hopkins University Press, 1990.

Netzley, Ryan. *Reading, Desire, and the Eucharist in Early Modern Religious Poetry.* Toronto: University of Toronto Press, 2011.

Neusner, Jacob, ed. *Sifré to Numbers: An American Translation and Explanation.* Vol. 2. Lanham, MD: University Press of America, 1986.

Nevalainen, Terttu. *An Introduction to Early Modern English.* Edinburgh: Edinburgh University Press, 2006.

The New American Bible. Rev. ed. Oxford: Oxford University Press, 2011.

Newhauser, Richard. "The Parson's Tale and Its Generic Affiliations." In *Closure in "The Canterbury Tales": The Role of the Parson's Tale,* edited by David Raybin and Linda Tarte Holley, 45–76. Kalamazoo, MI: Medieval Institute Publications, 2000.

Newhauser, Richard G., and Susan J. Ridyard, eds. *Sin in Medieval and Early Modern Culture: The Tradition of the Seven Deadly Sins.* Woodbridge: York Medieval Press, 2012.

Nicolson, Marjorie Hope. *A Reader's Guide to John Milton.* Syracuse: Syracuse University Press, 1963.

Northrup, Mark D. "Milton's Hesiodic Cosmology." *Comparative Literature* 33, no. 4 (1981): 305–20.

Norwood, Gilbert. *Pindar.* Berkeley: University of California Press, 1945.

Otten, Charlotte. "Homer's Moly and Milton's Rue." *Huntington Library Quarterly* 33, no. 4 (1970): 361–72.

Ovid. *Metamorphoses.* Translated by Arthur Golding. Philadelphia: Paul Dry Books, 2000.

Pagel, Walter. *Paracelsus: An Introduction to Philosophical Medicine in the Era of the Renaissance.* 2nd ed. Basel: S. Karger Publications, 1984.

Paracelsus. *The Hermetic and Alchemical Writings of Paracelsus.* Translated by Arthur Edward Waite. London: J. Elliot, 1894.

Parish, John E. "Milton and the Well-Fed Angel." *English Miscellany* 18 (1967): 87–109.

Parker, William Riley. *Milton: A Biography.* 2 vols. Oxford: Oxford University Press, 1968.

Partner, Jane. "Satanic Vision and Acrostics in *Paradise Lost.*" *Essays in Criticism* 57, no. 2 (2007): 129–46.

Paster, Gail Kern. *The Body Embarrassed: Drama and the Disciplines of Shame in Early Modern England.* Ithaca, NY: Cornell University Press, 1993.

Pender, Stephen, and Nancy Struever, eds. *Rhetoric and Medicine in Early Modern Europe.* Burlington, VT: Ashgate, 2012.

Peterson, Brandon R. "Augustine: Advocate of Free Will, Defender of Predestination." *Notre Dame Journal of Undergraduate Research* (2005). Web.

Pico della Mirandola, Giovanni. *Oration on the Dignity of Man.* Translated by A. Robert Caponigri. Washington, DC: Gateway, 1956.

Plato. *Complete Works.* Translated by Donald J. Zeyl. Edited by John M. Cooper. Indianapolis: Hackett, 1997.

Plotinus. *Enneads.* Translated by Stephen MacKenna. Revised by B. S. Page. London: Faber and Faber, 1956.

Plummer, John Francis, ed. *The Summoner's Tale: A Variorum Edition of the Works of Geoffrey Chaucer.* Vol. 2. Norman: University of Oklahoma Press, 1995.

Poole, Kristen. "With Such Joy Surcharg'd: The Predicament of Satiety in Patristic Theology and *Paradise Lost.*" *Milton Quarterly* 49, no. 1 (2015): 1–22.

Pope, Alexander. *The Dunciad.* Oxford: Clarendon Press, 1928.

Prescott, Anne Lake. *Imagining Rabelais in Renaissance England.* New Haven, CT: Yale University Press, 1998.

Prose, Francine. *Gluttony.* New York: Oxford University Press, 2003.

Psellus. *On the Operation of Daemons.* Translated by Marcus Collisson. www.esotericarchives.com/psellos/daemonibus.pdf. Accessed May 16, 2017.

Pseudo-Chrysostom. "Homilia quinta ex capite quarto." In *Opus imperfectum in Mattheum,* edited by J.-P. Migne. The Electronic *Manipulus florum* Project. web.wlu.ca/history/cnighman/OpusImperfectum.pdf. Accessed June 26, 2017.

Rabelais, François. *The Histories of Gargantua and Pantagruel.* Translated by J. M. Cohen. London: Penguin, 1955.

Raymond, Joad. *Milton's Angels: The Early Modern Imagination.* Oxford: Oxford University Press, 2010.

Raymond of Peñafort. *Summa de poenitentia et matrimonio cum glossis Joannis de Friburgo.* Rome, 1603.

Reid, David. "Spirits Odorous." *Milton Quarterly* 25, no. 4 (1991): 140–43.

Reiss, Timothy J. *Mirages of the Selfe: Patterns of Personhood in Ancient and Early Modern Europe.* Stanford, CA: Stanford University Press, 2003.

Revard, Stella P. *Milton and the Tangles of Neaera's Hair: The Making of the 1645 Poems.* Columbia: University of Missouri Press, 1997.

Reynolds, Rickey J. "Milton's Adam and the Angels: A Dialogue between Classicism and Christianity in *Paradise Lost.*" PhD diss., University of Dallas, 1980.

Ricks, Christopher. *Milton's Grand Style.* Oxford: Clarendon Press, 1963.

Roberts, Jeanne Addison. "Animals as Agents of Revelation: The Horizontalizing of the Great Chain of Being in Shakespeare's Comedies." In *Shakespearean Comedy,* edited by Maurice Charney, 79–96. New York: New York Literary Forum, 1980.

Roebuck, Thomas. "Milton and the Confessionalization of Antiquarianism." In *Young Milton: The Emerging Author, 1620–1642,* edited by Edward Jones, 48–71. Oxford: Oxford University Press, 2013.

Rogers, John. *The Matter of Revolution: Science, Poetry and Politics in the Age of Milton.* Ithaca, NY: Cornell University Press, 1998.

Rosenwein, Barbara. *Generations of Feeling: A History of Emotions, 600–1700.* Cambridge: Cambridge University Press, 2016

Rousseau, Jean-Jacques. *The First and Second Discourses.* Edited by Roger D. Masters. Translated by Roger D. and Judith R. Masters. New York: St. Martin's Press, 1964.

Rovang, Paul. "Milton's War in Heaven as Apocalyptic Drama: 'Thy Foes Justly Hast in Derision.'" *Milton Quarterly* 28 (1994): 28–35.

Rubarth, Scott. "Stoic Philosophy of Mind." *Internet Encyclopedia of Philosophy.* 2011. www.iep.utm.edu/stoicmind. Accessed June 26, 2017.

Ruck, Carl A. P., and Danny Staples. *The World of Classical Myth.* Durham, NC: Carolina Academic Press, 2001.

Rudolph, Hartmut. "Hohenheim's Anthropology in the Light of his Writings on the Eucharist." In *Paracelsus: The Man and His Reputation, His Ideas and Their Transformation,* edited by Ole Peter Grell, 187–92. Leiden: Koninklijke Brill, 1998.

Rumrich, John Peter. *A Matter of Glory: A New Preface to "Paradise Lost."* Pittsburgh: University of Pittsburgh Press, 1987.

———. "Uninventing Milton." *Modern Philology* 87, no. 3 (1990): 249–65.

Rumrich, John P., and Gregory Chaplin, eds. *Seventeenth-Century British Poetry: 1603–1660.* New York: Norton, 2006.

Samuel, Irene. *Dante and Milton: The "Commedia" and "Paradise Lost."* Ithaca, NY: Cornell University Press, 1966.

———. "Milton on Comedy and Satire." *Huntington Library Quarterly* 35 (1972): 107–30.

Saurat, Denis. *Milton: Man and Thinker.* New York: Dial, 1925.

Schmidgen, Wolfram. *Exquisite Mixture: The Virtues of Impurity in Early Modern England*. Philadelphia: University of Pennsylvania Press, 2012.

Schmidt, Michael. *Lives of the Poets*. New York: Alfred A. Knopf, 1999.

Schoenfeldt, Michael C. *Bodies and Selves in Early Modern England: Physiology and Inwardness in Spenser, Shakespeare, Herbert, and Milton*. Cambridge: Cambridge University Press, 1999.

Schultz, Howard. "Christ and Antichrist in *Paradise Regained*." *Publications of the Modern Language Association of America* 67, no. 5 (1952): 790–808.

Schwartz, Louis. *Milton and Maternal Mortality*. Cambridge: Cambridge University Press, 2009.

Schwartz, Regina. *Remembering and Repeating: On Milton's Theology and Poetics*. 2nd ed. Chicago: University of Chicago Press, 1993.

———. *Sacramental Poetics at the Dawn of Secularism: When God Left the World*. Stanford, CA: Stanford University Press, 2008.

Scodel, Joshua. *Excess and the Mean in Early Modern English Literature*. Princeton, NJ: Princeton University Press, 2002.

Segal, Charles. *Tragedy and Civilization: An Interpretation of Sophocles*. Norman: University of Oklahoma Press, 1999.

Shakespeare, William. *The Norton Shakespeare*. 3rd ed. Edited by Stephen Greenblatt et al. New York: Norton, 2016.

———. *The Riverside Shakespeare*. Edited by G. Blakemore Evans et al. Boston: Houghton Mifflin, 1997.

———. *Twelfe Night*. In *A New Variorum Edition of Shakespeare*, edited by Horace Howard Furness. Philadelphia: Lippincott, 1901.

Shawcross, John T. *John Milton: The Self and the World*. Lexington: University Press of Kentucky, 1993.

———. *Milton 1732–1801: The Critical Heritage*. London: Routledge and Kegan Paul, 1972.

Shelley, Percy Bysshe. *Defence of Poetry*. In *English Romantic Writers*, edited by David Perkins, 1072–87. New York: Harcourt, Brace, 1967.

Shifflett, Andrew. *Stoicism, Politics and Literature in the Age of Milton: War and Peace Reconciled*. Cambridge: Cambridge University Press, 1998.

Sidney, Philip. *An Apology for Poetry and Astrophil and Stella: Texts and Contexts*. Edited by Peter C. Herman. Glen Allen, VA: College Publishing, 2001.

Singer, Irving. *The Nature of Love: Plato to Luther*. 2nd ed. Vol. 1. Cambridge, MA: MIT Press, 2009.

Sirluck, Ernest. "Milton Revises *The Faerie Queene*." *Modern Philology* 48 (1950): 90–96.

Song, Eric. *Dominion Undeserved: Milton and the Perils of Creation*. Ithaca, NY: Cornell University Press, 2013.

Spenser, Edmund. *The Faerie Queene*. Edited by A. C. Hamilton. London: Longman, 1977.

Stavely, Keith W. F. "Satan and Arminianism in *Paradise Lost*." *Milton Studies* 25 (1990): 125–39.

Stock, George William Joseph. "A Guide to Stoicism." *Project Gutenberg*. www.gutenberg.org/ebooks/7514. Accessed June 26, 2017.

"Stoicism." *Internet Encyclopedia of Philosophy*. www.iep.utm.edu/stoicism. Accessed June 26, 2017.

Strauss, Leo. *Jewish Philosophy and the Crisis of Modernity: Essays and Lectures in Modern Jewish Thought*. Albany: State University of New York Press, 1997.

Suetonius. *The Twelve Caesars*. Translated by Robert Graves. London: Penguin Books, 2007.

Sugimura, N. K. *"Matter of Glorious Trial": Spiritual and Material Substance in "Paradise Lost."* New Haven, CT: Yale University Press, 2009.

Summers, Joseph H. *The Muse's Method: An Introduction to "Paradise Lost."* Cambridge, MA: Harvard University Press, 1962.

Svendsen, Kester. *Milton and Science*. New York: Greenwood Press, 1956.

Swift, Jonathan. *A Tale of a Tub*. Oxford: Oxford University Press, 1984.

Tatlock, John S. P. "Milton's Sin and Death." *Modern Language Notes* 21 (1906): 239–40.

Taylor, Jefferey H., and Leslie A. *The Influence of Boethius' "De consolatione philosophiae" on John Milton's "Paradise Lost."* Lewiston, NY: Edwin Mellen, 2017.

Tertullian. *De cultu feminarum*. Edited by Josephus Marra. Turin: Paravia, 1930.

———. *De jejuniis*. *Intratext Digital Library*. www.intratext.com/y/lat0249.htm. Accessed June 26, 2017.

———. *On Fasting*. Translated by S. Thelwall. In *Ante-Nicene Fathers*, vol. 4, edited by Alexander Roberts, James Donaldson, and A. Cleveland Coxe. Buffalo, NY: Christian Literature Publishing, 1885. Revised and edited for *New Advent Encyclopedia* by Kevin Knight.

Thomas à Kempis. *Imitation of Christ*. New York: Dover, 2003.

Tigner, Amy L. "Eating with Eve." *Milton Quarterly* 44, no. 4 (2010): 239–53.

Tillyard, E. M. W. *Milton*. London: Chatto and Windus, 1949.

———. *The Elizabethan World Picture*. New York: Random House.

———. *The Miltonic Setting: Past and Present*. London: Chatto and Windus, 1957.

Totaro, Rebecca. *Suffering in Paradise: The Bubonic Plague in English Literary Studies from More to Milton*. Pittsburgh: Duquesne University Press, 2005.

Turner, James. *One Flesh: Paradisal Marriage and Sexual Relations in the Age of Milton*. Oxford: Oxford University Press, 1987.

Ulreich, John C., Jr. "Milton on the Eucharist: Some Second Thoughts about Sacramentalism." In *Milton and the Middle Ages*, edited by John Mulryan, 32–56. Lewisburg, PA: Bucknell University Press, 1982.

Urban, David V. "Speaking for the Dead: C. S. Lewis Answers the New Milton Criticism; or, 'Milton Ministries' Strikes Back." *Milton Quarterly* 45, no. 2 (2011): 95–106.

Vaughan, Henry. "The World." In *Seventeenth-Century British Poetry, 1603–1660*, edited by John Rumrich and Gregory Chaplin, 599–601. New York: Norton, 2006.

Vaughan, Thomas. *Magia Adamica*. In *The Magical Writings of Thomas Vaughan (Eugenius Philatethes)*, edited by Arthur Edward Waite. London: Redway, 1888.

Vaughn, Mark. "'More than Meets the Eye': Milton's Acrostics in *Paradise Lost*." *Milton Quarterly* 16, no. 1 (2007): 6–8.

Vaught, Jennifer C., ed. *Rhetorics of Bodily Disease and Health in Medieval and Early Modern England*. Burlington, VT: Ashgate, 2010.

Venner, Thomas. *Via recta ad vitam longam*. London, 1650.

Virgil. *The Aeneid*. Translated by Robert Fitzgerald. New York: Vintage Classics, 1990.

Vision of Tundale. In *Three Purgatory Poems*, edited by Edward Foster. Kalamazoo: Medieval Institute Publications, 2004. TEAMS Middle English Texts. www.lib.rochester.edu/camelot/teams/vtfrm.htm. Accessed June 26, 2017.

Voss, Paul J. "Debris from Heaven in *Paradise Lost*." *English Language Notes* 35, no. 3 (March 1998): 37–40.

Waddington, Raymond B. "The Death of Adam: Vision and Voice in Books XI and XII of *Paradise Lost*." *Modern Philology* 70 (1972): 19–21.

Waldock, A. J. A. *"Paradise Lost" and Its Critics*. Cambridge: Cambridge University Press, 1947.

Walker, Julia M. "'For each seem'd either': Free Will and Predestination in *Paradise Lost.*" *Milton Quarterly* 20, no. 1 (1986): 13–16.

Ward, A. W., and A. R. Waller, eds. *Cambridge History of English and American Literature.* 18 vols. Cambridge: Cambridge University Press, 1907–21.

Warrick, John A. "The Medieval Theatrical Hell-Mouth: Ritual/Colonial Formations and Protestant Transformations in Anglo-Saxon and Early Modern England." PhD diss., University of Washington, 2006.

Waters, D. Douglas. "Milton and the 'Mistress-Missa' Tradition." *Milton Quarterly* 6 (1972): 6–8.

Watkins, W. B. C. *An Anatomy of Milton's Verse.* Baton Rouge: Louisiana State University Press, 1955.

Werman, Golda. *Milton and Midrash.* Washington, DC: Catholic University of America Press, 1995.

West, Robert H. *Milton and the Angels.* Athens: University of Georgia Press, 1955.

Whiting, George Wesley. *Milton and This Pendant World.* Austin: University of Texas Press, 1958.

Wimsatt, William K., Jr. and Cleanth Brooks, eds. *Literary Criticism: A Short History.* New York: Random House, 1957.

Wittreich, Joseph A., Jr. "Pico and Milton: A Gloss on Areopagitica." *English Language Notes* 9, no. 2 (1971): 108–10.

——. *Visionary Poetics: Milton's Tradition and his Legacy.* San Marino, CA: Huntington Library, 1979.

Wright, F. A. "The Food of the Gods." *Classical Review* 31, no. 1 (1917): 4–6.

Wright, Thomas, ed. *Gesta Romanorum; or, Entertaining Stories Invented by the Monks as a Fire-side Recreation, and Commonly Applied in Their Discourses from the Pulpit.* 2 vols. Translated by Charles Swan. London: J. C. Hotten, 1871.

Yeager, R. F. "Aspects of Gluttony in Chaucer and Gower." *Studies in Philology* 81 (1984): 42–55.

INDEX

Abdiel, 4, 78, 109, 123, 263

abstinence, 43, 44, 129, 279–80n3;
Adam and Eve and, 48, 58, 68, 71;
excessive, 8, 27, 74, 294n49; Milton
and, 21, 273; sexual, 43, 130

Adam and Eve, 1–2, 8, 65, 70–73,
176–78; Aquinas and, 285n48;
clothing of, 296n61; and death,
129, 130, 202; diet in the garden,
9–10, 186, 189, 224; dominion over
animals, 309n51; excess of, 60, 61,
62; expelled from paradise, 119, 176,
201; and the Fall, 13, 91; and felicity,
223, 263; and folly, 83; in the garden,
260, 309n49; gluttony and, 34, 42,
44–45, 52; and obedience, 125,
200; prayers, 57, 143; Raphael and,
141, 175, 192, 259; in relationship,
64, 85, 211; repentance, 206, 207;
Satan and, 126; sin of, 128, 290n17;
sleep and, 59; and temperance, 49,
243; translations of, 53; and tree, 53,
291n23

Aesop's fables, 51, 52

alchemy, 111, 159, 305n15

Alighieri, Dante, 135, 139, 246, 269;
Convivio (The Banquet), 247; *Divine
Comedy*, 103, 210, 243; and gluttony,
2, 18, 34–37; *Inferno*, 105, 128, 130;
influence of, 13, 240; Milton and, 3,
49, 210–11, 247, 326n11; *Paradiso*,
256–57, 317n105; *Purgatorio*, 37, 196,
271, 321n7; and Urania, 257, 259

Ambrose of Milan, 28, 209, 227,
283n36, 284–85n48; 320n4

ambrosia, 14, 142, 245, 252, 317n105,
318n121; fruit of, 176, 192–94, 202,
315–16n94; Homeric conception
of, 190–91; Milton and, 196–99;
offering, 234, 242, 276

Anaxagoras, 158–59, 314n89

angels, 61, 139, 141, 176, 189, 204, 215;
administering to others, 30–31,
69–70; bread of, 191, 317n104,
317n105; choir of, 211; and
corporeality, 98, 142–55,
304–06n15; and digestion, 80,
294n50, 319n122; eating, 153–55,
160, 191–99, 214, 238; existence of,
306n16; expressions of, 94, 121, 214,
299n27; faithful, 78, 122, 123, 141,
172, 263; food of, 91, 141, 176;
G. K. Chesterton and, 102; God's
words to, 173, 192; as guests, 82, 171;
humans and, 14, 29, 91; intelligence
of, 177–78; invisibility of, 303n1; the
naming of, 156–57; palates of, 11, 21;
routines of the temperate, 132; and
transformative ascent, 161–67, 169,
177, 212, 233, 235; unfallen, 116–17,
135, 178; and violence, 77, 111. *See
also* ambrosia; fallen angels; manna;
names of individual angels; War in
Heaven

Aphrodite Urania, 219, 257, 259,
323n27